HD 1698 S644 D46 2007 c.2

DEMOCRAT
WATER GO
IN THE MEKONG REGION

WITHDRAWN

This volume is the first of a three-volume multi-author book series on water governance in the Mekong region as part of the **Mekong Program on Water, Environment and Resilience (M-POWER)**.

The series provides critical perspectives and addresses water governance issues of contemporary relevance including contested discourses, policy directions, alternative development scenarios and action-research agendas in sharing, developing and managing water resources. This first volume provides a baseline, state of knowledge review of the politics and discourses on water governance; volume two is on planning, assessment and decision-making processes; volume three is on social justice, gender and knowledge with case studies on watershed politics, fisheries, urban/municipal and public works.

Mekong Press was initiated in 2005 by Silkworm Books, Thailand with support from the Creativity & Culture Division of Rockefeller Foundation's Southeast Asia Regional Office in Bangkok, to encourage and support the work of local scholars, writers and publishing professionals in Cambodia, Laos, Vietnam and the other countries in the Greater Mekong subregion. Books published by Mekong Press are marketed and distributed internationally. In addition, Mekong Press holds seminars and training workshops on aspects of book publishing and helps find ways to overcome some of the huge challenges for small book publishers in the region. Mekong Press is funded by the Rockefeller Foundation's Learning Across Borders in the Greater Mekong Sub-region progam.

DEMOCRATIZING WATER GOVERNANCE IN THE MEKONG

Edited by

Louis Lebel, John Dore
Rajesh Daniel, Yang Saing Koma

USER
MEKONG PRESS

Series title: M-POWER book series on water governance in the Mekong region
Series editors: Louis Lebel and Rajesh Daniel
This publication is funded by The Rockefeller Foundation.

© 2007 by Unit for Social and Environmental Research (USER)

All rights reserved.

No part of this publication may be reproduced, stored in a retrieval system, or transmitted, in any form or by any means, electronic, mechanical, photocopying, recording or otherwise, without the prior permission in writing of the publisher.

ISBN 978-974-9511-25-1

First published in 2007 by
Mekong Press
6 Sukkasem Road, Suthep, Chiang Mai 50200, Thailand
E-mail: info@mekongpress.com
Website: http://www.mekongpress.com

Cover photo © by Jim Holmes
Type set in Janson Text 10 pt. by Silk Type
Printed in Thailand by O. S. Printing House, Bangkok

CONTENTS

List of maps, figures and tables	vi
Acronyms and abbreviations	viii
Acknowledgments	xi
About the Mekong	xiii
Preface	xv

1. Introduction: Water governance in the Mekong region   1
   Masao Imamura

2. Irrigation and water policies: Trends and challenges   9
   François Molle

3. Politics of floods and disasters   37
   Louis Lebel and Bach Tan Sinh

4. China's energy reforms and hydropower expansion in Yunnan   55
   John Dore, Yu Xiaogang and Kevin Yuk-shing Li

5. Electricity sector planning and hydropower   93
   Chris Greacen and Apsara Palettu

6. Mathematical modeling in integrated management of water resources: Magical tool, mathematical toy or something in between?   127
   Juha Sarkkula, Marko Keskinen, Jorma Koponen, Matti Kummu, Jussi Nikula, Olli Varis and Markku Virtanen

7. Forums and flows: Emerging media trends   157
   Po Garden and Shawn L. Nance

8. Gender myths in water governance: A survey of program discourses   177
   Bernadette Resurreccion and Kanokwan Manorom

9. Multi-stakeholder Platforms (MSPS): Unfulfilled potential   197
   John Dore

10. Synthesis: Discourse, power and knowledge   227
    Antonio P. Contreras

Reference list	237
About the contributors	263
About M-POWER	267
Index	269

LIST OF MAPS, FIGURES, AND TABLES

Maps
Greater Mekong subregion — xii
Map 4.1 Yunnan's major rivers — 57

Figures
Figure 3.1 Floods may be beneficial, harmless or disastrous — 39
Figure 5.1 Peak demand in 2000 and projected peak demand year 2020 — 95
Figure 5.2 Planned and existing hydropower projects in Laos — 104
Figure 5.3 Hydropower projects planned or under implementation in the Salween River basin — 107
Figure 5.4 Chinese hydropower projects (planned and existing) in the Lancang-Mekong — 109
Figure 5.5 Comparison of base case Thai load forecasts to actual demand from 1992 to present — 116
Figure 6.1 Model flow chart from model input to impact analysis in the Tonle Sap area — 143
Figure 6.2 Tonle Sap Lake and its floodplain as a part of Mekong system — 145
Figure 6.3 Calculated average oxygen conditions in the Tonle Sap Lake and floodplains — 146
Figure 6.4 Calculated sedimentation results for different land use classes (agriculture, grassland, shrubland, forest and water) — 147
Figure 6.5 Framework for impact assessment and integration of hydrological, ecological and socio-economic information together with different WUP-FIN Project components — 151
Figure 9.1 Key concepts of MSPS — 200

Tables
Mekong region country overview — xiv
Table 3.1 Talking about floods — 40
Table 3.2 Talking about flood disasters — 43
Table 4.1 Hydropower potential of major rivers in China — 58
Table 4.2 Hydropower production versus potential—China, Western Region, Yunnan — 59
Table 4.3 Mekong region hydropower potential — 59
Table 4.4 China's projected supply of primary energy 2000–2020 — 60
Table 4.5 Projected supply of primary energy 2000–2020 — 66
Table 4.6 Energy production 1999 — 67

Table 4.7	Hydropower dam plans—Nu, Lancang and Jinsha rivers	71
Table 8.1	Gender discourses in fisheries management programs in the Tonle Sap Lake	189
Table 9.1	Major river basins of the Mekong region	199
Table 9.2	Desirable MSP characteristics	201
Table 9.3	Governance forums—tracks 1–4	203
Table 9.4	Recent regional water-related governance forums (tracks 1–2)	207
Table 9.5	Recent regional water-related governance forums (tracks 3–4)	213

Boxes

Box 2.1	Thailand and the "Water Grid" project	12
Box 2.2	The South-North transfer project in China	14
Box 4.1	Energy demand management options for China	63
Box 4.2	China energy industry reforms: Critical steps between 1996–2003	69
Box 4.3	Huaneng power International (HPI)	78
Box 4.4	Fish and Cambodia's Tonle Sap Lake (TSL)	81
Box 4.5	Financing the Three Gorges project	82
Box 4.6	Central issues in the dams debate: Past and present	86
Box 4.7	A new framework for decision-making on large dams	88
Box 5.1	IFIS and Mekong hydropower development	98
Box 6.1	Four main model categories	132
Box 6.2	Mathematical models	132
Box 6.3	Example of standardized models in the United States	134
Box 6.4	Models in development cooperation	139
Box 6.5	Bayesian Network	149
Box 7.1	Challenges for media development	171
Box 7.2	The greening of China's media	172
Box 7.3	Pak Mun Dam	175
Box 9.1	Recent civil society-led local/national MSPS	208
Box 9.2	Politics of participation: MSPS in Thailand	223

ACRONYMS AND ABBREVIATIONS

ADB	Asian Development Bank
ADPC	Asian Disaster Preparedness Center
APEC	Asia-Pacific Economic Cooperation
ASEAN	Association of Southeast Asian Nations
ASPL	Agriculture Sector Program Loan
AUSAID	Australian Agency for International Development
AWSJ	*Asian Wall Street Journal*
BBC	British Broadcasting Service
BDP	Basin Development Plan
BOI	Board of Investment
BOT	Build, operate and transfer
CASS	Chinese Academy of Social Sciences
CCGT	Combined Cycle Gas Turbines
CCTV	China Central Television (or Chinese Central Television)
CPR	Common Property Resource
CYEPC	China Yangtze Electric Power Corporation
CYTGPDC	China Yangtze Three Gorges Project Development Corporation
DDPM	Department of Disaster Prevention and Mitigation
DEDE	Department of Alternative Energy Development and Efficiency
DHP	Department of Hydroelectric Power
DOF	Department of Fisheries
DSF	Decision Support Framework
DSM	Demand Side Management
EGAT	Electricity Generating Authority of Thailand
EGCO	Electricity Generating Company of Thailand
EIA	Environmental Impact Assessment
EP	Environment Programme
EPPO	Environment Policy and Planning Office
ERI	Energy Research Institute
EU	European Union
EVN	Electricity of Vietnam
FAO	Food and Agriculture Organization
FMMP	Flood Management and Mitigation Programme
FWUC	Farmer Water User Communities
GDP	Gross Domestic Product
GEF	Global Environment Facility
GIS	Geographic Information System
GMS	Greater Mekong Subregion

GNP	Gross National Product
GOL	Government of Lao PDR
GRP	Gross Regional Product
GW	Gigawatts
HPI	Huaneng Power International
IBFM	Integrated Basin Flow Management
IDC	Indirect Cost
IEA	International Energy Agency
IFI	International Financial Institution
IRP	Integrated Resource Planning
IUCN	The World Conservation Union
IWRM	Integrated Water Resources Management
JBIC	Japan Bank for International Cooperation
LOLP	Loss of Load Probability
MARD	Ministry for Agriculture and Rural Development
MEA	Metropolitan Energy Authority
MEG	Medium Economic Growth
MEPE	Myanmar Electric Power Enterprise
MER	Medium Economic Recovery
MNRE	Ministry of Natural Resources and Environment
MOU	Memorandum of Understanding
MOWRAM	Ministry of Water Resources and Meteorology
M-POWER	Mekong Program on Water, Environment and Resilience
MRC	Mekong River Commission
MSPS	Multi-stakeholder Platforms
MT	Million Tons
MW	Megawatts
M-POWER	Mekong Program on Water, Environment and Resilience
NDRC	National Development and Reform Commission
NESDB	National Economic and Social Development Board
NGOS	Nongovernmental Organizations
NPC	National People's Congress
NPIMP	National Pump Installation Management Project
NSO	National Statistics Office
NWRC	Natural Water Resources Committee
O&M	Operation and Maintenance
OECD	Organisation for Economic Cooperation and Development
ONWRC	Office of Natural Water Resources Committee
PC	People's Committee
PDP	Power Development Plan
PEA	Provincial Energy Authority

PIM	Participatory Irrigation Management
PIMD	Participatory Irrigation Management and Development
PPA	Power Purchase Agreement
PPIAF	Public Private Infrastructure Advisory Facility
RBO	River Basin Organization
ROIC	Return on Invested Capital
RPTOA	Regional Power Trade Operating Agreement
RWS	Reform of the Water Sector
S.H.A.N.	Shan Herald Agency for News
SEPA	State Environment Protection Administration
SERC	State Electricity Regulation Commission
SPC	State Power Corporation
SRDC	State Reform and Development Commission
TLFS	Thai Load Forecast Subcommittee
TSL	Tonle Sap Lake
TWH	TeraWatt Hour
UNDP	United Nations Development Program
UNEP	United Nations Environment Program
UNESCO	United Nations Educational, Scientific and Cultural Organization
USAID	United States Agency for International Development
USER	Unit for Social and Environmental Research (USER)
USTVA	United States Tennessee Valley Authority
VNWRC	Vietnam Water Resources Council
WB	World Bank
WRB	Water Resources Bureau
WUA	Water User Association
WUG	Water User Group
WUP	Water Utilization Programme
WUP-FIN	Water Utilization Programme funded by Finnish Ministry for Foreign Affairs
YHLLHC	Yunnan Huaneng Lancangjiang Hydropower Company
YMEC	Yunnan Machinery & Equipment Import & Export Co. Ltd.

ACKNOWLEDGMENTS

This book has been conceptualized, shaped and written by the Mekong Program on Water, Environment and Resilience (M-POWER) water governance network with authors from across the Mekong region. The editors acknowledge and thank all the writers for their efforts, and the many that provided constructive feedback on early drafts. Special thanks to Chin-Wei Tang for her assistance at Chiang Mai University's Unit for Social and Environmental Research (CMU-USER).

We are grateful for the financial support generously provided by Swedish Environmental Secretariat for Asia (SENSA) which is a knowledge-based entity within the Swedish International Development Cooperation Agency (Sida), The Rockefeller Foundation, and The World Conservation Union (IUCN) via the Water and Nature Initiative. Their support enabled the authors to meet, write and edit this book. In addition to the efforts of all partners, key support is provided to M-POWER by the CGIAR Challenge Program on Water and Food, with funding from Echel-Eau and the International Fund for Agricultural Development (IFAD). The Rockefeller Foundation is also a supporter of the Mekong Press who chose to publish this book.

We thank Trasvin Jittidecharak, Susan Offner and the publishing staff at Silkworm Books/Mekong Press for supporting the production and distribution of the book. We are grateful to Dayaneetha De Silva of Mekong Press for showing confidence in this project and providing continuous encouragement and invaluable editorial assistance.

Greater Mekong Subregion

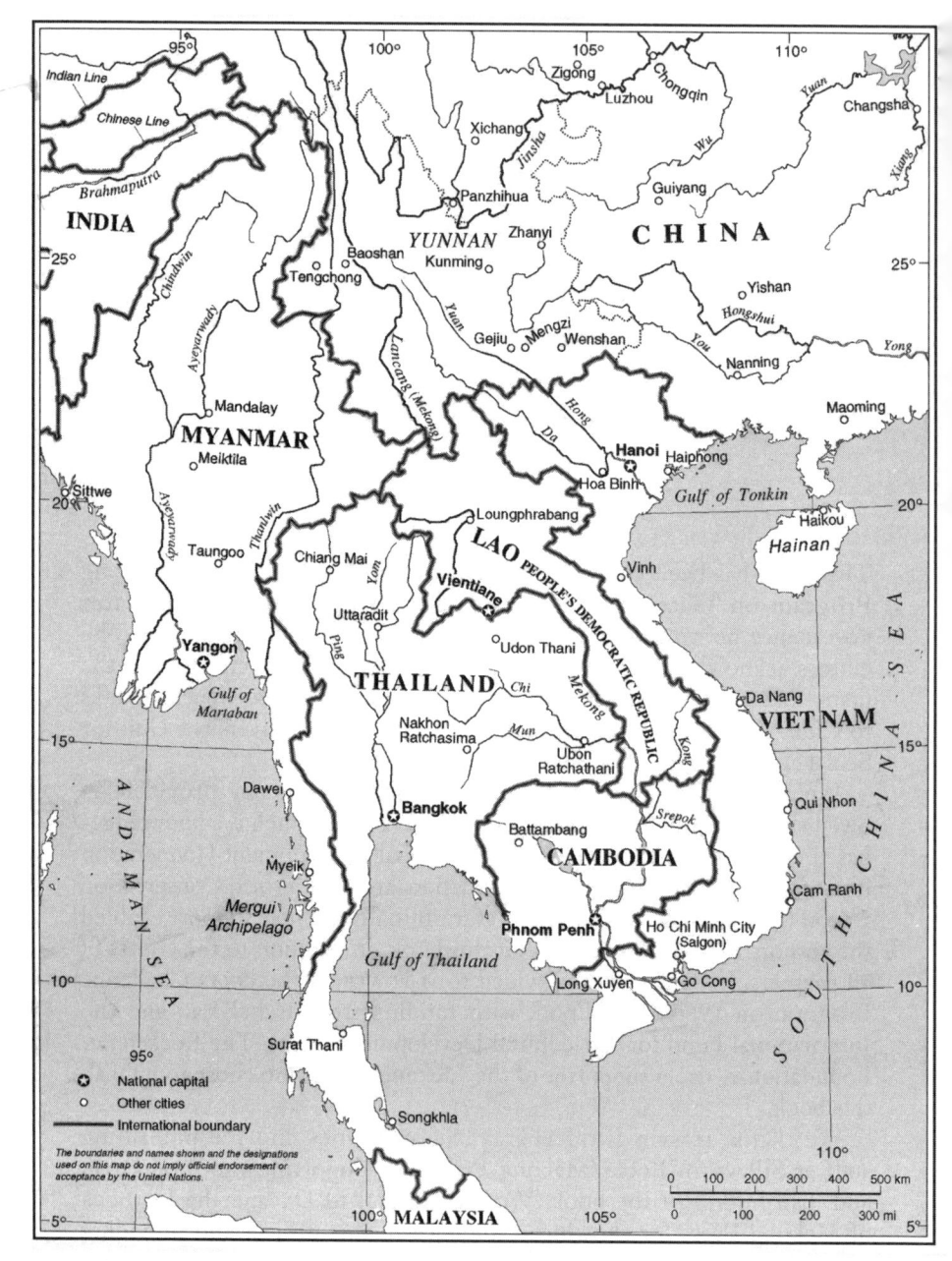

SOURCE: Map No. 4112, Rev. 2. January 2004. The United Nations Cartographic Section, New York, US

ABOUT THE MEKONG

There are many Mekongs—the river, the river basin and the region.
The Mekong River is the longest river in Southeast Asia and, with a length of approximately 4,800 kilometres, is the eighth largest (in terms of amount of water) and the 12th longest river in the world.
The Mekong River basin (or watershed or catchment) is 795,000 square kilometres, which comprises a very small percentage of the territory of the People's Republic of China, four percent of Myanmar [Burma], 97 percent of Lao PDR, 36 percent of Thailand, 86 percent of Cambodia and 20 percent of Vietnam. Obviously the river and its associated basin represent biophysical realities, with the basin being considered by natural scientists as a logical management unit.
The Mekong region is not the same as the Mekong River basin. This region—an area of 2.6 million km^2, home to approximately 300 million people—is spatially larger than the basin/watershed, and is a political construct with wider social and economic implications. It is mostly conceptualized as including all of Myanmar, Thailand, Vietnam, Cambodia and Laos, plus China's Yunnan province and (most recently) Guangxi province. In addition to the Mekong River basin, the "region" includes the Irrawaddy, Salween, Chao Phraya, and Red River basins.
Since the early 1990s the region has been enjoying an unprecedented period of relative peace between the countries, remarkably so given the tumultuous recent history of the region. However, conflicts continue inside countries such as between ethnic groups and the military regime in Myanmar with the ensuing displacement of peoples internally and across borders.

The present dynamic of the Mekong region is heavily influenced by its shared and overlapping regional history. As elsewhere, the borders of the modern nation-states do not neatly subdivide cultural affiliations. The numerous indigenous cultures of the region were heavily influenced by a fusion of Indian and Chinese (Han) culture beginning two thousand years ago. The ethnic Mon, Karen, Chin, Burman, Kachin, Khmer, Tai, Viet, etc. had their languages, religions and other customs heavily shaped, whilst of course retaining their own distinctive elements.

Significant parts of the region were isolated for much of the latter half of the twentieth century as a result of a series of wars and internal turmoil. In the last seventy years the Mekong region has been a battlefield for the Second World War, post-Second World War independence struggles against colonial powers, ideological struggles between the communists of Vietnam-Cambodia-Laos (and their allies, including at different times the former Soviet Union and China) versus other parts of Mekong societies and the United States (US) who had another wide range of "allies." New nation-states were created in Myanmar in 1948, China in 1949, Vietnam and Laos in 1975, and (effectively) Cambodia in 1993. In the last twenty years there have been various invasions and skirmishes between Cambodia and Vietnam, China and Vietnam, Thailand and Laos, and Thailand and Myanmar. These and the earlier conflicts have left many scars and continue to influence regional perceptions.

Current social and economic conditions, ethnicity, intra-regional and international negotiating powers all vary enormously. Aggregated national statistics do not adequately reflect the cultural and political diversity of the region, nor the gender and environmental complexity, but they do highlight some obvious similarities and differences (see table).

Mekong region country overview[4]

		Cambodia	China[1]	Laos	Myanmar[2]	Thailand	Vietnam
Area	'000 km²	181	9,561	237	677	513	330
Population	Millions	13.4	1,285.0	5.4	48.4	63.6	79.2
Gross Domestic Product	US $ billion	3.4	1,159.0	1.8	4.7	114.7	32.7
GDP per head	US $ in PPP[3]	1,790	3,950	1,540	1,500	5,230	2,070
Median age		17.5	30.0	18.5	23.4	27.5	23.1

NOTES: 1. Excludes Hong Kong and Macau; 2. Estimated. Official figures are either unavailable or unreliable; 3. Purchasing power parity, adjusted for cost of living differences; 4. Data refer to the year ending December 31, 2001.

SOURCE: *The Economist*. 2004. *Pocket World in Figures*. Profile Books, London.

PREFACE
Yang Saing Koma

The countries of the Mekong region are facing many social and ecological challenges in sharing, developing and managing water resources and in delivering water services across the major river basins, the Irrawaddy, Salween, Chao Phraya, Mekong and Red Rivers, as well as in the numerous sub-basins—catchments or watersheds, natural lakes, aquifers, coastal river basins and human-built dams and reservoirs

Water-use, sharing, and management are facing complex pressures from various forms of economic integration coupled with tense and largely self-interest dominated relationships between the Mekong states. These pressures have major effects especially on ecosystems and the livelihoods of rural communities.

The region is being pushed and pulled by the unequal powers of different states and their complex institutional arrangements and dynamics. Disputes over water (both within and between countries) are on the rise— because of escalating industrial and agricultural demands for water and energy, interference with natural river flows from large hydropower dams and river-linking and diversion schemes, and altered sediment and nutrient loads due to widening of river channels and the accompanying blasting of the rapids and reefs in the river for increasing large-scale commercial navigation.

In addition, there is a mixture of: the individual policies of both states and non-state actors on energy, water and other natural resources; the interventions from external actors such as donor or financial institutions; corporate water privatization efforts; and the influence of nongovernmental organizations, local community groups and wider civil society.

With both conflicts as well as cooperation occurring across national borders, more discursive deliberation is being sought for transboundary river management and for its institutional arrangements. Meanwhile, new governance arrangements are providing, in different places, both reinforcement of domination, and new progressive possibilities for greater empowerment of previously marginalized interests.

At this moment in regional history, the democratization of water governance across the region seems to be both progressing as well as deteriorating. What can we do to promote the democratization of water governance? One key to the democratization of water governance is knowledge.

Let us consider a water and food related example from my own experience with Cambodian agriculture. When we introduce new varieties of rice seed to the farmers, we first discuss with them what the good seeds are, how these seeds are produced, and what is the knowledge and skills needed to produce this seed variety. The farmers then understand that actually they can also develop their own capacity. We also help them to think about dependence: if they always need seed supply from outside, will they have to depend on outsiders or not? If so, will they have to relinquish their control over seed selection, and ultimately, their farming systems?

We need to help people understand so that they can have an opportunity to look at both good and bad sides of these technologies, and then make a sound decision on whether to use or not, or to develop alternatives. We should not transfer or impose knowledge on societies without knowing first if there is a real need for it. The knowledge that is transferred and used should be applicable to the specific conditions especially when it concerns marginalized people, as it should not make them increasingly dependent on knowledge generated outside their community, and lose control over decisions affecting their livelihood options.

Technologies should help people to solve their basic problems, respond to their needs and not result in communities ignoring their own local resources and knowledge. In the Mekong region, large dams or large-scale irrigation schemes are technologies that are introduced by governments, big financial institutions, and engineering companies. The problem is that these actors (especially engineers) often do not want to listen to the people who are going to use this technology. They tend to think the local people do not know about how to put in place a dam or irrigation system; and ignore local knowledge about water flows and local capacity to contribute to the design of an appropriate system. Moreover, in the absence of good governance mechanisms, these large-scale technology systems can also produce large-scale problems, and in the past, have resulted in inequitable water use and sharing as well as conflicts.

We need science at different scales, and democratic governance at different scales. Science can either support or not support democratic water governance. If science is used only to build large-scale reservoirs and large-scale irrigation schemes, then investment may only end up serving the interest of the elite, industry, and a minority in government and donors but may not lead to democratic water governance. In a specific sense of the technology and knowledge in farming and irrigation systems, enabling environments can work towards local people improving their capacity and sense of ownership in using, sharing and managing water resources sustainably and contribute to democratizing water governance.

In a larger sense of the knowledge and politics in the Mekong region, democratizing water governance could begin with a better understanding of what this means in different contexts, to understand knowledge and power relationships and its interplay between actors such as the state, various water-users and in particular, politically marginalized groups including women, rural poor and ethnic minority peoples, and to study the dynamic context within and between each country in relation to water governance.

This is what we hope to achieve through this volume and the book series it is part of. This volume attempts an assessment (or state of understanding) of the region looking at the knowledge and politics of the development of the region's rivers, river basins and sub-basins, ecosystems that are crucial for livelihoods, and the future of the societies that depend upon these ecosystems. We address wider yet inter-connected issues of water governance that are of immediate relevance to the Mekong region: irrigation and power sector planning, critiques of modeling, sharing of risks and vulnerabilities, media functions, aspects of gender, and processes and platforms for dialogue and deliberation. By taking an interdisciplinary and multi-scalar approach, the chapters in this volume explore the equity and effectiveness of existing rules and options in water governance in the Mekong region.

CHAPTER 1

INTRODUCTION: WATER GOVERNANCE IN THE MEKONG REGION

Masao Imamura

We live in an age of technical and professional expertise. Water resources development and management has been established as an area of expertise, and it has been assumed that in modern society the state bureaucracy takes care of this area more or less exclusively. But over the past decades it has become increasingly clear that even well-intentioned and technically advanced agencies have frequently been unable, on their own, to explore, make and implement decisions about water in ways that are ecologically sustainable and socially just.

Neat technical solutions often fail to deliver promised outcomes precisely because they try to skip the process of deliberation and social learning which is necessarily messy and conflictual. A good hydrological model, for example, can present trade-off scenarios to be considered among stakeholders. But the model itself cannot conduct negotiation; such negotiation requires involvement of stakeholders on whom the burden of articulation and argumentation rests (Campbell 2005). The neglect of open debate and negotiation prevented societies from learning as much as they should from past interventions, and instead it led to polarized and entrenched positions. And it has had serious repercussions for the livelihoods of millions.

Lack of articulation and argumentation is evident in the way management paradigms come and go one after another (Molle in this volume). The integrated water resource management or IWRM is the latest of such a paradigm which has been effectively reduced to a catch-all phrase and empty motto; it has been appropriated by conferences and brochures rather than critiqued, cultivated and incorporated in more specific contexts

(Biswas 2005). The trouble with IWRM is not that there is something specifically wrong with it but rather that it is so vague and generic that it is so difficult to point out specifically what is right or wrong and that it is thus hardly useful in practical and operational contexts.[1]

It must be admitted that "governance" itself is often nothing more than a vague and fashionable term.[2] But the new vocabulary around governance is meaningful if it reflects the shift from the techno-centric and hierarchic model of management to more value-laden process and mechanisms in which making arguments and judgments are central and integral.

Mekong region

Today, mainland Southeast Asia as a whole enjoys the highest level of peace, stability and growth in at least a half-century. It is one of the fastest growing regional economies in the world. Aggregate figures of conventional economic development indicators for the national economies are impressive: the GDP growth figures for 2004 were all above 6 percent for Cambodia, Lao PDR and Thailand and 7.5 percent in Vietnam. China's rise has been staggering. Equivalent figures in the same year for Yunnan and Guangxi provinces—two provinces that are now formally part of the Greater Mekong Subregion (GMS) of the Asian Development Bank (ADB)—were 11 percent (World Bank and ADB 2006, 68).

Water resources development has assumed a central role for the region's economic growth. A 2004 World Bank study presents a "high development" scenario projecting that in ten years in the Mekong River Basin alone there would be extensive infrastructure expansion including: nearly 4 million hectares of new irrigated areas, nearly 42,000 million cubic meters (mcm) of new storage in the form of reservoirs, 2,200 mcm of new intra-basin transfers and 3,300 mcm of new inter-basin water diversions (World Bank and ADB 2006, 58).

While the increase of irrigated area is tapering off globally, the "hydraulic mission" is far from over in the Mekong region. In Cambodia, for example, it is just beginning; the country's irrigated area is projected to as much as triple in ten years (World Bank 2004). In Thailand where the Chao Phraya basin has been over-exploited, the government is proposing a grand "water grid," a network of dams, canals and tunnels across the country's river basins. This grid would also import water from neighboring countries. Bangkok is currently in negotiation with Yangon (Rangoon), Vientiane, and Phnom Penh for a number of specific diversion projects.

While agricultural development has a long history and remains the largest driver of water allocation, it is hydropower that is captivating development planners' attention as well as a vast amount of investment capital. "Southeast Asia turns back to hydro" reported 2005 International

Water Power and Dam Construction, a leading hydropower industry magazine (International Water Power and Dam Construction 2005).[3] Energy is considered to be a key to the region's infrastructure development and hydropower a most promising choice. The increased tradability of electricity through long, often cross border, transmission lines allows hitherto improbable locations to be included on the ever expanding list of projects. The plethora of such projects dotted across the region illustrates the centrality of hydropower in the prevailing development plans for the region (Ojendal 2002).

Hydropower development exemplifies how water is a multi-dimensional resource that is enmeshed in layers of political economy which operate in a variety of geographic scales (Greacen in this volume). The largest demand center for hydropower to be generated in the Mekong region is in fact outside the region. The purpose of the cascade dams—including some of the world's highest—that are being planned and built on the Mekong/Lancang and the Salween/Nu Rivers in Yunnan Province is to secure electricity supply to China's east coast where thousands of factories are manufacturing goods for the global market (Dore and Yu in this volume).

Indeed historically, foreign players have been the driver of very large-scale infrastructure projects in the Mekong. Not only water but also money moves in enormous volumes with these schemes. The cost of the Nam Theun 2 hydropower dam, a World Bank–sponsored project in Laos, is USD 1.45 billion, exactly half of the country's GDP for 2005 (World Bank 2006). The use and purpose of foreign development aid has been vigorously contested; the debate over the accountability and legitimacy of international financial institutions has been particularly intense. Having investigated a controversial project of a wastewater treatment facility in Thailand, the chair of the ADB's Inspection Committee attested that the ADB "enjoys an extraordinary degree of immunity for the consequences of the activities it funds under national and international law" (Focus on the Global South).[4] Indeed no one at the ADB has been held accountable for funding the wastewater project in Samut Prakan while twenty Thai state officials including three former ministers involved in the project have been charged with corruption in a Thai court (Gray 2004, Chang Noi 2002, *People's Daily* Online 2004).

The debate on aid for water resource development is usually focused around specific projects such as dams, and the quality and relevance of this debate is uneven. It is often heavily dependent on who the donor is and what kind of formal and informal accountability mechanisms they have. Close observations also reveal that often local stakeholders are only superficially engaged in the debate and negotiation even when there is no shortage of actors who claim to represent their interests (Resurreccion and Manorom in this volume; Hirsch 2002).[5] The dynamics of foreign aid to the Mekong region is changing with the dramatic ascent of China as a donor and investor and is inevitably changing the terms of engagement and debate.[6] Today the bilateral aid from Beijing to Phnom Penh matches that of the seventeen other foreign donors combined. Prime Minister Hun Sen of Cambodia speaks of China as a model partner for his country's development (Deutsche Presse-Agentur 2006, Perlez 2006).

We should not forget that apart from efforts to impound and divert water in large volumes, there are thousands of smaller-scale alterations in water usage across the region which does not involve large dams or long aqueducts. The Mekong delta in southern Vietnam is a better-known case of dykes, embankments, weirs, and shrimp farms making irreversible cumulative impacts over a very wide area. Small and low-technological devices that have been made available at a low cost—electric stunners and gillnets in fisheries, as pumps in irrigation, and PVC pipes and sprinklers in upland agriculture—have been adopted, often innovatively, in livelihood strategies across the region. These "silent revolutions" are collectively making profound impacts on the economies in the region and its freshwater ecology.

Across the Mekong region urbanization and industrialization is an unmistakably strong trend, profoundly altering land and water uses. The governments tend to prioritize urban and industrial demands for water allocation, creating competition with agriculture, as in the case of the eastern provinces of Thailand (*Bangkok Post* 2004).[7] Access to clean water for the urban poor also requires urgent attention in the rapidly changing city landscapes like Ho Chi Minh City and Phnom Penh. Urbanization also intensifies the problem of flood disasters. Here again structural measures put in place under the name of flood mitigation often shift, rather than reduce, risks to different populations (Lebel and Bach Tan in this volume).

Moreover climate variability will impact the region's water at all levels. How the impacts will be experienced at local levels has, to date, received scant attention, however. This is surprising since climate change is likely to impact and disrupt the development processes including the many infrastructure projects currently planned and implemented without due consideration of their risks (Thomas and Chasca 2005).

Governance challenges

While the region's economy is going through historical changes, knowledge and information gaps remain severe. There are not even reliable population figures for Myanmar [Burma], for instance, where there has not been a nation-wide census for decades. Our knowledge about the region's culture and environment is so rudimentary that scientists are still "discovering" languages and mammal species hitherto unknown to them.

Our understanding of the region's complex freshwater ecology remains seriously limited; the 2004 World Bank report states that the "present state of knowledge of the Mekong River environment is patchy. For some aspects of the environment there are reasonably good sets of collected data while for many others there is little or no information" (World Bank 105).[8] But even the Mekong River fares better than many other rivers in this part of the world. Much of the Salween River that flows across Myanmar is not gauged and where it is gauged the data are kept confidential, so there is virtually no hydrological data available from this 2,815-kilometer long international river.[9] With political and military concerns, border areas tend to be sensitive; they can be difficult to access even in Thailand, one of the most open of the region's countries. In Myanmar, most of the Mekong, Salween and Chindwin basins are off limits.

There are certainly many efforts to fill in these knowledge gaps. Generally speaking, however, the conduct of research in the region is dominated by professional experts; and access to the sophisticated instruments and the information generated by them is often effectively restricted to state officials and contracted consultants (Goldman 2001). Their dominance in the production of scientific knowledge has led to lack of confidence and trust among many stakeholders. The controversy and confusion over the unusually low water levels of the Mekong mainstream in the past years, especially in 2004, has highlighted the need for making relevant scientific data available widely to the public in an accessible manner (Mekong River Commission 2004, Macan-Markar 2004, World Wildlife Fund). When a letter appears in a Thai newspaper reading "Don't let the Mekong go way of Mexico's barren Colorado" and warns about the possibility of upstream dams in China drying up the Mekong River downstream, it is easy to realize that basic information about the river's hydrology and the reservoirs' capacities can easily dispel such hyperboles—if such information is actually disseminated to the public. But in reality access to relevant information about the dams and hydrology is legally, technically or practically limited to certain privileged actors, and this naturally leads to mistrust and fear (Nance and Garden in this volume). Even anger is understandable when information on environmental changes observed at a local level is dismissed as anecdotal, unscientific and unverifiable. In the case of the Se San River, a Mekong tributary, the burden of proof has been unfairly imposed on locals of the riparian villages in northeast Cambodia regarding the impacts of a dam built upstream across the border in Vietnam (Hirsch and Wyatt 2004).

Despite the known gravity of these crisis cases, there is a strong tendency among management bureaucracies to avoid discussing openly controversial cases such as the Se San. It is as if once an issue becomes contested and controversial, it immediately falls out of the scope of the work with the experts saying: "We are technical experts and now the issue is political, which can only be handled by politicians." It is a common wisdom of diplomacy that negotiators first build a basic level of trust and forward-looking attitudes prior to bringing up particularly contentious topics. But in the Mekong region today, the practice of avoiding controversial topics is more of a rule than an exception especially when it comes to transboundary issues (Jensen 2005). Part of this phenomenon is the de-politicization effect of the professionalized development bureaucracy (aptly described as the "anti-politics machine") observed around the world (Ferguson 1994). The practice is defended often in the Mekong region, at times even couched in cultural terms.[10] As a result, controversial issues tend to divide and polarize the public. Opinions are expressed and contradictory information is disseminated in a one-way, broadcasting style through separate networks; rarely do they meet and examine each other (Dore in this volume). When there is no functional mechanism of engagement and accountability, the damage is most usually imposed on politically weak groups.

As research and negotiation is conducted behind closed doors, the general public's confidence in scientific, technical and administrative expertise is destined to be low. Without more inclusive processes and lasting mechanisms of social learning and public involvement, even scientific findings, however accurate, fail to gain social legitimacy.[11] Again, mathematical hydrological modeling is a good example; they are extremely useful and often indispensable but the usefulness is so little understood by the public and clearly there is mistrust and fear towards it (Sarkkula in this volume). For it is very rare that underlying assumptions and uncertainties of the modeling's outputs are shared, explained and discussed openly among relevant stakeholders. Choosing a model is seemingly a technical task but this choice-making in reality is a matter not of calculation but of judgment; it is unavoidably subject to contradictory perspectives as well as competing values and interests. It is this collective labor of judging, bound to be messy and conflictual, which is persistently avoided and discouraged in the professionalized conduct of development work.

Rather than relying on resource management professionals (most usually foreign consultants) to present their sophisticated findings and "best practices," stronger efforts need to be made to strengthen our capacity to learn and negotiate. And this should be explicitly identified as a fundamental development goal (Evans 2004).

This volume on water governance

The Mekong region has been steadily transformed from the "battlefields to marketplaces." Today commercial goods and services enjoy faster and wider circulation than ever before. In contrast, however, a vibrant marketplace of ideas has been slower in coming. The values of open competition, comparison and shopping around among a wide range of ideas on offer have yet to take hold. Fair negotiation and bargaining remain rare.

As diverse societies are confronted by local water management challenges as a consequence of regional and global socio-economic and environmental changes, the need for more democratic approaches to water governance grows and deepens. Constant engagement of citizens in exchange of information, opinions and ideas—on how to use a particular hydrological model, on what needs to be assessed, or on how to interpret a new water law—is necessary to ensure that society as a whole possesses the capacity to cope with changes and uncertainties and to actively make choices for its future.

This volume on water governance wishes to contribute to the region's democratic search for promising options on water governance. We aspire to provide new perspectives to the Mekong region's water governance by opening-up some of the most salient issues and ideas to renewed scrutiny. We seek to redefine scientific, social and action research agendas to new possibilities in which a new generation of citizens and stakeholders in the Mekong region could engage. The authors here are a heterogeneous mixture of actors with a variety of backgrounds. The diversity is purposeful. There is a need to open the doors and curtains and let in the whispered perspectives that now float aimlessly on the breeze to drift more strongly around the table of attentive but critical listeners.

Notes

1 In an effort to revitalize lessons from IWRM and inject additional insights, Dipak Gyawali et al advocates "Constructively Engaged Integrated Water Resources Allocation and Management" or CE-IWRAM. See Dipak Gyawali, JA, Allan et al, 2006. EU-INCO water research from FP4 to FP6 (1994–2006)—a critical review, http://ec.europa.eu/research/water-initiative/pdf/incowater_fp4fp6_rapport_technique_en.pdf#search=%22eu-inco%20water%20research%20from%20fp4%20to%20fp6%22 (accessed on September 21, 2006).

2 For an overview of how "good governance" has been interpreted in Thailand, see Barbara Orlandini 2003. "Consuming 'Good Governance' in Thailand," *The European Journal of Development Research* 15 (2): 16–43.

3 In 2005 alone, Vietnam and Lao PDR respectively began the construction of the country's largest dam on the Da River at Son La in the north of Hanoi and on the Nam Theun River, a Mekong tributary, in central Laos. Also in 2005, Thailand and Myanmar signed a Memorandum of Understanding to build a series of large dams on the Salween River. The most symbolical of the hydropower revival in the lower Mekong basin countries is Pa Mong dam on the mainstream of the Mekong River not far south of Vientiane, which was originally proposed by the former Mekong Committee in the 1970s (International Water Power and Dam Construction, 2005).

4 Frank Black, Asian Development Bank, "Interventions by Directors representing various Countries at the ADB Board meeting held on 25th of March 2002. Excerpts from the Minutes of the Board Meeting" contained in Focus on the Global South. *Too Hot to Handle: The Samut Prakan Wastewater Management Project Inspection Process.* May 2002, www.focusweb.org/publications/Books/too-hot-to-handle.pdf (accessed on September 21, 2006). Black spoke as an Alternate Director representing the United Kingdom, Germany, Turkey and Austria.

5 Bernadette Resurreccion and Kanokwan Manorom in this volume; Philip Hirsch, 2002, "Global Norms, Local Compliance and the Human Rights-Environmental Nexus: A Case Study of the Nam Theun II Dam in Laos". In *Human Rights and the Environment: Conflicts and Norms in a Globalizing World* edited by Lyuba Zarsky, London: Earthscan.

6 It has been reported, for example, that the Nam Theun 2 hydropower project in Lao PDR, the most controversial infrastructure project in the Mekong region in the last decade, went ahead with the World Bank's endorsement at least partly because of the fear that otherwise China would take over the project in place of a Franco-Thai consortium. See Martin Stuart-Fox, "The Paradox of Laos," *Australia Financial Review,* March 18, 2005, http://afr.com/articles/2005/03/17/111091373 3278.html. A rare in-depth report on China's aid to a Mekong country is Qian Xiaofeng, "China's Aid Flows Downstream to Laos," http://www.newsmekong.org/china_s_aid_flows_downstream_to_laos (accessed on September 21, 2006).

7 *Bangkok Post,* "Govt Solution to Water Crisis 'Killing Farmers,'" 2004.

8 The World Bank, "Mekong Regional Water Resources Assistance Strategy,".

9 "Stream flow data for the Salween River are very sparse. There are only two gauging stations, namely, SWN14 in Thailand and Hpa-An in Myanmar, on the mainstream of the Salween River. However, several gauging stations have been established on the tributaries in the territories of Thailand." Choolit Vatcharasinthu and M. S. Babel, Hydropower Potential and Water Diversion from the Salween Basin (September 1999), Panya Consultants, http://www.salweenwatch.org/news/No.05.php (accessed on September 21, 2006).

10 For a detailed analysis focused on the Mekong River Commission, see "Chapter 7: The MRC and Southeast Asian Political Culture." In *National Interests and Transboundary Water Governance in the Mekong* edited by Philip Hirsch, Kurt Mørck Jensen et al., http://www.mekong.es.usyd.edu.au/projects/mekong_water_governance2.htm 2006 (last accessed September 21, 2006).

11 Op. cit. 3. pp. 19.

CHAPTER 2
IRRIGATION AND WATER POLICIES: TRENDS AND CHALLENGES

François Molle

Introduction

In the past several years, water has moved up on the agenda of most countries in the Mekong region. This is due to several interconnected factors. First, recurring water shortages and crises (scarcity, droughts, pollution, interstate or intersectoral competition around the Mekong River, etc.), although often local and temporary, have instilled a sense of vulnerability. These shortages have typically affected irrigation and, in some cases, have also threatened urban supply. Second, numerous global initiatives and networking focused on water management (World Water Forums, etc.) have also contributed to giving water issues greater public salience. Third, these initiatives have been paralleled by persuasive insistence from development banks—most notably the Asian Development Bank (ADB) and the World Bank—that borrowing countries develop regulatory frameworks, water policy, white papers and water legislation. Fourth, there has been increasing involvement of the private sector, notably in hydropower generation and in urban water supply, which has changed the situation of virtual state monopoly over water resources. Water policy reform processes generally contemplate a blend of the following recommendations and measures:

1. Poor water distribution in irrigation networks, epitomized by efficiencies of between 30 and 40 percent, is addressed by trying to instill greater participation from users through designing service agreements in which agency and farmers act as service provider and clients, rather than as supplier and recipients.
2. Concern for cost-recovery and financial sustainability generally leads to making provision for the levying of a water charge.
3. Embracing Integrated Water Resource Management (IWRM) leads to putting emphasis on river basin management that, in turn, leads to proposals for River Basin Organizations (RBOS) or other types of interfaces between concerned line agencies and users.
4. The distinction between operating the hydraulic network, resources management, and policy-making/regulation is emphasized, which leads to proposing three nested layers of institutions with clear and distinct mandates.

These trends in the water sector give rise to several questions: how pressing was the need for such reforms and how sound have been the steps taken? To what degree have national bureaucracies and ruling political parties shared this concern for reordering the water sector and added their will power to the solicitations of outsiders, and how does this vary from country to country? How do expectations from these formal and state-centered initiatives compare with reality on the ground? Are policies derived from blueprints or based on a sound analysis of local problems, and to what extent do top-down approaches crowd out the emergence of endogenous and condition-specific solutions? More generally, what are the patterns of governance emerging in the water sector, and how do they shape policy-making, planning, and management of water resources?

This chapter documents current irrigation and water policies in the Mekong countries.[1] It successively reviews planning issues, water policies and legal frameworks, the setting up of water policy "apex bodies," participatory policies, and IWRM/river basin management. It comments on the underpinning of these policies, their discursive dimension, and how they fit the reality of the countries concerned. The aim is to pave the way for further research on water governance in the Mekong region.[2]

Review of main irrigation and water policy development

Planning and development of water resources
The development of reservoirs and irrigation schemes has been, and still is, prominent in the Mekong region. The situation, however, differs sharply according to the country. Thailand, China and Vietnam have extensively

developed their irrigation infrastructure and investments have declined in the last few years but hydropower development is in full bloom (especially in Vietnam and in the upper Mekong in China). Lao PDR, because of its scarce population, and Cambodia, due to the war and political turmoil, and to some extent Myanmar [Burma], still have a low degree of infrastructural development and options for the future are subjects of debate (notably in the Salween River basin).

According to Sacha et al. (2001) Thailand's irrigated area is around 30 million rai or 4.8 million hectares (ha), that is, approximately 20 percent of the total farmland. Its dams can now store 70 billion cubic meters (Bm^3) of water and most major dam sites have been exploited. A number of reservoirs are still under planning or construction, but their typical size is around 250 million cubic meters (Mm^3) and they face growing opposition from civil society, forcing the Electricity Generating Authority of Thailand (EGAT) to look for ventures and alternative sites in neighboring countries (Hirsch 2001). Nevertheless, in July 2003, the Government of Thailand announced that it would target 200 billion baht or USD 5 billion to solve the problem of water scarcity in Thailand and allow the irrigation of cultivable land not yet supplied with water. The northeastern region was to be the major beneficiary of the project conceived as a part of the plan to "eradicate poverty" in the country (see box 2.1).

Justifications for such large-scale investments are usually fuelled by alarmist surveys or reports on the impact of droughts and floods (*Bangkok Post* March 24, 2004, *Bangkok Post* February 18, 2004). Nothing is said about how scarcity is defined, and whether it is a result of climatic variability or, perhaps, slack management. These numbers are used to call for the construction of new dams and other infrastructures. Since irrigation areas tend to be overdeveloped in relation to storage capacity, a sense of scarcity is artificially created: "water distribution doesn't completely cover those irrigation areas; we've lost a balance between storage and distribution," commented a high-level official (*Bangkok Post* December 28, 2003). Focus on benefits rather than on cost/benefit ratios was exemplified by the then-Prime Minister Thaksin Shinawatra, who reportedly said: "It would not be a problem if the (water grid) project required a lot of money because it would be worthwhile eventually," and by the then Deputy Prime Minister in charge of the project, who saw the project as "a worthwhile investment because it will benefit 30 to 40 million people nationwide" (*The Nation* June 23, 2003).

The gigantism and the ambition of the project have been met with skepticism by many water professionals and with dismay by environmentalists (*The Nation* September 24, 2004). It strains the imagination to envisage how the irrigation area, which has been developed to 22 million rai or 3,520,000 ha in over one century, could be trebled or more in five years. From the governance point of view, the whole process is characterized by secrecy, with only a few statements (mostly contradictory) being delivered to the press. Despite the dramatic projected impact on populations, livelihoods and the environment (in terms of benefits, costs and externalities), no participatory mechanism has so far been observed.

Box 2.1 Thailand and the "Water Grid" project

The government of Thaksin Shinawatra announced in July 2003 that it would pursue a 200 billion[3] baht (USD 5 billion) venture to bring water to un-irrigated farms, notably in the northeast, and help "turn Thailand into an agricultural powerhouse" (*The Nation* September 14, 2003).

Project targets are still ill-defined and contradictory but all point to a dramatic increase in irrigated land. A recent study by Khon Kaen University asserts that water will be provided to 60 million rai (9.6 million ha) of farmland and confirms that there is not enough water domestically and that "water diversion from neighboring countries and international rivers is an essential part of the water grid project" (*Bangkok Post* June 13, 2004). In addition to that, according to a senior irrigation officer, "300 new large and medium-sized reservoirs and 25,000 community reservoirs are needed to support the project" (*Bangkok Post* May 03, 2004).

Thaksin was reported to believe "northeastern provinces have enough water resources and the problem is the irrigation and distribution system, which needs to be improved" and had instructed the "Irrigation Department to fix the lack of water in northeastern provinces and report to him on ways to solve the problem within one month" (*The Nation* April 24, 2004). According to a professor at Khon Kaen University involved in the feasibility study, the delay in the project was "the result of a row between the former Natural Resources Minister Suvit Khunkitti and former Agriculture Minister Somsak Thepsuthin over who should oversee the project," adding that "both ministers want to supervise the project because it could be promoted in their election campaigns" (*Bangkok Post* June 13, 2004). Pilot projects worth USD one million (40 million baht) are expected to be start soon and will consist of a diversion of water from Mae Klong to Phetchaburi and Prachuap Khiri Khan. Recent political changes probably means the project is going to be shelved, although specific projects are likely to be implemented.

Vietnam is still involved in massive investments for rural and water infrastructures. The Red River and Mekong deltas require huge outlays for works on dikes (flood protection) and channels, notably the Mekong, with further reclamation of land in the Plain of Reeds and closing off of the seashore, allowing freshwater irrigation during the dry season. Significant investments are also being made in rehabilitation and modernization, since most of the schemes developed in the 1960s and 1970s are now in a severe state of degradation (Tu n.d., World Bank 2004), but also because "further crop diversification and increases in productivity require modern hydraulic infrastructure and more efficient delivery of irrigation and drainage services" (Tiep 2002).

The area of irrigated land is currently around 3 million hectares, out of 7.4 million hectares cultivated. According to Tiep (2002), water used for agriculture was 47 Bm^3 in 1990 and increased to 61 Bm^3 in 2000. Average demand increases 3 percent per year and "requirements" for 2010 are estimated at 74 Bm^3 (Tu n.d.). Other large investments are made in the dam sector, mostly for purposes of energy generation (Song Da on the Black River in the northwest, and Mekong tributaries flowing westward into Cambodia).

In Cambodia, water policy as a whole and irrigation in particular are seen as crucial elements of the development of agriculture, leading to food security and poverty alleviation, the main objectives pursued by the state in a country where agriculture amounts to half of the gross domestic product and 90 percent of employment (Sinath 2001). Less than one percent of Cambodia's water is diverted and only 200,000 hectares (16 percent of the total cultivated area) are irrigated. The country counts only one medium-scale dam for hydroelectricity. During the Khmer Rouge regime, numerous schemes composed of dikes serving as reservoirs and of crude canals criss-crossing paddy lands were built but most of them have been destroyed and can only be transformed to efficient schemes with considerable redevelopment (Sinath 2003). In other words, Cambodia is presumably only at the beginning of substantial investments in the water sector. The main debate revolves around whether priority should be given to the development of small-scale water resources or to conventional large-scale irrigation schemes (Öjendal 2000), with investments relying heavily on forthcoming loans and grants from international banks and donors (MOWRAM and ADB 2001).[4]

Laos exhibits a similar low level of investment/infrastructures that contrasts with the fact that the agriculture sector provides the largest share of foreign currency income (40 percent), about 52 percent of the GDP, and 85.5 percent of the employment. The government stresses that: "The national economic development process is to be based on the wealth of natural resources, especially water and water resources," which includes in particular irrigation and hydropower (Phonechaleun et al. 2002). Significant improvements have been achieved in the agriculture sector, with an increase in dry-season rice area from 2,700 hectares in 1976 to 110,000 hectares in 2000,[5] and irrigation shifting the average rice yield from 1.43 t/ha (rain-fed) to 3.27 t/ha during the same period. In 1999/2000, there were 19,170 irrigation schemes with a service area of about 295,000 hectares in the wet season, a number still rising due to heavy investment in the National Pump Installation Management Project (NPIMP), mostly along the Mekong River in the southern part of the country (Khamhung 2001). Large-scale public schemes are confined to the main valleys, notably the Nam Ngum valley near Vientiane, which has a reservoir with a capacity of 7 Bm^3. Hydropower production is still low, i.e., 2 percent of a "potential" estimated at 30,000 megawatts. Development of hydropower dams has been subject to intense environmental debate and lobbying by nongovernmental organizations (NGOs) and activists from outside Laos, as epitomised in the Nam Theun 2 Dam controversy. New investments including large dams are contingent upon loans by development banks and private sector involvement, both explicitly welcomed by the government (Richardson 2002).

China's water economy has long been dominated by a strong engineering approach, but significant efforts are being made towards accommodating new concepts of environmental sustainability, demand management, rational pricing and institutional power-sharing (Boxer 2001). Although construction-based policies have decreased in importance, in the past years China has been a focus in the global news because of two major projects: the Three Gorges dam, and the south-north diversion, which diverts water from the Yangtze to the Yellow River (Berkoff 2003). This project includes three transfer canals that are expected to inject 50 Bm^3 into the Yellow River basin (see box 2.2). Dam construction on the upper Mekong River has been less publicized but has stirred debate on their current and future impact.

Box 2.2 The South-North transfer project in China

The south-north transfer project includes three different routes (the east, middle and west routes) that are to interlink the Yangtze River (which has relative "surplus" water) and the Yellow River (which is severely overcommitted). The North China plain is home to a population of over 300 million and is undergoing critical water scarcity, with the common patterns of declining aquifers, reduced allocation to agriculture, shortages in supply to cities and severe environmental problems of pollution and siltation. The first phase aiming at the diversion of 20 Bm^3 has started, with an estimated cost of USD 17 billion and the likely displacement of 300,000 people.

Although the environmental and economic dimensions of the project are not attractive, political and pragmatic arguments are likely to prevail. At stake is the alleviation of the enormous stress distributed between agriculture, cities and, last but not least, the environment in a region with high population densities and booming economic development (From Shao et al. 2003, Berkoff 2003).

Water policy and water laws

In past years, the Mekong region has witnessed several initiatives aimed at updating and strengthening national water laws and regulations. China enacted its first water law in 1988, which was revised in 2002. Laos and Vietnam had laws passed in 1996 and 1998, respectively, while Cambodia's draft is to be examined by its Parliament. Thailand has been considering several versions of a water law over the past fifteen years or so but the process still continues. These legal documents, and related decrees, have often been designed with significant contributions by foreign consultants hired by the World Bank, ADB or the Food and Agriculture Organization (FAO). As such they invariably borrow from a corpus of issues and strategies seen as "best practices" or "modern"[6] international standards, sometimes overlooking local constraints or specificities. Even where the role of foreign consultants has been more modest, as in China, a new generation of water specialists has reportedly embraced what is seen by Boxer (2002) as "internationally accepted strategies and methods." Recurring features include the separation of the water regulation, management and service provision functions (with, in particular, the establishment of an apex body); definition of permits for water use; mechanisms for cost-sharing; watershed management; polluter-pays principle; and emphasis on participatory and integrated land and water resources management; these two latter issues are examined in more detail in the following sections.

In Laos, the Water Resources Law and the Environmental Protection Law were approved in 1996 and 1999 respectively, and some ministerial decrees and regulations have been approved recently. The Water Law has ten provisions and forty-nine articles focusing on the protection of water resources and watersheds, water resources planning and prevention of water pollution (Khamhung 2001). An apex body, the Water Resources Coordination Committee (WRCC) was established in 1999 within the Prime Minister's Office, with the active support of the ADB (Khamhung 2001). The law includes some vague provisions for the establishment of water use permits which some observers see as little realistic (Pheddara 2003). There has been little domestic discussion or awareness of the law and its implications, and no civil society input into the policy process.

In Cambodia, a first draft was issued in 1999, one year after the establishment of the Ministry of Water Resources and Meteorology (MOWRAM), and revised in 2001. It failed to be examined before the political stalemate of 2003 and is expected to be considered when the national parliament reassembles. While one cannot prejudge what adjustments are going to be made,[7] the draft puts emphasis on several principles (KOC 2001): article 9 stipulates that "the diversion, abstraction and use of water resources for purposes other than those mentioned in article 8 [domestic uses and gardening], and the construction of the waterworks relating thereto, are subject to a license by the MOWRAM." These licenses "may be transferred by its holder to another user, whether totally or in part, subject to the prior approval of the MOWRAM" (article 13) and will be granted against a water fee. Accordingly, MOWRAM will keep and update a "centralized inventory of the water resources of the Kingdom of Cambodia"[8] and will also "record all water use and wastewater discharge licenses." Beyond granting the state the power to exact water fees from users, it is not clear why such a complex device is recommended in a context where allocation conflicts are hardly an issue and hydrological measurements are almost nil.

In the aftermath of the 1997 financial crisis, Thailand obtained a USD 600 million loan from both the ADB and Japan Bank for International Cooperation (JBIC) under the name of ASPL (Agriculture Sector Program Loan), conditional upon acceptance of some principles and a Reform of the Water Sector (RWS). A policy-matrix was defined, showing commitment and successive milestones to be achieved. The RWS was designed by consultants to the ADB and issued in March 2001. It included several components (Halcrow et al. 2001), including:

- Strengthening of the Office of the National Water Resources Committee (ONWRC) and its transformation into an apex body.
- Decentralization of water management to river basins.
- Watershed protection strategy.
- Setting of performance indicators and service standards.
- Participatory irrigation management and definition of farmers as clients of a service rather than beneficiaries.
- Cost sharing of O&M (Operation and Maintenance).
- Reorganization, decentralization and privatization of the Royal Irrigation Department.

In parallel, the National Water Resource Committee (NWRC) worked on the draft Water Law (that has been revised several times during the past years), which was supposed to encapsulate many of the crucial aspects of this ambitious reform, notably the establishment of River Basin Committees (RBCs), and the separation of the policy, management and O&M functions.

The reform process initiated under the ASPL has been phased out during 2002 and 2003, at the behest of the then-Prime Minister. Pilot projects have been implemented partially and without supervision, leading to no real change. Cost-sharing policies and service agreements have disappeared from the front scene. The draft Water Law is still in limbo. The restructuring of RID has been limited to measures such as the non-replacement of retiring staff. Only the setting up of RBCs has continued as planned, under the guidance of the ONWRC (now the Department of Water Resources of the MNRE). At present, however, they still lack the formal recognition that would give them a role beyond that of a mere consultative forum. On balance, although the reform process built in the ASPL was in general sound on paper, it suffered from being introduced through loan conditionalities, without paying enough attention to the acceptance or preparedness of the bureaucracy and of the political leaders, as well as of the civil society (which, for example, vehemently opposed conditionalities over water pricing). Involvement of the latter was minimal, although some stakeholder analyses and workshops were carried out by academics hired by the ADB.

Vietnam's 1999 Water Law vests all power in the state and "State agencies, economic organizations, political organizations, People's Army Forces units and all individuals in the protection, exploitation and use of the water resource ... have the responsibility to implement legislation on water resources" (Water Law, article 4). "The People's Committees at all levels and the competent State organizations" are entrusted with most of the tasks, from planning, regulation, emergency works, implementation, to control and management. The law introduces the user-pays and polluter-pays principles. Users must register and get a permit from the competent State agencies except for "small scale [use] for the family in agricultural, forestry production, aquaculture, small industry and handicraft production, hydropower generation and other purposes" (article 24). The law reviews in detail and prohibits a large number of actions that are "harmful to water resources and their quality." In 2001, the government set up the National Water Resource Council and also a provision for basin management, although little detailed. Control of water management by the state apparatus is almost absolute.

China's 1988 Water Law was meant to serve as a regulatory framework for rationalizing water use in a context of transition to a market economy (AIRC 2003). The law includes the user-pays principle[9] and compensations for third-party impact in case of flow alteration but often reads like a policy document since application is left to subsequent decrees. The 2002 revamp of the law draws on the 1988 act but gives greater emphasis to themes such as conservation, environmental preservation and allocation by quota. The major issue of river basin development and management is also given more salience (Shen 2004) but largely remains a matter of bureaucratic and centralized planning. Yet, the law provides for a relatively high degree of autonomy to local authorities (Saleth and Dinar 2000) and several experiments with bulk water allocation and pricing (Mollinga et al. 2003), intersectoral reallocation of water rights (Fu and Hu 2002), for example, are reported. Local administrative units, notably provinces (such as Yunnan, which has its own dam agenda), prefectures and county governments all have Water Resources Bureaus with large latitude for water management.

Myanmar has not yet considered updating any of its laws related to water. However, as part of its recent effort to define a National Water

Vision to Action, it is considering working on "a unified water resources law so as to promote a more effective legal framework for coordination and management of water resources" and establishing a national water authority (Ti and Facon 2004).

In the Mekong region, pressure from external agencies to pass water acts have tended to generate a process whereby these laws are watered down, leave state control intact or increased, pay lip service to the fads of the day (Biswas 2001, Jonch-Clausen and Fugl 2001), and need further decrees to be put into action.[10] Phonechaleun et al. (2002) emphasize "the urgent necessity to implement laws, decrees, regulations for integrated and sustainable management and development of water resources," but admit "that the enforcement of the Water and Water Resources Law and related regulations [in Laos] is still very weak." One may question whether such emphasis on legal aspects is warranted or not. Pessimists argue that the regulation established is wholly inadequate, at best innocuous and at worst counterproductive, echoing Ostrom's (2000) warning that "the worst of all worlds may be one where external authorities impose rules but are only able to achieve weak monitoring and sanctioning." Optimists tend to retort that despite the idealized view enshrined in the laws, these have to be seen as a set of principles meant to underpin future decisions and policies over a long time period. To be sure, both tend to overestimate the power of the state to control the water regime.

Institutional reform processes equated to policy and law formulations tend to be highly prescriptive, presenting models for desired end stages and list policy recommendations (Mollinga 2001). They rest on static[11] and managerial views of the world that deny heterogeneity and uncertainty (Mehta et al. 2000) and leave little room for flexibility and stakeholder inclusion.

Apex bodies and three-tier institutional design

Apex bodies are intended to advise governments and improve coordination between the various water-related sectors and ministries (Birch 2004). They have emerged recently as part of what Wright (1999) sees as "modern water management arrangements" to separate as much as possible the three complementary roles that constitute water management:
- Standard setter and auditor/reporter (*apex policy body*).
- Water resources manager or *regulator*.
- Water *operator* (for example, irrigation providers or water-supply utilities).

In Asia, apex bodies have been promoted as "best practice" by the ADB[12] which has supported the inclusion of a three-tier structure in national water policy reforms. According to Birch (2004), the focus of apex bodies is at the interministerial level and they are meant to influence national debates and reforms, instilling a degree of IWRM thinking and practice into decision making. ADB advocates that apex bodies "are needed in the developing countries of Asia to bring together government, civil society and nongovernmental stakeholders to promote effective water policies and guide national water sector reforms" (Arriens 2004), although it is not clear how interministerial committees can achieve much participation of the civil society.[13]

One reason why apex bodies proposed by ADB are relatively well accepted by the different countries might be that they understand the need to improve coordination and overall decision making in issues related to water resources. Yet, setting up such bodies, which are intended to be committees, not operational entities, does not automatically ensure that they will have a strong influence over water issues. Initially at least, they are likely to either remain largely cosmetic, or to appear as a threat to irrigation and other agencies, especially if they try to influence decisions in a way perceived as detrimental by these agencies. These bodies are, in general, an emanation of the higher levels of the bureaucracy and as such unlikely to preside over a drastic redistribution of power.

In Laos, the Water Resources Coordination Committee (WRCC) was established to "provide advice to the government on matters related to water and water resources and to coordinate the planning management, follow-up, inspection and protection of water and water resources aimed at sustainable development and utilization of water and water resources in line with the government policy of socioeconomic development" (Phonechaleun et al. 2002). In 2001, the Vietnamese government set up the Vietnam National Water Resources Council (VNWRC), to provide consultancy to the government "in the important decisions on water resource that come under the tasks and powers of the government." The VNWRC's achievements have so far been rather modest (Birch 2004, Lai 2002).[14] In Thailand, the ONWRC has been set up without legal backing and its record is modest. Despite the dedication of some officers, the committee's outreach is constrained by limited staff and resources, and its lack of power when dealing with long-established line agencies. Birch (2004) acknowledges that apex bodies must take a step-by-step approach and gradually build their capacity and legitimacy, and that they eventually critically depend on leadership and on the existence of a "champion" dedicated to pushing the new IWRM agenda.

The separation of the management/regulatory and water provision roles is a much more touchy issue because it meddles more deeply with the existing distribution of power. Therefore, it is no surprise that little, if any, progress is recorded on this point. The management function is generally being entrusted to Water Resource Management Departments established in new ministries responsible for natural resources or water as a whole. This is the origin of the MNRE in Thailand, Vietnam and, to some extent, of the MOWRAM in Cambodia.[15] So far, the experience has been inconclusive because powerful irrigation agencies have remained under the Ministry of Agriculture in Thailand, and the Ministry of Agriculture and Rural Development (MARD) in Vietnam. The new Water Departments have generally been staffed with individuals transferred from the irrigation agencies, who then found themselves in a delicate situation vis-à-vis their professional communities of origin.

On balance, it is too early to draw conclusions from these attempts to reorder roles and responsibilities in the water sector. However, regardless of whether the new concept is sound or not, it has not yet proved to be effective and it remains to be seen whether traditional structures will accept and adapt to these changes. The separation of roles has many benefits (Abernethy 2005) but it hinges on the assumption that water management can be expressed in terms of service agreements, abstraction licenses, allocation rules, enforcement, etc., which is often a far cry from the reality on the ground.

Participation and turnover

The ideology and rhetoric of participation have long infused development theory and practice (Cleaver 1999, Nelson and Wright 1995). The underpinning of the concept is that participation is conducive to greater efficiency and equity in management; that problems are better solved by those who experience them, and that projects are better maintained and more sustainable when designed and taken care of by the direct beneficiaries. Participation can be conceived as a tool (for better management) or as a process (with view to empowerment). In the water sector, there have been repeated and widespread attempts to replicate the traditional organizations for water management, observed in small communal systems, adapting them to large-scale schemes. Experiences with Participatory Irrigation Management (PIM) or management transfer (turnover) have had mixed results (Vermillion 1997, Samad and Vermillion 1999, Kolavalli and Brewer 1999, Meinzen-Dick et al. 1994), mostly because of a lack of genuine farmer empowerment and redistribution of roles, and of limitations in hydraulic infrastructure (Facon 2002).

In Cambodia, participation principles are reaffirmed in the draft water policy in a standardized and politically correct manner. The main policy line is the transfer of small- and medium-scale irrigation systems to Farmer Water User Communities (FWUCS). A long-term program called Participatory Irrigation Management and Development (PIMD) has been launched by the MOWRAM to establish FWUCS as legal entities with the right to own irrigation systems, hold bank accounts and enter into legally binding contracts. They are to be responsible for the O&M of their scheme; however, it is also clear that the "essential principle of PIMD is cost sharing" (Sinath 2003). After rehabilitation of the scheme (if needed) the FWUCS are to collect a fee: this is, initially, supported by the government, with a participation that decreases each year by 20 percent, over a period of five years. This income is to be re-injected into maintenance activities (that still need the approval of the Ministry) while possible surpluses can be used for collective investments such as tractors, threshing machines, pumps or seeds. The project is still at the initial stage and includes setting up one pilot project in each of the twenty-two provinces, while provincial teams are trained to establish and assist FWUCS.

The PIMD is a top-down program where farmers are considered as recipients of the knowledge and advice of the administration and experts, and are sometimes considered not to fully understand the issues at stake. The declared objective is "to catch the big benefits via using the participatory approach to mobilize, organize and explain to the farmers how important are the FWUCS, the responsibility for further O&M" and to instill a sense of ownership after rehabilitation of the irrigated system (Sinath 2003). The challenge of the project is to build up mechanisms of financial sustainability at the scheme level to avoid recurrent state expenditures or rapid deterioration of infrastructures. Several other similar initiatives have been launched by different NGOS (Roux 2004). Some anthropologists and political scientists dispute the adequacy of participatory approaches in Cambodia's socio-cultural context (Chandler 1996, Ovesen et al. 1996): the social structure is reputedly loose, with an all-pervasive notion of hierarchy and a strong control by the state on local life; communal work is associated with forced collective labor; marked inequalities and lack of personal security foster traditional patron-client relationships, etc.

The state-centered Water Law of Vietnam is parsimonious with regard to participation. It contains seventy-one occurrences of "state," forty-nine of "government," but none of "participation" or "participatory." This can be attributed to the particular conception that people are effectively represented by local People's Committees (PCS) and other official organizations. This may appear as a practical way to sideline civil society but such conception is also genuinely ingrained in local political discourse and culture, and the writers of the law did not feel the necessity to pepper its articles with participatory rhetoric. In that sense the notion of "civil society" is redundant. It is abundantly clear from official documents that the statement: "involvement of stakeholders is important for integrated water resources management" (Lai 2002) refers to the involvement of all ministries and provinces concerned. Likewise, China's water laws also make no mention of participation other than that of the concerned department and layers of the bureaucracy. The concept of civil society is absent and the same conception of people represented by their administration prevails.

In Laos, new policies are said to include "fully decentralized and bottom-up participatory planning with the governmental system" (Khamhung 2001) but there is little sign that this translates to giving people more say on, for example, the large infrastructures that are planned in the country (e.g., Nam Theun 2 or the Theun-Hinboun project; see Hirsch 2001, Pahlman 2000). The fact that NGOs are not allowed in Laos also gives a measure of the limits within which civil society is allowed to participate. According to Khamhung (2001), the rationale for the policy to transfer ownership and associated costs of irrigation to farm users is based on the belief that "traditional irrigation systems have been efficiently managed by farmers' communities" and also on the economic necessity for the government to reduce agriculture-sector subsidies.

In Thailand, the ideology of accountability and participation finds some common ground with that of self-reliance, cooperation and participation co-opted by governmental (in line with the 1997 Constitution) and academic circles, as well as with the rhetoric of the NGOs on grassroots democracy and community-centered development (Rigg 1991). It is thus little contested but the underlying conceptual understanding or assumptions of the different actors are often at variance.

Molle et al. (2002) have reviewed the Thai experience with Water User Groups (WUGS) and WUAS in large-scale public schemes and identified several reasons for their repeated failure. Most reforms focused at the tertiary level because irrigation agencies usually have little interest in what is occurring beyond the tertiary turnout. When supply at the tertiary level generally depends on allocation and distribution at higher levels in the system and cannot be made predictable, farmers soon discover that there is nothing to be managed and the WUGS become apathetic. Rather than issues of O&M at the tertiary level, the problem that has gained prominence in a context of water scarcity is the allocation of water in the dry season. The definition of (seasonal) entitlements in which users have a say (as a first step to defining water rights) is the preliminary step to the definition of service agreements, but nothing of the like has so far been attempted.

Attempts at joint management of natural resources (Heyd and Neef 2004) or to institute participatory irrigation management are still perceived locally as state-initiated and state-oriented, without real benefit for the farmers in terms of improved access to water. The contradiction between the decentralization rhetoric and the very nature of the Thai bureaucracy prompted Rigg (1991) to state that "a truly decentralized, grass-roots development approach comes into conflict with bureaucratic methods and Thai society."

More generally, in the whole region, the rhetoric of participation in official discourses and the prevailing cultural representations of farmer/ official relationships are often at odds. This can be clearly sensed during workshops and seminars, where officials are given the opportunity to express their viewpoints: "UNDP, UNEP, MRC, ADB, everyone who cares about environmental sustainability is a stakeholder, *even* the people themselves are stakeholders" (a Cambodian official);[16] "you have to make people understand your will" (a Thai RID official). These and many other declarations reveal deeply ingrained conceptions that are often at loggerheads with the intended activity and cannot be uprooted overnight.

IWRM and river basin management

IWRM and river basin management are definitely ubiquitous attributes of a "modern" water policy. They have received wide and consensual support from all quarters and feature prominently in all legislations. The underpinning of these concepts lies in the recognition that basin-wide interactions between upstream and downstream, surface water and groundwater, quality and quantity, and among uses and users, require integrated and systemic approaches to water management, as opposed to the sectoral and fragmented approaches followed in the recent past.

In Cambodia, the four priorities listed by MOWRAM include the establishment of a pilot RBO for the Prek Thnot River basin, which includes Phnom Penh. As for now, no activity is reported and the objectives and targets set up remain very general (Tara et al. 2003).[17] Myanmar, as part of its recent attempt to define a national Water Vision, has targeted the Sittoung River basin (Ti and Facon 2004). Likewise, in Laos, the Nam Ngum River basin (NNRB) has been selected as the first river basin to demonstrate the usefulness of IWRM approaches, because of the existing and planned water-sector investments as well as its proximity to the capital, Vientiane (ADB 2004). The National Water Vision for Laos (Phonechaleun et al. 2002) stresses not only the participatory nature of the RBO but also that management is under the control of the government.

In Thailand, the Seventh National Plan (1992–1996) provided strong incentive to the development of guidelines for water resources management in all twenty-five basins of Thailand (Sacha et al. 2001). This appears to be a desirable policy, especially in the basins where intra and inter-sectoral competition for water is highest. Basin studies, with detailed analyses of existing resources, uses, and problems were carried out for each of the twenty-five basins during the period of the plan. These studies were followed by a policy to gradually establish RBOs in these twenty-five main basins, the task of setting them up being incumbent upon the ONWRC. Farmers were grossly underrepresented in the earlier eight pilot RBOS but the ONWRC (now the Department of Water Resource) has worked to correct this imbalance. Three pilot RBOS that had received early support from the World Bank (Pasak River) and from the ADB (Upper Ping and Lower Ping rivers) are showing some interesting evolution (Apichart 2004). From an early composition heavily biased towards administrative representation, some RBOS have now been divided into subbasin committees, which choose/elect representatives at the village level, with further cooption of some of these representatives at the subdistrict, subbasin and basin levels successively. However, the lack of political and institutional support, with no formalization or recognition by law of their roles and power, is likely to affect these RBOS in the very same way they affected both the ONWRC ("upstream" of them) and the WUGS ("downstream"). The odds are high that these proto-RBOS will remain paper organizations with limited power and a consultative role rather than strong participants in arenas of negotiation and decision making.

It is also interesting to note how well the rhetoric of IWRM has been seized by consultant firms. Two consultants, for example, recently (2003) drew a Master Plan for the Ping River on behalf of the MNRE and claimed that "it was the first time basin management and integrated plans for water resources management were applied to solve the problems of drought, flood and water quality." An integrated plan is to establish both structural and nonstructural measures but while both are comparable in numbers the budget planned for the former ends up being only 1.3 percent of the total. Problems are to be "mitigated" by the implementation of both basin-level and local measures: numerous meetings with communities were used to produce a list of 5,056 desirable investments (mostly for domestic supply) "requested" by local people. These claims of a largely participative process are used to enhance the plan legitimacy but there is no mention of discussions/dissent about any of the large-scale plans envisaged, which seems to have been removed from debate.

China's 2002 law (CIECN 2004) stipulates that the "state shall, with respect to water resources, adopt a system that organizes the administration by watersheds as well as by administrative areas" and that comprehensive watershed plans[18] will be "formulated by the department of water administration under the State Council." The functions of river basin management focus on data collection, planning and interprovincial management on the key rivers. The Ministry of Water Resources retains a central role through its provincial departments but no role is granted to other stakeholders in the possible negotiations for water allocation or development plans. Shen (2004) believes that the law is "a milestone" but that its application is likely to face several problems, notably the equilibrium between river basin management and jurisdictional management, the lack of integration between water quality and water quantity, unclear separation of the regulator, manager and provider functions, and a low degree of participation.

Vietnam enshrined river basin management in its 1999 Water Law. In 2001, it started to build up RBOS for the Red, Dong Nai and Mekong (Delta) river basins (Wright 1999). As mentioned earlier, RBOS "must fit in the country administrative system" (Phan 2003). For the government, there is no question that official bodies, in particular at the local level, like districts, communes and People's Committees, do adequately represent the people, their needs and interests. The River Basin Planning Management Boards (RBOs in short) are seen as coordination institutions between different administrative scales/levels made necessary by the fact that river basins do cut across provinces and that interaction through the hydrological cycle requires management at an upper level (Phan 2003).

The Cuu Long RBO, for example (Mekong Delta), supported by Australian Agency for International Development (AUSAID), is focusing its work on gathering data and improving cooperation and integrated planning/management over the twelve provinces concerned (Cantor 2003). That it is part and parcel of the administration is strikingly illustrated by the fact that "the standing members of the RBO have been selected almost exclusively from Central Government Agencies based in Hanoi, more than 1,000 km from the delta, with non-voting representation from the provinces" (Cantor 2003). The need for coordination between provinces has become crucial to address the combined impact of land and water development on the river flow in the dry season (and resulting salinity intrusion threats).

The Vietnamese case well illustrates the dialectic of basin governance that, on the one hand, demands decentralization/participation, and where, on the other, integrated management also requires a degree of recentralization of decisions and command, or at least some high-level coordination. It is recognized that empowerment of local authorities in the 1980s has produced a fragmentation of water planning and management that created negative impacts (Wright 1999, Cantor 2003). Each province operates with a strong local perspective both in terms of management and planning of future works. The administrative structure is very hierarchical and provincial services are linked to MARD. As reported by Wright "any major issue affecting more than one province becomes a sensitive issue within MARD and is usually handled by separate discussion with each province." As some shortcomings of this fragmentation gradually appear, the RBOs might be seen as the place for the central government to reassert its authority regarding issues that eventually prove to transcend local boundaries, or to special interest-groups to promote narrow-focus development (Barrow 1998).

The way consultant firms or bureaucracies seem to ride the wave of IWRM supports the claims of Biswas (2004) that "because of the current popularity of the concept, some people have continued to do what they were doing in the past, but under the currently fashionable label of IWRM in order to attract additional funds, or to obtain greater national and international acceptance and visibility." Likewise, Jonch-Clausen and Fugl (2001) fear that IWRM may have "degenerated into one of these buzzwords that everybody uses but that mean many different things to different people." Just like participation, IWRM appears as something desirable and uncontroversial, and official documents can resort to it abundantly and at "no cost."

National policies, management of the Mekong River and other international issues

The Mekong River itself remains surprisingly pristine and undammed in its lower course, despite grand plans drawn up in the 1960s and 1970s to transform the basin to a sort of Tennessee Valley Authority. This can be partly ascribed to the difficulty of building reservoirs along the course of the river and also to the political instability of the region during the past four decades (Radosevich and Olson 1999, Mingsarn and Dore 2003).

National policies and development of water resources in the many tributaries of the river directly affect the flow in the Mekong, in terms of timing, quantity and quality. So far, interventions in the Chinese part of the basin have been limited but this has now changed with the construction of four dams (out of a total of eight reservoirs planned) (Dore et al. this volume). Forthcoming impacts of the Chinese dams are still unclear but opinions vary from alarmism (TERRA 2002) to relative confidence that sustained dry-season flows will benefit the basin (Adamson 2001). However, the main impact of a change in the hydrological regime (especially from the daily fluctuations in dam releases following electricity requirements), is likely to be on fisheries, since several species have reproduction cycles attuned to the current water regime and since the size of the fishery is directly related to the size of the flood. While Laos has only one major dam (Nam Ngum), Thailand has intensively developed its tributaries on the Korat plateau and has carried out studies on the possibility to divert significant parts of the Kok River, in Chiang Rai Province, before it reaches the Mekong, as well as some Mekong tributaries located in Laos (by siphoning under the river). Vietnam is also moving ahead with an aggressive hydropower development plan.

Potential for conflict from further direct abstraction from the Mekong or excessive use of its tributary streams is therefore high (Öjendal 2000), but efforts by the Mekong River Commission (MRC) have so far contributed to staving off divisive actions (Frederiksen 1998). In 1995, after three years of intense negotiations, the "Mekong River Agreement" was signed by the riparian countries (except China and Myanmar). The focus of the agreement is on "reasonable and equitable utilization" and "prevention and cessation of harmful effects" (with concern for environmental protection, ecological balance, pollution, fisheries, etc.). The touchiest section of the agreement is article 5, which constrains diversions from the mainstream and from tributaries (Radosevich and Olson 1999). Analysis of the agreement and consequences for riparian states are beyond the scope of this report. What needs to be noted here is that development of dams and diversions in each country is, in theory, constrained. Although the recent events in the Se San River (Vietnam/Cambodia) (Hirsch and Wyatt 2004, Öjendal et al. 2002) bode ill for the future, there are signs that the agreement acts as a deterrent to transbasin initiatives in Thailand.

Discussion

This brief review of policies in the water and irrigation sectors of the Mekong countries has yielded a number of both commonalities and discrepancies. It is apparent that the different countries are at different levels of water resources development. Laos and Cambodia are still at an early phase of infrastructural development and face the challenge of adopting better and more inclusive decision making processes than their neighbors were able to devise. Thailand and China have already significantly developed dams and irrigation schemes and are expected to move towards improved and more environmentally sensitive management. Vietnam and, probably, Myanmar stand somewhere in the middle and still have extensive plans to develop hydropower. Here, participatory decision making and willingness to manage water with a view on other uses need to be strengthened.

A global toolbox?

The development and evolution of water policies in all these countries[19] also bear, at least superficially, a number of similar features. They embody, tentatively or permanently, formally or informally, several traits that are part of the global "toolbox" of what is being promoted as "best practices," "internationally recognized principles," or "modern management." The hegemony and popularity of such principles, according to Biswas (2004), has something to do with their vagueness. "Integrated," "participatory," "decentralized," "pro-poor," "transparent" or "accountable" practices signal a "brave new world" and are at a certain level consensual, but their reification into a set of standard policy prescriptions may stymie or preclude the search for more flexible, adapted and negotiated outcomes.

The apparent uniformity of these water institutions partly stems from their promotion by bilateral and multilateral agencies, and also through mainstream literature and international conferences (Merrett 2003), or through influential NGOS such as WWF or IUCN. On the one hand, ADB discards the one-size-fits-all approach and acknowledges that "there is no standard approach that fits all the needs" (Arriens 2004). On the other hand, it proposes a quite unambiguous model of water regime, whereby "modern" water legislations are enacted, the state is confined to a regulatory role decentralized down to RBOS, while irrigation and urban waters "services" are assured by providers and utilities, duly paid by their clients in order to ensure full cost-recovery (Arriens 2004). Irrespective of the merits or limitations of such a water regime, this approach tends to "freeze" the range of arrangements and site-specific mix of communities, state and private management that are precisely what needs to be defined endogenously.

Mainstream approaches fostered by development banks or international agencies/think tanks and aimed at disseminating "best practices," organizing regional seminars and cross-country field visits do have positive aspects. They enable the formation of a wider community of water decision-makers who may learn from each other by putting their own context into perspective; they allow the diffusion of general principles and the identification of common problems and solutions at a generic level; they offer support/expertise and foster national processes of reflection on policies and the establishment of priorities; they sometimes elicit dialogues between segments of the administration or ministries that share responsibilities on water issues but do not coordinate their actions.

But policies are often top-down prescriptions consisting in identifying "lacks" and failures and then "providing" what has been identified as missing. Rehabilitation programs look for "technical fix," PIM policies or administrative reforms for "institutional fix," and new laws and regulation for "legal fix." All these approaches include a good deal of naïve social engineering that purges social processes of their political dimensions.

A corollary of the standard policy toolbox approach is that changes are evaluated based on the formal existence of particular administrative devices or institutions, without looking too much at contents and at processes. This is reinforced by the requirement for development banks and project managers to "measure" the impact of their interventions. They thus run the risk of finding themselves in the situation where the success of participative programs is supposedly assessed by the number of Water User Groups or RBOS set up (by the government), or by the number of meetings held with "stakeholders." It is obvious that the mere formation of an RBO does not ensure integrated management (Schlager and Blomquist 2000) nor does a water law reorder a water regime by itself (Shah et al. 2001). As Jasper (2001) noted with regard to the situation in Zimbabwe, it is becoming "painstakingly apparent that it takes more than good legislation to guarantee a change for the better."

Transposition of experiences and mindsets

The question of the transposition of experiences from one setting to the other is central to development theory and practice.[20] Are "success stories," "best practices," or "promising technologies" readily transferable to other contexts? Many analysts observe that the water sector appears to be largely littered with well-intentioned and rationalistic reforms that have failed to fully appraise the context of their implementation (Sampath 1992, Pigram 2001, Shah et al. 2001, Molle 2001). This raises two questions: is a particular reform element sound or indeed relevant in a particular context? And can this element be readily introduced by a voluntary and formal administrative fiat? In other words, even if a particular policy is likely to bring benefits, has its introduction any chance of success within the particular political-economic context?

It is interesting to note that reforms prompted by outsiders are never literally implemented but rather "absorbed" and always "digested" in some way: laws that include general principles always need application decrees that remain largely at the discretion of concerned ministries; conditionalities set by the multilateral banks are often watered down into pilot projects which evaporate with the next government or policy change; the transit through different governmental spheres may allow draft laws (once translated into local language) to be aptly modified before they are voted; participatory reforms are steered off course by peculiar conceptions of bureaucratic top-down "participatory" interventions; the rhetoric of IWRM is hijacked by line agencies repositioning themselves within the new discourse and by consultant firms proposing conventional structural projects under the disguise of "people's request" or integrated approaches.

All in all, two opposite attitudes seem possible:
1. One may simply dismiss attempts to set RBOs in contexts that are arguably unfit, and sometimes adverse, or legislation/reforms that seem overambitious and are unlikely to be put in practice. This leapfrogging syndrome often leads to failed and untimely policy reforms and make further attempts more difficult (Shah et al. 2001).[21] As Thomas and Grindle (1990) noted, with regard to economic and political reorganizations, "Reforms have been attempted when the administrative or political resources to implement them did not exist. The result has generally been misallocated resources, wasted political capital, and frustration."
2. But one may also adopt a more optimistic stance, whereby RBOs, apex bodies, cost-sharing arrangements, etc., are considered as necessary, if not sufficient, foundations towards a longer-term objective of establishing IWRM, redefining line agencies as service providers and water users as clients, in self-financing and sustainable arrangements. Initial effectiveness of the measures taken may often be limited or nil but there is confidence that, with time, adjustments to local reality lead to viable and adapted institutions. The gradual evolution of RBOs in Thailand (Apichart 2004), or the recognition by ADB that fully independent regulators

may not necessarily be the most effective (Arriens 2004), are examples of evolution by learning.

Both positions have their weaknesses. Sticking to the former may lead to inaction because settings are rarely easily amenable to change; it denies the possibility to seize opportunities or the necessity to adjust to changes. Sticking to the latter, on the other hand, may be tantamount to subscribing to the fallacy that some blueprints and alleged "best practices" can be easily transplanted, without burdening oneself with a thorough analysis of each situation. As pointed out by Evans (2003), with regard to economic reforms, "institutional monocropping" premised on the presumption that "the most advanced countries have already discovered the one best institutional blueprint and that its applicability transcends national cultures and circumstances" is a sure recipe for frustration. What is important to acknowledge is that none of the best practices promoted are inherently good or bad. Beyond the formal nature of a particular proposition, what counts is the substance of the corresponding process. For example, RBOS can be pivotal platforms for representations of different users and values about water, for information sharing and knowledge building, and for decision making about crucial issues of infrastructural development or water allocation. But they can also just as well be limited to consultative meetings masquerading as participatory processes, or be a handy way to sanction and give legitimacy to business-as-usual strategies. The two logics are at work and the constant but antagonistic shifts towards either genuine participation and democratization, or institutional reordering and capture by more powerful actors, is ultimately a political struggle, or process, shaped by many factors. This invites us to somehow reconcile the two approaches by looking for a middle path between prescription and a wait-and-see attitude.

Instilling or enabling change

Whether reforms are about the design of a water policy or water law, the establishment of basin or catchment organizations or platforms, the turnover of irrigation management to users, or the financial sustainability of a domestic water supply scheme, the main ingredients of these reforms are various and generally conflicting values, discourses and interests, which reflect the diversity of the people having a stake in water and the way they try to secure both personal and common interests. The smaller the scale, the more "wicked" the problems are: no omniscient representative of the public interest, enlightened planner, or expert-based model, will ensure an optimal social outcome (Wester and Warner 2002, Lachapelle et al. 2003, Clark 2002). Where heterogeneities and uncertainties prevail, "processes of mediation, bargaining, conflict and power become key" dimensions of institution building (Mehta et al. 2000). Robust arrangements combine (often lengthy) trust building, confrontation of worldviews and social learning, informed and supportive science, political space for the representation of all stakeholders, and must allow for a degree of "messiness and unpredictability" that is usually not recognized in classical approaches to Common Property Resource management (Cleaver 2000).

A more inclusive and balanced development path is, however, largely contingent upon societal changes and democratization, whose dynamics lie beyond the scope of the sole water sector. The vision of a shift from supply-oriented, paternalistic development to process-oriented approaches leading to "informed consent" (Delli Priscoli 2004), however attractive and desirable, certainly remains on the far horizon rather than something that can be conjured up by fiat or mere good will. Deliberative development enables a better definition of social choice but can only develop in a political environment whereby some "messiness" in the process of choice is allowed and where a degree of redistribution of existing power is made possible (Evans 2003). Multi-stakeholder dialogues are one way to engage government, business and civil society stakeholders in processes of learning and negotiation (Roling and Woodhill 2001).

In that sense, "check-box" approaches which merely aim at establishing formal and static structures or laws miss the crucial point that institutional building is an evolutionary and socially embedded process: human systems must adapt not only because surrounding ecosystems change but also because the actual distribution of a resource is always contested and generate conflicting claims that need to be reconciled (Both Ends 2000, Miller and Hirsch 2003, Cleaver and Franks 2003).

The definition of more inclusive and equitable governance patterns is also hampered by scale constraints. Local communities and NGOs emphasize the use of local and traditional knowledge to address problems and this knowledge and corresponding institutions are often quite effective at a micro scale. However, communities have rarely developed means to address issues at a wider scale because there was no such necessity and because they may not have the understanding of environmental changes occurring at a larger scale. They, therefore, have difficulties to scale-up their knowledge, organizations and interventions in a context of growing hydrologic interconnectedness across scales. To some extent it can even be stated that the principle of subsidiarity is antagonistic to macro-level basin management. Conversely, state agencies have a better understanding of macro-level constraints and allocation, have access to more data and technical tools, but struggle to understand the heterogeneity and discontinuities, both physical and human, of the real world, and have mixed success in their application of ready-made solutions. Their problem is scaling-down their understanding and management practices (Roth 2004).

Emerging governance patterns and main actors
What is the overall governance pattern emerging from the ongoing development planning and water policy reforms, and who are the main actors? While a quite vibrant civil society has developed in Thailand in the past fifteen years (Hirsch 2001), and is now emerging in other Mekong countries through the growth of NGOs (Dore 2003), grassroots movements and citizens as a whole have yet to be incorporated in decision making processes. Advocacy groups have recorded a few successes in their opposition to dams, for example, but they tend to be considered by governments more as an unavoidable nuisance than as "partners in development" to be reckoned with. Participation of "stakeholders" in meetings related to water policy or the setting up of RBOs has often remained cosmetic and largely been a way to legitimize state action.

NGOs, local activists and academics have generally adopted stances putting forward local traditions, culture and knowledge, but these have not been factored in policies (see Watershed 2001, for Thailand). These civil society organizations are also not homogeneous. Conservationists sometimes see the preservation of nature or biodiversity as an objective, which must take precedence over productive activities of poor people. The debate between conservation and production (e.g., protecting forests *from* people vs. protecting forest *by* people, see Johnson and Forsyth 2002) is persistent, although environmentalists have also borrowed from the livelihood framework in order to find compromises. Marked differences are also apparent between NGOs, which systematically oppose taxation of peasants, and organizations like IUCN or WWF, which have largely bought into the mainstream discourse of pricing and markets as a way to regulate the use of natural resources.

ADB and other funding agencies have also found difficulties navigating between their borrowers/client states and organized advocacy groups, despite unremitting calls for participation. While willing to balance government power through a more democratic process of decision making, they fear that projects (and disbursement of funds) may be paralyzed by uncompromising NGOs. Current affairs provide signs that both multilateral agencies and states are nevertheless, willy-nilly, gradually moving towards a more cautious approach to planning (Öjendal et al. 2002). However, traditional expert-driven approaches to development problems and a reluctance to engage in lengthy and uncertain planning processes set a limit to the changes one should expect.

If water policies owe a lot to mainstream general concepts, one must also question the role of national decision makers. Are these merely passive receivers of concepts crafted in other arenas? Is there a struggle between state departments, schools of thought (e.g., big vs. small projects), lines of thinking, or ideologies? The material reviewed earlier does not allow us to fathom policy-making processes in all these dimensions but the general impression is that disagreements are more related to political or administrative in-fighting, struggle for power, budget, or prerogatives than to differences in vision. Yet, it is also apparent that each line agency taken in isolation is not homogeneous. Some segments favor the status quo and oppose changes but others are open to reform and sometimes champion them.

Most bureaucracies or line agencies have difficulties in dealing with more deliberative or participatory approaches. They feel threatened by what they perceive as a loss of control, challenge to their legitimacy, or denial of their competence (Lachapelle et al. 2003, Wester and Warner 2002). The limits of the participatory rhetoric are also apparent in the fact that large-scale projects with massive potential impact on population and the environment and are still being devised in secrecy (e.g. the Thai "water grid" or the plans for "river interlinking" in India).

Research issues

This review of the water sectors in the Mekong region has unearthed more questions than answers. Failed reforms have a cost not only in terms of time and money but also in terms of lost opportunity and distrust. Research should address both theoretical issues (e.g. what governs differences in policy responses to similar challenges) and practical ones, providing insight on what governs success and failure, and on implementation, while emphasizing the need for the contextualization of options (see Bery 1990). Because of the centrality of water in many activities and livelihoods, relevant research questions on water governance in the Mekong region span a large spectrum of issues. Those more specifically related to irrigation and water resources management, either on a general plane or in relation to a particular project, could include:

1. What are the most pressing issues regarding water and irrigation practices and policies, and in which locale are these issues more salient (establish spatial and thematic priorities; do not apply policies across the board)?
2. What are the measures that can, realistically, be successfully taken and enforced by the state, given its current power and the political-economic environment?
3. What changes can be gradually instilled by a bottom-up approach that creates a sense of ownership and generates incentives through clear benefits to the population concerned? At the same time, what are the costs and limitations of bottom-up approaches? Most importantly, what avenues are there for a multi-scalar approach, co-management and so on that accommodate both state and civil society interests and agendas?
4. What is the scope for a "professionalization" of line agencies? What incentives to managers and officers can be designed?

5. What are the intrinsic limitations of local stakeholders (knowledge limited to local scale, nonawareness of scalar interactions, varied cohesiveness, etc.) and can leadership and accountability be fostered?
6. What can we learn from the ongoing implementation of policies on the ground? What scope is there to enhance social learning, build trust and favor endogenous processes?
7. What is the underlying structure of power and interests, within the bureaucracy, political parties and other stakeholders, and what bearing does this have on the options available and possible outcomes? How can this be rebalanced? And what is the nature of bureaucratic competition within and between state structures?
8. Genesis of reform and ideas: what type of knowledge and legitimacy are used, to what degree can experiences elsewhere be recontextualized?
9. How can the support of external development banks and agencies be made more efficient and better blend support to both the government and the civil society? How to avoid ready-made "best practices" to crowd out more endogenous responses? How to reconcile the slow pace of sociopolitical processes and the short time frames of state or bank projects?
10. How pressing was the need for such reforms and how sound have the steps been taken? To what degree (and why) have national bureaucracies and ruling political parties shared a concern for reordering the water sector and added their willpower to the banks' solicitations, and how does this vary from country to country? How can we get beyond the infamous "lack of political will" explanation?
11. What is the nature, and what are the implications of private sector involvement? How are community and private conceived in each case as alternatives to state roles?

In sum, water policy appears as a contested domain where varied interests (e.g. financial or political dividend of projects), values (e.g. local development or large projects), and strategies to access water conflict with each other. Two main lines of tension have been identified. The first is the conflict between water policies largely derived from international references, presumed internationally sanctioned practices and, on the other hand, the need for a more endogenous definition of priorities with emphasis placed on the specifics of each locale. The second line of tension is between the conventional top-down mode of action of state agencies and the general principle that puts the active participation of concerned populations as the point of departure for designing interventions that are more efficient, fairer and less-prone to externalities. Crafting or, rather, enabling governance patterns for water management in the Mekong region will be a journey towards bridging these divides.

Notes

1 China is mentioned but not dealt with in full detail because the diversity of situations warrants an extensive treatment beyond the ambition of this report.

2 In particular, it is meant to orient research of the water governance network of M-POWER.

3 The cost of the project fluctuates between 200 and 400 billion baht, depending on the official sources. The former Prime Minister Thaksin pledged to set aside 100 billion baht "for solving water problems in the Northeast" (*The Nation* April 24, 2004).

4 MOWRAM's current financial resources only ensure (very low) staff salaries and 10 percent of needed operation and maintenance (O&M) funds (MOWRAM and ADB 2001).

5 Numbers given by Khamhung (2001) differ: "The irrigation area in dry season has rapidly increased from 29,000 ha in 1996 to 197,000 ha in 2000." This increase has mostly been based on pump irrigation.

6 The introductory note of the Cambodian draft stresses that the document was "well conceived, in line with modern trends in water resources management" (KOC 2002).

7 The 2002 draft has been translated in Khmer and is to be submitted to the Council of Ministers, the Parliament, the Senate and the King before being translated back to English after its approval. This "black box" process ensures the appropriation of the law by national decision-makers, but sometimes also harbours some surprises, as was observed with the earlier fisheries and forest laws.

8 "This inventory shall indicate the location, quantity and quality of the resources during the year, each year," A massive task that seems to ignore the current poor status of data/knowledge of the overall hydrology in the country.

9 But this principle has been a principle of Chinese irrigation (as well as Vietnam's) for many years dating back to the 1960s.

10 As reported by Malano et al. (1999), the Vietnamese Water Law states general principles but provides no details on the modalities of their application. This will meet development banks' conditionalities for further funding in the water sector, while possibly deferring concrete actions for an indeterminate period of time. China's laws, too, let application modalities to be defined by ulterior decrees.

11 A similar static and bureaucratic view of river basin management appears graphically in IWMI (2003), where "right" policies, laws and administration are the three "pillars" supporting the temple: "sharing river basin water resources."

12 See http://www.adb.org/Water/NWSAB/default.asp.

13 The compositions of the apex bodies of Vietnam (Anonymous 2004b) and Laos (Anonymous 2004a) do not show any inclusion of non-state participants. Arriens (2004) sees an initial role of apex bodies at "multi-stakeholder forum at the highest level" which does not accord with their composition, unless stakeholders are assumed to be limited to the state apparatus.

14 An official report in 2002 on ONWRC (Lai 2002) states that "there is a perception that ONWRC is small and poorly supported... and inactive."

15 But Cambodia also has a Ministry of Environment (in addition to the Ministry of Agriculture and to the Ministry of Rural Development).

16 Southeast Asia Water Forum, Chiang Mai, December 2003, emphasis added.

17 Or sometimes utterly unrealistic: "Increasing water production two times in five years," "Decreased conflict in the river basin in two years" (Tara et al. 2003).

18 "The 'comprehensive plans'... shall refer to the overall arrangements, formulated according to the needs of economic and social development and the present situation of the development and utilization of water resources, for the development, utilization, preservation and protection of water resources, as well as for the prevention and control of water disasters" (CIECN 2004).

19 To a lesser degree in Myanmar because of its particular political situation.

20 There has been, for example, a flourishing literature on the conditions and possibility to transfer Australian experience to other regions of the world, notably to the Mekong River basin and Sri Lanka (Chenoweth 1999, Pigram 1999, 2001, Malano et al. 1999, Birch et al. 1999).

21 "Uncritical 'copycat' replication of successful institutional models—either by enthusiastic national governments or at behest of enthusiastic donors—is the sure formula for failure" (Shah et al. 2001).

CHAPTER 3

POLITICS OF FLOODS AND DISASTERS

Louis Lebel and Bach Tan Sinh

Introduction

People are never satisfied with the weather they have. For the farmer overseeing her rain-fed crop of rice, the wait for the next rains at the start of the monsoon is tense and hopeful. The monsoons of East Asia, predictable within bounds, have framed the adaptation of agriculture and social organization in the Mekong region. Large variations in rainfall, run-off and river flows between the end of the dry and wet seasons have shaped the way societies use land, build their houses and shuffle livelihood activities through the annual cycle.

Not all years are alike. Some have been drier than others; now that there are more water users, those drier years can be sources of intense local conflicts. Some have been wetter than others; now that there are more houses, roads and shops built on the flood plains those wetter years cause damage to property and loss of life. For the urban storm water manager the satellite images of a depression forming over the sea hundreds of kilometers away leads to more sleepless nights.

Global warming is adding another complication: the weather your grandmother's society experienced and learnt how to live with is likely to be different from that of your daughter's (Few 2003, Kundzewicz and Schellnhuber 2004). The question is: will today's infrastructure be appropriate for tomorrow's weather?

Societies have had to learn to live with both too much and too little water. As their skills and confidence in their engineering capacities have grown they have looked more and more towards solutions in concrete for managing floods. These feats have allowed governments to treat floods and disaster management as technical and administrative issues (Lebel et al. 2006c). The ecological impacts of river regulation, channel modification, and floodplain manipulation have been assumed to be small and worthwhile in the grander scheme of modernization. Upper tributary watersheds are the only part of the landscape for which the value of ecosystem services needs to be acknowledged.

Forgotten are the people in the lowland whose livelihoods depend on the ebb and flow of floodwaters to enrich soils and fisheries. Despised and discriminated against are those in the uplands whose livelihoods depend on the watershed soils for their farms. Blamed for their vulnerability to floods the poor in squatter settlements in the city tolerate poor sanitation and no access to drinking water so they can reach the jobs in factories and the informal sector. In this chapter we argue that the security of already marginalized households in the mountains and floodplains is being undermined by state approaches to flood and disaster management that increasingly serve elite and business interests and fail to address the opportunities provided by economic growth. We attribute this state of affairs to a lack of overt politics.

This chapter is about the politics of floods and disaster in the Mekong region. First we explore how people talk about floods and ask: when is a flood a disaster? Second, we describe some of the ways societies make choices about: who and what should be at risk? And, what are the underlying causes of vulnerability? Third, we look at how societies respond to major floods, asking: Are new risks and vulnerabilities being created? We end with suggestions that go beyond the logic of risk management to focus more on negotiating ways of building and maintaining adaptive capacities in society. We conclude with a concise action research agenda aimed at improving how floods are governed.

Talking floods: Events and discourses

Floods as a physical event vary greatly with respect to their velocities, onset, and high flow duration and recession dynamics, in their impacts on debris flows and water quality, and in their unusualness with respect to the historical flood regime. Floodwaters may come from rainfall and run-off, from failures of water retention structures, and in coastal areas, from tidal surges and wave extremes (figure 3.1).

Some floods are treated by society as potentially harmful; some turn into disasters (figure 3.1). Although most attention is given to maximum water levels, other factors like nutrient and sediment loads may be more critical to the level of benefits obtained from floods and factors like velocity and debris flows most important to risks of damage (Dixit 2003).

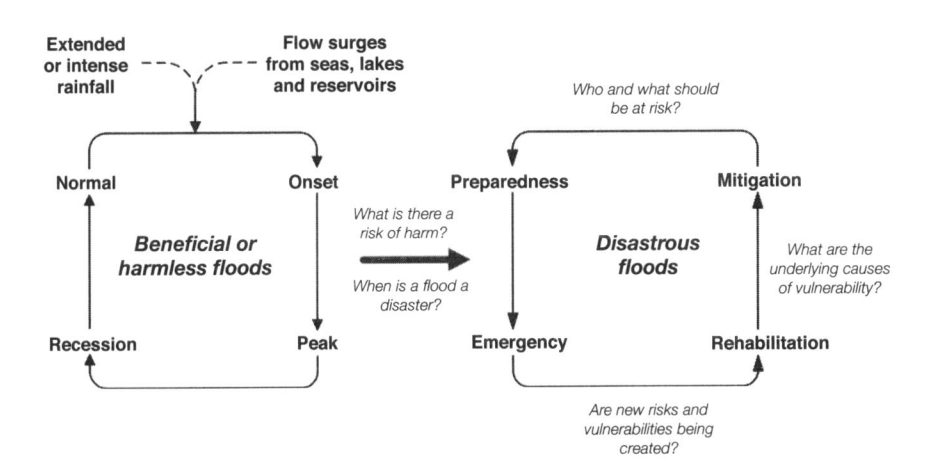

Figure 3.1 Floods may be beneficial, harmless or disastrous

```
Extended                Flow surges
or intense  -- -\ ,---- from seas, lakes
rainfall         \/     and reservoirs      Who and what should
                  |                            be at risk?
                  ↓
    Normal      Onset        Preparedness              Mitigation
                          What is there a
              Beneficial or  risk of harm?      Disastrous      What are the
              harmless floods   →                 floods        underlying causes
                          When is a flood a                     of vulnerability?
                              disaster?
    Recession    Peak         Emergency               Rehabilitation

                                     Are new risks and
                                     vulnerabilities being
                                         created?
```

Floods have adverse impacts on poor people in different ways, each of which requires different social institutions and policies to handle (Fox 2003). First, they can cause death and injury. Second, they can result in loss of homes, crops, livestock and means of livelihood. Third, they can increase risks of water-borne diseases (Few et al. 2004). Fourth, floods can disrupt economic activities.

The attributes of concern to different groups vary and the same flood event can be viewed very differently by people with contrasting interests. Floods look very different when you climb out of a boat onto the roof of your suburban house than to a farmer casting his fishing net over an inundated field. But even for the farmer the familiar flood that comes well after harvest is seen very differently than the unseasonally early event that strikes before harvest. Throughout the region local languages often have several terms to describe different kinds of floods. In Thai for example flash flooding in the mountains is called *nam paa lai lak* (literally the coming of fast forest water) whereas river bank overflow in usually described as *nam tuam* (with the sense of overflowing and covering with water).

The diversity of floods within the Mekong region is reflected in the range of arguments offered to explain their occurrence and rationalize different approaches to flood management (table 3.1). In traditional rice-growing cultures of the plains and deltas, wet season floods were a cause for celebration. It was a time of plentiful fish and of renewal for the paddy fields. A discourse of living with floods is part of such cultures (Wong and Zhao 2001).

Table 3.1 Talking about floods

Discourse	Main argument
Living with	Floods are natural events that arise from high rainfall. Living things are adapted to flood regimes and it is difficult to do much to prevent floods. Therefore, we should learn to live with floods.
Control	Floods are natural events that can and should be controlled with properly constructed and operated dams, embankments and spillways.
Adjust	Floods are caused by people, from how they use watersheds and floodplains, and how they regulate and modify river channels. We need to adjust land-and river-use in ways that don't cause floods.

Urban lifestyles and industrial or service-sector livelihoods are changing all of this, especially in the traditional rice-growing deltas of the region, and the wider acceptance of the "control" discourse. At the same time authorities may make nostalgic appeal to the "living with" discourse as an excuse for inaction or when protection efforts fail.

The "adjust" discourse (table 3.1) usually sits somewhere between the "living with" and "control" discourses when it comes to need for structural responses. It argues that "control" measures taken were somehow wrong or incomplete because they did not pay sufficient attention to human behavior and activities. In the real world combinations of or compromises between the extreme forms of the discourses listed are also articulated by some actors.

The interplay of discourses is perhaps most neatly illustrated by the divergent viewpoints of people from the north and south of Vietnam. In the mountainous north, floods are known as *lut*, characterized by rapid flow speeds and sudden increases in water depth. Floods are seen as a threat from which societies must protect themselves and they have done so with an impressive system of dykes constructed over millennia. Legends depict an epic struggle over a princess (*my nuong*) between gods with powers to raise mountains (*son tinh*) and water (*thuy tinh*); a battle that the loser renews each year with floods and which the people fight against with their dykes.

By contrast, in the large flat delta areas of the south, floods are known as *nuoc noi*. Flood speeds are sluggish and water depth increases are modest and slow. The dominant philosophy was of living with floods. During the flood season people did not cultivate rice but moved back to villages on higher ground leaving the low-lying areas empty each wet season. Floods were not perceived as causing disasters and hence needing to be prevented and controlled until very recently.

After reunification in 1975 the Government of Vietnam introduced resettlement policies that brought people from the north to the less densely populated areas of the Cuu Long delta. The new settlers lived permanently in the new economic zones and began cultivating three rice crops per year including one during the flood season. Now the government is trying to cope with the damage caused by floods through dykes and embankments around residential clusters.

Sharing the benefits

For rural households that continue to benefit from floods that renew agricultural soils and stimulate productivity of aquatic ecosystems that support fisheries the "living with" floods argument still makes the most sense (table 3.1).

The high dependence of livelihoods on the natural flood regime for the Tonle Sap region in Cambodia (Varis and Keskinen 2003) is often used to articulate concerns about the impacts of upstream dam construction on flood regimes downstream. The importance of flood regimes is not just restricted to the supply of water to major wetlands but is also connected to the life cycles of fish and other aquatic organisms. Moreover, the reversals of flow towards the Tonle Sap Lake during the high mainstream flows of the Mekong River mean that the lake naturally redirects floodwaters away from downstream Delta areas (Bakker 1999), thus underlining the importance that its capacity must not be decreased as a result of, for example, changes in sediment delivery or in timing of peak flows. Competing discourses about the naturalness, benefits and adverse impacts of floods are also central to political conflicts over the management of natural resources in the seasonally flooded forests in the floodplain of the Songkhram River in northeastern Thailand (David Blake, unpublished manuscript).

For fish the predictable alteration between dry and wet seasons is a flip between resource scarce and glut conditions (Dudgeon 2000). Many species have evolved life cycles synchronized to this periodic flood pulse that expands and retracts waters across extensive floodplains. In this setting the prevention and tempering of floods is an alteration of the natural flood disturbance regime and should itself be thought of as an external perturbation with likely adverse impacts on those ecosystems (Dudgeon 2000).

Societies also build dams and reservoirs to hold back floodwaters for use in times of scarcity, for example, dry season irrigation. Less directly, but as important, societies through the development of land resources for agriculture often reduce tree cover increasing run-off and sedimentation. Although it is popular for those outside the region to call this "deforestation" and "degradation" it must be recognized that this is an assessment made narrowly from the perspective of conservation of biodiversity and watershed functions; from the perspective of food production, the gains may still be seen as overwhelmingly positive by large segments of rural society. In Ayutthaya Province in the central plains of Thailand we have observed how the switch to higher yielding but less flood-resistant varieties of rice has resulted in flood protection measures being taken to protect farmer's paddy rice fields at the expense of rural towns (Manuta et al. 2006).

From flood to disaster

When is a flood a disaster? (figure 3.1) Floods are not automatically "natural" disasters: it can depend on who you are, and how you make your living. It can also depend on suddenness and timing. Flash-floods at night may be particularly dangerous to life. The characteristics of a flood event relative to preparedness, early warning systems and flood control structures also matters. Even in societies with long history of experience with flood regimes some flood events lead to regrettable losses of life and damage to property. Flood events that are unusual in their timing, speed of onset, depth or duration pose the largest problems for society. Extreme events, rare by definition, may lie completely beyond the experience of most people and memories of most organizations and cultures.

The way floods are talked about and classified is important to the shaping of expectations and responses of governments and other organizations to particular events. Once a flood is considered a disaster many new questions related to decision-making in disaster management become salient (figure 3.1). The language of disasters brings with it, for example, the peculiar logic of crises: the need to act quickly and decisively and sacrifice consultation and debate. Just as there are major discourses around floods that help different groups classify events as floods or disasters so there are different arguments about the causes and appropriate responses to major, potentially disastrous, flood events (table 3.2).

The "injustice" discourse is usually associated with groups—both state and non-state—concerned with the plight of poor people, for example, those living in informal settlements along waterways in the major cities of the region. The "incompetence" argument is a favourite of mass media in countries where such criticism of the government is tolerated, for example, within limits, as in Thailand. The "ignorance" argument is a nearly universal one used by responsible officials and a common one among community leaders.

Understanding the diversity of interests in flood management helps understand the different ways people talk about floods and disasters.

Table 3.2 Talking about flood disasters

Discourse	Main argument and favored responses
Injustice	Flood disasters are caused by social and political factors that result in disadvantaged groups having to live in high risk areas with poor emergency relief and recovery support. Reduce inequities and poverty.
Incompetence	Flood disasters are caused by the incompetence of state agencies to effectively warn about, respond to and rebuild after natural events. Re-design coordination mechanisms; train officials.
Ignorance	Flood disasters are caused by the forgetfulness or ignorance of people about potential risks. Educate the public.

Reducing risks

Risk management

States no longer just respond to disasters; they also claim to manage disaster risks (Lebel et al. 2006c). Most efforts at reducing risks from floods (and of flood disasters) focus on, to the extent that financing allows, technical assessments and structural measures (Takeuchi 2001). The "risk management" discourse is intentionally apolitical, reducing issues of differences in vulnerability and risks to static maps that avoid having to address the social reasons why people live and work where they do.

Assessments of risks and vulnerabilities in the Mekong region have mostly been made by international consultants (e.g. MRC-GTZ Cooperation Programme 2003). The Pacific Disaster Centre, for example, recently completed vulnerability mapping exercise for the Lower Mekong Basin in which spatial information about places where floods occur were combined with other development indicators and used as proxy measures for social vulnerability (PDC 2004). Opportunities for public participation in planning for floods and mitigation of flood-related disasters are rare. The need to take swift action in emergency situations may have left people "blind" to the longer-term needs of effective mechanisms of governance for reducing risks and vulnerabilities to floods in the first place.

Urbanization and economic growth, for example, have resulted in rapid increase in value of public and private property in flood-prone areas of Bangkok, Hanoi, Ho Chi Minh City (Schultz 2002). The very high cost of protecting these low-lying areas has driven states into choices about acceptable risks that are often high with respect to losses of property and human lives if extreme events were to occur. The non-transparent priority setting, as we will see in the following sections, can also result in flood and flood-related disaster reduction programs being turned into processes of risk redistribution and recreation.

Dams and reservoirs are used by water resource managers to moderate size and frequency of peak floods downstream (Schultz 2002). In Thailand, the large Bhumipol Dam in the Ping River and Sirikit Dam on the Nan River have reduced peak high flows downstream in the Chao Phraya by about 60 percent and through releases altered the hydrological cycle substantially (Tebakari et al. 2005). Other common structural measures for managing floods include construction of levees and embankments.

No country in the region can afford to take a purely structural approach even with the underlying ideology of control. Although references are made to land development guidelines most of the practical institutional effort is aimed at coordinating near event preparedness and short-term post-event emergency relief. The 2018 Chao Phraya Flood Management Master Plan in Thailand, for example, is filled with proposed structural measures and few basic institutional suggestions (Government of Thailand 1999).

The primary focus of flood management in Vietnam is in enhancing mitigation and prevention capacities. The focus is on infrastructure financed through loans. The main organizational innovation has been the establishment of a Department of Dykes Management, Flood and Storm Control at the central level with provincial branches and Disaster Management Units. There is no private flood insurance system because of the difficulties in negotiating state guarantees but a Disaster Self Reliant Fund system is being developed with assistance from the United Nations Development Programme.

A basic component of hazard-preparedness is the monitoring and forecasting of potential disasters with as long a warning time and as accurate a forecast as possible. The formal state system of weather and storm forecasting in Vietnam is centralized and functional. However, for some users, it is slow and can be improved with cross-validation. We have observed that some communities and users get additional weather and meteorological information from the Internet. The Cam Kim commune, Dien Ban district, Quang Nam Province in Vietnam, for example, uses a computer to receive news of a looming storm through the Internet well before they receive news from the steering committees at the province and district levels. In another case, the Mekong River Commission (MRC) is assisting with developing better early warning systems in vulnerable locations along the Mekong River in Champassak Province, Lao PDR.

Community and private sector participation are often critical for effective responses to disaster-threatening situations and emergency relief operations (Few 2003). A good reason to look beyond the state is that its capacities may be mostly on paper.

Thus the mandate of the Department of Disaster Prevention and Mitigation (DDPM) in Thailand greatly exceeds its financial and human resources (Manuta et al. 2006). The Laos disaster reduction strategy is primarily based on Decree No 158/PM (August 22, 1999) and the National Disaster Management Committee formed after assignment No 97/MLSW (June 30, 2000). The committee contains representatives from twelve ministries and oversees a conventional hierarchy on paper of units at provincial, district and village levels. Lower level units, however, are still very poorly linked with national system. In Vietnam, the current government regulation concerning mitigation of disaster damage is simply the one on the individual's responsibility for prevention and protection from harms caused by storms and floods (article 6 of the Ordinance of Storm and Flood Control, 2000).

In all countries in the region much work still needs to be done to get local government more closely involved in flood disaster management preferably in close partnership with communities in their jurisdiction. Local government is potentially very important to disaster mitigation as they are in a good position to assess local needs, take quick actions in emergency situations, and make requests for assistance from other government agencies on behalf of their constituencies. Moreover, as accountable officials they have responsibilities and legitimate authority to take action in crisis situations which other volunteers and community leaders lack. So far very little attention has been paid to the role of local government in flood disaster management in the Mekong region.

Creating opportunities for meaningful participation in disaster preparedness, relief and rehabilitation is essential for groups already disadvantaged and marginalized by development (Lebel et al. 2006b). Supported, prepared and warned they can help design and undertake actions that build on their own capacities and skills.

Risk redistribution

Disaster risk reduction often means risk redistribution. Large differences in vulnerability among people are in part being created and reproduced through institutional apparatuses designed to reduce risks to certain subsets of the population.

Some of the best examples relate to the protection of capital cities. Flood protection measures to protect the central business district in Bangkok frequently result in prolonged flooding of surrounding suburbs and districts. Having the option to use agricultural land for storage of flood waters in extreme events could reduce risks to built infrastructure but would require proper insurance or compensation schemes to be in place (Fox 2003).

In October 2006, the Thai government had to divert flood waters to agricultural fields upstream to protect key parts of Bangkok. A lack of pre-consultation and negotiation of compensation, and even a proper institutional mechanism for such discussions, made it very difficult to take action in time to prevent serious flooding and led to serious conflicts with, and stress in, farming communities. The ensuing conflicts among various local authorities have had domino-like effects with the transferring of risks further and further outwards. The Vietnamese government has had a particularly challenging task of protecting the rapidly urbanizing region around Hanoi given the huge seasonal differences in the water levels of the Red River. Decisions about the use of dams and dykes for diversion into other areas are very sensitive and require discussions about compensation. Similar issues exist for many major cities in the region, but little consideration has been given to what governance arrangements may help reduce conflict and introduce some fairness to the outcomes.

Deforestation and wetland destruction were blamed for the 1998 Yangtze River floods that killed more than three thousand people and destroyed more than 5 million homes (Lang 2002b, An et al. 2005). Total damage costs exceeded USD 20 billion. The state responded with bans on logging in large parts of Sichuan Province and then extended the bans to seventeen more provinces, autonomous regions and municipalities (Economy 2004). Such events in China have a major impact on fears and perceptions throughout the region. One of the indirect impacts of the logging ban was the shift of extraction activities from China to other countries in Southeast Asia (Lang 2002b, Lang and Chan 2006).

Ultimately the goal should be to link measures for disaster and vulnerability reduction to broader efforts for sustainable development (White et al. 2001). Otherwise the prospect is that risks will continue to be reshuffled and may even increase in the aggregate in response to the political pressures of the time.

Risk creation

Flood disasters are not just about having "too much water in one place at one time," but also the products of social relations and structures that make people vulnerable and place them at high involuntary risks (Blaikie et al. 1994, Bankoff 2004, Blaikie and Muldavin 2004). Some flood disasters are caused by "development." Land development by removing trees and increasing sedimentation of rivers may alter risks of severe flooding by raising river beds (Lang 2002a, Lang and Chan 2006).

Dams can be a source of risks because of sudden releases of stored water (Bakker 1999) or structural failures. In March 2000 the Se San River in Ratanakiri Province of Cambodia rose sharply as a result of an unannounced release from the Yali Falls hydropower dam—the largest dam located upstream in Vietnam (Saroeun and Stormer 2000). Several people were killed, livestock washed away, and crops and property including fishing gear were destroyed. The incident triggered reports by media and campaigns by civil society groups (Saroeun 2000). Subsequently, following Cambodian NGOs and local communities textensively reporting and discussing the damage, the government of Vietnam issued an apology and assured the Cambodian government that such an unannounced release of water would not happen again. The ensuing debate drew attention to mistakes committed years before, during the initial Yali dam project planning process. In particular, planning for the dam had not included sufficient attention to potential environmental and social impacts across the border in Ratanakiri in Cambodia (Badenoch 2001).

Experiences in neighboring basins underline the contributions of structural failures in some of the largest catastrophes. After disastrous floods in 1950, the Huai River Basin Commission was created by the Chinese Premier Mao Zedong to manage the Huai River which runs through four relatively prosperous provinces in eastern China (Economy 2004). The Commission constructed 195 dams along the river. In August 1975, two large dams, Shimantan and Banqiao, collapsed and the resulting floods killed as many as 230,000 people in Henan Province alone. The catastrophe was also remarkable for the way it was kept hidden from the media and the public for decades (McCully 1998). The history of dam collapses in China is a very sensitive political issue, but clearly a point of justifiable concern for people living downstream both within China and in neighbouring countries (Bhattacharjee 2004).

Societies make choices about whom and what should be at risk. But many of these choices are not a result of deliberation or transparent decision-making processes. With little consultation and no overt politics where the merits and fairness of different interventions can be discussed and challenged, programs that aim to reduce the risks of adverse flood impacts can easily become ways to redistribute and recreate risks.

Quick relief, sustained recovery

Coordinating recovery

When floods threaten to turn into disasters, societies are challenged to act to save lives and property. They must also work to restore economic and livelihood functions of the community as well as natural ecosystems as quickly as possible once immediate emergency relief and post-disaster trauma measures have been taken. Relief and recovery operations frequently base their assistance programs on assessments of economic losses. Recovery should be also seen as an opportunity to address injustices (Boyce 2000).

Policy initiatives that provide poor households and individuals with greater livelihood security, for example through enhanced skills, capacities and rights, are an important component of rehabilitation efforts following disastrous floods. Participation of affected communities is needed to identify locally appropriate solutions.

The Asian Disaster Preparedness Center (ADPC) has promoted an approach that places vulnerability to disasters within a more general development framework. Community-based disaster management is seen as risk reduction programs designed primarily by and for people in disaster-prone areas (ADPC 2000). This view and approach, however, remains marginal from the mainstream discourses on floods in Thailand (Yodmani 2001).

Governments have so far been unable to come up with appropriate institutional measures and guarantees for the private sector to take on flood insurance schemes. Experiences in other countries suggest that, while insurance may be a viable protection mechanism for firms and wealthier individuals, low-income households typically do not take out insurance so other approaches will still be needed for disaster relief (Browne and Hoyt 2000). In Vietnam relief assistance remains with the Ministry of Finance; in Thailand the Department of Disaster Prevention and Mitigation (DDPM) under the Ministry of the Interior.

A recurrent contest between lower and central level of governments is about assessments of damages from disaster and estimates of costs for recovery. It is in the interest of local officials to overestimate—and thus improve the quota of their constituents—and of central administrators to underestimate and thus leave more funds available to be used elsewhere (Manuta et al. 2006). Much of this politicking takes place behind closed doors within state bureaucracies. Flood-affected peoples are given few opportunities to negotiate the valuations and assessments are open to creative accounting. Contest among bureaucracies is often intense around budget allocations as well as field responsibilities during recovery and reconstruction efforts.

In Vietnam, where harms are "beyond the capacity of the individual," local and central governments can consider providing support, at their discretion. No ministry or agency is responsible for the overall coordination post disaster. Each ministry actively implements its own sectoral government mandate making it difficult to coordinate efforts.

In Thailand, major disconnects are apparent among agencies responsible for reducing vulnerabilities and preventing disasters on the one hand, and organizations oriented towards relief and emergency measures on the other hand. Even agencies purportedly on the same "side of the issue" often appear to be in direct bureaucratic competition for funds, if not responsibilities. There also major "disconnects" across administrative scales. Tingsanchali et al. (2003) argue the need for more specific and agreed power sharing arrangements between local and central state authorities in the case of flood disasters.

The administrative challenge is to integrate the special services needed to handle disasters with normal periods of development. Measures to meet short-term as opposed to long-term goals are often poorly coordinated leading to ineffective policy transitions that hinder longer-term recovery and reconstruction.

The political challenge is to recognize the importance of flood disasters to the political landscape. Disasters can make or break politicians and policies. Disasters make good stories even in countries that try to keep things quiet. Politicians and other leaders respond to media interest. Disasters inevitably raise questions about mitigation policies and their limitations.

Opportunities in crisis

Disasters provide opportunities for improvement. They supply a rationale to break the control of powerful land-holders misusing flood plain areas or logging companies exceeding their cut and mismanaging their concessions. They expose problems with institutional development such as poor coordination of overlapping mandates as well as gaps in coverage (Manuta et al. 2006). Civil society and progressive parts of government can use the context of a disaster to bring about institutional changes that, for example, ensure better representation of the interests of the poor in rural and urban planning and in environmental management.

On the other hand some actors may also use disaster rhetoric as justification for repressive policies (Blaikie and Muldavin 2004). The discourse of environmental destruction in the mountains is common in the Mekong region. Floods provide a rationale to gain control of forest and land (Forsyth 1996, 1998, Walker 2003). A well-documented example is the sequence of events and rhetoric after the severe flooding and landslides in southern Thailand in 1989. This disaster effectively brought about a nation-wide ban on logging concessions, redistribution of forest concessions and led to increase in logging of forests in neighbouring countries by Thai logging companies.

The politics of blame conveniently points to the uplands where people have few rights and representation in the political process. Rarely does the public finger point closer to home or towards the growth of infrastructure on the floodplains, the modification of river channels or the removal of wetlands. Crises provoke questions and thus provide opportunities to explain causality, but it is a battle for media space where entrenched views can be hard to shift.

Recreating disasters

One of the challenges for communities and governments is to ensure that recovery and reconstruction activities after disastrous floods do not inadvertently recreate the underlying conditions for another disaster.

Effective coordination of health services in the aftermath of flood disasters is often particularly important to reduce negative health impacts. Risks of infectious diseases, such as cholera and dysentery increase almost immediately; mental health problems like post-traumatic stress disorder may take longer to become apparent (Sawitri Assanangkornchai et al. 2004, Liu et al. 2006). Women and the elderly are often more likely to be affected (Liu et al. 2006).

Conventional structural measures of flood protection may in some places increase vulnerability. Embankments in flood plains, for example, can exacerbate problems of drainage congestion, seepage and water logging (Dixit 2003). Highways constructed within flood plains disrupt drainage. Expansion of rice farming into the wetlands of the Mekong delta in Vietnam has been accompanied by construction of roads and dykes to protect households. These interventions re-distribute flood waters and, by prolonging flooding in some areas, may be creating new risks of disaster.

This can be illustrated by some of the challenges that arise in development. The Residential Cluster Program initiated by the Vietnamese government was specifically aimed to cope with floods and flood-related vulnerability in the Mekong delta (Adam Fforde & Associates Pty Ltd, 2003). The program failed, however, to adequately incorporate the local interests and knowledge of vulnerable populations. A survey by CARE International in three provinces of the Mekong delta has documented low levels of participation of the community in the planning, construction and management of the residential clusters. There were no community representatives on the boards directing and supervising the construction and approval process. The outcome was that residential clusters were poorly designed for the local context and conditions. Houses, for example, lacked toilets and other basic infrastructure like water, electricity and road access. Moreover, key public facilities such as schools, kindergartens, childcare, first-aid posts, and markets were frequently built far away from the new residential clusters. The layout and structures for protecting residential clusters in the Mekong Delta appear to be a case of reducing short-term subset of risks that in other ways may be creating conditions for another disaster.

In rivers with high sediment loads, re-deposition only on the stream bed and not on the flood plains will raise the height of rivers over time, requiring higher and higher embankments. Flood protection measures such as river embankments also encourage human settlement in flood-prone areas, so that although they reduce the frequency of disasters they may create the conditions for very serious events when water amounts exceed design limits.

Institutional mechanisms may also recreate the conditions for disaster. Failure to adequately address recovery and reconstruction may leave parts of society even more vulnerable to the next flood. Flood disasters are subject to bureaucratic competition and institutional capture. It is very important that the difficulties experienced by state agencies in coping with a disaster do not become institutionalized in ways that prevent improvements, i.e. the problems become "acceptable in the circumstances" (Manuta et al. 2006). Nongovernment organizations and community-level administrations may help breakdown some of these barriers by insisting on greater transparency and accountability of the bureaucracy. Such actions can help clarify who is or should be responsible. They can also help ensure that promises of quick relief are kept and turned into a sustained recovery.

Building adaptive capacity

Share knowledge

Despite huge increases in research about natural hazards globally the indexed costs of property losses have continued to rise (White et al. 2001, Gupta et al. 2003). In order to make decisions on where to live, what type of homes to build, and what form of livelihoods to engage in, individuals need reliable and practical information that assesses hazards and risks over the long term.

In Myanmar [Burma], Laos and China, floods and "natural" disasters have been treated as national security issues about which media and public should know as little as possible. For example, in mid-2004, the military authorities arrested a Burmese filmmaker for filming floods in the Kachin state capital (Seng 2004).

In Thailand floods affecting downstream communities are usually met with calls for greater control of upland land-use by governments and publics even where the actual extent of changes in forest cover is modest (and in the absence of direct correlative linkages to forest cover and rainfall patterns) and links of cause-and-effect are tenuous (Lang 2002a, Walker 2003, Bonell and Bruijnzeel 2005). This is not to dispute that land-use changes have significant impacts on flood regimes; but to underline that flood politics leads to an uncritical application of scientific findings without a parallel consideration of the issues of soil, forest types, and even the extent of real changes in forest cover. Neither do we argue against the value of protecting forests, but rather wish to highlight the abuse of political rhetoric, the distributional consequences of "risk reduction" and the usual lack or fairness and transparency in their handling.

In 2000, in Cambodia, the Mekong River had its highest flood in seventy years. Hundreds of lives were lost as well as almost 20 percent of the rice crop. This was impetus for the Cambodian National Mekong Committee to host a workshop on flood management strategies for the Mekong River basin (Sodhy 2004). In November 2001 the governments of Cambodia, Laos, Thailand and Vietnam signed the Flood Management and Mitigation Agreement undertaking to coordinate land-use policies, share water-management information and improve cooperation in cross-border flood emergency operations (Dosch and Hensengerth 2005).

Following another agreement signed between China and the Mekong River Commission in 2002, China has provided Lower Mekong Basin countries with daily water level and twelve hourly rainfall information from the upper Mekong or Lancang River since April 2003 to help forecast floods (MRC 2003). China also established a special data center in Kunming at the Provincial Bureau of Hydrology and Water Resources. Myanmar has also indicated it would share data from its station on the Mekong (Dosch and Hensengerth 2005).

Floods are a common phenomenon across the broader Mekong region. There should be more opportunities for practitioners and researchers in the various countries to learn from each other's experiences. This applies not only to studies of the adverse impacts of floods, but also the importance of floods and floodplains to the conservation of aquatic biodiversity research on which is meagre (Dudgeon 2003, 2005).

Acknowledge change and uncertainty

Acknowledging uncertainty and change is fundamental to appropriate flood management. Uncertainties vary with types of floods. Flash flooding in the mountains, for example, represents a much harder technical challenge to developing early warning systems than for slower onset events in downstream rivers. First instrumentation for making ground observations is often sparse. Second communication infrastructure is often limited, although the expansion of mobile phone services is overcoming some of these historical limitations. Third there is no way to know where intense rainfall events will occur next; at best it may be possible to indicate high risks of such events over broader regions. These difficulties and the low commercial value of most upland enterprise, has resulted in little investment by the public sector in creating or improving such services for people living in the mountains. The same also applies to emergency relief and rehabilitation operations (Manuta et al. 2006).

The uncertain impacts of climate change on flood regimes is an important constraint on long-term flood and flood-related disaster management strategic planning (Dialogue on Water and Climate 2004, Few et al. 2004, Kundzewicz and Schellnhuber 2004). The long life span of key water and flood protection infrastructure, however, makes such assessments and considerations more important than in many other sectors of public management.

Floods and flood disaster risks need to be incorporated into development framework and not as a knee-jerk response to individual events. This requires building social memory into communities and state agencies that is not lost between disasters. Empirical post-event surveys and mapping exercises of affected households and locations can be helpful for fine-tuning mitigation and preparedness measures, especially in urban areas where there is often some capacity to control water flows with canals, gates, reservoirs and embankments. It also requires creating spaces for the real implications of both institutional and structural measures for flood management can be scrutinized and debated. A pro-active approach by government agencies will often be necessary to protect the interests of vulnerable groups that have also been marginalized in the development agenda setting processes more broadly.

Finally, building and maintaining adaptive capacity to manage floods and flood-related disaster risks requires institutional settings that gather information about flood regimes and their impacts, and promote learning from major events, whether or not into disasters.

Deliberate and negotiate risks and benefits

The most profound way to strengthen adaptive capacities of society as a whole is to ensure that the needs and interests of highly disadvantaged and vulnerable groups are pro-actively addressed (Lebel et al. 2006a). In the case of flood management this means looking carefully at the beneficial aspects of floods and how efforts to control them may undermine or redistribute these benefits. It also means that in the case of mitigating harmful impacts and disaster risks pro-active engagement is needed with people placed involuntarily at risk by the wider processes of development (Blaikie et al. 1994).

Disaster mitigation and risk reduction planning should be carried out as an informed deliberative process. This might include explicit negotiations over compensation schemes (for example for losses of crops when farmer's fields are used to handle excess flood waters to protect cities). The institutional mechanisms for such negotiations should be in place as part of appropriate approaches to development that encompasses flood and disaster management. They should not be an ad hoc response to the last catastrophe.

Conclusions

The politics of floods has not been a central topic for those concerned with water governance in the Mekong region. Research and policy appear to have largely accepted a technocratic paradigm of disaster management.

In this chapter we have tried to illustrate and argue that floods and flood-related disaster management are important and intersecting arenas for the exercise of power. Public consultation, participation and deliberation, however, of flood management policies, institutional innovations, and infrastructure measures have been modest.

We believe that research, conducted with community, non-profit and government agencies could lead to much better understanding of institutions as causes and responses to unfair distributions of risks and vulnerabilities. We think that more careful scrutiny of discourses around the management of flood risks would highlight their interest-based foundations and hence need for more explicit political processes to help explore and decide what to do about floods. At the same time we remain deeply concerned with the capacity of existing institutions and procedures to involve and take into account the special needs and rights of disadvantaged and highly vulnerable groups.

CHAPTER 4

CHINA'S ENERGY REFORMS AND HYDROPOWER EXPANSION IN YUNNAN

John Dore, Yu Xiaogang, Kevin Yuk-shing Li

Introduction

Energy sector reforms in China have unleashed an explosion in power industry development proposals across the country. Nationwide there is an intention to almost double hydropower capacity by 2010. The reforms have led to a national surge in competition between corporate generators to secure actual and potential power-producing "assets." Nowhere are dam builders aspirations' greater than in the south-west, especially Yunnan Province.

In the past Yunnan has been seen as a peripheral province—both geographically and sociopolitically. However, in terms of both the Mekong region and China, Yunnan is an increasingly important part of the water governance story.

The purpose of this chapter is to provide a brief update on what is happening in Yunnan—looking at the Nu, Lancang and Jinsha rivers—and then situate this within the wider context of China's changing political economy.

Yunnan Province

Yunnan has a population of approximately 43 million people (2,000 population census). It is one of three Chinese provinces with an ethnic minority population of over 10 million people. In 1990, of China's officially recognized fifty-five ethnic groups, fifty-one were living in Yunnan, accounting for a third of the province's population. Of these, twenty-five ethnic groups were living in "compact communities" with a population of less than five thousand. It is China's most culturally diverse province, with fifteen of the ethnic groups being indigenous to Yunnan—the Bai, Hani, Dai, Lisu, Wa, Lahu, Naxi, Jingpo, Bulang, Pumi, Nu, Deang, Dulong and Jinuo. It is the eighth largest province in China, covering an area of 394,100 km^2 that is 4.1 percent of the country's mainland area. Yunnan shares 4,060 km of border with Myanmar [Burma], Lao PDR and Vietnam. It is divided administratively into sixteen prefectures and 126 counties. Eight of the prefectures have the status of ethnic minority autonomous prefectures—including the Nujiang Lisu Nationality Autonomous Prefecture.

In recent years Yunnan has rapidly industrialized, with the formal economy increasing markedly during the 1990s. Core industries are tobacco, machinery, metallurgy, agricultural products, chemicals and building materials. The main border trade partner is Myanmar—recently estimated as accounting for 80 percent of cross border trade. In 2002 cross border trade was valued at USD 371 million. However, overall imports and exports were USD 2.23 billion, 80 percent of which was with ASEAN economies (Rungfapaisarn 2003).

Agricultural production, whether for trade or subsistence, is still dominates the provincial economy. While the economy is growing fast, in 1997, 36 percent of the population was still classified by China's government as living in poverty (annual income less than USD 77). Despite the recent transformation in Yunnan, the economic gap between China's eastern and coastal regions and the western parts of the country has increased. This is for many reasons, including the coast's more attractive geographic location for investors and the willingness of the state to cede some control and encourage private sector-led economic development in eastern and coastal provinces.

As part of a general effort to reduce this gap, the national government is promoting the Western Region Development Strategy (ADB 2002), which includes Yunnan. The provincial government is promoting its cultural diversity, biodiversity, mineral endowments and strategic location as a "gateway to South East Asia." Boosting production of "clean green" hydropower is seen as a strategically vital sunrise industry to aid development of the province and country.

Hydropower and World Natural Heritage and local livelihoods

Yunnan has over six hundred rivers forming six major river basin systems: Dulong (Irrawaddy), Nu (Salween), Lancang (Mekong), Jinsha (Yangtze), Zhu (Pearl), Honghe/Lixian Jiang (flows into the Red in Vietnam). Rivers have multiple uses and are valued for many different reasons. In this section we wish to introduce the Yunnan hydropower context, but also make mention of World Natural Heritage sites and local livelihoods.

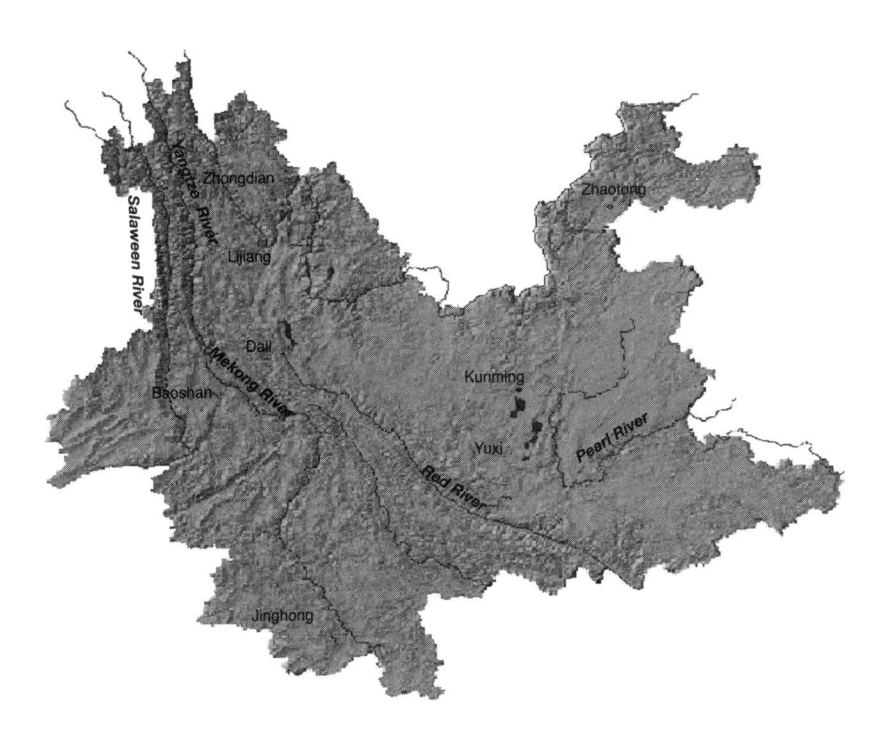

Map 4.1 Yunnan's major rivers

SOURCE: World Agroforestry Centre (ICRAF) & Centre for Biodiversity & Indigenous Knowledge (CBIK), Kunming

By one method of calculation, Yunnan is seen as having 24 percent of China's hydropower potential for medium- and large-sized projects. In terms of pure hydropower potential, Yunnan has more than any of the other five countries of the Mekong region. Each of the Nu, Lancang and Jinsha are in China's "top six hydropower rivers" (tables 4.1, 4.2, and 4.3).

Substantial hydropower expansion is part of national planning and Yunnan's role is a key one. One industry source claims that "China has planned to construct over 50 large and super large hydropower stations in the next 20 years" (Alexanders Oil and Gas Connections 2003). A deputy-director of the State Power Corporation, Chen Dongping, is reported as saying that China intends to spend nearly USD 40 billion by 2010 to double its hydroelectric capacity (China Economic Review 2002). This would involve increasing capacity to 150,000 MW by constructing the equivalent of another four dams the size of the Three Gorges dam. Chen Dongping assumes this is necessary to reduce current dependence on coal and to thereby "improve the environment." This remark is, to some extent, understandable given that one-third of China's territory is reported as being affected by sulphur dioxide (SO_2) related "acid rain" and about 40 percent of the contributing SO_2 emissions comes from coal-fired power plants (He Jing 2002). The seriousness of the acid rain problem was acknowledged in 1994 when the central government launched a seven-year spending initiative aimed at keeping SO_2 emissions at or below 15 million tonnes per annum. It was recognized that up to three thousand highly polluting plants would need to be closed, with their output replaced by more efficient generation units (World Bank 1998).

Table 4.1 Hydropower potential of major rivers in China

River	Potential installed capacity (MW)	Percent of the "top 18" Chinese rivers
Jinsha/Yangtze	210,810	49
Yalung Zangbo	54,960	13
Yellow	35,770	8
Lancang (Mekong)	28,930	7
Zhu (Pearl)	25,760	6
Nu (Salween)	30,410	7
Heilong (in China)	11,530	3
Subtotal	398,170	
Rivers 8–18	30,440	7
Rivers 1–18	428,610	100
Yunnan	103,130	24

SOURCE: State Power Corporation data for "medium- and large-sized hydropower projects" (He Jing 2002)

Table 4.2 Hydropower production versus potential—
China, Western Region, Yunnan

Territory	Actual (TWh)	Potential (TWh)	Exploitable (GW)
China	73	1,923.3	378.5
Western Region	38.4	1,567.8	290.9
Yunnan	6.9	394.5	71.2
Western Region (as percent of China)	52.6	81.5	76.9
Yunnan (as percent of Western Region)	18.0	25.2	24.5
Yunnan (as percent of China)	9.5	20.5	18.8

SOURCE: Data for 1999 from ADB report analyzing Western Region Development Strategy (ADB 2002: table 7-4)

Table 4.3 Mekong region hydropower potential

Country/region	Developed (TWH/year)	Potential (TWH/year)	Percent of potential already developed
Yunnan	7.9	450	1.8
Cambodia	0	41	0.0
Lao PDR	1.1	102	1.1
Myanmar	1.1	366	0.3
Thailand	4.6	49	9.4
Vietnam	5.8	82	7.1
Total	20.5	1,090	

NOTES: The figure for Yunnan is higher than the figure in table 5.2. The data set used in table 5.3 is older and from an ADB GMS energy sector study published in 1995. It refers to what is theoretically possible and is indicative only. What is practically and economically feasible is somewhat less.
SOURCE: Plinston and He Daming (1999, 26)

Although there has been an upsurge of plans for national and Yunnan hydropower-related dam building, there was already ample demonstration of China's commitment to a water resources development paradigm which sees large dams as integral (McCormack 2001). Elsewhere in the world this approach is being seriously challenged, most publicly in the outputs of the World Commission on Dams (WCD 2000). However, this paradigm is still thriving in twenty-first century China where about 280 large dams were under construction in the late 1990s (WCD 2000, 10), against a national backdrop of about eighty thousand large and medium dams, most of which were built since the success of the Mao-led revolutionaries in 1949 (Kattoulas 2001). Hydropower has long been a component of China's energy strategy and the new surge should be seen as an upscaling rather than as a new policy emphasis.

Table 4.4 China's projected supply of primary energy 2000-2020

	2000	2005	2010	2015	2020
Total (Mt, coal equivalent)	1092.7	1277.6	1481.1	1727.9	2016.4
Hydropower & nuclear (TWH)	227.8	320.2	435.1	544.1	682.0
Hydropower & nuclear (percentage)	20.8	25.1	29.4	31.5	33.8
Growth from 2000 levels (percentage)		16.9	35.5	58.1	84.5
Growth in hydropower & nuclear (percentage)		40.6	91.0	138.8	199.4

NOTE: He Jing (2002) notes the share of hydropower in 2000 had reached 24.8 percent.
SOURCE: 1) Data from 1999 in Asian Development Bank (ADB) report analyzing the Western Region Development Strategy (ADB 2002: Extract from tables 7-7, 7-8, 7-9).

However, rivers are more than just flows of water with hydropower generation potential. For example, the San Jiang or Three Rivers region is part of the upper watersheds of the Nu, Lancang and Jinsha. In July 2003 it was declared a World Natural Heritage site of the United Nations Economic, Social and Cultural Organization (UNESCO) in recognition of its rarity, beauty and ecological importance. Of course, rivers are also resources for local communities, dependent upon them—to a greater and lesser extent—to meet their livelihood and other needs. Conceivably, both hydropower development and UNESCO listing could provide a boost for local livelihoods but it does not automatically follow in either instance, unless priority is attached to local rights and development aspirations. Yunnan's hydropower development could provide increased local opportunities and prosperity; however, the threat to the livelihoods of millions in river dependent communities, mostly downstream, is also real. Recognition of opportunities and threats, and a more cautious approach, is required.

Driving forces for hydropower expansion

Key drivers for Yunnan hydropower expansion include the push for, and direction of, economic growth, China's associated energy security concerns, the Western Region Development Strategy and a political environment in which energy entrepreneurs have strong incentives to push ahead with expansion plans.

Globalization

The extensive medium and large dam building throughout China, especially in the past fifty years, and the new surge in Yunnan dam building can be seen as a by-product of the globalization[1] context in which it has and is taking place. Jan Aart Scholte (2000) argues that full-scale globalization from 1960s to the present has been grounded in four interdependent causes. First, the ascendancy of rationalism as the dominant form of knowledge that has privileged people over nature, science and solution-seeking. Second, capitalism: Scholte agrees with the Marxist analysis that capitalism, defined as structures of production focused on surplus accumulation, is the basic engine of globalization. As capitalist impulses have been given more freedoms, so the rate of globalization has increased. Third, technological advances: undeniably, there have been continued extraordinary improvements in engineering, transport, communications and data processing which have provided the infrastructure, or the "hardware," for globalization. Fourth, specific policy and regulation choices by which the dominance of arguments for removing business restraints, encouraging trade, and focusing on exports has shaped globalization. To a significant extent, these have been due to decisions taken by states, often willingly, but sometimes because they have perceived there were no plausible policy alternatives. Each of these causes also applies to China and has impacted on the focus and directions of development.

International economic integration and investors looking to China

International economic integration—just one part of globalization—is a highly significant factor, particularly in relation to providing the capital necessary for expensive hydropower development. A report publicized in August 2003 by the United Nations Committee on the Development of Trade noted that between 1980 and 2002 the world "stock" of Foreign Direct Investment (FDI)[2] increased more than tenfold to USD 7.1 trillion. Of this amount, in 2002 the Chinese mainland share was reported as being USD 448 billion (*Beijing Review* 2003b). This places China fourth worldwide in terms of receiving external investment, whether it is relatively fixed direct investment, or relatively mobile portfolio investment. In 2002 it absorbed USD 52.7 billion in FDI (*Beijing Review* 2003c). Chinese capital appears to have funded most of the large dams around the country. However, domestic and foreign investors are now more easily found to finance large hydropower. This is an important trend because by some predictions China will need to invest USD 800 billion for new power generating capacity over the next thirty years (IEA 2002b).

More than a shift to a market economy

The most recent wave of international economic integration wave, from 1980 to the present, has been an era dominated by neoliberalism, and Beijing's policies are no exception. Two significant elements include:

- Corporatization/privatization of public utilities implemented vigorously wherever possible due to a fundamental belief in greater business efficiency of the private sector. A first step of corporatizing public utilities would almost invariably proceed to partial or full privatization of ownership and management. Many countries that have embraced the neoliberal agenda—either willingly or reluctantly due to a shortage of other options—have proceeded rapidly to privatize many public utilities.
- Deregulation in the sense of removing impediments to business. Neoliberal regimes around the world have implemented competition policies which have invariably focused on economic issues such as: limiting anti-competitive conduct of firms, reforming monopolies to facilitate competition (for example, by restructuring energy utilities), compulsory competitive tendering of government contracts, etc.

This type of agenda has rapidly lead to the emergence of very new types of public-private partnerships being shaped, at least in part, by the activities of agents such as the World Bank's Public-Private Infrastructure Advisory Facility (PPIAF). In recent times PPIAF activities in China have focused on telecommunications reform, natural gas reforms and electricity generation. In each instance, the focus is on exploring ways in which the role of the private sector can be significantly expanded.[3] Chinese public policy-makers remain wary of unbridled privatization, and hence the efforts to retain state ownership and regulatory control. However, traditional ideas about what constitutes "public" and "private" are blurring and it is no easy matter for the state to find efficient and effective mechanisms for regulatory control.

Energy demand, trade and security

A key driver of Chinese government energy policy is the domestic demand estimates of key organizations such as the State Reform and Development Commission (SRDC). The SRDC's Energy Research Institute (SRDC-ERI) has released analysis in 2003 of three different scenarios. Coal demand is forecast to rise to somewhere between 2.1 to 2.9 billion tonnes per annum with the upper limit almost twice the current production capacity.[4] Oil demand is predicted to rise to 450 million tonnes of oil equivalent. Natural gas consumption is forecast to increase five-fold current levels, rising to 160 billion m^3 (*People's Daily* Online 2003b). Domestic energy demand is entwined with energy imports and exports. Imports are mostly oil, and more recently gas. Exports are mostly coal, but have an increasing hydropower component.

Earlier SRDC-ERI data published by the Asian Development Bank (ADB) presented a less nuanced picture portraying only one scenario. Domestic energy supply was projected to increase by 85 percent by 2020 (ADB

2002). Even if such massive increases in production were achieved, further imports would be necessary. The International Energy Agency (IEA), working in cooperation with SRDC, expects that China will become an even greater importer of oil and gas: "By 2030 Chinese oil imports will equal the imports of the United States today, while imports will meet 30 percent of the country's gas demands" (IEA 2002b). China is already a major actor in the global energy market as the largest oil importer outside the OECD. After the United States and Japan, it is the third largest consumer of oil (IEA 2002a). On the other hand, some parts of the country will continue and expand their international energy exports. It should be remembered that China is now the second largest coal exporter in the world, whereas only ten years ago it was primarily focused on supplying its domestic market (Ball et al. 2003).[5] And, as the plans for Yunnan's energy development come to fruition, the province will become a significant exporter of hydropower to other parts of China, Southeast Asia, and possibly South Asia. Entrepreneurs producing energy will sell to purchasers either inside or outside the country.

In addition, energy security for China, as for all other countries, remains an important influence on national policy (for still-relevant discussions see Medlock and Soligo 1999, Gao Shixian 2000, Stares 2000). The point being made is that not all of the planned increases in energy production are to meet domestic demand.

Box 4.1 Energy demand management options for China[6]
1. Imposing environmental taxes on dirty fuels
2. Further promoting electricity time-of-use tariffs
3. Reforming two-tiered pricing system for natural gas
4. Further regulation, upgrading and/or closure of inefficient power plants and coal mines
5. Promotion of clean coal technologies
6. Using advanced, combined-cycle technology in power generation
7. Promoting co-generation
8. Promoting renewable energy resources and technologies (including wind, geothermal and solar)
9. Promoting energy conservation
10. Encouraging more research and development in the energy industry
11. Phasing out hidden subsidies

Given its significance as a policy driver to those concerned about energy security and continued economic growth, it is important that the demand projections data, and their assumptions, are thoroughly analyzed. For example, does the data reflect the successful implementation of any demand management policy measures, or the development or wider adoption of new technologies?[7] It is important to clarify whether demand estimates are unnecessarily high and being used as justification to permit headlong expansion of energy production, perhaps with an over-emphasis on obsolescent technology.

China has rich potential in renewable energy sources, such as wind, solar, biomass (bio-gas and bio-fuel), geothermal, wave and tidal and etc. The Renewable Energy Promotion Law was approved in 2005 and enacted in March 2006, in order to respond to the increasing energy demand, diversify the energy sources and ensure energy security. However, the major power companies monopolize the renewable energy potential and the rights to develop. At present this is hindering investment and technology transfer from European countries with more experience in this area. For example, Guangdong Province alone could exploit as much as 20,000 MW of wind power potential by the year 2020. For the Eleventh Five-Year Plan period (2006–2010), the official government target is 6,000 MW.

However, even with this huge wind potential and the state's new law and policy, at present there is insufficient incentive to localize the technology and commence extensive production of wind turbines. The potential of wind energy will not be realized until there are more people in China familiar with the technology, and more local manufacturers engaged in turbine production. For renewables, including wind, it will be necessary for the same focused training and exchanges between countries which occurred in the past, for example with large hydropower production, from the 1950s between engineers of the former Soviet Union and China. Energy policy needs to have many elements, and all the options mentioned in box 4.1 have a role to play.

Western Region seen as key to increased energy production

Most evident to this proposed rapid and vast expansion of China's energy production is the importance of the Western Region. In short, "Rising demand for energy is a very significant factor in the economic development of the PRC, especially the Western Region" (ADB 2002, 147). The Western Region is intended to become an increasingly significant energy supplier.

The Western Region comprises the provinces of Sichuan, Guizhou, Yunnan, Shaanxi, Qinghai and Gansu; the autonomous regions of Tibet, Ningxia, Inner Mongolia, Guangxi and Xinjiang; the municipality of Chongqing. In 1999 the Western Region contained 28.8 percent of China's population, 61.9 percent of total land area, but accounted for only 15.8 percent of gross domestic product (ADB 2002).

The Western Region Development Strategy 2000–2020 was adopted by the national government in February 2000 and was a key component of the Tenth Five-Year Plan (2001–2005). Its stated aims are to combat poverty, industrialize the western provinces, including all mountain areas, and promote the transfer of science and technology from the centre to the periphery (ADB 2002). It is focused on conventional economic development. The strategy stresses the need for infrastructure investment in the middle and western provinces of China with special emphasis on transport, telecommunications, pipelines, electricity and the national power grid and water conservation. In particular, transport investment is expected to focus on better economic integration between western, central and eastern China, and also on improving economic linkages with Southeast Asia.

Energy exports from the Western Region to the Eastern Region are projected to quadruple between 2000–2020, with coal accounting for 91 percent of the increase. Electricity will be a much smaller, but still significant, component of the exports. After allowing for more than a doubling of electricity demand within the Western Region from 394 to 878 TWH, it is still projected that exportable electricity supply would increase from 102 to 365 TWH (ADB 2002,155).

The dual objectives of the Western Region Development Strategy are "development" (of the West) and "transfer" (to the East). An example of what is proposed is that authorities intend to be transmitting 8 GW of power per annum from Yunnan to Guangdong by 2015, derived from both coal-fired plants and hydropower from various sites.

As the data being produced by SRDC-ERI shows, the planned energy production and transfer from West to East is significant. Already one-quarter of China's energy derived from coal and half from natural gas comes from the Western Region. These proportions are to be increased as policy-makers search for the energy believed required to sustain China's (primarily eastern and coastal) economic growth.

It is within this context that Yunnan hydropower production is being pushed along by national policy makers, local authorities, designers, construction groups, lenders and business entrepreneurs. The province already provides about 10 percent of China's hydropower but exploitable reserves are considered to be ten times larger than current generation. If this potential is exploited, Yunnan could eventually supply closer to 20 percent of national hydropower production, to be fed into national or regional grids. For example, Guangdong Province is now assigned to purchase power, mostly hydropower, from western provinces, namely Yunnan, Guizhou and Guangxi. Power purchase agreements have been signed to ensure power transfers during the implementation of the Eleventh Five-Year Plan (2006–2010).

In summary, China's economic reforms, coupled with the development/transfer priority being attached to the Western Region, have catalyzed a substantial increase in the dam building aspirations of developers in southwest China. This is being enabled by wide-ranging reforms to the power industry, to which we now turn.

Table 4.5 Projected supply of primary energy 2000–2020

	2000	2005	2010	2015	2020
China					
Total (Mt, coal equivalent)	1092.7	1277.6	1481.1	1727.9	2016.4
Hydropower & nuclear power (TWH)	227.8	320.2	435.1	544.1	682.0
Hydropower & nuclear[8] (percentage)	20.8	25.1	29.4	31.5	33.8
Total production growth from 2000 (percentage)		16.9	35.5	58.1	84.5
Hydropower & nuclear growth from 2000 (percentage)		40.6	91.0	138.8	199.4
Western Region					
Western Region (Mt, coal equivalent)	286.4	392.7	539.0	696.0	889.7
Western Region hydro &-nuclear (TWh)	104.0	165.0	260.0	342.0	446.0
Hydropower & nuclear (percentage)	36.3	42.0	48.2	49.1	50.1
Total production growth from 2000 (percentage)		37.1	88.2	143.0	210.6
Hydropower & nuclear growth from 2000 (percentage)		58.7	150.0	228.8	328.8
Shares of primary energy supply from Western Region					
Coal (percentage)	66.6	59.4	55.3	52.7	49.4
Oil (percentage)	13.8	12.7	11.8	11.9	12.4
Gas (percentage)	6.2	12.1	14.0	14.0	12.7
Hydro & nuclear (percentage)	13.3	15.3	17.9	17.9	18.3
Renewable (percentage)	0.1	0.4	1.4	3.5	7.1
	100	100	100	100	100
Projected electricity supply					
PRC	1233.1	1729.3	2292.4	2995.5	3822.5
Western Region	281.1	495	693	956.3	1242.2
Western Region (as percentage of PRC)	22.8	28.6	30.2	31.9	32.5

SOURCE: Energy Research Institute data published by Asian Development Bank (2002 Extract from tables 7-7, 7-8, 7-9, 7-11).

Table 4.6 Energy production 1999

	Coal (Mt)	Oil (Mt)	Gas (GL)	Hydro (TWH)	Total Power (TWH)
China	1,045	160	25.2	196.6	1,239.3
Western Region	267	27.7	13.4	103.6	278.6
Yunnan	26.6	0	0.1	18.5	29.8
Western Region as percentage of China	25.6	17.3	53.2	52.7	22.5
Yunnan (as percentage of Western Region)	10.0	0.0	0.7	17.9	10.7
Yunnan (as percentage of China)	2.5	0.0	0.4	9.4	2.4

SOURCE: Data in Asian Development Bank report analyzing the Western Region Development Strategy (ADB 2002: Extract from table 7-2).

China's energy industry reforms

China's energy industry reforms are the result of the government policy put in place to foster competition and marketization, via corporatization that, especially for the power generation companies, is almost indistinguishable from privatization. The formation of the State Power Corporation (SPC) was the first main step. With registered capital of USD 20 billion, it was a giant monopoly, one of the hundred largest businesses in the world. By 2000 it was working as a consulting company in more than forty countries. At the time its break-up was announced in late 2002, SPC had in the vicinity of 2 million employees, and owned 46 percent of the nation's electricity generation and 90 percent of the electricity supply assets (Alexanders Oil and Gas Connections 2003).

The start of the SPC reorganization has involved separation of SPC's actual and potential (such as the Nu River) generation and distribution assets and designation of eleven enterprises to "acquire" these assets (box 4.2). The next step involved creating a competitive market, which includes pooling and pricing reforms, plus grid creation. To keep oversight of the reform process, the State Electricity Regulation Commission (SERC) has been formed, responsible for making proposals on power pricing and issuing and managing power service licenses.

Business competition

Prior to the current reforms, large-scale hydropower development had already become characterized by complex ownership and financing arrangements. Examples from Huaneng and Three Gorges illustrate the scale of the business operations, diversity of funding sources and aspirations of their corporate leaders.

Since the major energy industry reforms were announced in late 2002 there has been a stampede by the big groups including the Three Gorges Development Group—to secure their assets, principally coal-related, and move to develop their new assets, including "rivers for hydro" in various types of partnership with local authorities. In the words of *Business Week*, "newly established power conglomerates are scrambling to construct generating plants across China" (2003). Enterpreneurial dam developers are in hot competition: for example, Huadian, Guodian, Datang and China Power Investment Company have, in partnership with Hong Kong's CLP Power Asia Limited, announced new investment of USD 4.89 billion to build thermal and hydropower plants in the southern region of Guangxi (*China Daily* 2003b).

Why the current scramble? The past increases in energy demand and projections for further huge requirements are acknowledged. State policy support and sector reform has also been mentioned. But the rush into hydropower is also being fuelled by the relative ease with which many social and environmental costs can be externalized from "return on investment" equations, and the competitive need for companies—in the new business operating environment—to retain market share and steadily expand generating capacity.[9] While some in government, such as the chairman of the State Electricity Regulation Commission (SERC) are reported as having "hinted that the government is considering slowing down the building boom in power plants" and noting that government should have a clearer overall plan for power plant construction (*People's Daily* Online 2003d), thus far there is no evidence of either. The authority of the SERC is limited to promoting market competition, endeavouring to ensure transparency and supervising service licences. Decision-making about electricity prices and approving construction and expansion of power plants remains with the State Reform and Development Commission (SRDC).

Box 4.2 China energy industry reforms: Critical steps between 1996–2003

1996		Electric Power Law passed which required reforms, including the creation of separated power producers and retailers in a competitive market. The law also stipulated that power prices should reflect all production costs, profit, tax and contribute to transmission costs and situations where some subsidy may be necessary to ensure supply. Part of the rationale was to ensure that the industry would become attractive to non-state investors.
1997	Jan 16	Establishment of State Power Corporation (SPC) to represent the state as owner of government-owned assets. This occurred around the same time as the passage of the Electricity Law and the abolition of the Ministry of Electric Power, dividing its functions between existing agencies.
2002	Apr 11	Announcement by what is now the State Reform and Development Commission (SRDC) of next phase of energy industry reforms.
2002	Dec 29	End of SPC monopoly with announcement that SPC assets are to be acquired/transferred to five independent electricity generating, two transmission and four consultant/construction companies. The impending creation of an industry regulator was also signalled. Not all energy assets were included in this restructure.

Power generation companies
Huaneng, Datang, Huadian, Guodian, China Power Investment Company

Distribution (grid) companies
State Power Grid Company that controls the operation of five regional power grid companies in the North, Northeast, East, Central and Northwest.

State Power Grid Company was also authorized to oversee the orderly transfer of five hundred power plants under the management of provincial power corporations as part of the reform commitment to separate generation from distribution (see below).

Southern Power Grid Company which controls the operation of the Southern Power Grid formerly controlled by SPC, plus the formerly Province-controlled Guangxi, Guizhou, Yunnan, Hainan and Guangdong grids.

		Between 2011 and 2030, Southern Power Grid is prioritizing hydropower development on the Nu, Lancang, Jinsha,Wu; and aiming to expand connections with surrounding grids (e.g. China's central and north, also the proposed Mekong region grid). ***Consultant/construction companies*** Hydraulic Power Designing Institute Electric Power Designing Institute China Water Conservancy and Hydropower Construction Group China Gezhouba Group ***Regulator*** State Electricity Regulatory Commission (SERC).
2003	Jul 31	SERC announces its intention to create six competitive regional power markets across China within three years in the East, North, Northeast, Central, Northwest and South.
	Sep 3	*Example:* Signing of MoU to transfer power plants in Jiangsu Province to Guodian.
	Sep 19	*Example:* Connection of the north and central China power grids (now world's largest). The grid spans 4,600 km across fourteen provinces and municipalities, with a combined installed capacity of 140 million kilowatts.
	Sep 23	*Example:* Signing of MOU to transfer to state shares to Huaneng in thirteen power plants (total capacity 4,640 MW). Huaneng becomes major shareholder in twelve of them.

SOURCES: *China Daily* 2002, Alexanders Oil and Gas Connections 2003, *China Daily* 2003a, *People's Daily* Online 2003c, 2003d, 2003e, Freshfields Bruckhaus Deringer 2003, Xinhua News Agency 2003.

Table 4.7 Hydropower dam plans—Nu, Lancang and Jinsha rivers

Nu	Elevation (meters above mean sea level) m	Watershed area km²	Average inflow m³/second	Average inflow mcm	Total storage mcm	Installed capacity MW	Annual energy GWH	Inundated area ha	Locally displaced No. of people	Wall height m	Status
Song Ta	1,950	103,500	1,200	-	6,312	6,200	17,870	312	3,633	307	Designed
Bin Zhong Luo	1,690	103,700	1,200	-	14	1,600	8,340	0	na	55	Designed
Ma Ji	1,570	106,100	1,270	-	4,696	4,200	18,970	1,654	19,830	300	Designed
Lu Ma Deng	1,325	107,200	1,330	-	664	2,000	10,080	441	6,092	165	Designed
Fu Gong	1,200	107,500	1,340	-	18	400	19,800	59	682	60	Designed
Bi Jiang	1,155	108,400	1,390	-	280	1,500	7,140	322	5,186	118	Designed
Ya Bi Luo	1,060	109,300	1,430	-	344	1,800	9,060	178	3,982	133	Designed
Lu Shui	955	110,400	1,500	-	1,288	2,400	13,740	395	6,190	175	Designed
Liu Ku	818	112,500	1,610	-	8	180	760	11	411	36	Site preparation in 2003
Shi Tou Zhai	780	112,000	1,580	-	700	440	2,290	66	687	59	Designed
Sai Ge	730	114,000	1,700	-	270	1,000	5,360	207	1,882	79	Designed
Yan Sang Shu	666	116,500	1,770	-	391	1,000	6,200	286	2,470	84	Designed
Guang Po	609	124,400	1,890	-	124	600	3,160	4	34	58	Designed
						23,320	122,770	3,934	51,079		

"Downstream of China—Nu/Salween"								
Ta Sarng	na	207,000	na	na	36,100	3,600	23,006	na	188	Building 2004+
Upper Salween	na	293,200	-	118,600	21,000	4,540	29,271	na	168	Building 2007–12
Lower Salween	na	294,500	-	119,200	245	792	5,422	na	49	Building 2007–12
Lancang								
Gonguoqiao	1,319	97,200	-	31,060	510	750	4,060	343	4,596	130	Designed
Xiaowan	1,236	113,300	-	38,470	14,560	4,200	18,990	3,712	32,737	300	Building 2001–10
Manwan	994	114,500	-	38,790	920	1,500	7,805	415	3,513	126	Built 1986–96
Dachaoshan	895	121,000	-	42,260	890	1,350	7,021	826	6,100	118	Built 1996–2003
Nuozhadu	807	144,700	-	55,190	22,400	5,500	23,777	4,508	23,826	254	Designed
Jinghong	602	149,100	-	58,030	1,233	1,500	8,059	510	2,264	118	Building 2003–10
Ganlanba	533	151,800	-	59,290	na	250	780	12	58	na	Designed
Mengsong	519	160,000	-	63,700	na	600	3,380	58	230	na	Designed
					15,650	73,872	10,384	73,324		
Jinsha								
Upper Hu Tiao Xia	1,950	na	na	na	18,345	2,800	10,523	10,413	100,000	216	Designed
Liang Jia Ren	1,810	na	na	na	43	4,000	16,314	2	10	99.5	Designed
Li Yuan	1,620	na	na	na	891	2,280	10,292	190	1,300	155	Designed
A hai	1,504	na	na	na	840	2,100	9,371	333	2,400	139	Designed
Jing An Qiao	1,410	na	na	na	663	2,500	11,411	140	2,000	156	Designed
Long Kai Kou	1,297	na	na	na	657	1,800	7,893	293	2,000	113	Designed

Lu di La	1,221	na	na	2,099	9,350	2,087	16,900	120	Designed
Guan Ying Yan	1,132	na	na	1,973	13,138	940	8,810	183	Designed
Wu Dong De	na	na	na	na	33,900	na	na	na	na
Bai He Tan	na	na	na	na	55,000	na	na	na	na
Xi Luo Du	610	454,000	na	12,960	57,600	8,933	50,000	na	Building 2004+
Xiang Jia Ba	380	458,000	na	5,060	29,300	na	118,000	na	Designed
				59,080	264,092	23,331	301,420		

NOTES: 1) Details of dams remain subject to negotiation, redesign and variation. Different figures are used by sources for many variables, especially total energy and displaced people; but also for dam height, area to be inundated, etc. For example, the developer of Jinghong is seeking approval to increase the installed capacity from 1,500 MW to 2,000 MW. The information has been pieced together from multiple sources, including developer proposals, researchers documents and media reports. The foundations are: for Nu data, the Hudian proposal; for Lancang, the published work of Plinston and He Daming (1999) and McCormack (2001); for Jinsha, the Three Gorges and Huaneng development company documents. 2) Total energy data is intended to refer to hydropower potential as part of the full cascade eg. Dachaoshan's output can rise from about 5,900 GWH/year to 7,021 GWH/year once the Xiaowan reservoir is completed. 3) Not all of the Jinsha figure is "in Yunnan" due to border sharing, and for a period traversing entirely through Sichuan Province. 4) Both the Nu and Lancang are international rivers flowing into other Mekong region countries. Some data for three Salween (Nu) dams downstream is included: Ta Sarng within Myanmar (Choolit Vatcharasinthu and Babel 1999), and two on the Thai/Myanmar border (Daniel 2003) . There are no plans by other countries for mainstream dams on the Mekong (Lancang), but extensive dam-building on tributaries is proceeding. 4) na = not available, or not available to authors, when finalising the data in 2006.

Hydropower status of the "Three Rivers"

It is the Nu River dams that, at time of writing, are the most controversial both within and outside of China. Decisions about the future of the Nu are taking place now; the Lancang dams are being built; the planned Jinsha dams are extra dams on an already significantly modified Chinese river. Our scope is restricted to the Nu, Lancang and Jinsha rivers. These are only a part of the Yunnan transformation, and we stress that Yunnan needs to be seen as part of the larger Chinese picture.

Nu River

The future of the Nu River remains in the balance. In the last months of 2003 and early 2004 much information filtered into the public domain outlining the extensive hydropower development proposed for the Chinese section of this river which—upper, lower and middle—extends for 2,018 km. There are advanced plans for a cascade of up to 13 dams[10] on the middle and lower Chinese reaches which, if built, would profoundly alter this presently undammed, almost pristine river. Some supporters of the dams are focused on local development needs, which they hope the dams will assist. Others are focused more on the energy production and income potential for other people and places. Opponents of the dam are doubtful about the need for such radical development and fear the irreversible changes that a cascade will have on the current, mostly undeveloped area. There are many different positions in the debate. The total installed capacity of these dams would be 23,320 MW. By 2004 a site office was operating, and road building had commenced to facilitate the construction of the Liu Ku dam.

There are also three dams being promoted for the lower section of the river downstream of China. The Ta Sarng site is within Myanmar and the other two are planned for further downstream where the Nu/Salween forms the border between Myanmar and Thailand (For a review featuring concerns, see Daniel 2003).[11]

The chief promoter of the proposed Nu River development in Yunnan is the China Huadian Corporation, a wholly state-owned enterprise, and the controlling shareholder of the Hong Kong-listed Huadian Power International Corporation Limited. It is one of the "big five" power generation companies receiving assets from 2003 onwards, which were previously owned by the State Power Corporation (SPC). The right to develop the Nu River is seen by Huadian as one of the transferred assets now in their "portfolio."

Pre–2003 the Chinese central government had funded preparatory planning and design work by the Kunming Hydropower Design and Planning Institute. But the real action took place after the major energy industry reforms were announced in December 2002. By mid June 2003, Huadian was able to announce the formation of the construction entity,

Yunnan Huadian Hydropower Development Company, with registered start-up capital of 200 million yuan (approx. USD 24 million). At this time, the shares were split between China Huadian Corporation (51 percent), Yunnan Development Investment Co (20 percent), Yunnan Electricity Group's Hydropower Construction Co (19 percent) and the Yunnan Nu River Electricity Group (10 percent).

A development proposal was submitted to the State Reform and Development Commission (SRDC) in Beijing. SRDC convened a meeting, attended by about 140 people from various ministries and elsewhere, which reviewed the proposal and approved it, in principle, in mid August 2003. This was just prior to the new Chinese Environment Impact Assessment (EIA) law taking effect on September 1. Since then, the proponents have been vigorously promoting the proposal.

The Beijing-based State Environment Protection Administration (SEPA) convened an expert panel, reviewed the proposal in more detail, and in early September 2003 announced that it had serious reservations related to: the world class canyon which would be irreversibly altered, threats to the largely unexplored rich biodiversity, the loss of an extremely valuable wild rice gene pool, and geological instability which raised serious safety concerns. More general concerns related to the expected cultural disruption, a lack of faith that promised poverty alleviation would necessarily result from dam construction, and disappointment that alternatives to hydropower, such as ecotourism, are not being genuinely considered. Nevertheless, the Yunnan and prefecture governments were keen to proceed and attempted to counter the SEPA opposition via a provincially convened "Yunnan experts" meeting in September 2003. Given the pre-meeting attendee selection process and the general pressure being brought to bear, it was unsurprising when this group found that concerns were manageable and damming should proceed. SEPA then had further field visits While being courted by Yunnan provincial and prefecture officials. Further expert meetings took place in Beijing and Yunnan, prior to a joint meeting held in Kunming, October 20–21, 2003. In the week before this meeting, Yunnan newspapers were used to actively promote the scheme, putting additional pressure on the SEPA opposers.

As the plans entered the public domain, broader civil society—beyond the usual, officials, business operatives and experts—became very involved. For example, in Beijing, a public petition calling for the protection of the Nu was organized in October 2003 by the China Environmental Culture Association. This was signed by sixty-two people—including prominent artists, journalists, environmentalists and well-known public figures —and widely circulated. This was a small, early sign of a resistance that has since grown. In November 2003 in Kunming, the nongovernmental organization (NGO) Green Watershed[12] used their regular Environment Dialogue forum to share information and stimulate wider public awareness and debate. Discussions of alternative development pathways are also being held within the Nujiang Lisu Nationality Autonomous Prefecture. In December 2003 a forty-five-minute television documentary was prepared by Central China Television (CCTV) which presented both sides of the debate. This documentary was shown nationally three times, including on Saturday and Sunday morning prime time in early March 2004. Universities in Chongqing and Kunming also became involved in "Save the Nu" campaigning. In sum, the case attracted significant media attention, fostering a much wider public debate than the proponents had ever envisaged.

Meanwhile in Bangkok, the Chinese Ambassador was petitioned on December 16, 2003 by more than eighty environmental, human rights and ethnic groups from Thailand and Myanmar voicing their concerns and calling for the inclusion of downstream country perspectives in the decision-making process. This effort was coordinated by the South East Asia Rivers Network (SEARIN), a regional NGO based in Chiang Mai. A wider international petition was organized in January 2004, coordinated by the International Rivers Network (IRN), an international NGO based in California. Learning exchanges between Thai, Burmese and Chinese NGOs have also taken place.

The various spheres of Chinese government—with the exception of some of the perspectives convened by SEPA—and the developers remain firmly committed to the cascade, with only peripheral changes to the July 2003 plan being countenanced. However, it is now clear to the developer that more detailed impact assessment work will need to be done, and resettlement plans prepared and made public. This already represents a considerable achievement by SEPA and others who are yet to be convinced of the wisdom of the proposal. Resistance to the plan, the decision-making rationale and the original governance process has been surprisingly strong and has rapidly gained momentum.

In April 2004, the Premier Wen Jiabao chose to intervene and suspend the plans for the Nu development until such time as a proper impact assessment process was undertaken. This was a remarkable intervention, and was claimed as a great victory by those committed to more informed and transparent governance. Since then, the optimism of opponents has been dampened by the impossibility of obtaining access to the impact assessment documentation. This is considered top secret and is unavailable for public scrutiny, even to an official UNESCO World Heritage site inspection team that went to the province in early 2006. At the time of writing, the development of hydropower in the Nu remains the dominant scenario, but there may be substantial changes made to the original development plan. The governance process remains unclear, with many actors—including various Chinese government ministries—unclear of their role, and Chinese civil society actors frustrated by the unwillingness of authorities to share information in the public domain.

Lancang River

The Lancang River flows for nearly 800 km in Tibet before entering Yunnan where it flows for another 1,247 km. The Lancang cascade is a huge project designed to take advantage of an 800 m drop over a 750 km river section in the middle and lower sections of the Yunnan stretch (Plinston and He Daming 1999). For dam builders this part of the river has been described as a "rich, rare hydropower mine for its prominent natural advantages in abundant and well-distributed runoff, large drops and less flooding losses of the reservoirs" (ICOLD 2001). The cascade is no longer speculation, but rather a fact. Regardless of whether all eight proposed dams are built, Manwan and Dachoashan are already constructed, Xiaowan is under construction and Jinghong is soon to commence.

Proponents argue that the dams have the potential to offer flood control, more assured dry-season flows, increased navigation options, reduced saline intrusion and create extra irrigation opportunities for downstream countries like Thailand. In addition to the rapidly expanding grid system within China, the electricity produced will be able to enter the Mekong region electricity grid.[13] A particularly sanguine view is that "upstream development of hydropower will not sharpen the conflict of multi-objective competitive uses and will give benefits to downstream for the development of irrigation, navigation, and hydropower, and for flooding control" (Plinston and He Daming 1999). However, the conclusion that the cascade will not "sharpen the conflict" between upstream and downstream users is wrong. For example, there was significant tension in the first months of 2004 in northern Thailand's river-dependent communities who are concerned at the very low flows in the river, and apparent fluctuations. At that time, there was a drought and so natural flows were already low, but the Thais were also unsure as to what effect the river flow is being altered by China's upstream dam managers. More information exchange is essential if cross border understanding and trust is to be built.

The first dam constructed on the Lancang mainstream was Manwan, finished in 1996. As of October 2003, the second dam, Dachaoshan, is in full operation, with each of its six 225 MW generators now installed. The third dam being constructed is Xiaowan, seen as an iconic project for the Western Region Development Strategy. The power production from Xiaowan is considered an essential element of the West to East energy transfer. It is the second largest dam in China after Three Gorges. When completed and filled, scheduled for 2013, its reservoir will stretch back 169 km from its 292 m high wall.

Huaneng is the dominant actor, having been granted the majority of the development rights on the Lancang, and the upper and middle reaches of the Jinsha. Huaneng is already operating Manwan and Dachoashan; Xiaowan will also be under Huaneng's management.

> **Box 4.3 Huaneng Power International (HPI)**
>
> In November 2001, Huaneng Power International (HPI)—at the time China's largest independent power generator—announced it intended to list on China's domestic sharemarket. The parent Huaneng International Power Development Company had already been incorporated as a Sino-foreign joint venture in 1985. After incorporation, the HPI offspring had been listed on the New York exchange in 1994, followed by a listing on the Hong Kong exchange in 1998. In July 2003, the parent HIPDC held 43 percent of the shares. As of September 12, 2003, the share price had increased to 115 percent from the previous year. A valuation (02/01/2004) listed HPI as the thirty-eighth largest company on the Hong Kong exchange, with its H-class shares being valued at HKD 20 billion. Li Xioapeng, chairman of the Huaneng Group, wants Huaneng to be the world's leading electricity producer, aiming to double its generating capacity by 2010 to 60,000 megawatts, and make it into the Fortune 500 list of the world's largest companies (*China Daily* 2003c).

The dominant developing entity for the remainder of the construction is the Yunnan Huaneng Lancangjiang Hydropower Company (YHLHC) Limited. In February 2003, the shareholders were Huaneng (56 percent), Yunnan Development Investment Company (31.4 percent) and Yunnan Hongta Investment (12.4 percent).[14] The predecessor to YHLHC was Yunnan Lancang River Hydropower Development Company Limited, created in February 2001. The original shareholders were State Power Corporation (27 percent),[15] Yunnan Electric Power Group Company Limited (29 percent), Yunnan Provincial Development & Investment Company Limited (24 percent) and Yunnan Hongta Investment 20 percent. As the numbers show, the shareholding has changed, with Huaneng now the major player.

To fund Xiaowan's construction, in February 2003 YHLHC borrowed 25 billion yuan (USD 3 billion) from several banks: China Development Bank 15 billion yuan (USD 1.8 billion) (CDB 2003), Construction Bank of China six billion yuan (USD 725.5 million), and Industrial & Commercial Bank of China four billion yuan (USD 483.6 million). Effectively this fully funds Xiaowan as the total investment is expected to be 27.7 billion yuan (USD 3.3 billion) (*China West News* 2003b).

The next dam is Jinghong, which commenced construction in 2003, albeit without yet having been fully approved by state authorities. Both Chinese and Thai officials and experts have been involved in all stages of planning since the early 1990s. It is expected to be built by YHLHC at a cost of about USD 1.2 billion and be fully operational within seven years. The Electricity Generating Authority of Thailand (EGAT) has already entered into agreements to purchase power from the station. The Jinghong dam is yet to receive official approval to do anything more than site preparation (road building, communications establishment, water and electricity supply), but regardless it has already commenced dam construction earthworks.

Gonguoqiao, Nuozhadu, Ganlanba and Mengsong are designed but yet to commence—the last three would also be Huaneng-built dams. The Gonguoqiao, or Dali, dam is particularly interesting. As the most upstream dam in the cascade, its synchronous operation with those downstream is obviously important. A private company believed it had already negotiated prior development rights that were contested by Huaneng. The dispute highlights the problems that could arise on any river if there are different ownership/operation regimes in place, each seeking to maximize their revenue in the new competitive era.

While the hydropower potential is unquestioned, there also huge concerns about the impacts of the dams on riverine ecosystems and local livelihoods (Roberts 2001, IRN 2002). There are major worries about altering the natural regime of the river in a way which will increase flow fluctuations, increase average downstream dry-season flows and decrease the normal flow downstream of nutritious sediments crucial for fisheries and agriculture production. When the cascade is completed, it has been suggested that dry season flows may increase downstream by up to 90 percent at Chiang Saen, 80 percent in Luang Prabang, 70 percent in Vientiane and more than 1,600 km from the cascade, 40 percent at Mukdahan. Predicting impacts in a complex system is difficult, but obviously this will flood large reaches of river rapids, integral to fisheries and radically alter the normal regime of seasonally flooded forests (Blake 2001, TERRA 2002). Large amounts of sediment will be trapped by the new dams, depriving the lower Mekong of its normal load. Negative impacts may also include increased downstream erosion, serious disturbance to fisheries ecology and the devastation of annual riverbank gardening enterprises. Those who stand to lose out include millions of people downstream— mostly beyond the Chinese border—reliant on fishing and riverbank farming (box 4.4).

While an international river, inter-state actors of many different types were unable to ensure anything approaching a thorough discussion of the project alternatives and likely impacts. It was linkages between Chinese and international academics, particularly from the mid 1990s (Chapman and He Daming 1996), which first brought project information into the wider public arena, although the rosiness of the possible scenarios they presented were greeted with wry suspicion by some (Hinton 2000). An International Rivers Symposium in Kunming in 1999 also aided an exchange of perspectives (He Daming et al. 2001). An ADB project on the sustainable development of the Yunnan part of the Lancang-Mekong Basin was also provocative and put new information into the public domain (Landcare Research New Zealand 2000).

Transboundary Environment Assessment (EA) protocols, and the UN Convention on the Law of the Non-Navigational Uses of International Watercourses have been ineffective in either fostering or forcing more extensive cooperation or dialogue. Thus far, other intergovernment forums such as the ASEAN-China dialogues have also ignored the issue. The concerns of downstream nations do not seem to have been taken into account but "this is no surprise given the reticence of any of the downstream government elites to make any serious representations to their more powerful upstream neighbour, and in several cases, increasingly important patron" (Dore 2003). Moreover, in the case of Thailand, EGAT and government officials have been participating in at least a part of the cascade development for about a decade, signing various Memorandums of Understanding (MOUs).

For related reasons, the regional member states have rendered the Mekong River Commission (MRC) relatively impotent as an intergovernment forum for addressing cross border disputes. However, it should be acknowledged that in the Kristensen era of 1999–2003 when he was head of the MRC, the secretariat tried harder than previously, for example via carefully worded indirect appeals through the international and regional media. Since 2004 there is no criticism of China permitted to emerge from the MRC secretariat, with the strategy shifted towards more constructive engagement, and downplaying of development risks. Others have also noted the general silence of the neighbouring state leaders in raising any objections to China's Lancang dam building program. In the case of Cambodia, with China now the major financial patron of the country, Prime Minister Hun Sen has specifically banned any criticism or public deliberation about the risks to the Great Lake (Tonle Sap).

Challenging the rationale and speculating about the possible negative consequences have been left to Thai, Cambodian and international NGOs and policy research groups. This has greatly enhanced knowledge and awareness, but has had no substantive impact on the implementation of the scheme.

The spokesperson from China's Ministry of Foreign Affairs, Liu Lichao, and the Deputy Governor of Yunnan Province, Bai Enpei, have both made public statements in response to the downstream concerns. They have reiterated China's position is to avoid harm to downstream countries in front of the friendship tie with neighbouring Southeast Asian countries. However, the statements have as yet not been followed by mechanisms to ensure full information exchange, and joint analysis of how the dams might best be managed so as to avoid harmful impacts. China does continue to engage as a dialogue partner with MRC and the annual meeting agenda is becoming increasingly substantive, after many years of discussing only peripheral issues.

Box 4.4 Fish and Cambodia's Tonle Sap Lake
There is a rich diversity of fish in the Mekong system. While the taxonomy is still being sorted out, most experts agree that there are more than a thousand freshwater species. Fisheries are vital to the livelihoods of most of the 12 million rural households in the lower Mekong (MRC 2003). Current estimates are that almost two million tonnes are harvested each year from the Lancang/Mekong fishery—1.75 million tonnes from the capture fisheries valued at USD 1.45 billion, plus another 250,000 tonnes from aquaculture (MRC 2002). It is assumed the dam cascade will harm the fishery due to the new flow regime, migration disruption, and temperature and sediment load changes. The Tonle Sap Lake (TSL) area includes the largest freshwater lake in Southeast Asia. The functioning of this unique hydrological and ecological system is critical to the fisheries and rice fields production—and therefore the livelihoods and economy—of Cambodia and southern Vietnam. The area also has other ecological values that are deemed to be of national, regional and international importance. The depth varies from 1 to 2 meters in the dry season to 9 to 11 meters in the flood and its surface area varies from 250,000 to 300,000 hectares in the dry to 900,000 to 1,600,000 hectares depending on the extent of the wet season. At high water level the TSL covers up to about seven percent of the area of Cambodia. The lake is connected to the Mekong River at Phnom Penh by the Tonle Sap River. In the dry season the Tonle Sap River empties into the Mekong River, whereas in the wet season the river reverses direction and flows back towards the lake. More than 60 percent of the floodwater of the TSL comes from the Mekong River, the remainder from the catchment areas of the lake. At full flood the TSL temporarily stores about 72 billion m^3 of water, which equates to 16 percent of the average annual discharge of the Mekong River (MRC et al. 1998). The present annual fish catch from TSL is estimated at 235,000 tonnes, depending on the season (van Zalinge et al. 2001).

The Lancang/Mekong provides 70 percent of the sediment load received by the TSL. The closure of the Manwan dam in 1993 halved the sediment load in the Mekong River water at Chiang Saen in northern Thailand. It is uncertain as to the extent to which sediment loads will be further reduced when Xiaowan and others in the cascade are completed, and how far downstream these effects will be measured. The relationship between source of sediment and nutrient availability is also unclear. However, the researchers producing this data are convinced of the threat. They summarize: "regional developments utilising the Mekong water, such as extensive damming of tributaries and the main river (in China), as well as irrigation, may lead to lower downstream flood levels and extensive trapping of sediments, and thereby have a negative effect on the fertility of the Tonle Sap system, which appears to depend on high flood levels with a high sediment load" (Sarkkula et al. 2003, 45).

Jinsha River

The Jinsha is the largest river in Yunnan and refers to a stretch of about 2,300 km from Yushu in Qinghai Province to Yibing in Sichuan Province. More loosely, it refers to the Yangtze upstream of the Three Gorges Dam project. The upper Jinsha refers to the 994 km reach from Yushu down to Shigu in Yunnan's Lijiang Prefecture. The last 360 km are within Yunnan. Before the famous first bend of the Yangtze[16] at Shigu the river heads south in parallel with the Nu and the Lancang, thereafter it winds its way generally eastwards, splitting China in two between "the wheat-growing North and the rice-growing South" (Winchester 1996). There are no serious plans for hydropower in the upper Jinsha but plans for the middle and lower reaches have been worked up over the past ten years.

Box 4.5 Financing the Three Gorges project

The Three Gorges project is a flagship, national project costing USD 22 billion. The China Yangtze Three Gorges Project Development Corporation (CYTGPDC) is responsible for the construction phase, which began in 1994 and is scheduled for completion in 2021. Finance has been found from a range of sources. In 1992 the Beijing government imposed a levy on power producers across the country of between 0.004–0.007 yuan per kwh. The project was also granted the revenues from the Gezhouba power plant. Over an extended period, China Development Bank has thus far contributed USD 3.6 billion. With rising confidence in the project over time, the managers have been able to raise USD 2.3 billion from bond issues on the domestic market for periods of fifteen, twenty and thirty years. A further USD 1.3 billion has been borrowed from commercial banks including the China Construction Bank, the Industrial and Commercial Bank of China, and the Bank of Communications (*Beijing Review* 2003a). The managers are confident that future funds will be found as required, with all options—domestic or international—open to consideration.

Not content with waiting to finish this gigantic project before starting any other, CTGPC has already announced plans to build four new hydropower plants further upstream on the Jinsha that will provide twice as much generating capacity as the existing Three Gorges. To manage power generation, sales and management, the China Yangtze Electric Power Corporation (CYEPC) has been created. This entity was gifted assets of the aforementioned Gezhouba to aid in its start-up. It obtained permission from the government's corporate regulator to list on the domestic stock market in November 2003. 29.6 percent of the company was sold with the share price rising 44 percent on the first day from the initial offering price. The offering was heavily oversubscribed and raised USD 1.2 billion.

From Shigu to the junction with the Yalong River is the 563 km middle Jinsha, most of which runs through northwestern Yunnan Province. There are major development plans for this stretch, with eight dams proposed. Huaneng is the main player, having effectively been allocated the concession for this section of the river, which is considered ideal for hydropower development. They are intending to develop seven of the proposed dams. An eighth is planned by the private company Huari, which had commenced negotiating with Lijiang prefecture and Yunnan provincial governments prior to the SPC break-up and asset distribution.

The lower Jinsha runs for 768 km to Yibing. Most of this section forms the border between Sichuan Province and Yunnan Province. A further four dams are planned for the lower Jinsha by the China Yangtze Three Gorges Project Development Corporation (CYTGPDC). These huge stations are reportedly planned to have an installed capacity 38,500 MW, which would be twice as much as the existing Three Gorges project (China West News 2003a). So, it would seem that there will be one river with three different owners, potentially making flow management more complex.

Issues

Particular dam projects in Yunnan appear to have taken on a life of their own, well beyond the visions/strategies emanating directly from the Beijing or Yunnan governments. The momentum now acquired makes it difficult to modify the development agenda, partly because government is now "less empowered" and/or compromised by its linkages with private investment. The lines between public and private have become extremely blurred, whether via formal or informal public-private partnerships. New forces for development are pushing projects, such as: international financiers and the increasingly empowered natural-assets rich state-controlled power companies. The political economy has shifted. Formal state policy and planning may no longer be the key driver as capitalist forces have been substantially unleashed. In such a situation, the regulatory role played by state and civil society becomes critical.

Consider the following statement: "In the view of some experts, repetitive construction is a natural problem occurring in the development of a market economy, so it should be dealt with by the market itself, rather than through administrative interference such as loan suspensions and banning projects" (Feng 2003). While made with particular reference to the electrolytic aluminium and iron and steel industries, reflect for a moment on its relevance to the hydropower industry. Imagine the consequences of unrestrained, over-zealous "repetitive construction" in the hydropower industry. Imperfect markets can be wasteful and destructive.

Investment driven by competition, supported by easily accessible finance and almost free access to public land and water assets may not yield net public benefit (regardless of how it is defined). It would seem that there is a dangerous brew of unrestrained competition policy, confusion about the regulatory role of the state, freely available investment funds and easy access to rivers that could lead to unnecessary and irreversible damage to ecosystems, natural and cultural heritage and local livelihoods. Many within China are concerned about this current headlong pursuit of hydropower development. Other values are being discussed, other decision-making processes suggested, and the sensibility of intense competition between energy business giants is being challenged.

Several key questions require revisiting:[17]

- *What type of development is preferred?* This strikes at the heart of development directions—the "conventional" economic development of modernity, or more sustainability-oriented conceptions where different values are prized? While pursuing economic growth for job creation and poverty reduction is still paramount, the "New and Scientific Concept of Development" being actively promoted by President Hu Jintao explicitly acknowledges other goals—human development, more efficient resource use and less pollution (*China Daily* 2004a). Within this new context a review of national energy policy, including the hydropower component, would be appropriate.

- *How are development goals to be achieved?* This is essentially about modalities and roles that should be taken by the state, business and general citizens. The current phenomenon where capitalist entities are assuming monopoly control over state-owned natural resources requires rapid review and adjustment. More detailed analysis is required of the impacts of China's energy reform policies and the related surge for substantial Yunnan hydropower expansion. There seem to be many risks associated with these recent policy changes. There are serious concerns about the impact of the policies that have led to the current competition between the large energy consortiums. It is not simply a case of healthy competition between business competitors within a framework which guarantees overall public benefit. Water resources are being monopolized by the large companies via the partnerships being negotiated with various national and local authorities. The wisdom of policy that permits this degree of control and exploitation by profit-driven entities is now being challenged.

- *How are decisions about setting and striving for these goals to be made?* This is about the concept of governance which "encompasses the complex and open network of authorities by which the life of society—its institutions, bodies, souls, canons, knowledge, news—is monitored and managed"[18] (Lambropoulos, 1996). When thinking about the directions taken by society, the governance processes by which we deal with conflict are what really matter. Are they adequate?

Hydropower development is a sensitive issue, not just in China, but also throughout the Mekong region. Numerous projects have become the subject of national, and in some cases regional and international controversies. Examples include: Vietnam's Se San, Sre Pok and Son La dams; Lao PDR's Theun Hinboun and Nam Theun 2 dams; Thailand's Pak Mun Dam; the Yunnan dams, and those further downstream on the Nu/Salween into Myanmar. In the Mekong region, as elsewhere, it seems that many costs of hydropower development are ignored or excluded from analysis and debate.

Advocates of hydropower tout its positive features: renewable energy, pollution-free, relatively low generating cost, flood reducing, navigation improving and increased irrigation opportunities. However, an assessment of large dams by the World Commission on Dams found that performance is very variable, with many dams falling short of economic expectations and most having large impacts, more negative than positive, on rivers, watersheds and aquatic ecosystems. They also found that resettlement and compensation schemes had often been inadequate, impoverishing millions of people. Moreover, they noted that "Since the environmental and social costs of large dams have been poorly accounted for in economic terms, the true profitability of these schemes remains elusive" (WCD 2000, xxxi).

In China and the other Mekong countries, the large dam paradigm remains a respected pillar of the energy industry and key offices within government. New construction is deemed essential to meet national and regional energy demands. Nevertheless, there is a series of key issues that have emerged around the world, which should also be considered by Mekong region decision-makers (box 4.6). There was an initial expectation world wide that Impact Assessment (IA) would be a key mechanism to solve development project problems and address many of these issues. However, as practiced, it has not met expectations.

Hydropower governance should be inherently inter-disciplinary and perspectives from the social and physical sciences, government and civil societies should all have a place. China's highest political leadership has endorsed more participatory forms of governance (*China Daily* 2004b). Therefore it would seem that a necessary national review of hydropower governance, presently rooted in a closed rather than open network, while difficult, is politically possible.

> **Box 4.6 Central issues in the dams debate: Past and present**
> - *Performance: costs and benefits*—much depends on how completely costs are internalized, and who bears particular costs compared to how the benefits are shared.
> - *Environmental impacts and sustainability*—fundamental controversy centers on how environmental considerations are valued against immediate human development needs.
> - *Social impacts and equity*—much concern about the basis on which trade-offs, such as potential benefits to many at the cost of hardship for a few, are invoked and decided.
> - *Economics and finance*—controversy also surrounds the limits and the ability of methods for economic assessment to fully capture and reflect the various social and environmental impacts and values.
> - *Governance and participation*—at the heart of debate is the degree of involvement of affected people and wider groups of stakeholders in needs assessment and project-level decision-making.
> - *Wider development impact of dams*—controversial issues go beyond the impact of the project itself and touch upon wider regional or national development choices.
> - *Alternatives to dams*—are alternatives to large dams genuinely considered?
> - *Cross-cutting issues*—which actors are the most powerful and most influential in decision-making processes? What and whose rights are prioritized?
>
> SOURCE: Dams and Development (WCD 2000)

Environmental Impact Assessment (EIA) is only one component of governance, but due to the attention it receives, for good reasons, some comment is required here. There are standard issues raised in criticism of EIA, as it is usually undertaken. Most EIA tends to focus on individual projects and is therefore relatively narrow in its scope. Impact zone analyses often stop at national borders.[19] EIA often occurs at a relatively late stage in the decision-making process, when choice of alternatives has already been limited and significant project investment has taken place. EIA often occurs when there have already been significant positions taken in terms of project advocacy or opposition. EIA often occurs after political decisions have already been taken to proceed. The project-EIA then becomes an exercise in ameliorating negative impacts rather than an exploration of possibly more suitable alternatives. Moreover, "environment" is used in a more and less encompassing way in different countries—sometimes excluding social and economic issues, sometimes including one or other of these realms.

These standard criticisms resonate when reflecting on the current EIA process for the Nu River development. There have been Chinese regulations about environmental protection since the late 1970s. A framework has evolved, the latest step being the law on EIA, which came into effect on September 1, 2003. Effort has also been put into Environmental Impact Assessment (EIA) by other Mekong region countries, with the exception of Myanmar.

The overarching term of Impact Assessment (IA) is conceptually preferable, as it reduces the likelihood of externalising important factors. IA may involve evaluation of economic, social, cultural, political, environmental/biophysical/ecological, transboundary and cumulative impacts. But key to being truly useful is that IA occurs before final decision-making, and at a time when alternative options can be genuinely considered.

A suggestion voiced by experts attending the ground-breaking January 2004 Beijing hydropower forum was that "like everything else, hydroelectric plants and dams have their pros and cons...only when the comprehensive impact in economic, social and cultural terms is calculated objectively can assessment be made" (Chen Hong 2004). This ideal has not yet been evident in Yunnan's massive hydropower expansion push. Neither has it been common in other parts of the Mekong region. A few examples will suffice to show that IA needs to be more rigorous.

Economic impacts of Yunnan's hydropower development are unclear and may have been substantially overestimated by information used in decision-making. The useful life of the dams may be much less than has been (presumably) expected and factored into economic calculations. While estimated construction and operating costs per unit of power produced may be attractive, sedimentation inflows into the first-completed Manwan dam are much higher than anticipated (Plinston and He Daming 2000). There are now concerns that without drastic corrective landcare measures, it may only be able to function as a power-producer for less than twenty years (Roberts 2001,150). Without the upstream construction of the sediment-trapping Xiaowan, the Manwan dam would have a very brief working life. The economics of the Yunnan dams need to be properly evaluated, and that evaluation widely shared.

Cross border social and environmental impacts in downstream Myanmar, Lao PDR, Thailand, Cambodia and Vietnam have yet to be factored into China's plans. Cross border cooperation protocols for dam operation will be necessary for ecological damage to be minimized. Almost inevitably this would require energy production to be less than the pure economic optimum. How will this be negotiated?

One new approach has been presented in the report by the Commissioners of the World Commission on Dams (WCD) which they released at the end of the process (WCD 2000, Dubash et al. 2001). The WCD was a multi-stakeholder dialogue process that heard many different opinions. Ultimately, the Commissioners wrote their own opinion and have offered it as their contribution to the large dams debate and to those with responsibility for influencing or making large dam decisions (box 4.7).

Box 4.7 A new framework for decision-making on large dams

The World Commission on Dams (WCD) process and the report are continuing to make a significant contribution to worldwide large dams debates. A key conclusion of the Commissioners was that it is imperative "to bring new voices, perspectives and criteria into decision-making" (WCD 2000,197), hence their advocacy for a process which "gives all key stakeholders a voice and a full opportunity to participate in decision-making, seeks the broadest reasonable consensus, and is transparent in the criteria used for reaching a decision" (ibid., 209).

The Commissioners advocated, as a starting point, clarifying the rights context by undertaking a transparent assessment of the constitutional, customary, international, human, ecological, etc. rights held by interested and affected parties. They pointed out that this is best undertaken in tandem with a substantial assessment of the risks borne voluntarily by "risk takers" and involuntarily by "risk bearers." They proposed a decision-making framework which pays close attention to the following priority areas:

- *Gaining public acceptance* which advocates genuinely participatory decision-making processes
- *Comprehensive options assessment* which advocates genuine consideration of alternatives, rather than just focusing on impact assessment and amelioration/mitigation of negatives
- *Addressing existing dams* acknowledging that there are many decisions which have to be made about managing existing dams
- *Sustaining rivers and livelihoods* is primarily concerned with protecting ecosystems
- *Recognizing entitlements and sharing benefits* is primarily concerned with human justice
- *Ensuring compliance* concentrates on checking that all commitments made in negotiations are subsequently adhered to
- *Sharing rivers for peace, development and security* is endeavoring to see that transboundary, crossborder or "between country" issues are acknowledged, recognising that all riparian states and their peoples may be stakeholders.

SOURCE: Dams and Development (WCD 2000)

The WCD framework is a useful guide increasingly being considered by different groups within China. Translation and dissemination of the WCD report is ensuring that the issues raised in the WCD process are being more widely discussed. This is a positive step forward, and could greatly aid any review of existing Chinese dam decision-making processes.

The rapid Yunnan hydropower expansion is already having a major impact on the national and provincial economy, the finance sector, the rivers and the people of the province. A detailed review and debate is urgently needed of the rationale, the processes, the options and the implications for the entire Mekong region.

Recommendations

First order—China Energy Policy and Energy Development Governance

There are two key messages this chapter seeks to deliver. First, there is a need for China to revisit the energy policy, including the hydropower component, in the light of the new direction signalled in the New and Scientific Development Concept announced in 2003 by China's political leadership, and reinforced by President Hu Jintao at the Tenth National People's Congress (NPC) meeting in March 2004. Second, there is a need to overhaul energy development governance processes including: option formulation, debate, evaluation, negotiation and monitoring. The approvals and impact assessment processes are key areas requiring strengthening.

Second order—Yunnan Hydropower Governance

Current controversy over proposed Nu River development provides opportunity to enhance the quality of Yunnan hydropower governance. The following Nu assessments would, if undertaken and widely shared, contribute sorely needed new elements to China and Mekong region governance forums. Similar analyses on the Lancang and Jinsha would also be beneficial.

Decision-making process assessment

It is nothing new to note that IA processes should contribute to decision-making and approvals processes, rather than follow afterwards as a "rubber stamp" to legitimize a decision already taken, perhaps making minor changes to implementation plans. The influence exerted when selecting and using "expert panels" also needs examination. Possibilities for more participatory, informed and informing processes should also be explored. Closed processes that have to be painstakingly prised open are surely not the best way to go. Detailed analysis of the current Nu development decision-making process would be instructive.

Political economy assessment

Further clarification of the substantial shift in the political economy of Yunnan hydropower is required. Research should particularly focus on the relative power relationships between and within states; and between states, business and civil society. Production and public debate of this analysis is necessary for more informed and equitable and decision-making.

Economic assessment

The economics of Yunnan dams need proper evaluation from different perspectives, but in a way which takes account of the reality of the new and fierce competition between developers, and improves upon past analytical approaches which have regularly externalized many costs and benefits, and hidden or ignored particular winners and losers.

Social/cultural impact assessment

Social and cultural impact assessment is not common in China or the rest of the Mekong region, but has been done recently (albeit only retrospectively) for Manwan dam. Entrenching this type of analysis before committing to particular development pathways would be a step forward.

Ecological/natural heritage risk assessment

There are conflicting arguments presented by Yunnan dam proponents and critics about the risks to ecosystems and the natural heritage of affected areas. Clarification of the risks is required.

Transboundary, cumulative and multiplier effects assessment

More consideration needs to be given to transboundary effects. Impact assessment should not stop at national borders. Consideration should also be given to cumulative and multiplier effects.

Notes

The chapter was first produced as a Working Paper in 2004 by Dore and Yu, with the financial support of the Swedish Environment Secretariat in Asia (SENSA), a part of the Swedish International Development Agency (SIDA). The authors are grateful to many people who assisted us with information for this chapter, and for recent careful reviews by M-POWER colleagues, Rajesh Daniel and Tira Foran, and by Kevin Yuk-shing Li who contributed as a co-author of this updated chapter.

The opinions expressed in this report are those of the authors who alone are responsible for errors that remain. The chapter does not necessarily represent the views of SIDA or SENSA. Our purpose is to provide a brief update on happenings in Yunnan, within the wider context of China's energy policy, energy industry reforms and changing political economy.

1   Globalization is used here in the sense of a compression of space and time in a new era of interconnectedness, where there is less local control (Giddens 1992).

2   The method of reporting foreign direct investment (FDI) still differs between countries and organizations. According to Dunning (1988) FDI comprises activities controlled or organized by firms (or groups of firms) outside of the nation in which they are headquartered and the principal decision-makers are located. When reporting foreign investment, Asian Development Bank (ADB) datasets separate direct investment (what Dunning calls FDI) and portfolio investment. This is not and has not always been done at the country level. To an extent direct investment is fixed, and hence considered more likely to be productive capital investment. Portfolio investment refers to supplying capital and/or taking a shareholding, but with debatably less control/fixed stake and more investment mobility. Portfolio investment can be seen as potentially more speculative. The FDI figures quoted here for China represent direct investment plus portfolio investment in China-based, exchange-listed companies, such as Huaneng and Huadian.

3   In November 2003, there was a workshop held in Kunming on Private Sector Participation (PSP) Options in Water and Electricity. The workshop was jointly organized by the World Bank and the Yunnan Provincial Government and paid for with a USD 120,650 grant from the Bank's Public-Private Infrastructure Advisory Facility (PPIAF).

4   About 80 percent of China's known coal reserves are buried in the north and northwest region (Jia Mulan 2003).

5   China both imports and exports coal. In 2002, China imported 10.8 million tonnes, nearly 1.0 percent of its total consumption. In the same year it exported 84 million tonnes, mainly to Korea, Japan and Taiwan (Ball et al. 2003, 42–43).

6   The demand management suggestions for China policy makers (box 4.1) are taken from an ADB report which overviews the Western Region Development Strategy (ADB 2002).

7   The evocatively named "Power to the People"(Vaitheeswaran 2003) provides an inspiring analysis of the impending "energy revolution." The author argues that promising new technologies, such as fuel cells and micro turbines, will lead the way to a revolution in micro power—putting small clean power plants close to homes and factories—which will displace grids which deliver power from big plants to often distant consumers. This recent addition to the literature builds on other work which reports on promising progress with new energy technologies for developing countries (for example, see Forsyth 1999).

8   China has been constructing nuclear power plants for more than twenty years. The China Atomic Energy Agency plans that by 2005, with capacity set to increase to 8.7 million kilowatts, nuclear plants will be providing 3 percent of the total national energy output (*People's Daily* Online 2003a).

9   The economic argument of analysts Guotai Junan Securities Co (discussed in *Business Weekly* 2003), and others, is that as electricity price drops generating capacity must increase if company profits are to remain stable. In an example they worked through, for a 3.55 percent price drop, based on an average national tariff of 3.4 US cents per kilowatt-hour, generating capacity needs to increase five percent to maintain profit-levels.

10 The Bing Zhong Luo component of the cascade does not actually involve a "dam," rather being designed as "run-of-river," hence there is no "inundation area."

11 During October 2003, the Electricity Generating Authority of Thailand (EGAT) was told by the Thai Ministry of Energy to suspend talks on this delicate

subject until after the APEC show had exited Bangkok (Watcharapong Thongrung 2003). However, EGAT confirmed in November 2003 that it is prepared to finance the entire project, although it would prefer to explore some form of partnership with the Myanmar military junta and Chinese government (Nareerat Wiriyapong 2003).

12 Green Watershed has contributed to lifting the standard and inclusiveness of the Nu River debate in several ways, via its own hosting of public meetings and discussion with officials in Kunming and Nujiang Prefecture, support to the TV documentary makers, radio spots, and co-organising with the Centre for Environment and Development and others, under the China Academy of Social Sciences (CASS), a Beijing symposium January 8–9, 2004 focused on reconsidering the place of dams in national development. The authors have also jointly presented the substance of this research paper in Kunming, and in November 2003 to the Southeast Asia Water Forum held in Chiang Mai, and a meeting of development agencies in Bangkok.

13 At the Phnom Penh 2002 GMS leaders' summit, Mekong region governments signed an intergovernment agreement which paves the way for regional power trading. This should also be considered within the context of the so-called ASEAN grid being promoted by EGAT

14 The original Yuxi Tobacco Factory in Yunnan Province was established in 1956. A major reorganization in 1995 led to the creation of the Yuxi-Hongta Tobacco Group (Hongta), which is China's biggest tobacco grower and cigarette producer. As part of its WTO obligations, from 2003 China has begun opening its tobacco market to foreign firms by abolishing special retail licences and reducing import taxes. Since its formation, Hongta has diversified into many different areas, including power production. Hence, it was no surprise to see it take an initial 20 percent stake in the original Yunnan Lancang Jiang hydropower development company when it formed in 2001. With the advent of Huaneng and the morphing into the Yunnan Huaneng Lancangjiang Hydropower Company Limited, Hongta reduced its share to 12.6 percent (as at February 18, 2003).

15 The assets transferred from the State Power Grid Company to Huaneng on September 23, 2003 include their 27 percent share in the Yunnan Huaneng Lancangjiang Hydropower Company Limited.

16 Winchester (1996) provides a brief account of the significance and mythology of the rock barrier (Yun Ling or "Cloud Mountain") which changes the course of the river, at the beginning of his book *The River at the Centre of the World*.

17 These were triggered by and adapted from similar questions posed by a journalist (China Power News 2004).

18 A narrow conception may focus on: administration, business practice, legal formalities or government.

19 The four lower Mekong countries are slowly developing a transboundary EIA protocol, based on the European Espoo Convention. The process is being facilitated by the Mekong River Commission (MRC) secretariat.

CHAPTER 5

ELECTRICITY SECTOR PLANNING AND HYDROPOWER

Chris Greacen and Apsara Palettu

Introduction

Long before the first explosives are detonated to initiate construction, hydroelectric projects (in the Mekong region as elsewhere) exist as abstractions—as engineering drawings, as line items in a list of national "hydropower potential," as some kind of notion that the electricity these dams may produce will be necessary and that these particular dams are a preferable way of meeting expected demand for energy.

How are projections of electricity demand constructed? How are decisions made about what kinds of power plants are chosen and where they are built? What types of assumptions are made about options and alternatives? How does hydropower in the Mekong region relate to decision-making processes in the power sector?

This chapter makes three main arguments. First, plans for hydropower projects in the region are largely justified by projections of high demand for electricity in Thailand, Vietnam and China. Second, Thai electricity demand projections are constructed in a closed process strongly influenced by monopoly electric utilities that are incentivized to overestimate demand—and have a track record of overestimating demand. Vietnamese and Chinese load forecasting arrangements may face similar governance issues. Third, the paper argues that many hydropower projects in the region are not possible without substantial subsidies which currently take the form of grants and risk guarantees, soft loans, and political intervention in Power Purchase Agreements (PPAS); and in the future may well take the form of a subsidized regional transmission grid. It is argued that these subsidies should be removed, and hydropower should be forced to compete on a fair, least economic cost basis with a broad range of cleaner and less expensive alternatives.

This chapter proceeds as follows. First, it discusses existing and planned hydropower capacity in each country in the Mekong region, and considers some key historical events in the development of their power sectors. This is followed by a critical analysis of the contemporary power development planning process (especially in Thailand),[1] with a focus on the actors that decide, the incentives they face, and the methods and assumptions they employ. It then considers how the ways in which these demand projections are used to determine the future mix of power plants—and the peculiar way in which hydropower enters into these plans. The chapter closes with recommendations regarding planning and governance in the sector, including stricter interpretation and implementation of "least cost planning."

Regional overview

Electricity demand in the Mekong region is forecast to grow rapidly in the next fifteen years (figure 5.1); and there are big plans to develop hydroelectric power to meet this projected demand. Increasingly, a pattern is emerging in which poorer economies such as Lao PDR and Myanmar [Burma] in particular are lining up to supply hydropower to wealthier neighbors like Thailand and Vietnam. International financial institutions such as the Asian Development Bank (ADB) and the World Bank (WB) are intimately involved in encouraging, funding, and supplying technical expertise for hydro development in the region (see box).

While hydroelectric dams play an important role in electricity production and in some cases) flood control, and irrigation (ICOLD 2000), these massive structures also cause serious damage to freshwater ecosystems, affecting both nature and people. Decimated fisheries, forced relocations of communities inundated by the reservoirs, and downstream impacts from changes in siltation and flood regimes are among the most serious side effects (World Commission on Dams 2000b, WWF 2004).

An ADB-funded study by Norconsult in 2002 identifies "expansion candidate" hydro projects in each country. In Laos, the study identifies twenty-nine sites, totaling 7,380 megawatts (MW), with the vast majority of electricity produced to be exported to Thailand and Vietnam (Norconsult 2002a). In Yunnan, hydropower already provides 5,150 MW of capacity. Seven more sites on the Mekong (Lancang) are planned or under construction totaling 14,050 MW (Norconsult 2002a, 2–24), and a thirteen-dam cascade of hydropower totaling 23,300 MW is under consideration for the Salween (Nu) River (Sharp 2004). The power from these new projects

Figure 5.1 Peak demand in 2000 and projected peak demand year 2020

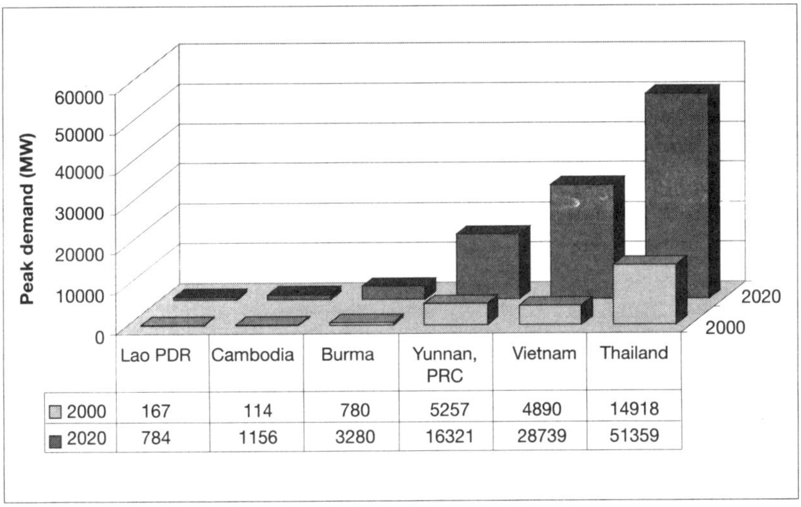
Peak demand (MW)
60000
50000
40000
30000
20000
10000
0
2020
2000
Lao PDR
Cambodia
Burma
Yunnan, PRC
Vietnam
Thailand
2000 167 114 780 5257 4890 14918
2020 784 1156 3280 16321 28739 51359

SOURCE: Norconsult 2003

will serve loads in China, Thailand and Vietnam. In Myanmar, the ADB study identified fifteen projects totaling 23,700 MW, with most power to be exported to Thai load centers. For Vietnam, the study lists thirty-four candidate hydro projects totaling 10,497 MW, mostly for domestic consumption. In Cambodia, the ADB study has identified sixteen candidate hydroelectric sites totaling 2074 MW (Norconsult 2002b, A2-15, tables A2-3).

Mekong River Commission: Hydropower visions

For decades, key decision-makers have held a common idea regarding rivers in the Mekong region: to develop water resources as hydropower for industrial expansion. In the corridors of political power, no strong competing vision for water resources has yet evolved to replace hydropower development. This widespread vision of large-scale hydropower development in the region began to take root during the Cold War, shaped by US, Soviet and Chinese planners who, despite differing political ideologies, shared a common vision of industrial development powered by big dams.

Starting in the 1950s, American economic advisors drew up plans for substantial regional infrastructure development in Thailand, Laos, Cambodia, and Vietnam. The planners envisioned Thailand as the launching pad for a Mekong development plan modeled after the US Tennessee Valley Authority (USTVA). The plan would have harnessed the Mekong River for electrical production to provide plentiful cheap electricity to drive industry and mechanized agriculture. Seven huge hydroelectric dams were planned which would have carved the Mekong River into a series of reservoirs over 2,000 kilometers long (Hirsch and Warren 1998). One dam alone, the High Pa Mong project upstream from Vientiane, would have required the resettlement of 250,000 people, flooded 3,700 square kilometers of land and reportedly would have cost USD 10 billion[2] (IRN 1994b, Dieu 2000). The project was investigated for thirty years, with at least USD 70 million spent on studies by 1984. The projected electricity generation capacity of the Pa Mong and three other related dams was estimated at almost four times the 1980 electric consumption of all of Thailand.

The Committee for Coordination of Investigations of the Lower Mekong Basin (Mekong Committee), founded under the auspices of the United Nations in 1957, was an intergovernmental agency consisting of government representatives from countries in the Mekong watershed. The mission of the Committee was the comprehensive development of the water resources of the Lower Mekong Basin, including the mainstream and its tributaries (United Nations 1963).

Regional conflict, disagreements among Mekong states over water management, and the economic non-viability of the proposed hydroelectric projects thwarted efforts to build any dams along the Mekong River. After 1978, the Committee functioned under an interim status, with only the government of Laos, Thailand, and Vietnam participating. During the 1980s, most of the long-range aspects of the Mekong scheme and its key basin-wide projects were abandoned (Hirsch and Warren 1998). In 1994, the Mekong Secretariat issued a study of nine proposed run-of-river dams for the Mekong mainstream. However, the plans were shelved following opposition by nongovernmental organizations (Imhof 2005).

Thailand: First to develop large hydropower, first to reach hydropower impasse

With increasing communist activity throughout Southeast Asia in the 1950s, the World Bank, the US Agency for International Development (USAID) and other international funding agencies turned their attention to regional economic development as a bulwark against communism. This played a crucial role in Thailand's energy history. Advice and concessionary financing were catalytic in the construction of a number of large power plants in Thailand starting in the early 1960s. Foremost among these was the Bhumipol (also called Yunhee) hydroelectric dam. The 100 MW dam (later expanded to 779.2 MW) was financed by a USD 69 million World Bank loan arranged in 1957. The loan was nearly three times larger than any Thailand had previously secured (Chatikavanij 1994, 33). Contemporary power sector investments facilitated by the World Bank included several thermal lignite (coal) power plants in north, central, and southern Thailand, as well as the beginnings of the Thai transmission grid, which allowed electricity generated in rural areas to be transmitted to industrial, commercial, and residential customers in Bangkok and the surrounding metropolitan area (Greacen 2004). The electricity authorities that built and operated these projects were later consolidated to form the Electricity Generating Authority of Thailand (EGAT), a state-owned enterprise under the Office of the prime minister.

After dozens of large hydroelectric projects had been built, most of Thailand's hydropower potential was realized. In the process, Thai society became increasingly concerned about the inundation of hundreds of villages and massive areas of farmland and forests caused by hydropower projects. Subsequently, when EGAT proposed to build the Nam Choan Dam in the western forest complex of Kanchanaburi Province that would inundate large areas of a wildlife sanctuary, widespread public criticism and protests followed. In 1989, after years of protest by villagers and environmental groups, the government under then-Prime Minister Prem Tinsulanonda halted the project (Phongpaichit 2000).

Following the cancellation of Nam Choan, EGAT built the Pak Mun project with most construction during the years 1991 to 1994. EGAT expected that the Pak Mun would face little opposition because as a "run of river" project it had a relatively small reservoir. Instead, the project became one of Thailand's most controversial projects with over a decade of protests by villagers whose fishing livelihoods were negatively affected by the project (World Commission on Dams 2000a). A World Commission on Dams case study on the project noted that actual dependable capacity of the dam was only 20.1 MW—vastly less than the 150 MW used in EGAT's options assessment. At the same time, costs escalated 68 percent in nominal terms over estimated costs (Amornsakchai, Annez et al. 2000).

Since then, EGAT has found it more difficult to develop dams in the face of greater public and community opposition. EGAT turned to greater reliance on natural gas and coal, which currently account for 70 percent and 12 percent of installed capacity respectively. Whereas hydropower accounted for 30 percent of installed generation capacity in 1986, by year 2005 domestic hydropower accounts for only 13 percent of installed capacity (Norconsult 2002a, Asia Today 2005, Federal Research Division of the Library of Congress).

Thailand also imports hydropower from Laos (currently equivalent to two percent of installed Thai capacity). The latest Thai government projections estimate demand will more than double from 19,326 MW in

2004 to 40,978 MW by the year 2015 (Thai Load Forecast Subcommittee 2004). These projections have sparked considerable interest among policymakers regarding increased imports of hydropower from Laos, Yunnan, and Myanmar.

Box 5.1 IFIS and Mekong hydropower development

International Financial Institutions (IFIS), particularly the ADB and the World Bank, have played an important role in the Mekong region's hydropower development.

Instead of financing projects with loans and government budgets, the IFI's have turned increasingly to the BOT mechanism: Build, Operate, and Transfer. Hailed as an answer to limited government and bank funds, BOT involves private companies constructing and operating power plants for periods of up to thirty years, and then transferring ownership to the government. In practice, however, private companies have been unwilling to develop hydropower schemes under BOT arrangements unless IFIS and governments provide a range of subsidies including bank loan guarantees, grants and low interest loans (IRN 1999).

IFIS have played a crucial role in promoting hydropower projects in a variety of ways. One is financial assistance—the World Bank and ADB have provided grants, guarantees, and loans for specific projects. Another role is generating, and engineering government approval of, key studies that support proposed dam projects. These studies include those that identify hydro potential and propose sites for dams, and then call for follow-on feasibility studies, initiating the hydropower development process in specific regions. An example is the ADB funded *Se Kong-Se San and Nam Theun River Basins Hydropower Development Study*—commenced in 1997 and completed in September 1998-that proposed at least six hydropower projects for further study. Financing for the study was in the form of a USD 0.5 million grant from the ADB, and a USD 2 million grant from France under the Channel Financing Agreement between the French government and the ADB through which the ADB proposes projects for funding by the French Government with the funds administered by the ADB (Lang 1998). Similarly, Vietnam's National Hydropower Master Plan was originally conceived by the World Bank, which even wrote the initial TOR for the study (Aylward, Berkhoff et al. 2001).

International forums held by the ADB starting in 1994 helped prepare rules for international joint ventures in Mekong hydropower projects. The ADB funded studies of hydropower resources in the region. In addition, the ADB has been very active in studying and promoting the Greater Mekong

Subregion (GMS) regional transmission grid, connecting Yunnan, Thailand, Laos, Cambodia, Myanmar and Vietnam. The cost of this USD 1.2 billion project will be incorporated into the tariffs paid by electricity consumers. The benefits, however, will primarily flow to hydropower developers by substantially decreasing the transmission costs they must bear in getting their electricity to market. It is not clear whether these cost decreases are sufficient to make hydropower competitive with natural gas, as feasibility studies for a number of projects in the plan have yet to be completed. Moreover, whether or not these benefits will ultimately trickle down to consumers in the form of lower electricity rates depends on competition between generators. Effective competition requires conditions such as free flow of information, lack of regional transmission constraints, large numbers of competing generators none of which has more than a few percent of market share, and effective and rigorous regulatory oversight to eliminate market manipulation. Based on experience with attempts to develop power markets in other countries, these conditions will be difficult to achieve in the GMS plans, according to a senior transmission planner who reviewed the documents (Garret 2005).

The motivations behind IFI involvement in hydropower in the region are not entirely clear. On the one hand, there appears to be a strong belief among leaders of these organizations that large hydropower projects are the best option available to help lift poorer countries in the area "out of poverty." "Only projects like this offer any possibility for development in the country," claims Homi Kharas referring to the Bank's involvement in the Nam Theun 2 (NT2) project in Laos (Balls 2005). The claim is that development requires large sums of money, and these countries have few other options for revenue generation.

Aid from multilaterals often comes at the behest of developing country leaders who share the bank's visions of development, or who see dams as national symbols of modernity and independence (Williams and Dubash 2004). Some lawmakers have raised concern that corruption may motivate funding requests in some cases: in 2004 witnesses testified to the US Senate Foreign Relations Committee under the chairmanship of Richard Lugar, that borrowing-nation bureaucracies and crooked contractors have stolen over USD 100 billion from the World Bank over the past five decades (Bhargava and Bolongaita 2005). However, IFI leaders claim that their involvement in big dam projects ensures a greater degree of transparency, accountability, and attention to mitigating or reducing social and environmental impacts than would have otherwise occurred, and point to unprecedented public meetings and a large amount of publicly available documents that characterize the World Bank involvement in NT2 (Porter 2005).

Some NGOs take issue with the argument that "IFI involvement increases accountability," pointing out instances of corruption that violate IFI lending policies (Environmental Defense 2003, Lang 2003). They also assert that IFI claims about increasing good governance are moot if these projects would not have gone forward in the first place without IFI involvement; many project developers are reluctant to get involved, or threaten to pull out, unless IFIs offer guarantees and other subsidies (Imhof 1997). The assertion is that had the IFIs not made the project possible, project-associated corruption would not have been an issue.

The IFI claim that "large revenues are essential for development" risks conflating "economic growth" with "development." Philip Hirsch observes that the impacts of dam development have to be seen in terms of unequal distribution of costs and benefits. These projects invariably entail sacrifices by one group in the name of benefits to other groups. Problems of unequal sacrifices are compounded by lack of access to a balanced and impartial justice system, lack of freedom of speech in non-democratic governments—Laos, Myanmar, China—and by the problem that resource tenure and property rights are ill-defined in these countries and especially in more remote locations where dams are planned (Hirsch 1998). IFIs claim that these issues are well addressed by dam-related social and environmental programs (see, for example, the set of "safeguard documents" on the World Bank's Nam Theun 2 website: www.worldbank.org/laont2).

Some opponents of big dams argue that IFI involvement in large hydropower projects is explained best not by altruism, but rather by the interest of the Banks in preserving their raison d'etre. The World Bank returned to lending for mega-projects after a decade-long attempt to reinvent itself as a standard bearer for corporate governance and economic reform. However, in an internal review completed in 2003, the World Bank determined that the empirical results of its private sector-led electricity reforms were poor (Dominguez, Manibog et al. 2003). In many cases, World Bank power sector privatization initiatives led to substantially increased tariffs—not to decreases promised by privatization promoters. Increased tariffs were accompanied by labor and public opposition to various features of the reform package, especially those seen to unfairly pass excessive risks to consumers and government (Williams and Dubash 2004).

In the wake of power sector crises in India, Indonesia, and the Philippines in the late 1990s, many governments declined Bank advice on power sector liberalization. At the same time, large economies like Brazil and India that previously were major World Bank clients have shifted to other sources of capital (Mallaby 2004). In this light, critics argue that the Bank is attempting to use large infrastructure projects in countries like Laos to prevent a decline in the Bank's financial base and to bolster justifications of its own existence (Imhof 2005).

Critics of IFI involvement in big dams point out that there are plenty of countries whose development have arguably been hindered, not helped, by exploitation of energy resources for export. The economy and government of Algeria, Angola, Ecuador, Indonesia, Iraq, and Nigeria, for example, are arguably worse off because of excessive focus on extraction of a single energy resource. Critics are concerned that corruption and lack of democracy in Mekong countries will be increased rather than decreased by revenue streams from large hydropower projects. Some analyses argue that even if one disregards their failure to fully account for social and environmental costs, key Mekong region hydropower projects are still uneconomic (IRN 1999, Ryder 2004).

One significant question is whether or not other financiers would have been found if the IFIs had never supported and promoted these projects. One need look only as far as Myanmar, Vietnam, or Laos to see substantial bilateral hydropower development assistance and/or private investment for projects that the World Bank and ADB refuse to touch (Akimoto 2004). Similarly, many of China's own dams are built without IFI assistance. These projects receive considerably less NGO attention, and proceed with substantially less environmental and social impact assessment—but likely higher environmental and social impact—than dams in which IFIs are involved.

China's large dam building industry is of particular concern in this regard. Evidence suggests that Chinese developers may be able and willing to take on projects that do not look financially attractive to other investors. The ADB-funded Norconsult document reports that Chinese investment costs for hydropower projects are "very low" compared with those in Thailand and Vietnam (Norconsult 2003). Chinese hydropower developers are already active with a number of smaller projects in Laos, Myanmar, and Cambodia. NGOs and IFIs alike have raised concerns that Chinese hydropower developers and financiers with fewer environmental and social safeguards than IFIs would step in to build these dams if the IFIs pulled out (Osborne 2004, Balls 2005).

Vietnam: Hydropower development in high gear

Hydropower development in Vietnam followed a path somewhat similar to that of Thailand, but with the former Soviet Union broadly playing the role that the US and World Bank played for Thailand. Contributions from Russia to the Vietnamese electricity monopoly Electricity of Vietnam (EVN) included technical capacity building, financial, and construction management aid for many of the country's major hydropower dams including the 1,920 MW Hoa Binh and the 720 MW Yali Falls hydropower dams. The former began operations in 1988 and the latter in March 2000. Russian aid and technical assistance continues to be important, particularly for environmentally controversial projects such as the 2,400 MW Son La[3] and the 586 MW Se San 3 hydropower dam which IFIS will not touch (Wyatt 2002).

By the late 1990s, Vietnam relied on domestic hydropower for about 70 percent of its electricity. *Doi moi tu duy* or "renovation thinking" economic reforms in 1987 initiated a transition to a "market-based socialist economy," and the dominance of the EVN in the power sector came under criticism by IFIS in the 1990s. One consequence was increased deployment of electricity generation from natural gas, which foreign investors found more profitable and less risky than hydropower because of lower capital costs, fast construction times, and (at the time) low natural gas prices (Wyatt 2005). By 2000 Vietnam's reliance on hydropower decreased to 49 percent of installed capacity, while natural gas rose to 20 percent (Norconsult 2002a). Nine new thermal and gas fired power plants currently under construction with a total capacity of 3,620 MW are expected to come online in 2006–8 (Socialist Republic of Vietnam 2004).

Unlike Thailand, however, Vietnam continues rapid development of large hydropower projects. Within three years, from 2002 to 2004, construction has started on seventeen medium and large hydropower plants with total capacity of 2,952 MW and about twenty small hydropower plants with total capacity of 500 MW. Like Thailand, Vietnam is looking to buy additional hydropower from Laos and China. Vietnam and Laos have signed an "accord on energy cooperation" in which Vietnam will purchase 2,000 MW of electricity from Laos. Vietnam is planning two 500 kv lines and two 220 kv lines to transmit this power. In December 2005, the Vietnamese government licensed a Vietnamese company to build a 250 MW hydropower project in Sekong Province in Laos. The project is expected to cost USUSD 271.3 million (Xinhua 2005).

In August 2004, Vietnam signed a contract to purchase 40 MW of electricity from China via a 110 kv line, and is currently engaged on a joint study to connect the transmission networks of the two countries. Another 2,000 MW import from China is planned by 2014 (Socialist Republic of Vietnam 2004).

The Vietnamese Ministry of Energy's year 2000 *Master Plan on Power Development of Vietnam* projects electricity sales to increase from 38.8 TWh in 2005 to 61.5 TWh in 2010 and 146 TWh by year 2020 (Socialist Republic of Vietnam 2000). Projections from EVN are even more aggressive: EVN forecasts demand to double from 39.95 TWh in 2004 to 81.9 TWh by the year 2010. By 2020, demand is projected to more than double again, reaching 180.3 TWh (Lam Du Son 2005). The differences are indicative of the uncertainty that underlies these types of predictions.

Laos: "Battery of Asia"

Though very little hydro capacity has been built so far, Laos has substantial hydropower potential. Laos also has inadequate enforcement of environmental laws, an undemocratic political system, and a population unlikely to mount effective protests against damaging hydropower projects (Anonymous 2005). National leaders in Laos—as well as some key leaders in Thailand and Vietnam), working together with project developers, IFIs, bilateral organizations, and private financiers, have placed high hopes on future fat revenue streams from hydropower export from Laos to wealthier Thailand and Vietnam.

Norconsult lists twenty-three possible hydropower projects in Laos totaling 7,383 MW. Thus far, Laos has a total installed electricity generating capacity of just 642 MW, of which 628 MW comes from hydropower projects.

The Government of Laos (GOL) has been selling hydropower to Thailand since 1971, following the completion of the 150 MW Nam Ngum Dam (Ryder 1994). In 1998 the 210 MW Theun Hinboun Dam began selling power to Thailand as well. Theun Hinboun has come under criticism from environmental advocacy groups who report a decline of 30 to 90 percent in the quantity of fish caught downstream of the dam, substantial loss of agricultural land both above and below the dam, and damage to fragile ecosystems (Shoemaker 1998).

"Battery of Asia" is the new moniker for Laos employed by Thailand's former Prime Minister Thaksin Shinawatra referring to future plans to develop hydropower in Laos for export (Associated Press 2005, Petty 2005). Laos is featured strongly in Thai Ministry of Energy plans which include an additional four planned hydropower dams and a lignite project totaling 3,300 MW (see figure 5.2 below, available from the Government of Laos).

One of the most controversial mega-projects in the Mekong region in recent times is the Nam Theun 2 (NT2) Dam currently under construction. In March 2005, the World Bank decided to provide grants and a partial loan guarantee up to USD 270 million for NT2. In November 2003, EGAT

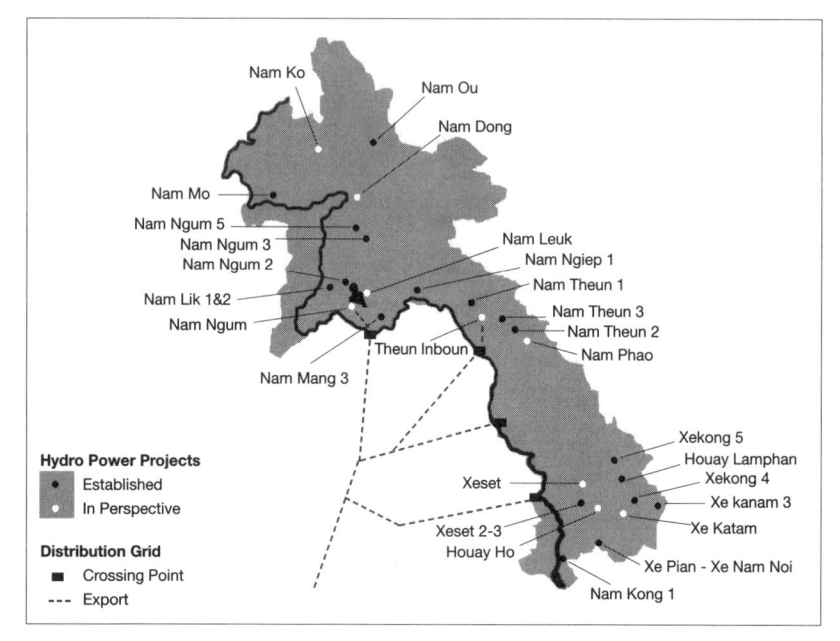

Figure 5.2 Planned and existing hydropower projects in Laos

[Map of Laos showing hydropower project locations: Nam Ko, Nam Ou, Nam Dong, Nam Mo, Nam Ngum 5, Nam Ngum 3, Nam Ngum 2, Nam Leuk, Nam Ngiep 1, Nam Theun 1, Nam Lik 1&2, Nam Ngum, Nam Theun 3, Nam Theun 2, Theun Inboun, Nam Phao, Nam Mang 3, Xekong 5, Houay Lamphan, Xeset, Xekong 4, Xe kanam 3, Xeset 2-3, Xe Katam, Houay Ho, Xe Pian - Xe Nam Noi, Nam Kong 1. Legend: Hydro Power Projects (Established, In Perspective), Distribution Grid, Crossing Point, Export]

SOURCE: Lao PDR Ministry of Industry & Handicraft, Lao National Committee for Energy www.poweringprogress.org/Lao-energy/projects/indexprojet.htm

signed a contract to buy 995 MW of electricity, guaranteeing a market for most of the electricity from the planned 1,060 MW project (IRN 1994a).

NT2 will create a 450 km² reservoir that will flood the Nakai plateau, an area of rich biological diversity. The project requires displacement of some 6,200 villagers, most of them members of ethnic minority groups, and affects some 40,000 to 170,000 villagers living downstream who rely on the rivers for fish, agriculture, water supply and many other aspects of their livelihoods (Osborne 2004, 36; Balls 2005; Perrin 2005).

The project is built by a consortium of investors led by Electricite de France (with a 35 percent share). Electricity Generating Company of Thailand (EGCO) is a subsidiary of EGAT, and holds 25 percent of the shares of the project. In addition, the Thailand-based Ital-Thai Development Company holds 15 percent and the Lao government holds 25 percent.

EGCO's part ownership in NT2 raises the specter of significant conflicts of interest. EGAT has a 25 percent stake in EGCO.[4] But EGAT also is the main customer for NT2 power. As such, EGAT may have faced a perverse incentive to engage in lackluster negotiations in their power purchase agreement (PPA) for NT2 power. At the time the contract was signed, the price that EGAT agreed to pay for NT2 electricity—USD 0.047/kwh (1.974 baht/

kWh)—was 16 percent higher than the price that EGAT agreed to pay for power from gas-fired combined cycle plants—USD 0.04/kWh (Baht1.70/kWh) (Permpongsacharoen 2005).[5]

This is not the first instance that potential conflict of interest involving EGCO and EGAT has been flagged. In year 2001, an anonymous source within EGAT leaked data that EGAT paid about 20 percent more for power from EGCO's natural gas power plants compared to power from other natural-gas fired private power producers (Anonymous source within EGAT undated circa 2001). EGCO's director was a former EGAT deputy director (Greacen and Greacen 2004).

Proponents claim that the NT2 project will provide revenues of up to USD 150 million per year to the GOL, which they claim is essential for helping the country to eradicate poverty and protect the environment. According to World Bank advisors, "The NT2 proposals, taken as a whole, represent the most promising development package before Laos at this stage in its evolution for the net environmental, economic and social benefits substantially outweigh the downside costs" (*Business Day* 2003).

Opponents of the project, on the other hand, point out that the "up to USD 150 million" statement is disingenuous. The International Rivers Network notes that "between 2009, when project revenues come online, and 2020, net revenues for the GOL will total only USD 20 to 29 million per year, or approximately three percent of total projected government revenue." Throughout the twenty-five-year concession period ending in 2034, revenues are expected to amount to around five percent of projected GOL revenues. According to environmentalists, past experience shows that benefits will not "trickle down" to affected people, that the project's studies on environmental and social impact, hydrology, resettlement plans, and project economics are seriously flawed, and that the project violates World Bank policies; they argue that the project developers should have been left to sink or swim without World Bank assistance (Ryder 2004, Environmental Defense 2005). A critical analysis of the project economic appraisal by Thai economists and this author argued that the World Bank project appraisal used unjustified fine-print assumptions to make NT2 appear to be economically preferable to natural gas fired generation (Greacen and Sukkamnoed 2005).

Myanmar: Hydropower for export to Thailand, China and India

International Water Power & Dam Construction featured Myanmar as "Southeast Asia's last great hydropower frontier" (Sharp 2001). The Burmese Ministry of Electric Power has identified 268 sites with a total capacity of 39,720 MW, and Norconsult identifies 35 candidate hydro projects totaling 23,700 MW (Norconsult 2002a). The importance of hydropower to the Burmese military junta is underscored by the creation, in January 2002, of a high-level Department of Hydroelectric Power (DHP) reporting directly to the Deputy Minister in the Ministry of Energy (Myanmar Ministry of Electric Power 2004). The DHP reportedly employs a staff of three thousand including over four hundred engineers (*Hydropower & Dams* 2005).

At least 60 percent of hydropower potential is in the eastern and central regions, mostly in Karen and Shan states (*Hydropower & Dams* 2005), and construction of reservoirs would flood Karen, Shan, and Karenni communities that the Burmese army is currently fighting (Earthrights International 2005). Construction of dams has reportedly used forced labor, relocations at gunpoint, and the use of landmines to prevent displaced populations from returning (Akimoto 2004). Planned dam sites are all located in non-ceasefire ethnic areas where war continues, which is contributing to deteriorating livelihoods, worsening food security, people becoming internally displaced and thousands of political refugees fleeing to Thailand. Human rights activists argue that the proposed dams would exacerbate this already desperate situation through increased militarization by the SPDC and through forced relocation, land confiscation, forced labor, and environmental injustices (Noam 2006).

As in the case of Laos, very little hydropower has actually been developed in Myanmar: total hydropower capacity is 745 MW (*Hydropower & Dams* 2005), much of which is built in ethnic minority areas such as the Baluchaung No. 2/Lawpita 168 MW dam in Karenni State, sending generated electricity to Yangon and Mandalay. As of 2002, Myanmar's total installed capacity was 1,240 MW (Norconsult 2002a) with the non-hydro capacity being mostly natural gas turbines.

Most of the country's planned hydropower capacity, including the 7,000 MW Ta Sarng Dam, the 1,200 MW Hat Gyi (or Hut Gyi) Dams, the 500 MW Lower Salween dam (Dag Win), the 4,000 MW Upper Salween (Wei Gyi) dam, and the 600 MW Tennasserim Dam are expected to be built to export power to Thailand (*Bangkok Post* 2005, *Hydropower & Dams* 2005).

In July 1997, Thailand and Myanmar signed a Memorandum of Understanding (MOU) on cooperation to develop hydropower and natural gas power plants in Myanmar for export to Thailand. The MOU specified power export of up to 1,500 MW by 2010 (Norconsult 2002a). In March 2005, the Burmese DHP of the Myanmar Electric Power Enterprise (MEPE) and the Thai MDX Group of companies signed an agreement for the joint-development of a 7,110 MW dam at the Ta Sarng site in Shan State; another MOU between MDX and the Burmese regime was secured in April 2006. Another MOU was signed in December 2005 between EGAT and the MEPE. The latest serious development for dam construction on the Salween River to secure investment occurred in June 2006 when EGAT

Figure 5.3 Hydropower projects planned or under implementation in the Salween River basin

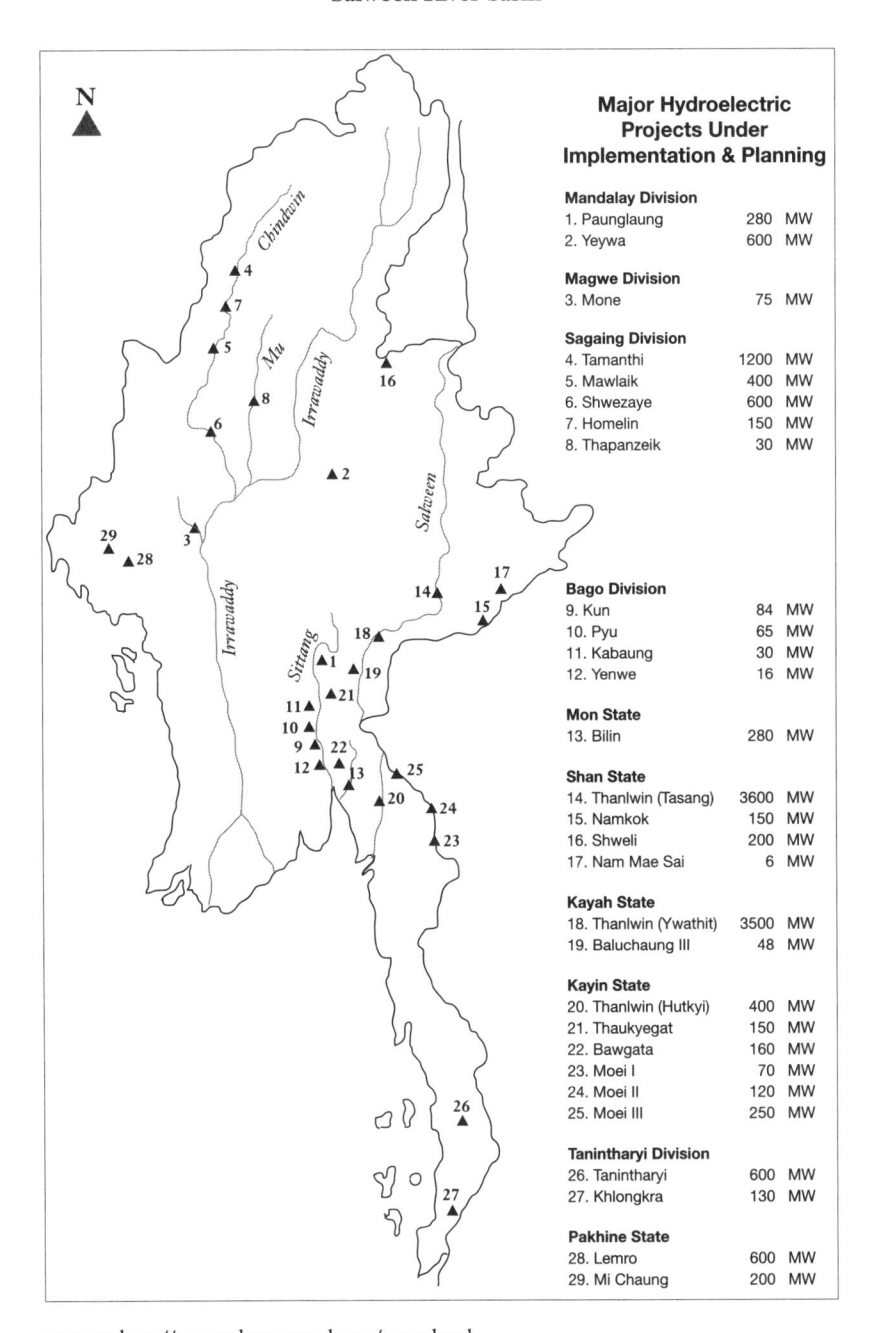

Major Hydroelectric Projects Under Implementation & Planning

Mandalay Division
1. Paunglaung	280	MW
2. Yeywa	600	MW

Magwe Division
3. Mone	75	MW

Sagaing Division
4. Tamanthi	1200	MW
5. Mawlaik	400	MW
6. Shwezaye	600	MW
7. Homelin	150	MW
8. Thapanzeik	30	MW

Bago Division
9. Kun	84	MW
10. Pyu	65	MW
11. Kabaung	30	MW
12. Yenwe	16	MW

Mon State
13. Bilin	280	MW

Shan State
14. Thanlwin (Tasang)	3600	MW
15. Namkok	150	MW
16. Shweli	200	MW
17. Nam Mae Sai	6	MW

Kayah State
18. Thanlwin (Ywathit)	3500	MW
19. Baluchaung III	48	MW

Kayin State
20. Thanlwin (Hutkyi)	400	MW
21. Thaukyegat	150	MW
22. Bawgata	160	MW
23. Moei I	70	MW
24. Moei II	120	MW
25. Moei III	250	MW

Tanintharyi Division
26. Tanintharyi	600	MW
27. Khlongkra	130	MW

Pakhine State
28. Lemro	600	MW
29. Mi Chaung	200	MW

SOURCE: http://www.salweenwatch.org/maps.html

and the Chinese Sino Hydro Corporation signed a MOU to jointly develop five large hydroelectric dams in Myanmar with an estimated total output of 12,700 megawatts, starting with the Hat Gyi Dam (Noam 2006). This MOU followed on the heels of a Thai Ministry of Energy Plan, released in a November 2005 seminar chaired by the former Thai prime minister, that included five large Burmese hydropower projects by the year 2020 (Thai Ministry of Energy 2005). Further export possibilities are planned with China and India (*Hydropower & Dams* 2005).

Currently, hydropower in Myanmar is largely financed by Chinese and Japanese bilateral loans, as well as private investors from China, Thailand, and Japan (Akimoto 2004). Chinese firms have a long history of involvement in hydropower in the country and Chinese finance and construction of dams has a history. Myanmar has about 30 hydro power projects either operating or being built that involves China in some capacity. For example, the MEPE and the Yunnan Machinery & Equipment Import & Export Co. Ltd. (YMEC) in China signed a MOU to implement the Upper Paunglaung Hydro-electric Power Project located east of Pyinmana, the new government capital of Myanmar. According to the MOU, Myanmar will buy the necessary machinery and equipment for the project worth USD 800 million from YMEC. Also, the military junta signed agreements recently to purchase equipment from a consortium of state-owned Chinese companies to build the Ye Ywa hydropower plant. The MEPE also agreed to purchase equipment from China's CITIC Technology Company Ltd. and Sino Hydro Corporation worth USD 125 million.

China (Yunnan): Targeting the Upper Mekong and the Salween rivers

Discussed in depth in a separate chapter (Dore & Yu) in this volume, hydropower development in Yunnan is driven primarily by high and increasing domestic demand for electricity, and secondarily by perceived opportunities to sell electricity to Thailand and Vietnam. Much of Yunnan's electricity production is sent through China's southern power grid to fuel industrial development in Guangdong Province, where GDP has been growing at 13 to 15 percent per year. Guangdong's economic growth has outstripped available electricity, and unmet demand in 2005 was estimated at 4,500 MW (Li 2005).

Yunnan is home to the upper portion of the Mekong and Salween Rivers; and while considerable hydropower has already been developed, an even greater potential is claimed as undeveloped. China began building a series of large dams on the upstream of the Mekong River starting in the early nineties. The 1,500 MW Manwan Dam was completed in 1996. Limited information was available to the general public about the project,

ELECTRICITY SECTOR PLANNING AND HYDROPOWER

Figure 5.4 Chinese hydropower projects (planned and existing) in the Lancang-Mekong

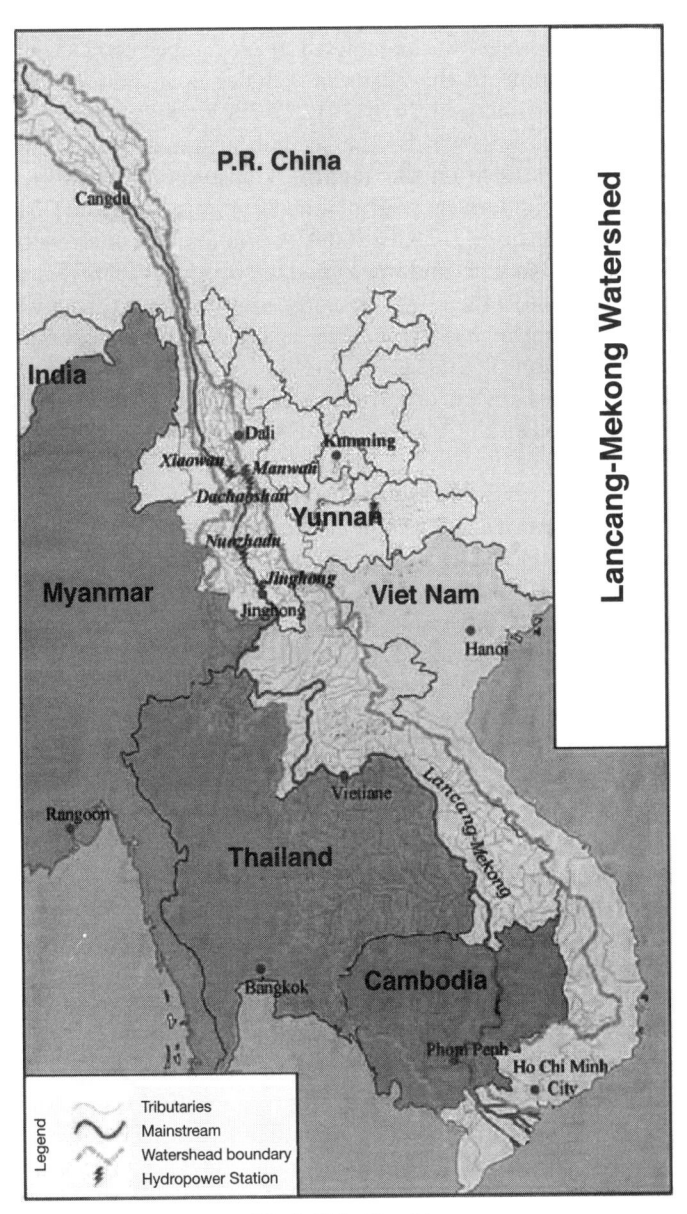

SOURCE: Image courtesy of Kevin Yuk-shing Li

109

and project developers sought no international finance. By the time news of Manwan was generally known, the dam was nearing completion and work was being initiated on a second dam, at Dachaoshan. The 1,350 MW Dachaoshan project was completed in November 2003 (Samabuddhi 2004). Construction on the Xiaowan was begun in January 2003 with expected commissioning in 2010–2012. With a projected power output of 4,200 MW, Xiaowan will be the second largest dam in China, after the Three Gorges Dam on the Yangtze. Construction on the 1,500 MW Jinghong is also underway, with planned commissioning in 2012–2013 (Norconsult 2002a, page 2–24, Li 2004). A MOU for sales of electricity from the Jinghong dam to Thailand was signed in November 2000 (Samabuddhi 2004). A fifth project, the Nouzhadu, has an even larger capacity at 5,500 MW, and according to Norconsult has a planned commissioning date of 2013–2016 (Norconsult 2002a).

In addition to dams on the Mekong, a 23.3 GW thirteen-dam cascade has been proposed on the upstream Chinese portion of the Salween River, an area that was also declared in 2003 to be a UNESCO World Heritage site. In March 2004, Chinese Prime Minister Wen Jiabao surprised the world by rejecting a National Development and Reform Commission (NDRC) proposal for the cascade, citing environmental and social concerns (Sharp 2004). However, development of the Salween's hydropower potential remains a priority of Huandian Corporation, one of China's "big five" power generating companies.

Cambodia: Facing hurdles to hydropower development

Like Myanmar and Laos, Cambodia has very little installed electrical generation capacity. Electricité du Cambodge operates about 130 MW of total installed capacity, the vast majority of which is expensive diesel generation (Norconsult 2002b). Though much of Cambodia's topography is flat with little hydropower potential, a recent review concluded that Cambodia had the technical potential for sixty-five hydropower projects, mostly located in the mountainous western part of the country, with a combined installed capacity of 5,300 to 8,135 MW and total energy generation as high as 41,400 Gwh/year (CPEC & ACT 1995). The Norconsult study funded by ADB identified 16 candidate hydroelectric sites totaling 2,074 MW (Norconsult 2002b, A2-15, table A2-3). Compared to sites in Lao, Myanmar, and Yunnan, however, little Cambodian potential is economically competitive (Norconsult 2002a). Lack of personnel and financial resources limit Cambodia's ability to build hydropower. In the short or medium term, most hydropower development will likely be fairly small, used to supply domestic consumption.

Regional summary

The previous sections can be summarized as follows:
1) Thailand faces difficulties in developing new hydropower projects, because most sites are already exploited and new dam projects are highly controversial.
2) Hydropower construction in Vietnam is significant and growing, mostly to meet domestic demand.
3) Dam construction is intense in the upper reaches of the Mekong in China's Yunnan Province, both for providing electricity to domestic loads largely in southeastern China), and for export to Thailand and Vietnam.
4) Laos and Myanmar, together with hydropower project developers and investors, are moving towards extensive development of hydropower inside their borders, primarily for export to Thailand, and secondarily to Vietnam.

What dam proponents say

Proponents of dams cite a number of reasons why hydropower development makes sense in the Mekong (Nam Theun 2 Power Co. Ltd. 2004, Regional Power Trade Coordination Committee 2004, Chantanakome 2005):

- There is a lot of hydropower potential in the region
- Demand growth is high and many new power plants need to be built to keep up
- Hydropower is inexpensive
- Dams provide fuel diversity
- Hydropower is reliable power
- Hydropower helps reduce greenhouse gas emissions
- The environmental and social downsides of hydropower can be mitigated without destroying the economics of the projects.

These is little dispute about the first claim, as discussed in the previous section. The other claims, however, have been contested. The remainder of this paper addresses the claims regarding projections of demand growth and the costs of hydropower in the Mekong region context. Based on historical records and on an analysis of the process of constructing demand projections in Thailand, it is likely that actual demand will be considerably less than projected demand. Regarding the claims that hydropower is low cost, it is noteworthy that power development plans in Thailand consider hydropower as foregone conclusions, not options—that is, hydropower comes into the plans without having to compete on a cost basis with other approaches. Furthermore, hydropower projects under consideration are all a great distance from major load centers. Even the closest of these projects, the NT2 Dam in Laos near the Thai border, requires 500 km of expensive transmission lines. While some hydropower projects may be able to generate electricity at competitive costs, this electricity is worth little if it cannot reach markets. A World Bank-commissioned study concludes that even in the NT2 case other options such as energy conservation are considerably less expensive (du Pont 2005a). Under these circumstances it is not surprising that there is a significant movement to subsidize transmission costs by constructing a rate-payer-funded regional grid that would transfer electricity from dams to distant loads.

The remaining claims are discussed in a variety of other publications (McCulley 1996, Sant, Dixit et al. 1998, Hildyard 2000, World Commission on Dams 2000b, Environmental Defense 2003, Environmental Defense, Friends of the Earth et al. 2003, WWF 2004) and, while deserving special attention in the Mekong context, are beyond the scope of this paper.

Load forecasting in Thailand

As discussed in the country-by-country review, much of the hydropower development in the region is justified by expectations of high demand growth in Thailand, Vietnam, and Yunnan. How is demand for electricity projected? Who decides how much power will be needed and what types of power sources will be exploited to meet demand? How does hydropower fit in?

When the Bhumipol Dam was built in Thailand in the late 1950s, a small handful of Thai power sector planners, having little hard data to work with, used guesswork and a "build it and they will come" philosophy to justify new generation capacity additions. Kasame Chatikavanij, the "father of EGAT" wrote in his autobiography about the process he and a few colleagues used in defending parliamentary approval of the World Bank loan for the Bhumipol Dam: "We looked for ways and means to solve the puzzle and in the end decided to use the 'supposition' method. We supposed for everything—what if this house had this appliance and that house another. We included every possible appliance into our calculations until we felt we were safe" (Chatikavanij 1994, 34).

The process is notable in several respects: first, the conception for the project paved the way and, indeed, guided the "quantitative" assessment of the need for it. Second, it was fundamentally based on speculation about what electrical loads people might use in the future.

More recent power sector planning by the Thai government and by EGAT is considerably more sophisticated than this early "stab in the dark" approach, but the fundamental uncertainty about future electricity demands that characterized Chatikavanij's guesswork remains an inescapable part of Thailand's power development planning process. Specifically development planning is based on power demand projections that, in turn, are based on projections of future economic growth. In the long term, (greater than 5 years) these projections can only be regarded as speculative. Problems with the speculative basis for projections are compounded by potential conflict of interest: key decision-makers in developing load forecasts benefit from high forecasts. The devil is in the details:

Since 1993, the process used in Thailand's generation planning is as follows:

1. The Thai Load Forecast Subcommittee (TLFS) develops projections of future electricity demand. The TLFS reports to the Committee for the Administration of Energy Policy chaired by the Minister of Energy. The TLFS includes representatives from the three Thai monopoly utilities (EGAT, MEA, PEA), the Energy Policy and Planning Office (EPPO), the Department of Alternative Energy Development and Efficiency (DEDE), the NESDB, the National Statistics Office (NSO), the Federation of Thai Industries, the Thailand Chamber of Commerce, the Association of Private Power Producers (APPP) and consultants/academics appointed by the Minister of Energy (Thai Load Forecast Subcommittee 2004).
2. EGAT uses the TLFS demand forecast to determine, in its opinion, the most cost-effective power plants to add to meet the expected demand plus a safety margin.

The TLFS uses a variety of methodologies depending on its distribution utility, the Metropolitan Electricity Authority (MEA) (in the Bangkok metropolitan area) and the Provincial Electricity Authority (PEA) (in the rest of the country); on customer class residential, commercial, industrial, etc.); and on the forecast horizon (long-term or short-term).

Future electricity use of residential customers is estimated based on surveys conducted in 1998 on appliance use in households of different income levels (Vernstrom 2004, du Pont 2005b). The predictions adjust for expected growth in number of households, appliance saturation, and expected appliance energy efficiency improvements. Similarly, predictions of electricity consumption in office buildings in Bangkok are based on year 1998 surveys on energy use per square meter of several varieties of office buildings, adjusted to account for new building construction or demolition and changing occupancy rates. In the short term, utilities also use information from the Board of Investment (BOI) and applications for new service hookups from large industrial customers.

Since Bangkok office buildings and residences comprise only 30 percent and 20 percent of Thailand's electricity consumption respectively (du Pont 2005b), these bottom-up models account for about half of electricity demand projections. The remaining methods are "top down" in the sense that they are derived from macroeconomic trends. One top-down method employed by the TLFS focuses on energy intensity and is essentially a spreadsheet that lists GDP data disaggregated by region and business sector. Total electricity consumption is estimated based on historic consumption per unit of gross regional product (GRP), combined with forecasted growth in each sector. This approach is used for long-term modeling for business and industrial loads for both utilities. Econometric regression modeling, which is even further removed from bottom-up data, is used for remaining types of customers (small businesses, water pumping, etc.)

Fundamentally, economic forecasts drive the Thai load forecast, especially long-term forecasts (Vernstrom 2004). In the short term (less than five years) these economic forecasts are issued by the Government of Thailand's National Economic and Social Development Board (NESDB).

TLFS long-term electricity demand forecasts are based on long-term economic forecasts developed by a non-profit policy research institute, the Thailand Development and Research Institute (TDRI), and funded by the three Thai electric utilities EGAT, MEA and PEA (TDRI 2005). Although the methodology employed by TDRI is similar to that used by the NESDB for short-term forecasts, because of the inherent uncertainty of predicting technical, political and social determinants of economic growth in the long-term (more than five years), these forecasts can only be regarded as speculative. This last point is of crucial importance since most power projects, and especially hydropower projects, have lead times longer than five years.

The TLFS assembles short-term and long-term forecasts for different customer types and sectors and issues its official electricity load forecast. In Europe and North America, forecasts are contested in public rate cases, or in market price referent proceedings. There are lots of interveners that have their own points of view, and the final result is determined through an open, transparent and participatory process. Not so in Thailand. There is no room for interveners in the TLFSs official forecast—the forecast is concluded behind closed doors and presented as a done deal. The closed nature of the proceedings means that there are insufficient checks and balances in this speculative and interest-ridden process.

Thai utilities play a lead role in the TLFS by providing most of the key data used in the forecasts. They are clearly not neutral actors: they exist in an industry structure that perversely actually rewards overestimates. As is common with regulated monopolies worldwide, the Thai electricity tariffs are set according to a "cost plus" structure with a guarantee of sufficient utility revenues to expand. The more those utilities spend to expand the system, the more they are allowed to collect.[6] These arrangements provide incentives for continual system expansion—and may lead to a proclivity to overstate demand. If demand for electricity is less than expected, Thai utilities are protected by mechanisms that allow the cost burden of over-investment to be passed through to consumers in the form of higher tariffs.

Not all demand overestimation is attributable to lopsided incentives of TLFS members, however. A significant source of load forecast overestimation in the short term arises from proposed industrial loads that apply for new hookups, but later are not built or are delayed (*Bangkok Post* 2002).

To summarize, in the case of Thailand most electricity demand forecasting is based on top-down models, the accuracy of which depends to a large extent on the accuracy of economic forecasts. In the long term, these economic forecasts are very uncertain. A minority of the forecast (residential and commercial floor-space) is based on outdated surveys and demographic/business expansion forecasts, or on applications for service hookups. All of the data is brought together to create an overall load forecast in a closed, non-transparent process with leadership and key data provided by monopoly utilities. These utilities tend to benefit from high electricity consumption projections, while at the same time being buffered from the negative consequences of overestimating demand.

One would expect from this arrangement that demand forecasts in Thailand would tend to overestimate demand. The evidence shows that this has indeed been the case.

Track record of load forecast overestimation in Thailand

Figure 5.5 below shows successive base-case forecasts over the past thirteen years in which the TLFS has issued demand forecasts. The thick red line in the graph below the other lines is the actual demand. Demand forecasts for Thailand have tended to overestimate actual demand—sometimes by as much as 48 percent. Out of nine "base case" forecasts, all nine have substantially overestimating current demand.

There are two interpretations of the past record. Defenders of the TLFS forecast argue that the discrepancy between forecasts and actual demand can be largely explained by the Asian financial crisis in 1997–98 and the repeated but excusable failure of the TLFS to predict the severity of the downturn (Vernstrom 2005, 19). Those who challenge the forecasts claim that the overall record highlights the long-term bias of influential members of the TLFS (Permpongsacharoen 2005). The "Asian financial crisis excuse" does not work for the most recent demand forecasts. The current January 2004 forecast already overestimated 2006 peak demand[7] by 1,674 MW, or about 1.7 times the planned import from the Nam Theun 2 Dam. A new April 2006 forecast has been issued but is not yet official. The forecast was issued just two weeks before the actual 2006 peak load occurred. Remarkably, this forecast overestimates actual 2006 peak demand by 899

Figure 5.5 Comparison of base case Thai load forecasts to actual demand from 1992 to present. MER = "Medium economic recovery"; MEG = "Medium economic growth."

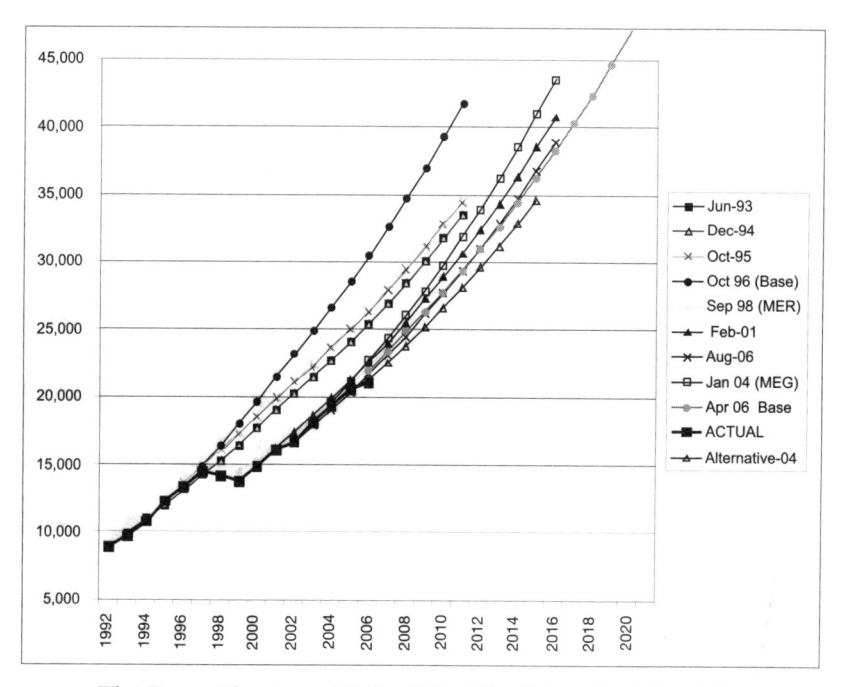

SOURCE: Thai Energy Planning and Policy Office. The "Alternative-04" load forecast was developed by citizen's groups concerned about the systematic bias in official TLFs forecasts.

MW. The 2006 load forecast is based on a projection of average economic growth of 5.38 percent per year for the next fifteen years. By comparison, the actual average annual GDP growth rates over the past ten and fifteen years were only 2.8 percent and 4.7 percent respectively (Bank of Thailand 2006), and the size of the economy was much smaller then.

While Thailand's economy has been recovering—economic growth in 2005 was 4.5 percent (Bank of Thailand 2006)—it is unclear that this recovery can be sustained. The World Bank, among others, has noted that Thailand's recent economic expansion has been driven mostly by private consumption (fueled in part by double-digit growth in personal credit), and that private investment's contribution to growth has been less than in previous economic recoveries and lower than in many other countries in the region (Malaysia, Indonesia, Korea, and Singapore). The World Bank concludes that Thailand will have to become more productive and competitive in order to convert the current recovery into sustained high economic growth (World Bank 2003).

Load forecasting in Vietnam appears to be broadly similar to that in Thailand, with even less reliance on detailed household and commercial survey data, and more reliance on economic growth projections (Socialist Republic of Vietnam 2000). The authors have no specific data on how load forecasts are constructed in China, but it would be surprising if they were not also fundamentally based on economic growth assumptions.

The considerable uncertainties of these electrical demand forecasts are forgotten by most observers. The TLFS (or its Chinese or Vietnamese counterpart) issues a precise sounding prediction with five significant figures such as "40,978 MW demand by year 2015," and this number, stripped of its uncertainties and caveats, forms the basis of big plans.

Thailand's Power Development Plan (PDP)

The biggest of these plans in Thailand is EGAT's Power Development Plan (PDP). The PDP is a fifteen-year investment plan that specifies which power plants are to be added at what time. A new official PDP is issued about once every two years by EGAT. EGAT's PDP is reviewed by the Ministry of Energy and approved by the National Energy Policy Council, and then by the Council of Ministers. In practice the Ministry of Energy seldom questions the fundamental underpinnings of the PDP. After the approval of its PDP, EGAT then undertakes to develop and expand the power system according to the plan.

The methodology is as follows: in a computer modeling program called STRATEGIST, power plants are added to the system in a way that seeks to optimize lowest overall costs including investment costs, fuel, operation and maintenance (O&M) costs, and financing subject to two criteria: the planned reserve margin is at least 15 percent, and the loss of load probability (LOLP) is less than one hour per year. The reserve margin indicates the amount of generating capacity available in excess of the annual peak demand which occurs once a year in early afternoon sometime during the hot months of March, April or May. When EGAT defines its reserve margin, it counts only plants that it considers "dependable." The amount considered "non-dependable" includes certain percentage of hydroelectric projects since the availability of hydropower during the dry season differs from year to year.[8] The LOLP addresses the fact that there are regional differences in the availability of transmission and generation and everywhere in the country should have sufficient generation and transmission to have power 99.99 percent of the time.

Journalists and consumer groups have raised concerns that EGAT has virtually no oversight in developing the PDP (Crispin 2001). EGAT decides what power plants to install and, because of the cost-plus tariff structure, all costs are borne by consumers. If EGAT is wrong and costs are underestimated they are still allowed to recoup most, if not all, costs through tariffs. In practice, planned costs and actual costs can differ significantly, as in the Pak Mun dam example discussed above.

From a societal perspective, another shortcoming is that the PDP is determined by considering commercial costs from EGAT's perspective, and not economic costs from society's perspective. Thus, although an energy solution could be beneficial for Thai society, it will not be chosen if it costs EGAT more money. Energy efficiency provides an excellent example: many studies have shown thousands of MW potential to save electricity (du Pont 2005a). Implementing these savings would cost a small fraction of the cost of new power plants. But EGAT has little incentive to invest in energy efficiency because its revenues are based on the amount of electricity sold, and energy efficiency leads to lower electricity sales. In contrast, worldwide many utilities[9] have made decisions on the basis of economic costs using a decision framework known as Integrated Resource Planning (IRP) (Swisher and Jannuzzi 1997). IRP requires utilities to consider all options, including energy conservation, and choose the package that has least overall economic costs.

Energy activists in Thailand also criticize the PDP for considering only capital-intensive options such as coal, gas, oil and big hydropower plants for future energy generation. Demand side management (DSM)—systematically improving efficiency of electricity use or shifting load to off-peak periods—renewable energy, and cogeneration, are not considered as options that STRATEGIST can pick, even if they are less expensive than conventional options. In Thailand, EGAT's own DSM program with a variety of programs launched in the mid-1990s) has provided over 735 MW of demand reduction[10] by year 2001 at a cost of US 0.0125 or 0.5 baht per kwh (Phumaraphand 2001). This is about one-third the economic cost of electricity generation from natural gas combined cycle gas turbines which are currently the "low cost" generation source from EGAT's planning perspective. A report commissioned by the World Bank estimates that 1,225 MW of DSM in Thailand is "economic and achievable" by 2015 that is not included in the 2003 PDP (du Pont 2005a).

Taken together, the load forecast, the PDP, and the cost-plus structure form a vicious circle: demand forecasting that tends to overestimate actual demand, power development planning that favors capital-intensive supply-side solutions, and tariffs that pass costs on to consumers. In 2003, then-Prime Minister Thaksin Shinawatra estimated that accumulated unnecessary investment in the power sector totaled 400 billion baht or USD 10 billion (*The Nation* 2003).

How do hydropower imports end up in planning?

The demand forecast and planning methodology discussed above describes the process by which "least cost" power plants like combined cycle gas turbines (CCGT) are added to the power mix. But, while the discussion provides useful context for hydropower power additions, it does not fully explain them. What does this mean? EGAT's 2006 PDP makes an assumption that power imports will account for 20 percent of all new capacity (EGAT 2006). In EGAT-STRATEGIST modeling, specific projects such as Nam Theun 2 are entered into the PDP assumption matrix as foregone conclusions, not just as candidate options (Vernstrom 2005, 27, EGAT 2006).

Convincing EGAT to sign power purchase agreements from these projects in the past may have involved government pressure as part of regional economic cooperation initiatives. But increasingly, EGAT's business interests are aligned in ways that encourage imports from neighbors. In the case of the EGAT subsidiary EGCO's involvement in NT2 (discussed earlier in this chapter), EGAT may have had incentives to sign because it is part project owner. With the formation of EGAT International Co., a wholly-owned private subsidiary of EGAT, the potential for this type of conflict of interest may increase. EGAT International Co. will invest in a 23-kilometer transmission line from Lao and Udon Thani in Thailand, another hydropower project in Lao, and two power plants in Myanmar—with all electricity sales to EGAT (Dow Jones Newswires 2006).

Wires on the horizon

Transmission costs are very large for hydropower projects distant from large load centers. For example, the Nam Theun 2 Dam in Laos, although located very close to the Thai border, still requires over 500 km of new 500 kv line to reach the closest tie-in to Thailand's transmission grid located near Nakon Sawan. At a cost of USD 300,000[11] to 800,000 per km[12], the transmission cost for bringing NT2 power from the Thai border to the Thai grid exceeds USD 150 million. In the case of NT2, EGAT will pass these costs directly on to consumers.

Considering the competitiveness of alternatives such as natural gas power plants, or even better, combined heat and power plants which can generally be sited much closer to existing transmission networks and load centers, it is likely that many hydropower projects are financially unfeasible unless hydropower developers avoid paying the bulk of transmission costs.

Plans for a regional transmission grid offer just this opportunity: a massive transmission network funded by ratepayers, reaching near to hydropower sites, but with accounting separated from the financial calculations of hydropower projects. In July 2005, leaders from Mekong countries gathered at the Second Greater Mekong Subregion (GMS) Summit in Kunming, China to sign a MOU on the Implementation of Stage 1 of the Regional Power Trade Operating Agreement (RPTOA). Stage 1 is the first of four stages that promoters envision leading to a region-wide transmission network spanning Thailand, Lao, Myanmar, Yunnan, Cambodia, and Laos. In addition to the GMS plans, a separate ASEAN grid, championed by EGAT, includes all of the countries in the GMS plan plus Malaysia, Indonesia, Brunei, and the Philippines.

In both the GMS and ASEAN plans, the claimed benefit of the scheme is that sharing electricity will lower costs: while Thailand's peak electricity demand occurs during the middle of a hot day in April, Thailand's neighbors' greatest power needs might occur at other times and all will in theory be better off by sharing with others when they need it.

But GMS studies concede that interconnection will enable a regional coincident peak load reduction of only 2.5 percent (Norconsult 2003). An independent transmission expert who investigated the ADB study found that the hope that the scheme will pay off is actually based on the assumption that lots of "cheap" hydropower will be built in Laos, Myanmar, and Yunnan, and that this hydropower will displace electricity generation from gas and coal (Garret 2005). But whether the hydropower is actually "cheap" is anybody's guess, given that no one knows what these projects will really cost. The RPTOA's final report confesses that "there is not enough base information to estimate costs for developing hydropower plants;" yet a companion document, the Indicative Master Plan on Power Interconnection in GMS Countries, somehow derives a set of favorable hydropower cost assumptions to conclude that the scheme will save USD 914 million (baht 36.6 billion) (Norconsult 2002a).

As of August 2004, only five of eight Lao hydropower projects even had feasibility studies. Without feasibility studies for all the main proposed projects, the economic benefit of the projects, and thus the entire interconnection plan, is uncertain. Indeed, even having feasibility studies offers no guarantees of economic benefits: a World Commission on Dams study found that the average cost overrun for 248 large dam projects was 54 percent (World Commission on Dams 2000b).

The uncertainty in estimating hydropower project costs is just the tip of the iceberg. Equally important, the expert said, is a profound underestimation of the costs, time, and leadership required to harmonize technical planning and operating standards across the region, as is required to operate an interconnected power grid that must respond without fail to any disturbances, within minutes, in a coordinated fashion, twenty-four hours a day, seven days a week (Garret 2005). Though the technical challenges are formidable, the political ones are even tougher. It takes good neighbors to share a transmission link. The Canadian economy, for example, lost USD 400 million in August 2003, when a US utility caused a massive cascading blackout throughout the east coast of North America that literally pulled the plug on Ontario's industries. This example indicates how tying transmission systems of different countries together can introduce new power stability risks.

The proponents of the grid such as the ADB and dam developers are publicly confident that it will "yield benefits" (Norconsult 2003). But promoters are not the ones who will be left footing the bill. The additional USD 1.2 billion in costs for the transmission scheme, embedded in electricity tariffs, go directly to the electricity consumers. The benefits go to the private sector electricity producers. If there is sufficient competition to force producers to forego some of their profits, then the resulting lower costs trickle down to consumers. But experience in California showed all too clearly that the two relatively unique traits of electricity—its non-storability and the "obligation to serve" of utilities effectively eliminating price elasticity for short-term price movements—that allows even small suppliers to gouge customers when supplies are tight (Duane 2002).

If governments are not willing to agree to the regional grid plans, then many hydropower projects are likely not to be cost-competitive. Projects will have to proceed as bilateral "international cooperation" initiatives rather than as commercially viable business propositions. Considering the low economic projected returns, it is perplexing that countries would sign on to a large risky project such as the GMS regional transmission grid. But there may be significant extenuating factors. The ADB has done an effective job of encouraging "buy in" by key decision-makers in the region, with little critical discussion of the risks and costs involved. Another extenuating factor is that while the overall economics are not great, there are significant profits to be made by well-placed players. Client politics may play a significant role and the process may be challenging to stop, especially as all key decisions occur in restricted, non-transparent settings.

Needed: strong independent regulation and integrated resource planning

Without a strong independent regulator and a regulatory process that guarantees public involvement and scrutiny, there is little reason to believe that the interests of the consumers and other vulnerable stakeholders will be protected with respect to hydropower development. In this sense, "strong" means that the regulator has the authority to enforce the law, and has the political will to do so. "Independent" means free from political influence, and not "captured" by special interests. So far, electricity sector governance in all countries in the region is far from this ideal. In Thailand, Laos, Myanmar, and Vietnam there is no regulatory authority[13] (Chantanakome 2005) and the utilities in these countries are largely self-regulating. While China and Cambodia have official regulatory bodies, analysts have raised questions about the independence and authority of these organizations (Yeh and Lewis 2004, Shi 2005). In no countries in the Mekong can there be said to exist a strong, independent, public-accountable regulatory authority.

Perversely, the RPTOA report recommends against implementing "a highly independent regional regulatory agency" because "the introduction of liberalization and truly competitive markets is not a short or medium-term objective of GMS countries." This makes little sense. It is precisely the lack of competition that is a primary motivation for strong and independent regulation, as has been the case for regulated monopolies in the US and elsewhere for almost a century. Without competition, an independent regulator is essential to ensure that monopolies or oligopolies do not gouge ratepayers, and that regional transmission investments are prudent, timely and in the best interests of consumers.

While an independent regulator is not, in itself, sufficient to guarantee positive outcomes, it is a necessary step. Another essential step is effective public hearings, which would allow for a degree of transparent oversight of power sector investments. Public hearings are an essential safeguard mechanism for meaningful intervention by consumers and other vulnerable stakeholders in decisions that will ultimately become their lasting economic and social burden.

Finally, the regulatory process should include a mandatory Integrated Resource Planning (IRP) decision framework that selects risk-adjusted economic least-cost alternatives. The options considered should include demand side management (DSM) and clean distributed generation, which have proven again and again to be cheaper and less risky than building massive transmission and centralized generation (Swisher and Jannuzzi 1997, D'Sa 2005).

Strong and fair independent regulatory authorities, public participation, and IRP have been three pillars of successful utility practice for decades in developed countries, have saved consumers billions of dollars, and helped minimize social and environmental impacts of power sector infrastructure. But every country in the Mekong region is currently lacking in all of these practices and institutions. Strong progress in these areas is desperately needed considering the aggressive plans currently underway for the many dubious massive hydropower and transmission projects discussed in this paper.

How can electricity needs be met fairly and sustainably in the region? This chapter suggests several hypotheses that warrant further study:
1. Hydropower development is based in part on ideologies of river basin development that were transplanted from the US and former Soviet Union during the Cold War era and have largely remained unchallenged.

2. Future plans for hydropower projects in the region are justified in part by uncertain projections of high demand for electricity in Thailand, Vietnam and China.
3. Thai projections are led by utilities that generally have self-interest in, and a track record of, overestimating demand. Vietnamese and Chinese load forecasting arrangements may face similar governance issues.
4. Hydropower selection occurs outside of cost-based planning e.g., as part of socio-politically-constructed bilateral or regional "cooperation."
5. Many hydropower projects in the region are not economically competitive and therefore would not proceed were it not for substantial subsidies—which currently take the form of grants and risk guarantees, soft loans, and political intervention in PPAs; and in the future may well take the form of a subsidized regional transmission grid.

In closing, we consider the question, "how can electricity needs be met fairly and sustainably in the region?"

1. Governments should adopt power sector reforms designed to promote public oversight, rigorous least-cost planning, effective environmental and safety regulation, respect for citizens' rights, and consumer protection. Such a campaign would build on citizens' ongoing attempts to demand open and honest government, recognition of local rights to resources, environmental, public health and safety regulations, and, respect for citizens' property rights in the development of new electricity and fuel supplies.
2. Governments and/or ratepayers in the region should not subsidize large hydropower by shouldering the cost burden of building a regional transmission grid.
3. Citizens of countries in which hydropower is built must be guaranteed the right to question and oppose new dam construction, and have their concerns addressed in all phases of planning, construction and operation. As long as the regimes in Laos, Myanmar, and China remain strongly authoritarian, this will be a difficult challenge.
4. True least-cost economic planning and realistic demand forecast practices must become common practice among power sector planners. The current planning paradigm considers only large-scale coal, natural gas, and hydropower as options. True least-cost planning means a public planning process and a framework within which the costs and benefits of all options are considered. Thus demand side management and cogeneration or renewable energy would be considered on a level playing field with conventional

supply-side resources, and the options selected are those with the lowest overall cost to society. In many cases "least cost planning" is interpreted to include consideration of environmental and social damages caused by electricity supply/transmission, for example by including "environmental add-ons" in cost-estimation processes. IFIS must to provide detailed, transparent, competent studies of the economics of dam projects and comparisons of least-cost studies of alternatives. IFIS must be held more accountable for inaccuracies and misrepresentations in project appraisals.

Notes

The authors would like to thank M-POWER and the Robert and Patricia Switzer Foundation for financial support.

1 Thailand is chosen because we are most familiar with the Thai case, though even here our research only scratches the surface. We expect that key assumptions, methodologies, and conflicts of interest in demand forecasting and power sector planning are broadly similar throughout the region. Thailand is de facto of considerable importance as a major portion of the planned hydroelectric capacity in the region is earmarked for power exports to Thailand.

2 Dieu (2000) reports that the USD 10 billion Pa Mong project was highlighted in the Mekong River Commission's Indicative Basin Plan (1970–2000) published in 1971, suggesting that the USD 10 billion figure is computed using year 1970 dollars.

3 An estimated 91,000 will need to be resettled (Norconsult 2002a). Indicative Master Plan on Power Interconnection in GMS Countries III-A. June., Imhof, A. 2005. Personal communication." 26 July 2005.

4 http://www.egat.co.th/english/about_egat/.

5 With the current rapid escalation in gas prices, however, Nam Theun 2 electricity is now less expensive than electricity from natural gas.

6 Currently, the pricing principle states that tariffs should be sufficiently high that the return on invested capital (ROIC) should be 8.39 percent. Before 2005, the pricing principle stated that the net income after expense of EGAT should not be less than 25 percent of the investment budget self-financing ratio (not less than 25 percent). Either way, the more the system is tipped to expand, the higher the allowed tariffs.

7 Peak demand in Thailand occurs in the early afternoon (air conditioning load) during the hottest working days of the hot season (typically in March or April)

8 Grid-connected biomass fired generation that use fuels with seasonal variations in availability are also not included in the "dependable" reserve.

9 Search Google for "integrated resource planning" to see dozens of utility programs.

10 A 2005 Global Environment Facility (GEF)/World-Bank commissioned report provides updated figures for demand reductions. Demand reduction from lights, refrigerators and air conditioning alone currently exceeds 1000 MW (Marbek Resource Consultants Ltd. and G. C. S. International 2005). "Post-Implementation

Impact Assessment: Thailand Promotion of Electrical Energy Efficiency Project (TPEEE). Draft Report." Prepared for: World Bank–GEF Coordination Team. April 8.

11 500 kv, Double Circuit, four-bundled conductor per phase, using 1272 MCM ACSR/GA conductor costs 12.2 million baht per kilometer, according to personal communication with EGAT.

12 USD 800,000 per km figure is based on costs in British Columbia and includes materials, labor, project management, indirect costs (IDCS), and all substation and protection work.

13 As this chapter goes to press, the Thai government has appointed a seven-member interim regulatory body. The body has no legal authority to penalize, and citizens groups have raised concerns that the appointed commissioners are not sufficiently independent.

CHAPTER 6

MATHEMATICAL MODELING IN INTEGRATED MANAGEMENT OF WATER RESOURCES
MAGICAL TOOL, MATHEMATICAL TOY OR SOMETHING IN BETWEEN?

Juha Sarkkula, Marko Keskinen, Jorma Koponen, Matti Kummu, Jussi Nikula, Olli Varis and Markku Virtanen

Introduction

Are models useful for management and decision making on water resources? Are the efforts put into them justified? In this chapter we argue that mathematical modeling is one of the few options available to look at the questions of future changes and impacts of human activity on water resources. Models and their results, however, are often mistrusted, under-utilized or misused in management and decision making, and as a result the role of models in water management seems to be both controversial and unclear.

Critical questions related to the use of models in decision making on water resources include: What is the connection of modeling to social, economic and political aspects of water management? Do models provide an adequate representation of biophysical processes? Do models present their results in a form that addressed the actual needs of policy- and decision-makers? Do decision-makers and other "non-modelers" understand the limitations included in the models and their results? Are there strategies in model development and communication that can help allay unreasonable fear and mistrust of mathematical models? How can the perceived legitimacy, credibility and transparency of modeling be improved?

This chapter presents, drawing on examples from the Mekong region, our ideas and suggestions on responding to changing user needs, model content and user interfaces as well as on increasing the linkages between modeling and other critical issues in water management. We argue that further work is needed on linking hydrological and environmental issues with social and economic activities to facilitate balanced modeling and impact assessment, and consequently, decision making. This will require multi- and cross-disciplinary approaches for both modeling and impact assessment, and better communication and interaction between modelers and non-modelers. This, in turn, helps to produce more transparent and relevant information, and creates stronger scientific and social basis for impact assessment and management decisions.

Integrated modeling and assessment of water resources

Challenges for integrating multidisciplinary information

Successful implementation of environmental management policies requires thorough understanding of environment and its linkages with the surrounding society. Due to the complex nature of these issues and their interconnections, various kinds of mathematical models have been developed to support management and governance. Models are used to improve understanding of cumulative and aggregate effects, to provide forecasts, and to help to quantify scenarios, which in turn are helpful for long-term planning.

However, the role of models in environmental and water management is controversial. There appears to be two totally different schools of thought regarding the use of models. While some managers and scientists look at the models as basically mathematical toys of over-enthusiastic engineers with only weak connection to real problems, others value models above anything else trusting almost blindly their results. As a consequence, models and their results are often either poorly integrated in the decision making, or the management is based completely on their results without proper consideration of the limitations and uncertainties of the models and their results.

This chapter looks at the strengths and weaknesses of mathematical models based on the experiences from the integrated water management in the Lower Mekong Basin. Integrated and balanced management of water resources is an extremely challenging task, as it should take into account several different fields from environment to economy and society. Information needed in water management thus comprises not only hydrological but also environmental, social, economical and political information and data. Collecting information on these wide-ranging fields is an enormous challenge, not to mention actual analysis and comprehension of the issues.

The biggest challenge, however, is successful integration of these different types of information. It requires open and long-term cooperation between researchers from different disciplines, preferably as a multidisciplinary team working together from the very beginning of analysis work. This naturally necessitates also some sacrifices, such as sharing of financial resources and project achievements within the team. On the other hand, it also shares the workload and most probably brings new kind of ideas and approaches for the entire team. However, the success of integration may be threatened by the reluctance of the decision-makers to adopt new kind of information that conflicts with prevailing understanding and management strategies. Achieving greater integration thus demands a change of mindset from both researchers and decision-makers, and it can be rather time-consuming and even frustrating experience for all the parties involved.

The authors note the valuable contribution by Somlyódy (1994) to the issues addressed above. He points out tremendous gaps in the integration of environmental management, technology and society, between different disciplines and professions, barriers in legislation, institutions and decision making, and lack of future visions supported by science. Related to this, Nancarrow (2005) addresses some interesting issues on modeling, and particularly on the relationship between modelers and social scientists. She points out some differences in their overall approaches (to simplify: modelers simply assume a problem and start by defining and collecting data needed to solve it, while social scientists start by identifying the different stakeholders and how they see and define the problem) and also addresses challenges related to working in multidisciplinary teams.

Over the past decade, many of the gaps have become narrower, through a number of scientific, institutional and other initiatives and cooperative efforts that have led to progress in integrated approaches. These include for example the concept of Integrated Water Resources Management (IWRM), EU-funded European Forum for Integrated Environmental Assessment (EFIEA), international conventions such as the Mekong River Agreement and its implementation by the Mekong River Commission (MRC) as well as activities by different research institutions and NGOs in developing more cooperative and integrative approaches.

Approaches for integrated modeling and assessment

Integrated Modeling and Assessment (IMA) has evolved rapidly over the last decade as a new scientific concept to address the need for more multi- and cross-disciplinary approaches. Rotmans (1998) notes the increasing recognition for the field of Integrated Assessment (IA) but at the same time recognizes that the methodological basis is lagging behind the expectations from the outside world. Parker et al. (2002) give a review of state and position of IA modeling, concluding that the science behind IA modeling is often not new and in many ways it can be considered to be the combining of old areas of science and research to consider problems in new, more holistic ways.

One of the main methodological problems in IA modeling is the scale, and the resolution of different scales for different system components. Jakeman and Letcher (2003) point out some important considerations within IA modeling; appropriate time periods and time steps to choose over which to model the highly variable ecosystems, handling model complexity by keeping the level of integration of issues and disciplines manageable and developing methods to characterize model uncertainty.

Janssen and Goldsworthy (1996) discuss the importance of attributes of multidisciplinary teams and research efforts, that are required for success in IA modeling. They emphasize the importance of the teams developing their own sets of norms and values and conclude that attitude, communication skills, education and experience are all important attributes. Communication is a central issue both internally among the team members and externally with decision-makers, stakeholders and other scientists. Parker et al. (2002) and Jakeman and Letcher (2003) highlight that the process of IA and modeling is actually as important as the product of any particular project. Learning to work together and recognizing the contribution of all team members can create a strong scientific and social basis created to address the environmental problems of the twenty-first century.

In this chapter, we seek to illustrate what models are, how they are used and how different people perceive them. Experiences are derived mainly from work done in the Mekong region, and in the Tonle Sap Lake in particular. The use of modeling tools for supporting sustainable environmental, social and economic development is underlined. An essential part of this work is capacity building for future use and maintenance of the developed tools by the end users in the region. We also discuss standard as well as tailored models and try to see how they fit to different kind of needs of problem solving.

There is a great number and variety of models developed for the Mekong basin, with overlaps and weak connections between the models being the rule rather than the exception (annex 7.1). This can be seen to illustrate the common difficulties to coordinate between individual modeling approaches as well as lack of proper understanding of the capabilities of different models by many managers and decision-makers. The Mekong River Commission (MRC) has a key role and opportunity to create a solid model and information base for hydrological, environmental and socioeconomic impact assessment to support the development planning in the Mekong basin. To this end, this chapter also discusses the ongoing work on MRC's Decision Support Framework (DSF).

Specific attention is paid to the questions and problems of integrated assessment and modeling. The case study in the Tonle Sap Lake and its floodplains offers a complex, challenging and important task in this respect. Finally, conclusions are drawn to identify barriers and possibilities for developing the integrated assessment and modeling platform, for bringing the new information to the disposal and use of the decision-makers, and for linking modeling better with other aspects of water management.

Modeling: The outline

What are models?

Contemporary methodological literature on natural resources management presents a wide array of analytical and computational approaches, most of which are closely related with modeling. The different approaches range from various statistical techniques (empirical) to process models with difference or differential equations (mechanistic), and from decision making models and optimization (pragmatic) to checklists and impact matrices (verbal). Much of the practical application of these models is in one way or another related to various administrative needs.

In environmental and socioeconomic modeling, the planning and management component is typically crucial. This is simply due to implicit role of human being in such systems, since the concept of "environment" per se without a human being is equally as absurd as "socioeconomy" without a human being (or, at least in the context of the Mekong region, without environment). Sutherland (1983) sees the combined use of models in decision making as "an art of getting things done." For this purpose, he has categorized decisions and consequent modeling approaches into four main categories described in box 6.1.

Water and ecosystem model use can be divided into research, engineering, environmental management and socioeconomically orientated branches. Typical uses in research are, for instance, comprehensive ecosystem models describing detailed nutrient and carbon cycles and large number of species or classes of species. Engineering applications can for example include design of control structures such as embankments, culverts and gates, or finding optimal dredging solutions.

An individual working with environmental problems, decision making, and environmental policies, inevitably comes across persons whose approaches and conventions to scientific problem solving and decision making are very different. This is partly due to the constantly evolving state of the field, and partly due to the great interdisciplinarity; environmental studies is at the cross-roads of several tradition-rich pure and applied sciences.

Engineers, economists, biologists, sociologists, etc., have all their own paradigmatic backgrounds. Communication problems and intolerance, and even prejudice concerning approaches are very common. Take as an example the word "model" itself which has several different meanings. Synonyms such as ideal, exemplary, and perfected can be found among adjectives, miniature, saint, idol, representation, symbol, prototype, example, and replica among nouns, and pose and mimic among verbs (cf. Somlyódy and Varis 1993). The exact interpretation depends on context and convention. A brief description of water and ecosystem modeling is given (box 6.2).

Box 6.1 Four main model categories

Operational models: Provide enhanced possibilities and support for real-time management and decision making through automated data retrieval from the water body in question. Such data is often being used in real-time operations such as reservoir operation, flood protection or treatment plant operation. Models for short-term predictions are needed. Typically, the most essential features of data stream are filtered out.

Tactical models: The basic task is to find input-output relations between key variables of the system. In surface water modeling, monitoring data is usually used to construct models, which allow for instance "what-if" type of scenario analysis and trade-off analysis between different stakeholders and water users.

Strategic models: By definition, a strategic analysis should be used to project current situations to states, which have a significant probability of occurrence. Environmental and social impact assessment, medium-term planning and other tasks in which the system is exposed to potential structural changes are typical situations for the use of this category of models. Game theoretic models, simulation, probabilistic risk analysis and scenario analysis are typical computational approaches.

Directive models: Problems such as sustainability, adaptivity, resilience, and description of possible future events are included in planning and management of the evolution of the system in the long run. The problems and data sources of the systems are essentially more expert-judgment based, policy and politics related, and subjective.

Box 6.2 Mathematical models

Numerical model is itself a simplification of the reality and it attempts to describe the real world phenomena based on the physical and chemical laws, and functions derived from biology, ecology and socioeconomics. It offers an extension and tool for brainwork to analyze complicated processes and their interconnections.

With the model, it is possible to simulate processes that are difficult or impossible to describe or research any other way, including analysis of the probable future changes and their impacts. The model can describe various phenomena and analyze the effects of changes in independent (i.e. explanatory) variables on dependent variables.

Who develops, who benefits?

Among the biggest challenges within the environmental modeling is the gap between modelers and potential model-users i.e. environmental planners and managers. This gap has often been large due to various reasons, the lack of communication and prejudice towards models and their results being among the simplest but biggest hindrances. Modelers and model-users often speak different languages, with modelers far too often resorting to too technical terms and/or not explaining clearly the basic principles and assumptions behind the models. Modelers and model-users also have usually different needs and demands: while modelers want to develop more advanced models with long-term perspective, planners and managers actually need quick and simple model results that are accurate enough. Although modelers put a lot of effort into developing advanced models, they rarely put equal amount of time to transferring the model outputs into simple—and simplifying—results that planners and managers could more easily use. This kind of imbalance between time allocated for modeling on one hand, and for communications and cooperation on the other, is also unfortunately prevalent in other stages of the modeling.

Consequently, the role of model-users has become increasingly important and has led to increased efforts in user training and development of more user-friendly model interfaces. The successful transfer of model results to the end-users is naturally an absolute necessity for sustainable use of the models. But the information exchange must happen both ways: model developers also have to listen to the decision-makers and managers from the very beginning of model development—only in this way the models will be able to answer to the most urgent problems and questions that the managers face. As a result, in recent years there has been a general tendency to involve environmental managers and planners, limnologist, biologists and other "non-modelers" better into model use and even development. This diminishes the gap between the "non-modelers" and the modelers and improves the usefulness of the models for both management and research and development.

The dialogue between the modelers and model-users is particularly important because managerial decisions on natural and environmental resources are usually bound to forecasts and assessments with very high uncertainty. Due to economic, time-related and other practical constraints, it is often difficult or impossible to collect thorough enough empirical data, especially in developing countries where existing resources and information are usually more limited. The MRC has been no exception on this, and is still facing wide gaps in its environmental information on the Mekong region. However, the MRC is still to be commended for promoting a basic research programme in the Mekong region, developing the data and information bases, and building the capacity of the national institutions in its member countries.

Standard or tailored modeling?

Regulatory needs. In practice, environmental modeling is still a relatively heterogeneous field with a great number of commercial and public modeling tools available. This is as much due to the rapid evolution of the field as the wide gap between model developers and end-users. This problem is particularly valid in planning and management settings. There are almost as many models as there are modelers and there exist few "best-approach" guidelines to help select the most suitable model for the issue at hand.

On the other hand, the diversity must be tolerated otherwise no progress is possible. Moreover, the tasks to which models are being used are diverse enough that no generic environmental models are realistic. Many large government agencies or commercial companies have developed selections of environmental modeling tools to address various needs. Some actors include the United States Environmental Protection Agency (EPA) and the European Commission (EC) from the public side, and the Haestad Methods and Danish Hydraulic Institute (DHI) from the business side. Such standardization is justified as certain model products become well-known and the communication around them becomes easier. However, such models are often understood as being more general-purpose tools than what they actually are and often leads to ignoring the case specificity of the actual problem to be solved.

Box 6.3 Example of standardized models in the United States

The USA has established and implemented a Data Quality Law (Public Law 106-554, 2001) to improve standardization and legitimacy of environmental information. Its objective is to "ensure and maximize the quality, objectivity, utility and integrity of information (including statistical information) disseminated by federal agencies." Mathematical models have been also classified to this category and a list of models that fulfill the quality criteria of the law has been published by the US EPA. In the best case, the law could add to the transparency and use of sound science in formulating regulatory policy.

The first experiences seem to be, however, rather disputable. Many citizens groups and environmental activists say that the act is biased in favor of industry, that it dismisses scientific information and will always be more useful to those seeking to decrease government regulation (Rick Weiss, *Washington Post* August 2004). It seems that the best results from the social and environmental development point of view are achieved by a continuing debate between the interest groups, active public media and awareness raised with the help of scientific information. Maybe science should not be disputed in courts of law, except in cases of misuse or falsification of information.

Limits of standardized model packages. The uses of standardized model packages are justified due to the transparency and reliability requirements that are particularly important in sensitive political settings. Many environmental changes and problems impact various different stakeholders and can even be internationally sensitive issues. Many standardized model packages are also relatively strong in presenting and communicating the model structure and model results to the decision-makers and other non-users, thus potentially decreasing the possible gap between modelers and non-modelers. In addition, standardized model packages that have a strong training component may offer relatively easy way to start exploring the basic possibilities—and limitations—of modeling. However, there are cases in which quick modeling implementations with standard modeling packages do not necessarily go hand in hand with credible modeling results or development of sustainable planning tools.

The authors of this chapter are of the opinion that tailoring of models to a specific case usually pays off. The reasons are fundamental: The use of a standard modeling tool confines research approach to the limits of the tool. The problem-solving aspect and production of the most useful information becomes a secondary goal, and fitting the problem to suit the standard approach the primary one. In this case, the inherent limitations of a standard model and approach constrain the whole modeling process from the model construction to the end use of the results.

Standard tools can undermine the reliability of the modeling results. It is relatively easy to assume that a use of a standard tool is more or less "automatic," the results will be practically always correct, and that application doesn't require any special experience or understanding of modeling principles. This may lead to fallacious assumptions in setting up the model, passing erroneous data to the model and accepting results without proper checking. Finally, the model results are likely to be used without the user's proper understanding about the limitations of the assumptions that the models are based on. Tailoring necessitates the modeller to dwell deeper into the problem at hand and the modeling techniques applied to it. In this way, it protects against at least the most blatant negligence.

The cases where using tailored models instead of standardized model packages can be more beneficial are further illustrated by the following examples:
1. A modeling case may contain elements that are impossible or difficult to model with any standard approach. An example where major tailoring is needed is a case where different areas need to be coupled: this kinds of areas include e.g. floodplains, river channels, reservoirs, lakes and coastal areas.

2. Standardization may stifle local model development. The best way to train and maintain competent modelers is to involve them in model development. If research and development is externalized, also the quality of the modeling work that any institution is involved in suffers. For this reason, even if an institution is planning to use only standard tools, it is strongly recommendable that it is still involved at least on some level on model research and development as well.

When using tailored modeling tools, it is naturally important to involve decision-makers and other users of the model results in the tailoring of the model. However, their role is not always that straightforward, as they may not always be even able to formulate the problem or required outputs in concrete terms. It is therefore no wonder that they may not be eager, or able, to guide in deciding on the exact approach for modeling. In this kind of case, probably the best option is to first have thorough discussion between the modelers and end users on the expected outcomes of the modeling, and then produce a pilot version of the model with some sample outputs so that the user can comment on them and be thus better included in model development.

Standardized model selection and evaluation. More important than model standardization is to standardize model selection and evaluation procedures. In weather forecasting, standard evaluation methodology has helped model comparison and development. In environmental modeling, however, globally accepted evaluation procedures are still lacking. Because of this, model users and project evaluators have often great difficulties in selecting the right tools for their work, and in ranking different approaches.

There are areas such as applied meteorology where complicated, well-established numerical models are in operational, everyday use, and are used to give predictions i.e. weather forecasts to people. However, the interpreters of the results that the meteorological models provide are still there. Experts in meteorological processes that are able to translate the forecasts of often several different numerical models to the language of an ordinary person—in this case for example, decision-makers operating under the considerable uncertainties of weather—are still a prerequisite for successful use of meteorological models, and consequently good weather forecasts,

In operational cases such as flood forecasting of rivers, the situation is not very different from the meteorological model use. Well-established hydrological models—often a combination of statistical, physically-based, risk-analytical etc. tools—are operated by a hydrological service. This service then communicates forecasts to different stakeholders and users in forms that are (or at least should be) easily understandable.

Way forward for modeling

In order to look at ways to improve the utilization of models and model results in actual management and decision making, and therefore to define the possible way forward for modeling, we should also understand the different kinds of experiences—both positive and negative—with modeling.

In a positive experience on modeling, model development and use facilitates cooperation and dialogue between wide range of disciplines and sectors from computational physics to socioeconomics and environmental policy-making. This kind of multidisciplinarity enables an extensive use of the tools in assessments, encourages making an analytical approach in problem formulation and solving, and directs and stimulates information collection. In this way it may also potentially offer an important platform and basis for transboundary water management.

Frustration with model development can be experienced, for example, in cases where model results are not trusted or seriously taken into account, or are omitted from decision making because of political reluctance or other short-term interests. This kind of situation does question the efficiency of the vast efforts made for developing technically high quality models, and also underlines once again the importance of open communications between the modelers and decision-makers. How can we better link models and other research activities with governance practices? How can we lower barriers for better penetration of scientific and technical information into decision making? These questions deserve serious attention in the research on integrated assessment and modeling.

Finally, it is very important to state the obvious fact that no model, whether for water management, economics or other fields, is an appropriate reason for replacing a human being. Models are like any other tools that require a skilled user, and are useful only if conducted and operated properly but could otherwise even be dangerous. A model without a competent user is like a car without an experienced driver.

Modeling the Mekong River

The Mekong River basin is no exception among the world's rivers as it has been subject to a broad spectrum of modeling efforts over the years (a bulk of the resulted model products are listed in annex 6.1). Many models have been developed and used, and many players are working with them. What are the main questions in the Mekong region that modelers are trying to answer? Why are these questions important? Is anybody coordinating the work or is coordination needed at all? Why there are so many models? Is there something that the old models have not been able to answer, and if so, why? Managers and planners don't actually need new models that are even more elaborate, but rather a single model that is simple but accurate enough. How could this be achieved?

Key lessons learnt from past modeling exercises

Why do various agencies and actors still keep developing models for the Mekong? To what end? In this short summary, there is little possibility of making a thorough scrutiny and thus provide answers to all these questions. However, some general outlines can be provided.

First, it is important to notice that the different models developed for the Mekong region serve many fundamentally different purposes. Most of them have been used either in scientific investigations or as planning and management instruments. Thereby they belong in some cases to tactical, but in most cases to strategic level, often used also in scenario analyses. Typically, the data and knowledge management properties are very crucial and numerical models are used in combination with geographic information systems, statistical models and risk-analytic tools. The accuracy and precision of such tools cannot reach the same level as those models that are used for operational purposes—in a data-affluent, single-purpose setting. Rather, they are more analogical to regional or global climate models used, for instance, in climate change research than to operational weather models.

Second, the field of actors in the basin is diverse. National agencies are active in this regard particularly in Vietnam and Thailand. The Mekong has been an attractive and important topic to for research. There has been tens of academic modeling studies carried out, for example, in the Mekong delta alone. In addition, the Mekong region has been a major target of an array of bilateral and multilateral development co-operation efforts over decades. This has resulted in great diversity of activities which are very difficult to manage; coordination and synthesis are seriously needed.

In these and several other regards, one of the key organizations in the Lower Mekong Basin is the MRC. Therefore, we will focus here on the MRC's concurrent modeling efforts. Donor-driven organizations such as the MRC are particularly challenging since externally driven development initiatives do not easily get rooted in the region. For obtaining sustainable results, the riparian experts and institutions should feel that they are the "owners" of such modeling tools. This is easier in cases in which the initiative comes from inside the countries. However, countries such as Laos and Cambodia have had considerable capacity shortcomings and external input has been seen as an important contribution in the field of water and environmental management. The contribution of the MRC has been considerable here, although it has not been fully capable of creating sufficient links to local experts in the riparian countries. The extension of the training efforts to a wider community of modelers and model users, including academics, is seen as way to increase sustainability and utilization of the modeling tools, as discussed repeatedly in this chapter. This would also shore up the MRC's efforts to recruit modelers.

Box 6.4 Models in development cooperation

Many of the Mekong-related models have been realized as development cooperation projects or programs. Bringing "western" models and modeling approaches into the projects also brings several new things into modeling and model use. One of these is the definite need to integrate social and economic analysis and impact assessment tools with traditional engineering. The problems of the most vulnerable and poorest people cannot be addressed without social considerations and participatory approaches. The great challenge in most cases is to integrate qualitative social information with traditionally quantitative nature-scientific and technological data. In addition, many development co-operation projects have also not properly understood the political, institutional and cultural context where they have been working.

Perhaps the greatest challenge is to provide sufficient training and capacity-building for the beneficiaries and to guarantee sustainable use and benefit of the developed modeling and assessment tools in future. Too many "products" of past development initiatives have been put aside without use. To be honest, full success in this respect also seems impossible. The problems do not lie only in the attitudes and capabilities of the supplier, but also in the barriers with and limitations of the receivers. Naturally there are gaps in technical skills and experience, but they are not the most difficult to overcome. Sometimes the limitations in language skills block a good part of the information transfer. Moreover, the poor countries are often unable to provide long-term work contracts and assignments for young people, and thus a reason for these staff to commit to learning and using this new knowledge.

Both the donor community and implementation agencies should therefore pay increasing attention to follow-up training and cooperation on modeling and impact assessment. This is best done with established trainee networks, preferably by coordinated and collaborative efforts with different actors and institutes. The Tonle Sap case presented later in this chapter shows one practical experience on the integrated modeling approach as well as capacity building and its challenges.

Modeling activities at the MRC

The MRC is one of the most powerful international organizations in the region along with ADB, Asia-Pacific Economic Cooperation (APEC), Association of Southeast Asian Nations (ASEAN), Greater Mekong Subregion (GMS), and various large non-governmental organizations. However, a lot is needed to merge their approaches closer to each other with more open collaboration and information sharing. Among the riparian countries, Cambodia, Vietnam, Lao PDR and Thailand are members of the MRC, but China and Myanmar [Burma] are only dialogue partners. A lively scientific-technological cooperation with these upstream countries is a necessity for comprehensive basin-wide hydrological, environmental, economical and social impact assessment. This issue is also well addressed by the MRC, and its new Strategic Plan 2006–2010 recognizes promotion and improvement of dialogue and collaboration with China and Myanmar as one central objective of the organization.

The contemporary MRC is based on the Mekong Agreement, which was signed in 1995 by the four member countries. Related to the Agreement, the following vision for the Mekong River basin was defined: "An economically prosperous, socially just and environmentally sound Mekong River basin." These strategic outlines that form the backbone of the MRC are very interesting. In fact, they are very much in accordance with the principles of Integrated Water Resources Management (IWRM). Therefore, the MRC's ongoing modeling efforts are performed also in the broad framework of IWRM.

The MRC is currently working on a comprehensive rolling plan and planning process for the Lower Mekong River Basin. This includes the basin's parts that are within the member countries. This comprehensive plan, the Basin Development Plan (BDP) is supported by a massive six-year background analysis—or a series of analyses—under the title Water Utilization Programme (WUP) funded mainly by the Global Environment Facility (GEF).

Water Utilization Programme (WUP)

The WUP aims at helping the MRC member states to implement key elements of the 1995 Mekong Agreement. It provides technical and institutional capacities required for longer-term cooperation to manage the basin's water and ecological resources in a sustainable manner. One of its core activities is the Integrated Basin Flow Management (IBFM), realized jointly by the WUP and the MRC Environment Programme (EP).

IBFM activities are designed to provide information to the decision-makers on the predicted benefits and costs of land and water development of the Mekong basin. This information is aimed at facilitating discussions between the countries to reach a balanced and sustainable economic, environmental and social development in the basin.

Numerical models play a key role in the IBFM process, leaning on the development of the MRC Decision Support Framework (DSF). The DSF comprises a set of hydrological models and flood analysis procedures. So far, the IBFM process has focused on hydrological characteristics as basis for the flow rules, leaning on the properties of the present DSF. However, for widening the scope of IBFM approach, more advanced analytical methods are needed. These include, for example, water quality models for simulation of material transports in the river and in the floodplain and assessing consequent environmental, economic and social impacts under various flow regimes.

Strengthening the model base for impact assessment

The model and knowledge base i.e. MRC's Decision Support Framework (DSF) is the cornerstone of IWRM as well as of the IBFM process. A major challenge for, and interest of, the MRC is to build a scientifically validated, credible and sustainable model platform to support basin development planning, hydrological forecasting, and integrated environmental, economic and social assessment. In this regard, there is still lot of work to do with the DSF. The MRC would benefit greatly from continuing validation and scientific review of the model system, which is necessary for its transparency and credibility, not least in the transboundary context. Widening the platform to an ensemble of models for different scopes, involving model comparison and cross-validation, would most likely lead to increasing credibility and additional usefulness of the DSF. Without doubt, all this would lead to more effective Mekong basin development planning and decision making by the MRC.

An elementary part of the model base is to build a riparian capacity to take care of its maintenance, development and future use, to effectively respond to any emerging development plan with regional importance. Building of wide national capacity and potential in the member countries is necessary, extending from MRC to national agencies and academic institutions. This allows continuing capacity forming and updating for this entire user community and resource. Moreover, international scientific and research networks offer wide range of possibilities for developing countries for training and R&D cooperation. The EU, among others, is showing a growing interest in the Mekong region and in becoming a noteworthy partner in this field.

Related to this, it is essential to make the model base architecture open and modular to facilitate capacity building and avoid possible risks of dead ends in system development. The model engines must be possible to change and be compatible with each other. Modeling is a continuous process and new generations of models appear frequently and need to be easy to use.

Consultants, who are largely responsible for developing models at the MRC, should share responsibility for developing tools which meet the needs of their clients. Moreover, open source software and license-free model systems would widen the possibility of national bodies, including universities, accessing and using the MRC-sponsored tools. This could add remarkably to the confidence on the models as well as their development. The extensive use of models, for a multitude of purposes and case studies in the riparian countries, would have a strong positive effect in the long-term sustainability of the developed tools.

Basin Development Plan

The model and knowledge base (DSF) also forms the foundation for the development scenario assessment of the MRC Basin Development Plan (BDP). According to the 1995 Mekong Agreement, the BDP is: "The general planning tool and process that the Joint Committee of the Mekong River Commission would use as a blueprint to identify, categorize and prioritize projects and programmes to seek assistance for and to implement the plan at the basin level."

The objective of the BDP is "sustainable development of the water and related resources of the basin for the mutual benefits of the riparian countries and people living in the Mekong River basin." In the medium term, the programme will develop a framework for regional cooperation among the riparian countries to develop the Mekong River basin through implementation of a well-defined and established BDP. The BDP is therefore a central planning tool for the MRC's new "Mekong Programme," a regional cooperation programme that, by using the concept of Integrated Water Resources Management (IWRM), aims to achieve more effective and balanced use of water and related resources in the basin. The knowledge and capacity building process and a dialogue with the public, stakeholders and political levels run parallel with the basin development planning process. The big challenge for the MRC is to develop and implement a holistic model system to serve as an integrated planning tool for its sub-regions as well as basin wide planning needs.

WUP-FIN tools supporting the MRC

Complementary to the MRC's Water Utilization Programme (WUP) is the WUP-FIN Project, which focuses on capacity building in modeling and impact assessment for socioeconomic and environmental analyses. This kind of multi- and cross-disciplinary approach, linked to national institutes, aims contributes to the development of enhanced hydrodynamic models as well as environmental and socioeconomic impact assessment tools for the Lower Mekong Basin.

Part of the WUP-FIN project is to develop an integrated modeling approach using a gridded, hybrid and multidimensional (1/2/3D) model. The river and floodplain system is characterized by slope, physical, chemical and biological gradients, horizontally and vertically. The GIS-type of system allows for integrating floodplain information, such as infrastructure and land use, with water and environmental parameters. This is complemented by socioeconomic data and information for further analysis and impact assessment.

In addition to WUP and national institutes, the Flood Management and Mitigation Programme (FMMP) as well as the Fisheries and Navigation sectors of the MRC are key users and beneficiaries of the WUP-FIN modeling and impact assessment tools. It is anticipated that the WUP-FIN Lower Mekong Basin hybrid hydrodynamic model will serve the FMMP for improved flood forecasting accuracy in place and time over the river and floodplain system. In addition, the three-dimensional hydrodynamic and water quality model can be an efficient tool in navigational planning and development, environmental impact assessment and management of accidental cases (e.g. oil spills) and contingency planning. The Fisheries Programme benefits from the integrated hydrodynamic and water quality models applied to the LMB floodplains and to the Tonle Sap flood pulsing system in particular. The WUP-FIN Project is continuing this work by creating a framework for modeling terrestrial and aquatic productivity of the pulsing system. The work focuses on the role of sediments and nutrient brought to the system by flood waters for maintaining its biological productivity, floodplain vegetation impacts, and the indicators of fish reproduction rates in the floodplains.

Figure 6.1 Model flow chart from model input to impact analysis in the Tonle Sap area

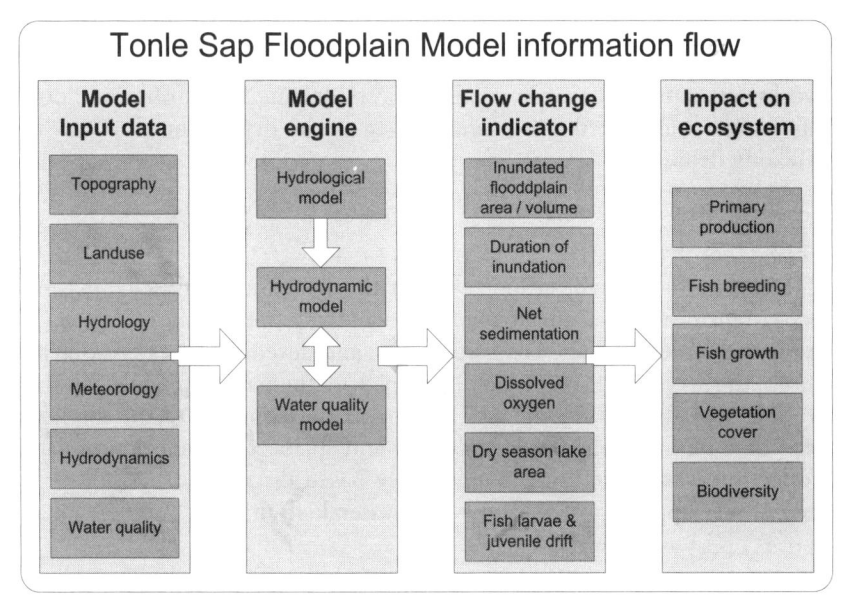

Integrated model of the Tonle Sap system

In the following, the application of the WUP-FIN models and analysis tools to the Tonle Sap system is presented as a practical example of integrated modeling and impact assessment process (figure 6.1). The application also shows the need and justification of developing an advanced model system for this kind of complex hydrodynamic, environmental and social entity. The model development and application work has been accompanied with training and capacity building given for the model users and decision-makers at the MRCS and at the national institutions, including both governmental and academic institutions. The mode of training has covered workshops and courses, on-the-job training, support to academic research and dissertations and curriculum development, joint publications and conference papers as well as support for the trainees to reach international training and study positions. All this has been aimed at increasing the skills of the trainees in modeling and impact assessment methodologies as well as enhance their knowledge in the functioning of the Tonle Sap Lake and floodplain system.

The Tonle Sap Lake in Cambodia is the largest permanent freshwater body in Southeast Asia and a very important part of the Mekong system (figure 6.2). The lake is among the most productive freshwater ecosystems in the world (e.g. Bonheur 2001, e.g. Lamberts 2001, Sarkkula et al. 2003). The high ecosystem productivity is based on the flood pulse from the Mekong and the transfer of terrestrial primary products into the aquatic phase during flooding. The pulsing system concept was developed and studied in great detail in the Amazon basin by Junk (1997), and it is a very useful concept also applied to the Tonle Sap. Due to the flood pulse and extensive floodplain, the lake offers many of the Mekong fish species ideal conditions for feeding and breeding (Poulsen et al. 2002). The lake also works as a natural reservoir for the Lower Mekong Basin, offering flood protection and contributing significantly to the dry season flow to the Mekong delta.

Ecosystem processes

Despite the extreme importance of the lake and its floodplains, its ecosystem processes and biological productivity are poorly understood. To better understand the lake's ecosystem and develop impact assessment tools, the WUP-FIN Project has developed mathematical models for the Tonle Sap Lake and floodplain. To support development of the models, extensive physical, chemical, biological and socioeconomic primary data collection was carried out. A physically based distributed hydrological model was applied to the Tonle Sap watershed and three-dimensional

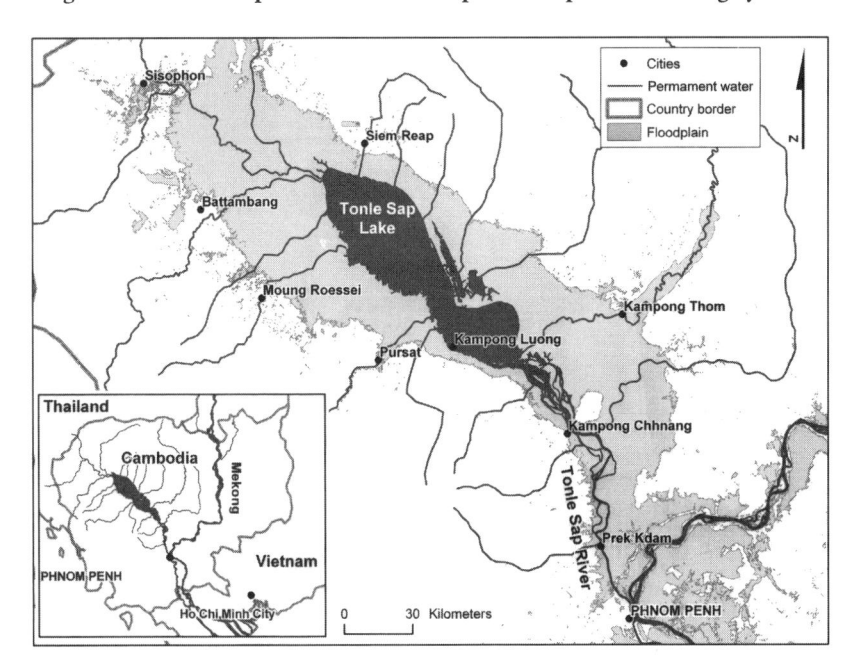

Figure 6.2 Tonle Sap Lake and its floodplain as a part of Mekong system

hydrodynamic and water quality model developed for the Tonle Sap Lake, floodplain and the Tonle Sap River up to Prek Dam.

The projected infrastructure development in the Mekong basin, including increased irrigation and hydropower construction at both local and regional levels, threatens the Tonle Sap's vulnerable ecosystem. For example upstream developments in the Mekong River such as dam construction have already led to significant trapping of sediments and nutrients (Kummu et al. 2006b), and may have significant impact on the flood regime and timing of the flood in LMB and Tonle Sap Lake in the near future (Adamson 2001). These changes may have a great influence on the productivity of the lake's ecosystem (e.g. Sarkkula et al. 2004, e.g. Sarkkula et al. 2003). The models developed during the WUP-FIN Project can thus be used to estimate possible impacts on the Tonle Sap Lake due to the local and upstream developments (Kummu et al. 2006a, WUP-FIN 2003).

Available model results from the WUP-FIN Project can be achieved for both natural and scenario cases, and include tributary inflows, flow speed and direction, flooding characteristics, dissolved oxygen concentrations (figure 6.3), sedimentation (figure 6.4), larvae and juvenile fish drift (Sarkkula et al. 2004) as well as pollution dispersion from floating villages.

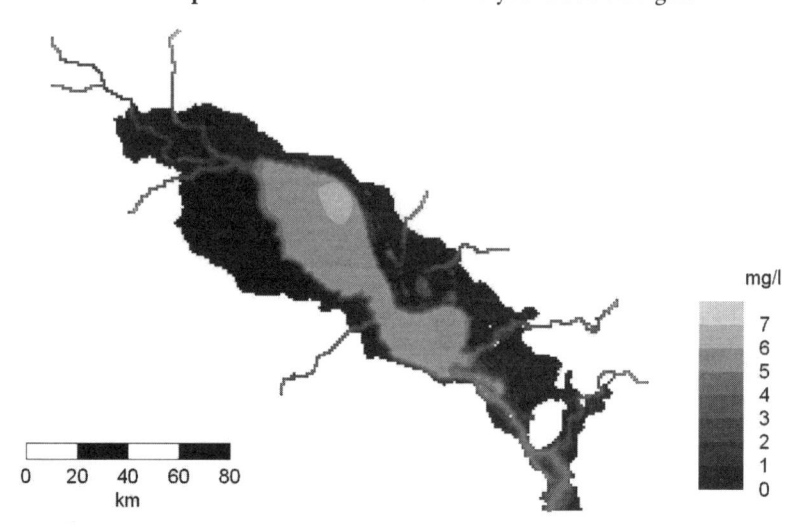

Figure 6.3 Calculated average oxygen conditions in the Tonle Sap Lake and floodplains. Year 1998 on left and year 2000 on right.

Socioeconomic analysis

In order to facilitate impact assessment and to link modeling better to social, economic and governance issues, the models developed within the WUP-FIN Project were complemented with socioeconomic and policy analyses. The socioeconomic analysis consisted of three main components: 1) analysis of the databases and creation of a new GIS-based socioeconomic database; 2) participatory village surveys and their analysis; and 3) analysis of other sources of information including literature reviews and expert interviews. The focus of the socioeconomic analysis is on water-related livelihoods and trends of natural resources (Keskinen et al. 2005).

The socioeconomic analysis thus consisted of two main phases: assessment and integration phases. Assessment phase was carried at the beginning of the project and it analyzed the most important water-related socioeconomic issues in the area, which then helped to set the focus for the actual modeling work and issues that the modeling aimed to tackle. The second phase was implemented at the latter half of the project, and it aimed to integrate the model results with social and economic information and this way to assist social impact assessment, and ultimately, to give balanced management recommendations (Keskinen et al. 2005a).

In order to facilitate the integration with the results of hydrodynamic and water quality models, the gathered quantitative socioeconomic data was arranged and analyzed according to topographic location (i.e. elevation) of the villages in GIS. All topographic zones were covered also by the participatory village surveys, although their small sample size meant

Figure 6.4 Calculated sedimentation results for different land use classes
(agriculture, grassland, shrubland, forest and water).
Diagram on top shows sedimentation for the western part and right
for the eastern part of the lake

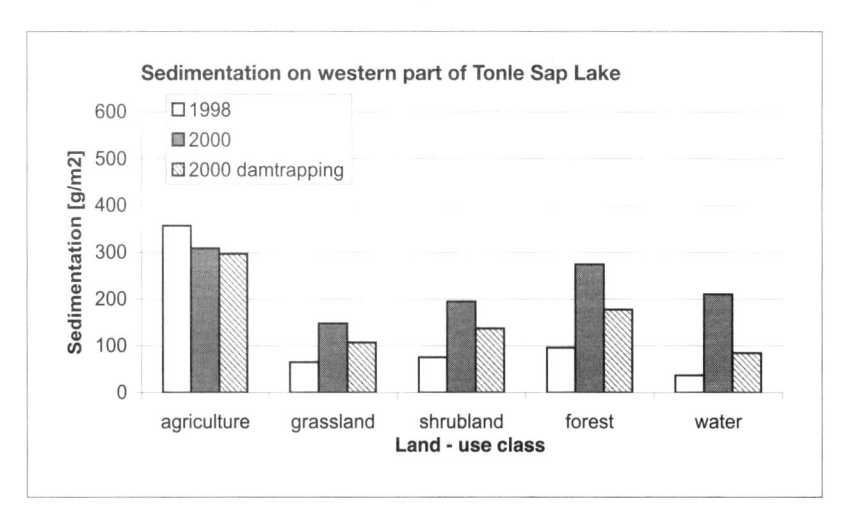

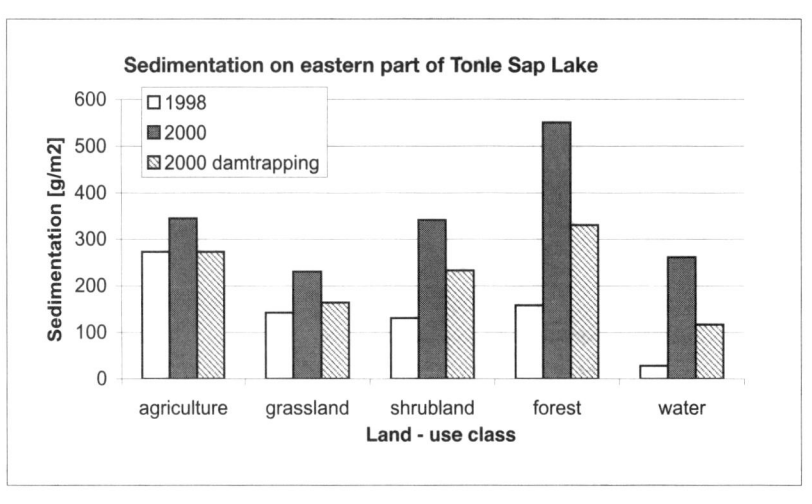

that this coverage was indicative only. Altogether four topographic zones were formed. In addition, urban areas were analyzed separately and they formed the fifth zone. The entire Tonle Sap Lake falls within Zone 1, and most of its floodplain within Zones 1 and 2. Exceptionally high floods like that in 2000 can also cover most of Zone 3 and parts of Zone 4 (Keskinen 2006).

Outputs from socioeconomic analysis derived from the above-mentioned activities include:
- increased understanding of livelihood structure in the area, including seasonal variation and diversity of livelihoods as well as livelihoods' connections to water resources and natural resources
- recognizing some recent trends of livelihoods, natural resources and water-related factors
- linking the achieved socioeconomic information with the topographic location, hence facilitating the connection with the hydrology of the floodplain
- detailed analysis of the different sector policies' impact to environmental sustainability, economic growth and poverty reduction (as part of policy analysis work)

It must be emphasized that although one part of the WUP-FIN Project also included modeling (see below), the analysis presented above was not carried out for modeling purposes per se, but rather to guide modeling through increased understanding of the socioeconomic situation in the Tonle Sap area, and together with model results and other information, to facilitate more balanced social and environmental impact assessment.

Policy analysis

Socioeconomic analysis within the WUP-FIN Project was complemented with policy analysis of different water-related sector policies in the Tonle Sap Area. For the purposes of policy analysis, the so-called WUP-FIN Policy Model was created. Although bearing the name "model," WUP-FIN Policy Model is actually very different from the hydrodynamic and water quality models as it is based on Bayesian Causal Networks (box 6.5), and aims to analyze in a broader manner the impact of different water management policies to society and environment (Varis and Keskinen 2006).

The policy analysis aimed thus to link the results of the hydrodynamic and water quality models with broader environmental, economic and social factors, and therefore to support management and decision making. The Policy Model based on Bayesian Causal Networks enables a systematic risk analysis of different types of factors, and also allows uncertainties to be taken into account in the modeling—characteristics that are often lacking but definitely needed when analyzing the complicated interconnections and impacts of different policies.

> **Box 6.5 Bayesian Network**
> The Bayesian Network methodology is based on the systematic analysis of causal interconnections in complex systems under high uncertainty. It allows the analysis of risks to various components of the environmental and social system under concern, as consequences of policy strategies under evaluation. Trade-off analyses between different development objectives can be made, and policy combinations that create win-win situations between the competing stakeholders can be sought (Varis 1998, Varis and Fraboulet-Jussila 2002)

The results from the policy analysis show that some, but not all, of the sector policies included in the analysis are crucial for both the economy and poverty reduction. The measures that decrease the huge shortcomings in education and governing institutions are obviously the ones that most strongly support these two goals. At the same time, with every scenario and sector policy, uncertainties related to their impacts remain very high and must therefore be appreciated. The reason for high uncertainties result partly from the lack of data, but even more importantly from highly complicated network of direct and indirect impacts that tend to be inconsistent in many cases, thus increasing uncertainty of possible impacts.

The sector policies included in the Policy Model appear, however, to be relatively toothless to environmental problems, particularly if defined as "environmental sustainability" as is done in the Mekong Agreement. This is most probably due to the following reasons. First, the concept of environmental sustainability is not easy to be conceptualized concretely enough so that it would be easy to treat analytically. Second, as the majority of the population of the Tonle Sap Area live in villages and make their living from the lake or the floodplain in a direct way, the environmental issues are closely bound to social issues. Social developments therefore are tightly bound to environmental impacts, and the improvements in social conditions tend to introduce both positive and negative environmental impacts which cancel each other, seemingly to a great extent. The situation would most probably be different if the area's governance system was more developed and transparent (Varis and Keskinen 2006).

Integration of socioeconomic, ecological and hydrological information

As was mentioned earlier, integrated management of water resources as well as impact assessment of different flow scenarios asks for a comprehensive approach that analyses and integrates information of various types. The identification of crucial issues in terms of policies, their interrelations, their social, economic and environmental impacts and the outcome to various vulnerabilities and stakeholder trade-offs is not a trivial thing, but at the same time it offers a unique learning experience. Often such a procedure reveals major new areas for research.

The social and environmental impact assessment requires thorough understanding of the linkages between hydrology, ecosystem and social and economic issues, as well as of the impacts that these different factors experience due to the changes in water regime. Figure 6.5 shows a simplified illustration of the interconnections between the three main factors together with different components of the WUP-FIN Project. Consequently, social and environmental impact assessment of the WUP-FIN Project builds on the integration of social and economic information with modeling results and information on environment, ecosystem processes, and land use.

The integration between hydrological, ecological, social and economic information can naturally be carried out in different ways, depending on the local setting and the overall context of the modeling and impact assessment work. Common to all of these different approaches is the challenge in facilitating the linkages between diverse socioeconomic information and other information sources and datasets, in particular with modeling results. This is partly related to the differences in type of information available: while mathematical models are based on quantitative data, socioeconomic analyses are commonly founded on both quantitative and qualitative information. Since qualitative information is practically impossible to include into conventional mathematical models, quantitative data is typically preferred when linking these different elements together. However, quantitative social and economic data has its own problems and biases, and utilization of both quantitative and qualitative socioeconomic information results in more comprehensive understanding of the social and economic situation in the area (Keskinen 2006).

The challenges described above can be tackled in different ways. As was explained earlier, in the case of Tonle Sap Area, the integration was facilitated by carrying out the socioeconomic analysis according to GIS-based topographic zones that could then be linked with model results (Keskinen 2006). Other possibilities exist as well, such as re-organizing existing social and economic information based on flood characteristics as was done in the Cambodian Mekong Floodplains (Keskinen et al. 2005b).

In the WUP-FIN Project, two different kinds of methods were used for integration (Keskinen 2006, Keskinen et al. 2005b, Nikula 2005):
 1. Quantitative integration of socioeconomic, land use and hydrological data with the help of GIS and topographic zones, and
 2. Descriptive integration combining quantitative and qualitative information on interconnections and causalities between hydrological, ecological, economic and social issues.

Figure 6.5 Framework for impact assessment and integration of hydrological, ecological and socio-economic information together with different WUP-FIN Project components

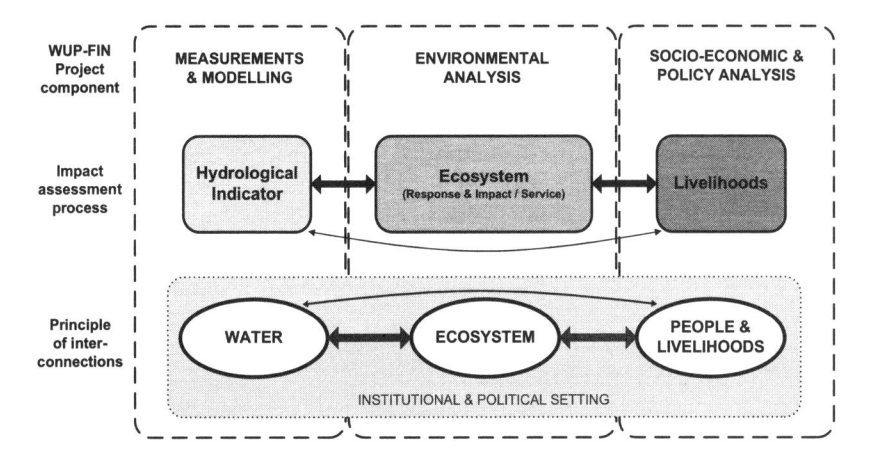

Initially, the idea was to determine relations between possible hydrological changes and their impacts on people's livelihoods at the lake largely quantitatively with the help of GIS and topographic zones. Soon it became clear, however that this kind of quantitative integration was not enough to understand thoroughly the intricate interconnections between hydrology, environment and social and economic aspects. The main reason for this are the limitations related to quantitative data: most of the interconnections remain poorly understood and analyzed, and many of them cannot anyhow be presented comprehensively in quantified terms. Also, the traditions of different disciplines from computational hydrology to participatory methods in sociology hampered the integration. This unease could have probably been reduced with a careful design of the project components in the early stages of the project. Consequently, also more conceptual approach for integration, descriptive integration, was applied.

The basic idea behind the descriptive integration is first to identify the most relevant hydrological indicators/parameters (e.g. flood level), then define the response of the ecosystem or ecological mechanisms that their potential changes cause (e.g. decrease in inundated habitats), then recognize their most important ecological impacts (e.g. fish production), and finally consider impacted livelihood activities, together with the immediacy that the impact is felt. This entire "impact process" is presented with so-called impact tables, where the direction and intensity of the impacts are specified based on data, information and knowledge available for this specific impact. For more information on descriptive integration, please refer to Keskinen (2006) and Nikula (2005).

Initial experiences from the integration work emphasize the need for a more comprehensive approach that makes use of a wide array of different methodologies and information sources, preferably together with a multidisciplinary team. Hydrological models contribute significantly to understanding the lake's complicated hydrological regime, but their usefulness for assessing social and environmental impacts is limited. To further work on impact assessment, more qualitative methods have to be applied. Local and expert knowledge is needed: when local and expert knowledge is combined with information from the measurements and models, the output of the modeling project will also be much more sustainable and better connected with local needs and expectations.

Conclusions and the way ahead

The chapter has discussed several issues related to water modeling: model technology and development, the relation of models to environmental and social impact assessments, and the usefulness of models in supporting planning and decision making. Examples have been derived mainly from experiences in the Mekong River basin, particularly within the context of the MRC. Some key conclusions and concerns have emerged for further research and practical applications on modeling and impact assessment:

- Modeling has potentially an important role in water management, particularly for analyzing future scenarios and their impacts as well as for complex, multi-dimensional systems such as the flood pulse of the Tonle Sap Lake.
- However, in order to link modeling with real world problems, the entire approach of modeling has to be updated: modeling projects must link better with the other dimensions of water management, most importantly with the society its is studying. This linkage should preferably be created from the very beginning of any modeling exercise, and enough time and resources should be allocated to it.
- Modelers and modeling projects need to focus more on cooperation and communications, by enhancing dialogue with decision-makers and other stakeholders, and by increasing the transparency and intelligibility of the models and their result. A way for the latter would be to provide decision-makers and other non-modelers possibility to actually try—and potentially also use—modeling and model applications by themselves.
- Related to this, bringing new information in a clearly understood form to the awareness of the managers, decision-makers and the

public calls for a professional skill. A modeler cannot usually replace a professional journalist in this task.
- Collecting primary information on hydrological, environmental and social and economic processes is a key for developing the model system and consequent, integrated impact assessments. All possibilities to cooperate openly with other research teams should be utilized.
- Model system needs to respond sufficiently to the complexity of the environment and context where model is applied; standardized and commercial approaches are not always the solution, so the possibilities should be open also for tailored model systems.
- One of the most difficult tasks in modeling work lies in training of the regional experts for long-term sustainability, maintenance and future use of the developed skills, technology and knowledge on modeling and impact assessment.
- Related to this, the risk of losing trained key personnel is a real threat in the Mekong region. Here the stability and long-term work of the MRC Secretariat's modelers group is of central importance for developing and maintaining technical skills both at the Secretariat and in the member countries.
- Risk of sustainability losses can be mitigated by continuous and effective cooperation between the model developers (presently mainly international consultants and the riparian experts) and the national line agencies, institutes and universities. The role of national universities in long-term capacity building cannot be over-emphasized, and they should be closely involved in the training and development of the models.

However obvious the needs for an integrated and cooperative approach for impact assessment in transboundary water basins are, there seems still to be a long way to go. Some progress in integration of teams from natural and engineering sciences has been made, but integration with the social sciences is still only dawning. To date, the approach adapted by modelers to address these more multidisciplinary connections has typically been just "to add some social stuff" to their models (Nancarrow 2005). This may have been predominantly just to satisfy the demands of the donors and/or decision-makers, but it doesn't really change the fundamental problems with modeling. The real change may come through establishment of teams for integrated assessment and modeling with balanced and equal participation by modelers, social scientists, policy experts and other non-modelers. This may help to formulate the right questions to guide model development and to end up with relevant answers and solutions from society's point of view. This may also help to bring new information and recommendations to the decision-makers.

Improving the connection with decision-makers is not without barriers and obstacles, either. Neither political attitudes and interests nor financial constraints are easy to overcome. The responsibility to rise above these barriers rests mainly on modelers, who need to develop models and present the model results in such a clear way that they are acceptable and understandable by planners, managers and decision-makers. This evident barrier makes one to think that a great deal of the effort put in modeling and its technical development should actually be released for collaboration and communication with decision-makers to ensure that the results achieved by (typically not cheap) modeling projects are really utilized in planning and decision making. The necessary resource for this could be easily released from scattered model developments, if only the decisions for more collaborative and concerted modeling work can be taken, and implemented.

The challenges described above lead one inevitably to think that the "spiritual side" of the long discussed and awaited—and still largely pending—integrated approaches has been mostly ignored. Reaching new milestones in the cumbersome road of integrated approaches thus necessitates identification of the mental and social barriers preventing true integration of the people involved. This does concern the research teams as well as the institutions and organizations, and also their governance methods and practices. The solution may rest in better mutual appreciation and listening between the involved individuals, teams, stakeholders and interest groups. The importance of multidisciplinary research for natural resources management is indeed obvious. As pointed out by Janssen and Goldsworthy (1996), to really achieve this, the most important attributes are attitude, communication skills, education and experience.

Annex 6.1. Selected modeling efforts in the Mekong region.

Hydrological Modeling

US Army Corps of Engineers (SSARR): first basin wide watershed model for Mekong region around 1960. Simulate runoff from rainfall and snow melt, and river systems including operations of reservoirs and diversions (Tanaka 1998).

MRC-DSF (SWAT & IQQM): SWAT, soil and water assessment tool, runoff for each Mekong sub-basin. IQQM, Integrated Quantity and Quality Model, movement of the runoff generated by SWAT model down the river system. Models are part of MRC's Decision Support System (DSF) (e.g. Jirayoot and Trung 2004; WUP-A 2003).

MRCS/WUP-FIN (HBV & VMOD): Tonle Sap sub-catchment and Songkhram watershed in Thailand, 1D lumped HBV model and 2D distributed watershed model (VMOD) (WUP-FIN 2003).

TSLV Project: WUP-JICA and Tonle Sap Vicinities project, 1D hydrological model down from Kratie to support the 2D hydraulic model (TSLV Project 2004).

University of Washington (VIC): Basin wide 2D distributed watershed model.

IWMI (SLURP): Basin wide Semi-Distributed Land-Use Runoff Process hydrological model (Kite 2000; Kite 2001).

Ibbit (TOP Model): Flow hydrograph model for Nam Gnouan Catchment in Laos (Ibbit 2000).

University of Yamanashi (YHYM): Basin wide Yamanashi Hydrological Model, 2D grid based distributed hydrological model (Kudo et al. 2004).

Tohoku University (BTOP/MC): Distributed discharge model used for sediment movement study, Middle Mekong Basin (Kudo et al. 2004).

Herath et al (IISDHM): flood hydrographs simulation up to Kratie (Tran 2000).

Nanjing Institute of Hydrology and Water Resources (LSM): Yunnan part of Mekong, Lancang river Simulation Model (LSM), lumped rainfall runoff model (Liu unpublished).

Hydrodynamic modeling

SOGREAH: Mekong delta model in 1963. Quasi 2D flow equations.

Delft (WENDY): Hydraulic model for Mekong Delta Master Plan.

Wolanski: 2D model for coastal erosion in Mekong delta (Wolanski et al. 1996).

SAL99: 1D hydraulic model to simulate flow, salinity intrusion, BOD, and propagation of acid water (Tran 2000).

HMS (KOD Model): 1D flood model for Mekong delta.

SIWRP (VRSAP): 1D hydraulic and water quality model for Mekong delta (Tran 2000).

HMS (HYDROGIS): Flood and salinity intrusion forecasting in Mekong delta.

Kyoto University (KYOTO): 1D river network & 2D overland flood model (Inoue et al. 2000).

MRCS/WUP-A (ISIS): 1D hydraulic model for Lower Mekong floodplains (from Kratie down to sea including Tonle Sap Lake) (Tes and Trung 2004).

MRCS/WUP-FIN (3D EIA Model): Applications for Tonle Sap Lake, Vientiane—Nongkhai section of Mekong, Nam Songkhram floodplains, Lower Mekong Basin floodplains (downstream from Kratie to the South China Sea), Chaktomuk junction in Phnom Penh, Tan Chau area, Tieu River Mouth, and Plain of Reeds (WUP-FIN 2003).

Tonle Sap vicinities (Mike 11): Used in Cambodia floodplains to study multifunctional hydrologic roles of Tonle Sap Lake and vicinities (TSLV Project 2004).

DHI (Mike21): 2D hydrodynamic model with curvilinear coordinate system applied to Chaktomuk area for understand the erosion and sedimentation characters

AIT (PWRI): Combined 1D and 2D surface-river flow model applied to Cambodian floodplains (Dutta et al. 2004)

Notes

All the authors are working for the Lower Mekong Modeling Project under the Water Utilization Program (WUP-FIN2) of the MRC. Finnish Environment Institute is leading the project in collaboration with the Environmental Impact Assessment Centre of Finland and the Water Resources Laboratory of the Helsinki University of Technology. The project is funded by the Development Cooperation Department of the Ministry for Foreign Affairs of Finland through the MRCS. The first phase of the project, called the Tonle Sap Modeling Project (WUP-FIN) started in June 2001 and focused on the Tonle Sap Lake of Cambodia. The second phase of the project, namely the Lower Mekong Modeling Project started in May 2004 and extends the work from the Tonle Sap to other critical areas in the Lower Mekong Basin. These hot-spot areas include Cambodian Mekong floodplains, the Mekong delta of Vietnam, and erosion-prone areas around Vientiane in Laos as well as the Songkhram Watershed in northeastern Thailand.

The authors would like to acknowledge all of the WUP-FIN team, particularly Seppo Hellsten, Mikko Kiirikki, Mira Käkönen, and all of the Cambodian co-workers, especially Mao Hak and Yin Than, Chit Kimhor and Bonvongsar Toch and trainees. Professor Pertti Vakkilainen is equally acknowledged. Critical and constructive comments during the writing process made by John Dore, Louis Lebel and Rajesh Daniel are greatly acknowledged. Masao Imamura is acknowledged for all the organizing efforts during the writing process.

CHAPTER 7

FORUMS AND FLOWS: EMERGING MEDIA TRENDS

Po Garden and Shawn L. Nance

Creative solutions and lower prices for media technology have enabled people in the Mekong region to get their messages across in media markets characterized by strict censorship and limited access. State governments have somewhat relaxed their grip on the media and have welcomed a degree of private and commercial ownership. But coverage of politically sensitive environmental issues is still far from free. Media reporting of debates and conflicts over water and its uses could be improved by doing more "listening to" rather than "speaking for" people at the fringe of nation-states—groups that are affected most by unfair water and development policies, especially ethnic communities and the poor. In response to these limitations, the region is beginning to teem with homespun media that provide a channel for minority voices to reach the public through regional distribution networks. Overall, however, it is still difficult for the interests of the poor and the environment to compete with the investments made in media messages by state authorities and private firms. These problems are shared for most development challenges, including those over water resources and management.

This chapter will first review the conditions under which the media operate before looking more specifically at how media cover issues of water governance in the Mekong region. This chapter will also review some of the unconventional mediums that are gaining popularity and effectiveness before finally considering various strategies to improve media conditions in the Mekong region in the face of daunting obstacles.

Prologue

The Mekong region is home to some of the most restricted media in the world. It is a milieu of monarchs, communist republics, parliamentary (semi) democracy, iron-fisted autocracy and military dictatorship, where governments, national armies and political parties control most of the region's airwaves, newspapers and cable lines. Newspersons and other dissenters operate under heavy surveillance and are commonly kept in line through intimidation, harassment, imprisonment, torture and death.

Press watchdogs have consigned the Mekong countries to the bottom of their annual press rankings. The Washington-based Freedom House, in its 2004 global press survey, ranked Myanmar [Burma] third from the bottom, tied with Turkmenistan and ahead of Cuba and North Korea. Vietnam, Lao PDR and China also scored near the bottom. Even Thailand, which once had one of the most progressive media in Asia, has taken a downturn, plunging from 59 in 2004 to 107 in 2005 in the yearly rankings for the most restricted media of the Paris-based Reporters Without Borders. Still, information manages to flow. Independent media offer at least some consumers alternatives to the official and semi-official news fare. Internet, radio, video disc and better transportation have helped news and information reach remote and poor audiences. Journalists and non-journalists alike expose corruption and government misdeeds, and by doing so, bring issues like land reform, resource management and pollution into the public domain. Environmental stories especially have been used as an instrument to discuss other issues such as governance and freedom. As Bach Tan Sinh, a Vietnamese environmental researcher puts it, Vietnamese reporters "feel comfortable discussing the environment" and they use their stories to "elegantly slip other issues in" (personal communication, January 2005).

Throughout the region there are reasons to be upbeat about the health of free and fair media. In China, with some two thousand newspapers, nine thousand magazines and two thousand television channels, only a handful are controlled by the government and communist party, while tolerance of dissent in the press and other public forums reached levels that were previously unimaginable. And prior to the recent military coup, Thailand's 1997 Constitution promised to turn its broadcasting frequencies into "national communication resources for public interest." Cambodia's press corps is notoriously feisty. For all the positive signs, however, the sad truth remains that in the line of duty journalists throughout the region still risk arrest by the police—often in the middle of the night—or assassination by a local thug.

Limits to free expression

In February 2003, Thai television and newspaper reporter Surapong Ritthi was killed by two bullets to the head at a convenience store in the heart of the resort island of Phuket. Santi Lamaneenil, owner of the *Pattaya Post*, was found dead in his car in November 2005, bound and blindfolded and shot several times in the back of the head. Both reporters had investigated local business scandals and illegal activities in the local gambling and entertainment industries and both had riled the local heavies. No suspects have been detained for either crime.

Cambodian reporters also pay with their lives sometimes. In October 2003, Chou Chetharith, a deputy editor at Radio Ta Pruhm, a station linked to the opposition royalist party, was gunned down by two men on a motorcycle as he was getting out of his car in front of the station's studio in the capital. A few days prior to the murder, Prime Minister Hun Sen, whose Cambodia's People Party and allies control several TV and radio stations, warned the royalist station that it should "control its programs better" (Reporters sans Frontier 2004 Annual Report, Cambodia).

More overt methods of intimidation are commonly used to keep journalists in line. In recent years numerous Cambodian journalists have been arbitrarily arrested on phony charges of inciting terrorism or of having illegal links to armed groups and then imprisoned unfairly.

The "world's largest prison for journalists," according to the New York-based Committee to Protect Journalists, is China, which has about twenty-five reporters and fifty cyber-dissidents behind bars. In Vietnam, Internet activist, Pham Hong Son, was sentenced to thirteen years in prison in 2003, after downloading an essay titled "What is Democracy" from the website of the United States (US) embassy in Hanoi and then distributing it to friends and government officials. He faces charges of spying and communicating with "political opportunists" at home and abroad.

There are less sinister methods to keep journalists in line too. In Laos, where the communist party and government control all print and broadcast media, journalists are essentially civil servants, and, as newspersons, are constitutionally bound to serve the party's polices and direction. Outright censorship is rare. Editors meet weekly with officials from the Ministry of Information and Culture to discuss the coverage of the past seven days and to decide what news will get covered in the upcoming week. A vague press law (ostensibly to intended to improve standards but used to tighten control) is only a couple of years old and has left reporters unclear on what boundaries they can cross without running into trouble.

In military-run Myanmar, the regime keeps a tight lid on dissent not only by arresting reporters but also through its peevish censors. The unfortunately-named Literary Works Scrutinizing Committee, which is managed by the home affairs ministry and monitored by intelligence forces, vets all material before publication. Since the military began ruling the country, the censorship board has screened everything from news articles, novels and poetry, to music, film scripts and artwork. Today, the board bans articles about human rights, environmental destruction, AIDS, and any other news that could cast the military regime in a negative light. Even the Motion Picture and Video Censor Board has gotten in on the act, ordering that movies cannot be shot on university campuses because of their association to the democracy movement. Popular movie stars with ties to the opposition movement are banned from the screen and their films are no longer available in stores. Pro-government writers and film directors, by contrast, receive financial assistance and privileges for their efforts.

Cash and regional media consolidation

The culture of censorship in the region is also fueled by a combination of limited cash and the consolidation of media outlets. The 1997 Southeast Asian economic meltdown felled many publishers in the region both large and small. In Thailand, the epicenter of the crisis, it is estimated that three thousand media jobs vanished as papers halved their staffs and expenses. Media outlets that survived now face increasing intimidation and economic pressure, in the forms of pulling advertising revenue, exorbitant lawsuits, or outright purchase of the offensive publication.

The former prime minister of Thailand, Thaksin Shinawatra, is widely accused of abusing his position to set the media agenda. His family maintained controlling interests in a vast communications empire ranging from mobile phones and newspapers to satellite broadcasting through the Shinawatra group of companies. As PM he also had direct authority over the state-owned TV stations. Families of other top politicians in his administration invested heavily in commercial media groups. Meanwhile, the Thai army, which along with the other armed forces once had a monopoly on the airwaves, controls two of the six TV stations and 120 or so of the 500 some radio stations. With bosses closely connected to the top echelons of power and with jobs scarce, self-censorship is rife. The few newspapers that have run afoul of the government have seen their advertising revenues dry up or have been sued for excessive sums of money.

The regional English-language media have been victimized by the global trend of media consolidation and dwindling advertising. Dow Jones's closure of its weekly *Far Eastern Economic Review* in late October 2004 cleared the competition for advertising revenues for the company's flagship publication, the *Asian Wall Street Journal* (AWSJ). It also signaled the end of the regional weekly format and to a touchstone of Asian news for the past six decades. A few years earlier, Time Warner folded its *Asiaweek* magazine, a rival of the *Time Asia* weekly, for similar reasons. Meanwhile, rumors persist of the impending closure of Time Asia and the AWSJ.

Finances also brought down the British Broadcasting Service (BBC) World Service's East Asia Today program, which aired for the last time in March 2004. It shut down so that resources could be diverted to the BBC's Arabic, Indonesian and Urdu services. The program's in-depth features and news reports on Southeast Asia were widely considered the best of any regular English-language broadcasts in the region.

Reaching your audience

Censorship is not the only obstacle to information flows. Access to news, particularly in print media, is another hindrance. In Laos, the combined daily print run of its three regular papers totals just over ten thousand. Most are distributed in the capital, and even there you have to know where to look to find one. Cambodia's best selling paper *Rasmei Kampuchea* (Light of Cambodia) has a daily circulation of about twenty thousand, about 70 percent of which is in the capital. The local press is further hampered by a shortage of trained reporters.

Internet also has limited reach. In the Mekong region, using the web is chiefly an urban pastime and is closely monitored by the authorities. Televisions are expensive and programming in much of the region is unimaginative. The four local TV stations in Laos, for instance, serve up the predictable fare of cultural performances and official meetings; so most viewers prefer to watch Thai television programs, which the Lao Information and Culture Ministry in May 2004 banned from being shown in public places. Lao Radio also must compete with foreign broadcasters. The fifteen provincial stations vie for listeners among Chinese and Vietnamese radio, as well as about ten Thai stations, which can be tuned in all over the country.

Access to international news has received a boost from cheap Chinese technology that has flooded the region, in the form of plastic radios, televisions and video disc players. Homespun efforts like Hmong Lao Radio, for example, airs news and propaganda from Minnesota back to the Lao hills via a transmitter in Uzbekistan. Region-wide, people already tune into nightly shortwave broadcasts from Radio Free Asia and the Voice of America, both based in Washington. The BBC broadcasts drama programs with health and education themes in Burmese and the languages of ethnic minorities from Myanmar. Major broadcasters—even as some scale back their programming in national languages, like BBC's closure of its Thai service—plan to ramp up their ethnic language programming. The Democratic Voice of Burma, a much smaller station, broadcasts daily news on Myanmar from Oslo in several local languages. Nongovernmental organizations (NGOs) in Chiang Mai, Manila and Kunming help Burmese ethnic nationalities relay shows in their native tongues back home, to refugee camps on the Thai-Myanmar border, and to inmates in Thai prisons. Typically ten- to fifteen-minute spots, a few days a week, the programs reach groups of people who struggle with Thai and Burmese languages and help some listeners get information on legal and health issues.

But the Thai government of the now deposed Thaksin Shinawatra took care not to damage relations with its counterparts in Rangoon and so, a few years ago, ordered Shan, Karen and other ethnic language radio producers in Thailand to the keep the hard news out and to cover only safer issues like health, drug-use prevention and forest conservation. Bangkok officials have also taken measures to exert control over the some 2000 recently established Thai community radio stations which serve Thais. The move to close or control community radio contravened the now defunct Thai Constitution which allowed for the creation of community-based radio stations to break the government and army monopoly over the national radio frequencies and to promote greater diversity of media ownership. Community radio is popular because it provides an important alternative to news and views presented by state-controlled media.

Radio remains a popular medium. Its appeal is that it is widely accessible and requires minimal personal investments of time, effort and cash to use and understand. Cheap Chinese batteries aren't too hard to find, and if they are, crank-powered radios could be introduced. Radio attracts a wide audience with combinations of entertainment programming, news and community bulletins and call-in shows. Some media training groups have already begun shifting their curricula away from print and toward broadcast journalism.

Challenges in water politics: Governance issues for the media

People whose livelihoods would be unfairly disrupted by the construction of big water-related infrastructure or by changes in water rights and access regimes are often those that are poor and at the fringe of the nation-state—peripheral either because of their remote locations or by their minority status within their own country (Hirsch and Warren 1998). The remote and poor, an audience to mainstream and alternative media alike, are difficult to reach owing to technological reasons and because of literacy, language, and cultural barriers. They pose the most difficult challenge for media when covering water politics.

As a source for journalists, the poor are usually accessed through NGO intermediaries and, ironically, the state's public relations strategists and private developers, to introduce the poor as "the other side" of the story. A common theme running through the dense file of stories on the Mekong River is that the marginalized are a naturally simple people, whose lives will be ruined by damage to fisheries, river flows or other resources; another is that this simple life and relationship with the environment will be enhanced by programs of NGOs, the state or private developers. The bulk of these stories are intended to justify more effort to conserve and protect natural resources, and by doing so, ostensibly arrive at a win-win solution for all.

Both types of story seemingly render this disaffected group as benign victims unable to grapple with the breakneck pace of modernization. It is a simplistic representation, given that rapid modernization has brought with it a history of colonization, dictatorship and war. Often overlooked is the complicated transformation of minority group politics that is unfolding in the Mekong basin as it becomes a geopolitical region. Whether the millions of people on the fringes of nation-states are satisfied with this representation is difficult to tell, as there has been scant effort to solicit their opinions.

In terms of functionality, a good story should help the audience understand the risks, benefits, and options to gauge what is best for their livelihoods. Media producers do that daily with the help of market research and by virtue of having similar socioeconomic backgrounds to their audience. However, it is tough to produce a story for someone with an entirely different worldview and dissimilar language from the producer. Tough because the stories about the disaffected are not likely to reach them, and feedback is never intended to be heard from them. With feedback loops being systematically absent, communicators who aim for strategic intervention to achieve their agenda of social change may find it a challenge to adjust their own performances to account for the responses and the needs of this audience—whether the needs are about economic decisions, natural resource use, political maneuvers, or empowerment.

Specific issues in accountability: Fostering (mis)understanding across borders

Generally speaking, neighbors are not news in the Mekong region. The media only have so much space, so that international reporters cover only a few of the world's conflicts and leave most others unreported (Hawkins 2000). Also, historical enmity and economic disparity fuel suspicions between people in neighboring Mekong countries and thus limit the prospect for cooperation across borders. Reporters, and especially editors, seldom "know" their subjects in their own country—who may hail from a different region or from a different economic class—and rarer still do they understand those from neighboring countries.

The Thai-language press, for example, publishes little news on Myanmar, but when it does the coverage is usually emotional and seldom flattering to the Burmese, who are widely associated with AIDS, illegal migration, refugees, murder, arrest, drugs. The stigmatization has made it difficult for Thais to sympathize with the plight of the Burmese. Burmese also have their own stereotypes of Thais, just as the Cambodians and Laotians have their own strong feelings towards Vietnamese. Stereotypes and suspicions of foreigners are deeply embedded throughout the region.

Under these conditions it can be expected that coverage of water politics, or any kind of regional politics in the mass media, would be nested in ignorance of the "other's" identity, ethnicity, and culture; it is much easier to play on established perceptions and ingrained feelings.

Left to the national media, coverage of the region's major issues is scant and usually framed by "national" interests. To serve those interests, news reporting is often unfair and usually fails to account for mutual interests across borders. Truly regional mediums hardly exist and the issues, either national or regional, are usually too small for, or beyond the reach of, international media. Chinese and Thai river traders who ply Mekong, for example, rely largely on their own networks of contacts extending along the river for news and information.

As the region is now integrating, greater effort is needed to address concerns that are shared across borders. Cross-country, cross-border and cross-basin irrigation schemes are also being conceived, meaning that the public in each country should have an increasing role in ensuring that their government officials or their energy companies act in the best interests of the well-being not only of their compatriots but also of citizens in neighboring countries—even though these schemes may generate valuable foreign exchange and energy for national governments.

Donor-driven media

To fill the news void, donor-driven broadcasters have tried to step in, but they are saddled with their own problems, especially limited funds. Donor-driven media (often called "independent" media) are an important source of stories that voice minority groups' views on politics, development and environmental issues. Sometimes, these stories are picked up by mainstream (advertising-driven) media; usually they are ignored entirely.

Still, donor-driven media fill a void in the region. As much of the mass media landscape is carefully groomed to suit governments and big business, donor publications and broadcasters generally serve audiences in search of alternative news. Many also provide space for aspiring younger journalists to learn the tools of the trade. The best of these media groups make a real impact on decision-making and on drawing a wider audience to pertinent issues in the Mekong region.

In Cambodia, for example, the Women's Media Center runs a popular low-power station in the capital, but doesn't have the funds to branch out into the countryside. More popular is Beehive Radio FM (*Sambok Khmum*), established in 1996 specifically to give Cambodians exposure to cultural ideas that were lost over decades of conflict. The station has been used to reunite thousands of Cambodian families who were separated after 1975 and has helped a few thousand find jobs. It has also encountered the usual problems with the authorities. Over the past few years the station has been shut down temporarily for inflammatory coverage of elections and for relaying international shortwave broadcasts. Another problem with Beehive is that it is largely funded from the pockets of its founder and with donations from charitable admirers. As such, its news scope is limited. A common complaint among Cambodians is that all stations broadcast the same news.

"Independent" (or alternative, or community, or grassroots, etc.) print publications are more numerous and diverse than radio, although they are similarly limited in their reach and funding. Dozens of periodicals of varying standards and credibility are published by Burmese and ethnic nationality exiles based in Thailand, often to serve a single ethnic group or political strategy. Elsewhere, magazines that focus on a specific topic, like health or environment, are common and have modest impact on people's lives. While many publications enjoy widespread popularity, they sometimes have difficulty adapting to the changing needs of their readers and the changing interests of their donors.

Thus, most donor-driven publications (whether they are independent, alternative, community, or grassroots) face the realization that the cash flow may one day dry up. Moreover, much of the existing independent media is aimed at lower-income consumers, who are either unable or unwilling to pay for their news. News journals and other publications funded by private donors have limited, if any, advertising, as local advertising markets are poor and small—and because of low literacy, limited distribution or range, and the lack of phone lines or electricity. Meanwhile, subscription revenues are not enough to finance operations. Without the capacity to generate their own incomes, such publications depend on the caprices of their funders and are thus not self-sustaining. They are sustainable only so long as they keep the favor of their donors.

Dammed if you do

If independent publications do stay afloat, the opinions that they are trying to push must vie with those of the state-approved news and the rigorous public relations offensives of private companies and multilateral institutions. The campaigns to sway public opinion in favor of mega-infrastructure development for water take different forms that are high-profile enough to attract the attention of the press.

The Nam Theun 2 Consortium, for example, that is building the 1,070 MW Nam Theun Dam in Laos, comprises a group of four partners: EDF International, a wholly owned subsidiary of Electricité de France; the Lao Holding State Enterprise, wholly owned by the Lao government: the state-run Electricity Generating Public Company of Thailand; and the private-sector Italian-Thai Development Public Company of Thailand. The consortium has an extensive and user-friendly website, on which curious browsers can access pages of press releases, photo galleries, papers about the Mekong River and watershed issues, as well as FAQs and links to other sites—all of which paint their project in positive hues.

The Asian Development Bank (ADB) provides another example of a well-coordinated and well-financed public relations offensive. The ADB staged a three-day water conference for journalists in Chiang Mai in 2003 to present its perspective on hydropower development. However, the ADB's opponents took the opportunity to stage a parallel conference at the same time. Both events were covered by the local English and Thai-language press.

Generally speaking, water issues (particularly on infrastructure building that involve big construction companies in the developed countries and international NGOs) are fairly well covered, at least in the English-language and international media. Type "Mekong" and "water" into a search engine and thousands of articles appear—environmental features, business and finance stories, construction and energy reports. Many give a platform to local voices; others, like those that run in the business page, usually don't. Local mainstream media, on the other hand, tend to ignore opposing perspectives, either out of negligence or of fear of reprimand from local heavies.

There are important questions to be asked about how independent media can empower the poor and the weak, particularly when livelihoods are at stake. The simple aim of alternative media is to provide that voice. More troublesome, however, is how "to represent" the poor and the weak.

Are they pitted against monolithic state forces in a battle over resource use, as unified peasants trying to protect their traditional way of life? Are the poor represented by the press as prehistoric savages whose knowledge systems will no longer suffice in the modern age and who can only be saved by the graces of foreign aid? Will the press act as a transmitter of news, an interpreter of it, or as an active participant?

The Chiang Mai-based Shan Herald Agency for News, or S.H.A.N., is in some ways all three. Closely associated with the insurgent Shan State Army, which is fighting for greater autonomy from the ruling military junta in Yangon (Rangoon), the news agency puts a pro-Shan/anti-junta spin on much of its content. Nevertheless, its exclusive reporting on events in the Shan state in Myanmar is an indispensable source of news for Shan and for others who take an interest in Shan and Burmese issues. More common, however, are less traditional, less newsy, media, which use the technology at hand to get a message across.

Creative solutions

Efforts at advancing media in the Mekong region so far have been limited in scope and impact, but they have planted seeds for media's further growth. Advances in communication technology like satellite and wireless devices could aid more progress in opening access to news to reporters and in secretive regimes. More likely, however, existing cruder forms of technology, like radio, word of mouth, and even film and music, seem best suited to the region's needs. Creative uses of these mediums so far have brought surprising results.

Burmese are famous for using non-written forms like cartoons to make veiled statements about their junta. And lately, music is becoming a popular medium for sedition. An overseas Burmese online rap group that calls itself Myanmar Future Generation is making strong political commentary with its music, sampling speeches from independence leader Aung San or from the 1988 anti-junta demonstrations played over apocalyptic hip-hop beats. The music is spreading through Rangoon's underground via illegal downloads from MFG's website—a triumph considering that Internet only reaches an estimated 0.02 percent of people in Myanmar—and by smuggled CDs from abroad. It has limited appeal so far, but enough to move the authorities to ban their music.

NGOs have had some success with other unconventional methods. To promote health awareness, Public Services International targets vulnerable populations with a combination of TV, radio and print but also with personal consultation, appearances at special events like beauty pageants and performances at nightclubs. Other novel approaches by PSI in Laos and Myanmar include placing TVs which air reproductive health news at bus stations, and a mobile video unit that brings multimedia and live programming to buses and boats. Sometimes PSI health educators ride intercity buses, where they perform songs, skits, and comedy routines that help educate passengers about HIV prevention and condom use. Some bring battery-powered video equipment to remote villages. But even PSI officials admit that their success in combating the HIV/AIDS problem in Myanmar has been limited.

The "mic" is mightier than the sword

A Shan singer recently teamed up with a Chinese entrepreneur in northern Thailand to produce a hit karaoke album. The songs and videos are not overtly political, but mostly aim to comfort the audience—much of which lives and works abroad in the Mekong region—that Shan music and culture still exist. On the video, as the sun sets over the river, he sings of leaving home to perform his duty (work or war). It's a romantic and nostalgic ballad of sorts that helps reassert Shan identity through the music, lyrics and images. Produced on a shoestring budget, the album earned the singer more than USD 1,000 (pirated copies notwithstanding). It is considered a major success for a vocalist who sings in the Shan language.

Amid the flood of media dominated by Thai, Chinese and Burmese (and indeed English) languages, the mere production of the karaoke CD in Shan empowers ethnic Shan. The accompanying images of home, particularly the recurring theme of free-flowing water (ethnic minorities are not likely to control a large dam project on any river in the Mekong region) provide symbolic links to their motherland. Thus, karaoke in ethnic languages is so far really the only medium that is widely available through commercial channels and widely consumed, and which reinforces ethnic identity.

Other Shan vocalists sing more explicitly nationalist songs and chant down the military system over footage, both real and re-enacted, of battles between the insurgents and the Burmese army. At Shan temple fairs, the young and middle-aged alike swarm around the TVs at stalls selling karaoke discs. Onlookers cheer the images of shoulder-launched rockets being fired, of Shan leaders commanding their troops in the field, and of dead Burmese soldiers. These discs are produced in Thailand by the political wing of the Shan State Army and are certainly biased. But they are distributed widely among Shan in northern Thailand and then carried inside Shan in Myanmar by returning migrant workers and others.

Karaoke has connected people across borders and strengthened political alliances among the Shan. The same is true also for other ethnic groups that have limited access to other media.

The Mon, an ethnic group that largely resides in Myanmar and near the border with Thailand, are undertaking similar efforts. The Mon Literature and Culture Association in February released its second karaoke CD of classical songs about Mon kings and traditions in a bid to strengthen the sense of Mon identity (www.kaowao.org, January 26, 2005).

Reinforcing ethnic identity

Reinforcing ethnic identity and uniting groups across borders is important for the members of that group, but it is also important because it elevates the visibility of that group. And people are more likely to care about those with a culture that they have seen and know something about.

The Ta Sarng Dam, for example, in the eastern part of Shan in Myanmar, is not far from Chiang Mai, the second largest city in Thailand and a major regional communications center. Since 1997, Thai power companies have explored plans to dam the Salween River, one stretch of which separates the two countries. The dam would generate at least 3,300 MW of electricity and cost more than USD three billion. Type "Ta Sarng" into an Internet search engine and hundreds of matches will show. Ask human rights and environmental groups and they'll tell you that the dam will displace hundreds of thousands of people, damage the environment and lead to the further militarization of nearby areas in Myanmar. Yet ask a Thai businessman in Chiang Mai for his opinion on the matter and he might answer, "I heard of Shan state once from a soap opera on Channel 7." No matter that his housemaid is an ethnic Shan woman from Shan state (personal communication, Chiang Mai, January 2005).

The Shan comprise roughly 10 percent of the population of 50 million of Myanmar and hundreds of thousands more live in Thailand, especially the north. Thais and Shan share common religion and border and related languages. But for most Thais, the Shan—and indeed, all people from Myanmar—are a fictional people from a fictional land. Thai homes and factories employ nearly one million workers from Myanmar but for the Thai public, the political dramas and human tragedies in that country are the stuff of television, or of disconnected news bits in the media which are randomly presented as otherworldly, "out there" events which can disappear with the turn of a page or dial (Spurr 1993). Because it will be built outside Thailand's borders, the Ta Sarng dam is not really news inside Thailand, except in the business pages.

But neither is it news in Myanmar, where the military junta tightly controls the media. Hydropower projects, irrigation works and other incidents that occur in the vicinity of water are deemed matters of national security and nation-building. In 2004, maverick filmmakers were imprisoned for taking footage of flood devastation in the north. Coverage of these sensitive matters is the preserve of the junta's official mouthpieces.

The state-run press, however, barely mentions such news. When the military junta agreed to open the Mekong River to bigger cargo ships by blasting the rapids and reefs in the upper reaches that separates the country from Laos, the ethnic Shan and Lahu living along the river only learned of the scheme when they heard the first explosions in March 2002. In preparation for increased river trade with China, Myanmar has beefed up its military presence along the river's west bank in recent years and in some cases relocated villages away from the blasting sites (LNDO 2003). But the media coverage of the events was scant.

The construction projects on the rivers in Shan state are externally imposed (Burman, Chinese, Thai), and as such, they represent the disempowerment of the Shan people and the loss of their homes. The Burmese military and Thai media might report the projects as national development but the millions of Shan people at home and in exile may claim these resources as their own and may want a say at the table to determine how they are governed—which often goes unreported in the mainstream press. This is true of people and water governance region-wide. For the Shan, rather than trying to voice their concerns amid the din of junta or big business opinion (which is amply covered) in the mainstream media, a better solution is to produce their own media solutions.

Take advantage of existing media: More producers and consumers

One effective strategy would be to create more media producers and consumers in dominant and minority languages, in the hills and lowlands. On one level, it would help perpetuate diverse languages and cultures. It would also generate interest and participation. Vast numbers of publications already serve some of these needs—ethnic language, political, environmental publications. The more promising ones could be incorporated into future programs to make them more effective.

Other mediums, however, may promise more immediate returns. Radio, for example, is cheap, accessible, and easy to use and understand. Crank radios solve the problem of limited electricity distribution or access to batteries. They can be operated on the spot or from remote locations. Exiles have access through Internet. Karaoke is a favorite pastime, thanks largely to cheap technology. Chinese video players and (usually pirated) video discs flood the region. Music videos are typically love songs or tunes about life on the farm and are available in ethnic languages. But just by having access to media in a minority language is empowering.

Networks of local people that use the simplest medium, word-of-mouth, are also effective. Events such as plays, concerts, parties and other gatherings seem the best method so far for environmental groups, ethnic insurgents or others for using local people to gather and disseminate news, photos, maps and medicine. Since local knowledge seems to serve these purposes best, donors should keep an open mind, a flexible agenda and trust.

A network of activists opposed to the Salween dam plans have met in Thailand regularly in recent years. However, comprising several different ethnic groups—Shan, Karen, Thais, Europeans, Japanese, others—and several different ideas of how the meetings should proceed, the group's work has been hampered by disagreements.

As for the mainstream mass media, Cambodia is also instructive for what can happen when a fledgling free press operated unfettered by regulations or professional ethics. Over the past decade or so, local newspapers, though expensive and reaching only a fraction of Cambodia's 12 million people, have blossomed and gained large numbers of readers in the countryside. Television is as popular as ever. A private FM news station has drawn a huge following in Phnom Penh and shortwave radio broadcasts bring local and international news to Cambodian farmers who tune into cheap Chinese-made receivers.

Many of the stations they listen to and the papers they read are owned by political parties and NGOs. And with so many competing voices and agendas on the market it is inevitable that much of the news is unbalanced or poorly written (frequently by hand), often by journalists who accept cash and gifts from their sources, unaware of their ethical transgressions. The media mayhem reached such heights in recent years that top information official Khieu Khanarith once famously quipped: "We have always said we have the freest press in the world, because everyone here has the right to make up reports out of thin air" (RSF 2004 Annual Report, Cambodia).

Box 7.1 Challenges for media development

Any projects to build on this must consider several questions:

Who will define the scope of news coverage? Locals, donors?

What is important, the medium or the message? To enable a counter-discourse or to enable multi-stakeholder platforms? To counter the discourse of big-infrastructure energy development with alternative development paradigms? To produce more papers and media trainings?

When developing the media, what units should be developed? Province, village, district? And how to determine the boundaries? Multiple, overlapping networks or isolated projects?

How do you share the risk of reporting?

How to sell these ideas to governments and legitimize media projects? Covering health and environment stories in political settings is good. Better yet, convince authorities that communication is good for business.

How can alternative media sources stand out? How can they make themselves heard, read or watched?

**Box 7.2 The greening of China's media
by Kevin Yuk-shing Li**

Much has been made of the recent "greening" of China's media. For most of the past fifty-five years of Communist rule, the state-run press has been little more than a mouthpiece of the Communist Party and state. But as China's industrialization gathers speed, so too do concerns about resulting environmental problems. And in the past decade or so, the authorities have allowed some public discussions of those concerns in the media.

Much of the opening has been driven by the commercialization of the media (without some degree of transparency, how can foreigners confidently invest their money?) but also by environmental NGOs and other elements of China's civil society. And through the media, they have taken the lead in exposing the environmental fallout resulting from China's industrial growth policies. Many of these activists, in fact, also work as reporters.

They have raised public awareness about the disasters resulting from massive dam projects and other infrastructure construction, as well as biodiversity protection and urban renewal. Initially, Beijing viewed environment issues as apolitical, safe for public discussion and unrelated to human rights and other sensitive matters. But the more that environmentalists and news reporters push, the more the state, or elements of the state, fight back.

In the 1990s, the government allowed international NGOs and foundations such as Worldwide Fund For Nature (WWF), to set up offices in China. And when the "new generation" Hu Jintao took over the Party in 2002 and became president the following year, analysts agreed that he tried to give consideration to the plight of common people and would put people first (*yi ren wei ben*).

In the summer of 2003, journalists reported that a dam project in Sichuan Province threatened to flood the 2,200 year-old Dujiangyan irrigation scheme, which was designated a UNESCO World Heritage site in 2003. The reports were published in a number of state-owned and non-state-owned newspapers and magazines including *China Youth Daily* and *Southern Weekend*. Web portals like sina.com and 163.com reprinted the story and then many other newspapers, web sites and online forums all over the country did too. A few months later the project was cancelled.

Other infrastructure projects such as the ADB's Greater Mekong Sub-region (GMS) project, hydropower development and damming the Lancang (Mekong) River, have also been reported by local, grassroots media, which have then been picked up by mainstream media outlets such as CCTV, Xinhua news agency, and other magazines. But developers and authorities presented these stories to the public, through the media, as a major step toward eliminating poverty by increasing revenue for local government. The projects are presented as crucial nodes in expanding China's trade, tourism and overall economic progress, while the potential social and environmental toll is ignored.

As more and more academics and activists speak out, authorities crack down, Internet "police" close websites, which then open up again later only to close down again. Academics may get away with more than independent critics, but they still lose their jobs if they push too far. NGOS are threatened with the removal of their registration status, and journalists face heavy censorship. Urban-based environmentalists are accused by authorities and developers as being indifferent to poverty.

The degree of media freedom in China in regards to environmental reporting ebbs and flows. Part of the opening can be attributed to the close relationship between environmentalists and reporters. But for the time being, state officials have awoken to the sensitivity and inter-connectivity of environmental issues. They also value social stability and economic growth above displacement, pollution and the other undesirable side-effects of dam construction and mega-infrastructure projects. And that's bad news for China's environmentalists, local and downstream communities.

Conclusion

Throughout the Mekong region, there has been a gradual opening of the airwaves and newspapers to multiple voices and viewpoints, particularly regarding environmental issues. Sadly, however, discouraging setbacks typically have followed promising signs of greater media freedom like the Chinese activists cum journalists who raised social and environmental questions with their coverage of big-ticket infrastructure projects. It seems the harder that journalists push, the more that rulers clamp down by arresting journalists or shutting feisty publications. State controls, strict censorship and thuggery still haunt the media throughout most of the region.

There are also problems of media consolidation, which in recent years has slashed the number of radio programs and news journals that serve the Mekong region. Deep-seated stereotypes still inhibit impartial coverage of transborder issues, like dam construction and other water diversion schemes. Even national news is beset by a similar degree of ignorance—as in the Pak Mun Dam controversy in Thailand, where reporters covered the news as a made-for-TV event of local protestors versus the state rather than as a prolonged struggle over resources and livelihoods. There are also problems of limited access, of untrained reporters and ignorance or disregard for people living on the other side of borders.

This chapter has briefly reviewed these difficulties facing the media in the Mekong region and also has presented some of the ways people have responded to these problems. Foreign-based broadcasting and publishing have provided one antidote to the state-controlled media. Whether big international news services like the BBC or smaller donor-driven efforts like the Democratic Voice of Burma and NGO publications, however, these services share similar downsides such as limited resources, specialized audiences, and constant struggles against massive state and corporate media offensives. Nonetheless, such media provide indispensable sources of news to the region.

This chapter has also argued that the solution for a freer and fairer media in the Mekong region may not lie in providing more of the same conventional mediums of newspapers, television, radio or Internet. Unconventional, less newsy, types of media have been quite effective in conveying messages and providing alternatives to information that comes from outside. Music recordings, karaoke albums and traditional word-of-mouth networks have all brought surprising results in informing and empowering people and reinforcing ethnic identity, particularly in Myanmar. Any efforts to democratize or open the media in the Mekong region must take account of these more recent homespun efforts that have flourished in recent years, thanks to cheap technology and greater integration within and among the Mekong countries.

As the region grows closer together through increased linkages and dependencies because of water development schemes and other transboundary infrastructure projects, people living on opposite sides of the border will begin to have more in common. Perhaps these shared concerns and experiences with water development could spur a greater effort towards a more inclusive and fairer media that will not only serve state-led national development agendas but also a wider range of interests that include the poor, remote and downstream communities.

Box 7.3 Pak Mun Dam

Located on the Mun River, the largest tributary of the Mekong River in Thailand, the Pak Mun Dam was built by the Electricity Generating Authority of Thailand (EGAT) and funded by the World Bank. Construction on the USD 24 million, 136 MW dam began in 1991 and was completed in 1994. In the process of building the dam, more than two hundred households were displaced; crucially, the dam destroyed riverine ecosystems and obstructed fish migrations leading to the loss of thousands of fisheries-based livelihoods. The Pak Mun Dam sparked vigorous protests and critical reaction from local village communities living along the Mun River. Most particularly, the villagers pointed to the fact that damming the Mun drastically reduced fish catches in the river by as much as 70 percent, despite the construction of a fish ladder at the request of the World Bank's fisheries experts. The dam wall effectively blocked many fish species that had once migrated up and down the river. In a remarkable victory for local political action, the Thai government in June 2001 gave in to continuing local protests and agreed to open the dam's gates. But the gates are allowed only open four months of the year, and local people assert that this is not sufficient for fish migrations and to regenerate the area's fisheries.

The story became most intensely covered just before the 2001 elections in Thailand, and during a time when debate raged about the proposed privatization of EGAT. The stories were allegedly "planted" in the press to discredit then Prime Minister Chuan Leekpai's administration, which was widely criticized for ignoring the demands of the Pak Mun protestors.

After the defeat of the Chuan administration in the elections, the Pak Mun Dam stories faded. The stories that did get published revolved mostly around issues of land compensation for displaced villagers and the failure to open the dam's gates.

The stories also failed to speak to the idea that Pak Mun is a controversial issue for the EGAT union (by closing the dam, EGAT would be forced to shed workers), as it faced pressure under EGAT's push to privatize and list on the Stock Exchange of Thailand.

Most reports also failed to address issues of potential "over-fishing" of the Mun River by locals as the area's fishery authorities had expressed "official" concern over this issue. It is possible reporters are influenced by timeliness, proximity, and human interest; over-fishing lacks the drama of state versus local conflict.

The television networks also were influenced by the availability of dramatic visual images and by geographical factors such as cost and convenience (Greenberg et al. 1989). Rather than report about issues of livelihood, conservation, health, the science or the aesthetics of dams, most local Thai television reporters covered the story as an event, comprising protests and protestors.

CHAPTER 8

GENDER MYTHS IN WATER GOVERNANCE: A SURVEY OF PROGRAM DISCOURSES

Bernadette Resurreccion and Kanokwan Manorom

Since the early 1990s, the consensus on water as a vital resource has been premised on the holistic view that its management should combine economic, social and environmental considerations as well as recognizing its multiple uses. Moreover, the consensus asserted greater involvement of direct users in the management of water resources through participatory approaches that recognized the central role of women. Official rhetoric at International Conference on Water and the Environment in Dublin in 1992 stated that "Women play a central part in the provision, management and safeguarding of water."[1] More than a decade down the line, donor-driven state and non-state water infrastructure and management programs have increasingly integrated both participatory and gender-responsive elements into their program designs and implementation (Cleaver 2003, Prokopy 2004, Singh et al. 2003) Additionally, sector-specific approaches were abandoned for more integrative approaches usually under the general rubric of "integrated water resource management" or in the case of riparian regions, "river basin development," such as the river basin development projects supported by the Asian Development Bank (ADB) in Thailand and in the Second Red River Basin Sector Project in Vietnam implemented by the Ministry of Agriculture and Rural Development (MARD).

The Mekong region has undergone decisive social, economic and political changes in the last twenty years. Over time, problems related to the use and management of water, infrastructure and existing river networks have called for greater collaboration among governments for concerted action. Originally envisaged to serve the infrastructural requirements of maintaining the Mekong River, the Mekong River

Commission (MRC), serves as a case in point where increasing attention is being given to social and geopolitical issues as well as to capacity-building in public participation. Multilateral organizations such as the ADB and the Food and Agricultural Organization (FAO), for their part, have emphasized gender-responsiveness in their lending programs and technical assistance packages.[2] The foregoing consensus by planners on women's important role as primary managers of water resources because of their "natural interest" or their involvement in the domestic care of their households continues to underpin much of the emerging programs on decentralized water management in this region. This often implicit assumption of multilateral and national planners about women's proximity to natural resources traces its origins to various approaches developed as early as the late 1980s, and which over the last two decades, have come to pervade water resource management programs in the Mekong region. A summary of the intellectual origins underpinning women's role and relationship with the natural environment is as follows.

Women, water and participation

A. Common property resources approach and local institutions

In natural resource management in general, the creation of local institutions is considered to be crucial in ensuring sustainability of the use of resources, economic production and to some degree, empowerment of communities. These ideas draw from literature on the Common Property Resources (CPR) approach that views local people and governments as being able to successfully manage common property resources through the creation of local institutions and rule-making. Development interventions, in this regard, aims to craft formalized community structures for purposive agendas (Ostrom 1990). As a result of this policy approach, in the last two decades, we have seen a proliferation of water user associations, water user groups, community fisheries, village user associations, community forestry groups, village development councils and other similar nomenclature in the development and natural resource management horizon. The main intent is to institutionalize cooperative and collective interactions among stakeholders for management of a common property resource, usually land or water.

Desirable results from the formation of such institutions at the local level, for example, include a clearly defined group and its boundaries, a system of sanctions and rules imposed on those who violate publicly designed regulations and an array of conflict resolution mechanisms (Ostrom 1990). There is also an emphasis on participation in institutions through democratic representation and the election of representatives.

Critique leveled at this approach points out its lack of attention to the complexity in local social relationships and practices that actually characterize and shape resource management situations and which formal institutional rules may often overlook. Second, the CPR approach also tends to gloss over the fact that fuzzy boundaries define informal and formal institutions and that natural resources are often managed in ways blurring such boundaries. And third, institutions are often viewed as static and ahistorical, instead of being rooted in people's actual and even ad hoc practices that shift or continue according to the ebb and flow of circumstances under which they live, and that do not necessarily conform to project rules and activities (Mehta et al. 1999, Cleaver 1999, Mosse 1997).

B. CPR and participation

Current emphasis on participation in natural resources management has combined with the CPR approach, incorporating the need for women to be part of local institutions in environmental governance.

"Women-and-environment approaches,"[3] meanwhile, were part of the discussions on sustainable development that peaked in the early 1990s and as a result, influenced much of the environment-related projects since then. Women's participation and involvement in natural resource management institutions continue to be regarded as pivotal to the sustainable use and management of resources partly due, on one hand, to assumptions of women's interconnectedness with nature, and additionally, on efficiency-driven arguments on the other.[4] Women are viewed as major stakeholders and therefore are often mobilized to participate in institutions created by such programs such as water user groups, community fisheries or village associations.

Current thinking, however, has been critical of the assumption that women's participation in these institutions is straightforward, unproblematic and will translate fully into empowering benefits for women. The work of Bina Agarwal (1997, 2001) on community-based natural resource management in South Asia, for instance, exemplifies this point in her discussion of women's experiences of participation, where they are involved yet simultaneously excluded due to traditional practices and established norms of gendered exclusion, formal rules of membership, social perceptions regarding women's ability to contribute to user groups and their household endowments. Interestingly, she refers to women's experiences in resource user groups as "participatory exclusions."

Just at the turn of the new millennium, scholars like Agarwal continue to unpack the problematic nature of including women in environmental programs, taking their arguments and research beyond the normative of gender-responsiveness in development programs today. This inclusion of women, they maintain, has been largely a result of the plethora of gender toolkits that tend to oversimplify and ignore women's *social worlds* of uneven power relations (Locke 1999, Cleaver 2003). Recent research has called attention to the absence or lack of understanding of the social and political conditions under which the women compelled to participate in these programs, often live. The outcome is reproducing gender stereotypes and perpetuating former gender myths about the nature of women's role in natural resource management. Cleaver (2003, 3) illustrates this further through a caricature on women's emerging responsibilities in water resource management programs:

> A prototype rural woman water user is "traditionally" responsible for fetching domestic water for her family should also become involved in planning and decision making about the management of integrated water resources, raising funds and contributing other resources for the construction of new supplies. Through membership in water user associations and groups, she should play a part in the maintenance of water supply infrastructure and in regulating the distribution of water. As a consumer she is empowered to exert sufficient pressure to demand a good service from water suppliers. Poverty targets are achieved through efficiencies achieved in the management and distribution of irrigation water which enable her to increase productive output; a possibility enhanced by the release of her time through the supply of improved domestic water supplies closer to home. Building on her productive roles this woman also assumes primary responsibility for financing and constructing household latrines and ensuring that the family will adopt safe water-related hygiene practices....

If women's real life situations are not addressed, women's involvement in water resource management may in fact add to their already long list of caretaking roles (Leach 1992). Further, this caricature associates women with economic productivity and efficiency without clearly addressing the benefits their involvement implies as well as the complexity of their livelihood problems and situations. In a related article for instance, Jackson (1998) shows how women from various contexts, by exercising their agency, deliberately evade participation in water resources management since for them, it means more work and paying more fees. In fact, they employ the discourse of "being women from poor households" to justify their non-involvement.

C. CPR and "efficiency"

Apart from the CPR approach that calls for the creation of local institutions that will manage resources, another argument that underpins policies of decentralization calls for greater efficiency. This aims at reducing central state aims for reducing central state authority in order to transfer costs, resource management, productivity and conservation responsibilities to local users to relieve the state of burdensome costs, at the same time bureaucratizing local communities into the orbit of greater state control and accountability (Mosse 2001, Gauld 2000). Institution-building, public participation and community-based programs are therefore the currency. Many, if not all, of these programs express the importance of women's participation in varying degrees.

The World Bank, for example, is a proponent of women's participation for efficiency ends: "Women who are trained to manage and maintain community water systems often perform better than men because they are less likely to migrate, more accustomed to voluntary work, and better entrusted to administer funds honestly" (World Bank 1992, 113). Investing in women has been critically described as instrumentalist by scholars, noting how women have been taken on board insofar as they could contribute to development and conservation objectives, yet sidestepping deliberate advances towards achieving gender equality or transforming existing gender/power structures (Jackson 2000, Cleaver 2003).[5]

The three approaches discussed above based on CPR and calling for greater institution building, women's participation and efficiency may therefore be: (a) be blind to the gendered nature of local and complex social dynamics and conditions in resource allocation and management and thereby result in gender-specific exclusions; and/or (b) instrumentally place more pressure on women to add resource management (or poverty alleviation) to their current workloads. These gender dimensions, however, must first be understood against the complex template of rules, roles and rights that define people's practices in using and managing water resources.

The foregoing arguments, however, do *not* call for the non-involvement of women in water governance programs. Instead, the authors advocate for women's greater and more meaningful participation in such initiatives provided that they are fully aware of the benefits of their involvement and are able to define the terms of their participation independently. Planners must rely less on the normative of participation and attune themselves more to the actual practices of women and men in water management, including the actual power relations that define such practices and result in uneven access and control of resources. Experiences of political struggle against state and corporate encroachments on women's rights to use water resources in parts of the Mekong region have demonstrated that women often take up many acts, both overt and less overt, of resistance and struggle to protect their sources of livelihoods once food security is at risk. While women's overt resistance often captures public attention, covert actions are usually downplayed, overlooking multiple and interconnected sites of struggle (Hart 1991). In this chapter, incursions into some experiences of struggle of women in parts of the Mekong region also demonstrate that women's environmental actions arise in connection with their defense of the family and community, most often for reasons of livelihood security, health and safety, as well as a sense of place. This underscores the fact that issues pertaining to common environmental resources such as water are inherently political, and decisions about the environment are not politically neutral. Depending on their stakes and their social locations, women may deem it important to engage in political struggles around water resources. However, this cannot be always assumed, *a priori*. Local power relations may constrain women's involvement and harnessing their presence for community participation will in turn reproduce the inequalities caused by these power relations—instead of transforming them.

Having discussed the key debates and approaches in gender, water and participation, we now turn to water governance programs in the Mekong region: water resource development, irrigation development and management, and community fisheries in Cambodia. Though we limit ourselves to a cursory examination of program discourses, these programs will be discussed to exemplify the foregoing conceptual points, thus offering critical perspectives to the increasing emphasis on women's participation in water governance.

Water resource development

This following section looks at various state and non-state water resource development projects in Thailand, Vietnam and Cambodia that have attempted to integrate the participation and involvement of women.

Thailand

In Thailand, the ADB's Technical Assistance (TA) Number 3260 is titled "Capacity Building in the Water Resources Sector." The objective of TA 3260 is to assist the Thai government in developing a unified water management system that will strengthen integrated water resources management and improve water service delivery in irrigation. Public participation has been envisaged as the cornerstone of ADB's country water sector strategies where institutional arrangements at the community level, will be strengthened. The creation of local institutions at the local level—river basin committees—has been the core strategy to achieve the objective of public participation and decentralization of water resource management, including the costs of privatizing water resources. A recent study on the Ping River basin in northern Thailand implementing TA 3260 (Resurreccion, Real, Pantana 2004) has shown that costs of privatizing water resources will be shouldered by farm households who were members of the river basin committees. Current practices show that it will probably be women's non-farm labor that will generate disposable household incomes to cover the privatization costs, largely by their trade in local markets. However, river basin committees are building on traditional water and irrigation committees that are male dominated, thus sidestepping women as stakeholders in water resource management. This is one example of gender-blind planning, where women's work and resources are being harnessed informally for covering the costs entailed in formal (male) membership in a water association such as the river basin committees.

However, in the Pa Sak River Basin Development Project, unlike the RBCs in northern Thailand, explicit attempts have been made to incorporate women in resettlement efforts. The main objective of the project is to improve agricultural production in the northeastern plains of Lop Buri and Saraburi provinces by managing the Pa Sak River through the construction of Thailand's largest earth-filled dam. As a result, villagers were relocated and subsequently, other livelihoods were created such as commercial fishing and intensive farming since rice land was no longer available for all those displaced by the dam's construction. Part of the resettlement scheme was to assist women "who formerly stayed home" by teaching them new home economics skills and learn how to do engage in cottage industries.[6]

Vietnam

Similarly, in Vietnam, the Second Red River Basin Sector Project implemented by the Ministry of Agriculture and Rural Development (MARD) from an ADB loan was designed as an integrated water resource management intervention in the Red River basin. The Red River Basin Organization (RRBO) was created in 2001 with an inter-ministerial Red River Basin Council responsible for approving the water sector action plan for the river basin. The chief task of the RRBO is planning investments for natural resource management including land, water and forest and coordinating water services delivery for agriculture, industry and domestic uses. It was created in order to ensure beneficiary participation in operation and management activities in the irrigation and drainage system. The project professes an explicit gender dimension and aims to ensure that poverty among rural women is reduced through income-generating opportunities, and that women's representation in decision-making for water management is increased. Women farmers are therefore expected to be dominant as project beneficiaries. The project will also promote stakeholder participation at local and basin levels, with an emphasis on women's participation.[7]

Social assessments have shown that village men out-migrate, that women and children have needs for safe water, that women are involved in periodic irrigation maintenance as pump operators and that they need credit to start income-generating enterprises. In response, the project aims to increase women's roles in water resources management, health and hygiene management and ensure that they make at least 40 percent of the membership of the Red River Basin Organization.

Discussion

Both the Thai cases show that creating institutions at the local level may inadvertently reproduce existing social and gender inequalities. In the case of the Pa Sak River Basin Development Project, it appears that the understanding of women's participation in livelihoods is confined to their roles in social reproduction. The assumption is that the project has managed to draw them away from being housewives into being cottage industry entrepreneurs especially during a period of displacement and resettlement when farm resources and incomes had fallen. Women are therefore viewed by the project as fallback and supplementary labor and whose skills reside and are being developed largely within female-ascribed enterprises such as influenced by home economics. Yet this change in women is being defined as being no longer content to sit by and that women are participating in setting up their new villages. The assumptions in this project are problematic in the first place: in real practice, women do not just sit by as they are probably involved in numerous productive tasks (formerly) in rice farming and in the domestic care of children and the elderly, food preparation and perhaps even petty trade as are most women in Southeast Asia. Similarly, in the Ping River project, overlooking sources of income in rural households assumes that there is only one income earner, usually male, and this entitles him to be household's representative to the RBC. Both projects therefore implicitly assume that women are housewives.

Just as in Thailand's Pa Sak River Basin Development project, Vietnam's Second Red River Basin Sector Project views women as bearing a disproportionate share of poverty. As men out-migrate, women are left behind to tend to farms. It is unclear whether decision-making power is actually exercised by women since much of the studies on male out-migration show that women usually only act as guardians of farmlands and production for their husbands but cannot really make decisive resource investments (Palmer 1985, Francis 1999, Hampshire 1999). In this project, poverty goals are addressed at the expense of gender equality goals—or inadequately addressing the low status of women in resource management in the first place. In reality, women are poorer and powerless mainly due to the local gender hierarchies and the assignment of gender-specific tasks that they perform in the face of resource scarcity. They thus shoulder a disproportionate share of the burdens of poverty compared with men. This assignment of gender-specific tasks is often not addressed by planners, who instead put in place income-generating programs for women that may add to their long list of responsibilities and may overlook their weak capacity for loan repayments and production investments.

However, under politically charged conditions of dispute over decreasing natural resources, women may become active in contesting resources and making demands on the state for action meeting their welfare needs.

Decreasing resources or resources under threat may open up a wider political space for women. For example, women have actively been involved in the opposition to government plans for dam construction in river basins—but are constrained by a number of factors, as will be discussed below.

Thailand

Gender relations have somewhat changed since women's access and control of river resources have been undermined after the Pak Mun and Rasi Salai dams were constructed in the northeast region of Thailand. The study by Ubon Ratchathani University scholars (2002) found that women worked both inside and outside their homes as fishers, farmers, fish traders and household caretakers. After the dams were built, women actively participated in the political negotiation over river management alongside male activists. The studies done by Kotavinon (2000) and Manorom (1999) have shown that women have persistently called the state's attention to declining levels of household food security as an outcome of deteriorating river resources caused by the dam's construction. In turn, women's self-confidence acquired through a training process provided by local NGOs strengthened their participation in the river basin management and negotiation. This also coincides with a decisive shift to the discourse of public participation pervading much of recent sustainable development programs, both national and international.

Cambodia

In terms of transboundary impacts within the catchment areas, the Yali Falls Dam located 80 kilometers upstream of the Se San River, with its headwaters in Gai Lai and Kon Tum provinces in the Central Highlands of Vietnam, consequently poses acute threats for the environment and local communities in the downstream areas of Cambodia in Ratanakiri and Stung Treng provinces. These people have not been fully informed and have had no access to decision makers in Vietnam prior to the dam's construction. After the dam was officially in operation in 2000, it has dramatically modified the river hydrological regime and water quality that adversely affects whole aspects of local livelihoods in Cambodia (Hirsch and Wyatt 2004), especially those of indigenous women that are totally based on the Se San River resources.[8] The study conducted by the Se San Working Group (SWG) cited unusual flooding, increased dry-seasonal flow, unpredictable fluctuations in river flow and height, loss of fishery resources, bad water quality and related health effects as being some of the impacts on some 50,000 people from ethnic groups.[9]

Leading organizations like the Australian Mekong River Commission (AMRC) have conducted policy research and capacity building in support of development paths that maintain the integrity, diversity and symbiosis of local livelihoods, cultures and ecosystems. The Se San Protection Network (SPN), associated with AMRC, has placed "gender" within its program framework "to maximize community involvement and to manage the Se San River such as using the existing decision making structure to involve women, using local language and using other networks that have importance for women, as well as inclusion of illiterate women and having one female representative from each village under the program (Both ends/Gomukh 2003). NGOF, a partner organization of SPN, released an annual report in 2001 which discussed the integration of gender concerns through gender training[10] as weak representation beyond village meetings in the SPN (ibid.).

Despite their involvement in assailing the dam's construction and effects on their lives, indigenous women however still have little space for negotiating the transboundary impacts of the dam's construction since this must be mediated by inter-state mechanisms, to which they have little access.

Thailand (northeast region)

Initiatives to include local actors in knowledge construction have also been part of river basin development. The Thai Baan research (or "villagers" research) is a case in point. The research was conducted by Assembly of the Poor (AOP), a coalition of farmers and local people's groups with the academic support of Southeast Asia Rivers Network (SEARIN), a nongovernmental organization. The main goal of the research was to influence the decision-making on the future of the Mun River's sustainable management and provide rich data for the public about the Mun River, its people and the impacts of the Pak Mun Dam to local communities and ecology. Local groups of women and men were trained to be local researchers. They were involved in gathering and analyzing data about their own livelihoods related to the Mun River resources and the effects of the Pak Mun Dam on their lives. Alongside their daily household activities such as fishing, making fishing gears, selling their catch to the market, collecting wild plants and vegetables, preparing food for the monks and so on, they collected data. They also analyzed how the experiment of the opening of the Pak Mun Dam's sluice gates dramatically improved the Mun ecology and their livelihoods. The Thai Baan research has shown that local women are able to engage in research and the analysis of their relationship with the river's resources

Thailand (northern region)

The second Thai Baan research is at Chiang Khong district in Chiang Rai province of northern Thailand. This research had been done after the rapids in this part of the Mekong River were partly blasted as an outcome of an agreement on regional trade among the Mekong countries and the Chinese government for improving navigation of large commercial vessels down the Mekong River. The research covered thirteen riverside communities in and around Chiang Kong and bordering communities in upper Lao PDR. The main objective of this research was to provide systematic information to the public and decision makers about local livelihoods that depended on the Mekong River's resources. The issues addressed in this research included 1) fisheries 2) river ecosystem 3) plants and vegetation 4) traditional fishing gears and 5) social, economic and cultural issues in the local context. It appeared that gender issues were not part of this research but women were included as key researchers and informants. Local villagers, both men and women, were participant observers, note takers, focus group discussants, in-depth interviewers, and local experts to validate all data that was gathered. They also analyzed why resources were so important to local living conditions and validated local knowledge on river ecosystems.

This research exercise was an attempt to demonstrate the importance of local knowledge in managing aquatic resources and the implications of this on local livelihoods. The apparent gap in this exercise was the lack of recognition that knowledge, as a social product, is gendered and that women and men may acquire and develop different types of knowledge on the use of resources based on their social locations, that is, their different livelihoods, access to resources and social status in communities. Policy-making in river basin development is about how people, the state and organizations employ and construct certain types of knowledge or information as being authoritative over others, a process also influenced by power relations with gender as being centrally one of them, and therefore may simultaneously be exclusionary of certain types of women and men.

Irrigation development and management

Laos

The creation of local institutional mechanisms such as water user associations (WUAS) is the main intent of the Decentralized Irrigation Development and Management Project supported by the ADB to be completed in 2006 in order to increase growth in agricultural production and to reduce poverty. About fifty-six well-functioning and appropriately trained WUAS will manage and operate irrigation infrastructure covering about 10,000 hectares of agricultural land. The program, supported by an ADB loan, employs a gender analysis which will ensure that women are not excluded from WUAS as part of the process of irrigation management transfer (IMT) by the government. The project briefly describes its strategy:[11]

The only way of avoiding this risk [of exclusion] is to encourage active participation of women farmers. A specific strategy will be adopted to increase women farmers' involvement and carry out systematic gender development training and integration program geared to a selection of women farmers for responsible positions in WUAS. About 20 percent of all posts are expected to be occupied by women. To ensure that women have adequate access to training and extension, the Government has agreed to increase the number of women extension workers in the district forestry and agriculture offices.

Discussion

The quota for women members in WUAS is commendable and is a decisive step in redressing the gender gap in membership in such organizations. Training and capacity-building of women for membership should however genuinely address existing gender/power issues that constrain women's meaningful and beneficial participation and seek strategies to transform these or consider alternative ways of involvement. Most training efforts have been geared to strengthen management skills and technical expertise while glossing over the real issues of power and domination of women. Capacity building programs were addressed by the study of Huyen (2003) that assessed the experiences and lessons from the Sida Environmental Fund Projects in Vietnam. The Sida projects provided opportunities for public awareness raising on environmental issues and environmental education. The Vietnam Women's Union in different parts of the country was involved in this training. It is not clear however whether gender issues of uneven entitlements, access and control of resources were part of the capacity-building efforts, and whether transforming this unevenness was an overriding concern.

Cambodia community fisheries

The Tonle Sap Great Lake is the largest freshwater body in Southeast Asia and is often referred to as a unique hydrological phenomenon, where local people fish and farm its rich fishing grounds and floodplains in seasonal cycles. In order to conserve fisheries resources in the Tonle Sap, the Royal Cambodian Government has recently recognized the role of local communities in managing common property freshwater and forest resources through the formation of community institutions—Community Fisheries (CFS). Community Fisheries are currently being created throughout villages in the Tonle Sap Region for the purpose of enabling local communities to use and manage fisheries and forest resources in sustainable and gender-responsive ways. Development program discourses have increasingly emphasized the central role of women in community fisheries management, such as in the Tonle Sap region in

Cambodia. Table 8.1 below presents some of the recent articulations on gender in major programs formulated by a multilateral lending agency, a government division of the Cambodian fisheries department and a local non-government organization for community fisheries in the Tonle Sap:

Table 8.1 Gender discourses in fisheries management programs in the Tonle Sap Lake

Multilateral Asian Development Bank (ADB 2002)	NGO Community Capacities for Development (CCD 2003)	State Community Fisheries Development Office Master Plan (CFDO-DOF 2004)
Women constitute about 51 percent of the population in the Tonle Sap region. Significantly, they also head about 15–30 percent of households (p. 4). Non-participation in community decision making, scarce opportunities for self-development and inadequate access to financial services keep the women poor (p. 4). About 40 percent of seats in community organizations will be allocated to women. Women will be organized for training and capacity building for participation and leadership. They will be selected for training in livelihood development, value-added activities, and establishing linkages with ongoing microfinance programs (p. 20).	The goal . . . is to enable community fisheries associations to manage natural resources effectively and sustainably and thereby improve livelihoods with the full participation of women The staff will conduct leadership training and provide small loans to (women) clients to be invested in a small business or used to buy an asset (p. 5).	Ensure that due consideration is given to gender issues (p. 2). Cooperation required with the Department of Women and Veterans' Affairs on gender concerns in fisheries (p. 7).

The program discourses in table 3 seem to be premised on the following assumptions: first, that participation in these programs and credit facilities will solve women's poverty; second, that women's participation will improve the management of fisheries in the Tonle Sap.

Discussion

The first assumption presupposes that poverty pointedly targets women only. In reality, countless women *and* men are poor. However, women experience the burdens of poverty more disproportionately since they are socially assigned specific roles and tasks that are understood as being rightfully female and on balance, consume more time and effort (e.g., reproductive work, food production, household debt management on top of farming and fishing, etc). Being women and considered as housewives, their time and labor are often assumed as being infinitely elastic, thus making them "available" for community activities. Participation in community organizations or credit projects, as such, will therefore not mitigate women's poverty for as long as culturally constructed notions of women's work and their assigned roles in society are not genuinely transformed and remain unequal both in terms of workload and status.

The second assumption is that mobilizing women for natural resource management will ensure project success and efficiency. This assumption is problematic for a number of reasons. First, recent studies on wider water-related projects have found that women's participation at the levels observed was found to have no relationship to project success (Prokopy 2003). Second, the same earlier notion of "investing in women" comes into play as fisheries management is being presented as being of interest to women despite their hectic pace in productive and reproductive work, and the prevalent notion in Cambodia that fishing is largely a male activity. Participation incurs costs to the participant in terms of time, labor, skills and resources. Without the full support of their households, their participation costs them valuable leisure time and increases their workload. Since gender organizes women's and men's work and responsibilities in society in unequal manner, it is gender inequality, therefore, that needs to be addressed and transformed.

Vietnam

The case of a fish sanctuary at Anbinh community located in the Mekong delta in Vietnam has emphasized the importance of women's involvement in the project management cycle and exemplifies how a gender equality approach has enabled women to widen their livelihood options. The fish sanctuary is supported by Can Tho University and Mekong Learning Initiative (MLI) and women have been involved in trainings and in the demonstration of organic farming methods, as well as pig-raising and biogas. Villagers have said:

They (the women) have been "liberated" from their families and have grown less dependent upon their husbands because the program approach frees up some of their time allowing them to engage in other income-generating activities. One female villager also said that there have never been better livelihood opportunities for women than in the last couple of years (Nguyen Huu Chiem et al. 2004).

Laos

In another project of fish sanctuary development, water supply and hygiene management project in Hanghee village, Champassak province, southern Laos, women have been identified as key stakeholders. Gender is inclusive in the project design and implementation. A gender workshop was conducted in Hanghee, Phnom Penh, and Bangkok in order for stakeholders to gain exposure to gender issues. The purpose of the gender workshop was to emphasize the importance of women's role in the success of community-based natural resource management (CBNRM) initiatives and community development in general to villagers, government officers and academics. One villager remarked: "Women already do a lot, and now they can participate in the project activities as well. They must be stronger!" After several workshops, women are now active partners in integrated agriculture/organic farming, food processing activities and the fish sanctuary. However, it remains unclear whether men also contribute to reproductive work or whether this remains to be women's work on top of all other project responsibilities. While women's role in the success of CBNRM has been rightfully underscored, it is not very clear whether inequalities based on their gender roles and social locations have been seriously redressed.

Program planners may in fact be well-intentioned in advocating for the inclusion of women in community fisheries or community-based natural resource management, as a reaction to former gender-blind planning. Yet by ignoring women's actual social worlds of uneven power relations that translate into a low social status and heavier workloads for them, they may inadvertently reproduce *gender* inequality. The result may burden women even more in the name of advancing sustainable development in fisheries and natural resource management.

Conclusion

The arguments and content of this article do not serve to advocate for a lesser role for women in water resources management. Rather, it makes a plea for a more holistic understanding of the disjunction between women and men's actual practices, rules, rights and roles in water resources management on one hand, and project assumptions, objectives and planning, on the other. People's practices are often shaped by their interests and particular conditions that circumscribe their actions. Some of these conditions are linked to their existing relations of power.

Although by no means representative of water governance programs in the Mekong region, the foregoing discussion of existing program discourses in different sectors of water resources management have demonstrated that assumptions on women's participation is largely driven by underlying efficiency-oriented considerations. The poverty/efficiency approach has been dominant in major development organizations for some time. It emphasizes decentralized management of resources and public participation devolving power from the central state to ensure more direct relationships with local users and harnessing them for local management as well as increasingly to shoulder the costs of privatizing former public goods. Thus, the creation of local institutions such as water user groups where quotas for women's representation have been set, and where gender unequal arrangements of workloads, time and labor have been overlooked. Women are therefore being increasingly harnessed for conservation activities without consideration of the actual conditions under which they may live: a disproportionate share of heavy productive and reproductive workloads, low social status, and a tradition of being "at the rear" rather than in key leadership positions. These are the effects of gender inequality, where established understandings of women's place in society define their daily responsibilities. Further, getting women involved in water governance, it seems, extends to their conventional reproductive roles and planners often assume that women are more reliable and trustworthy in attending meetings, maintenance of infrastructure and payments, especially in decentralized costs of water supply (Cleaver 2003, 2–3).

The efficiency approach is also an instrumental approach that justifies attention to gender in terms of how this will advance project objectives (e.g., poverty reduction, sustainable use and management of water resources and infrastructure, and so on) rather than transforming gender inequality. Women are often defined as being inferior due to poverty or scarcity of water resources and thus measures are designed to ameliorate poverty instead of addressing unequal gender relations. Poverty reduction and sound water governance cannot be achieved so long as women continue to occupy an inferior place in society. An implicit but flawed instrumental approach therefore ensures that gender issues are taken on board insofar as they are consistent with development goals and insofar as women are seen to offer a means to achieve these goals.

Additionally, the nature of women's involvement in these projects often assume their close association to social reproduction and being part of unpaid family labor. Their activities revolve around their traditional reproductive and caring tasks such as in managing water sanitation, cottage industries and home economics. They are also assumed as being supplementary labor for income-generation in the event of displaced farm livelihoods due to dam construction.

Local power/gender relations are generally overlooked. Planners assume that women can participate freely and willingly in community-wide assemblies and turn a blind eye to their social standing in communities and in households. They are also aggregated as a unified group, not suggesting that disparities among women may exist, where poorer women may be edged out by others less poor or by those better connected to positions of influence. Little attempt has been made to ascertain whether it is generally accepted by women to involve themselves actively in decision-making in traditionally male-dominated fields such as water resource development. Often planners assume that women are available or that they are a natural, logical constituency in resource management.

Furthermore, the conventional assumption is that women are generally available and that it is within their interests to "participate" in such programs. Women's time and labor are often assumed to be infinitely elastic since they are often regarded as sedentary, at home or "housewives." However, women perform farm and non-farm work, are fishers and water users, as well as care for members of their households. They have limited time and assets, and unless it is clear what benefits they will get out of their participation, they may opt to channel their efforts elsewhere.

In short, combining former conceptual threads of women-water-and-participation and efficiency thinking in water governance may prove, in the end, to be counterproductive for women and water governance in the Mekong region in the long term, as they are largely mobilized for top-down or instrumental ends to serve the "gender" requirements of state projects and multilateral or other development funding agencies. A thorough and consistent use of gender analysis that looks into the local social and power relations in which women are embedded is in order, disabusing conventional assumptions that women are "closer to nature," are "victims of poverty" and possess "unlimited energy and time" for projects that do not address the central reasons why women are disadvantaged in the first place.

Some experiences of women in the Mekong region demonstrate that women are actually involved in various struggles around water resources, especially when health and livelihood security are in great risk. This should not be ruled out as a reality. However, it would be more instructive for planners and development specialists to investigate under what particular conditions are women able to participate in struggles, engage with the state and negotiate for fairer, more just use and protection of resources. Women's actual practices of engagement, resistance and even compliance must be considered in order to fully understand the nature of women's participation in water resources management. That women are a natural constituency in water governance in the Mekong and elsewhere is more assumed than actually explored by experts and planners. Such assumptions may only serve to increase women's workloads, instrumentally make use of women's time and labor, and reproduce the inequalities that are attached to their gender roles and obligations in households and communities.

There is therefore need to re-position the "political" when bringing in "gender" to water governance programs and less of instrumentalizing women for efficiency, conservation and donor requirement ends for their own sake. In short, efforts to redress inequality and power relations between women and men should be centrally part of the program agenda and goals. Otherwise, women will continue being harnessed as a reserve army of labor under the aegis of poverty alleviation, conservation and participatory development.

Further research on selected intervention sites in the Mekong region would therefore require investigating (a) under what conditions are women (and men) enabled to engage in political struggles around water resources; (b) the actual and complex practices (roles, rights and responsibilities) of women and men in water resources management and how these might translate into policy responses instead of privileging women in resource management in *a priori* manner.

Notes

1 The consensus being referred to here is Principle No. 3 of the Guiding Principles of the International Conference on Water and the Environment Development Issues for the Twenty-first Century, Dublin, 1992.

2 http://www.fao.org/Gender/gender.htm; http://www.adb.org/Gender/default.asp.

3 The first conceptual approach is the "women, environment and development" (WED) approach, which basically argues that women are more dependent on environmental resources due to their principal role in reproductive work. The second strand of women-and-environment thought influential in gender planning for sustainable development is ecofeminism developed from a Third World perspective that posits women's close relationship with nature and argues for women's chief role in the conservation and management of natural resources. Both approaches have come under question in the last decade.

4 This is not to say, however, that sustainable development interventions are no longer gender-blind. Leach (2003) points out that after a decade or so "inserting women" into environment programs, they are increasingly reverting back to gender-blind approaches.

5 Jackson (2000, 40) adds quite succinctly: Gender concerns are justified by the World Bank and others with reference to economic growth, poverty reduction; UNFPA justifies gender in relation to population control and environmental agencies in terms of environmental management and conservation. Thus women are now a means of controlling population, of achieving sustainable development, of poverty alleviation. All these on top of their caring tasks in households.

6 http://www.fao.org/DOCREP/005/AC620E/AC620E00.HTM.

7 http://www.adb.org/Documents/RRPS/VIE/rrp_30292.pdf.

8 http://ngoforum.org.kh/Core/annual_report_2001%20text.html.

9 http://oxfamamerica.org/newsadpublications/news_updates/archive2003
10 http://ngoforum.org.kh/Core/annual_report_2001%20text.html.
11 http://www.adb.org/Documents/RRPS/LAO/rrp-30254-lao.pdf

CHAPTER 9

MULTI-STAKEHOLDER PLATFORMS (MSPS): UNFULFILLED POTENTIAL

John Dore

Introduction

Multi-Stakeholder Platforms (MSPS), or Dialogues, are a democratic governance technology that can assist society to reflect on the wisdom of past actions, more comprehensively explore and assess future options, and more openly negotiate workable strategies and agreements. The central ingredient is informed debate that gives ample opportunity for learning and possible reshaping of opinion. This may lead to the creation or strengthening of bridges of understanding between actors representing wide-ranging interests, and the satisfactory resolution of at least some differences. The MSP may also bring into sharper focus substantive differences of approach and priorities that may not be easily reconcilable. Either way, by articulating these differences in the public sphere, an MSP can contribute to a sounder basis for charting a forward path.

The vision for MSPS put forward in this chapter is for important transboundary water-related governance affecting Mekong region livelihoods and ecosystems to be more informed and influenced by public deliberation. In this vision MSPS would be accepted as a legitimate element of governance, providing a mechanism for many different stakeholders in the state-society complex to explain, defend and potentially adjust their perspectives. This is not a utopian vision constructed in ignorance of the daunting Mekong region political context where many substantive decisions are made without an airing in the public sphere. The power relationships embedded in this context, within and between countries, undoubtedly influences the extent that meaningful MSP participation and negotiation is possible. But, it is noted that there are some inspirational examples of MSPs at the local and national scales, and a new promising effort at the regional scale. The contention is that regional water-related MSPs can also display desirable characteristics, more conducive to socially just and ecologically sustainable development.

This chapter unfolds in the following way. First, the Mekong region is introduced. Second, the relationship between governance and MSPs is made clear. Third, the existing diversity of regional[1] water forums in the Mekong region is shown, but no claim is made that all "earn the label" of MSP. Some of the most prominent forums are discussed. Fourth, some key challenges for MSPs are identified, evident from current practice and debate. Finally, I point to several major infrastructure-heavy projects with transboundary dimensions. These include current plans for large-scale hydropower development in China's Yunnan province, a hydropower-reliant energy grid being promoted via the Association of South East Asian Nations (ASEAN) and the Asian Development Bank (ADB), a multi-faceted water grid recently explored by the Government of Thailand, and a "regional water strategy" being developed by the World Bank and ADB. The governance of each would be enhanced by a high-quality, transboundary MSP.

The core argument is that MSPs have unfulfilled potential in the Mekong region both within as well as beyond the realms of water-related governance. In 2006, steps have been taken to realize this potential via the launching of a Mekong Region Waters Dialogue.

Water concerns

In the Mekong region, disparate regionalisms have emerged from desires related to: peace, poverty reduction, disease control, infrastructure installation, drugs, wealth-seeking, and preference for ecosystem approaches, all of which may favor a regional logic which transcends state borders. These are reflected in various political solidarities between actors in the state-society complex—whether governments, bureaucrats, non-government organizations (NGOs), the private sector, militaries, ethnic minorities, relatively powerful lobby groups etc.[2] These are manifested in an array of rationalizations, identifiable via many regional organizations, initiatives, networks and coalitions. Actors in old and new rationalizations are learning how to co-exist, compete or combat with each other.[3]

One of the key social challenges for the region is to negotiate the reasonable and equitable utilization of water[4] in the major river basins of the region (table 9.1).[5] Conflicts exist and others are looming[6] over many, often-connected issues, such as: growth in water and energy demand, interference with natural flows via dams, timing of dam releases for energy or irrigated production, water diversions, altered sediment and nutrient loads, and reshaping rivers to rivers to make navigation easier and safer.

MSPs

Multi-stakeholder platforms are just one part of governance where actors with either a right, risk or general interest (stakeholders) are identified, and usually through representatives, invited and assisted to interact in a deliberative forum, aiming for all participants to learn, understand alternative perspectives, and possibly negotiate workable strategies and agreements (figure 9.1). An MSP may involve regular meetings between core participants, conferences/discussions open to the wider public, locally hosted field visits, electronic exchanges, government briefings, films, plays, historical texts, testimony, or commissioned research.

I favor the term multi-stakeholder "platform" over multi-stakeholder "process," whilst recognizing that many commentators are using the latter. The term Dialogues is also commonly used, and we have begun using it in the Mekong region. This is synonymous with the platform conception.

MSPs (or Dialogues) have been defined as: "… a contrived situation in which a set of more less interdependent stakeholders in some resource are identified, and, usually through representatives, invited to meet and interact in a forum for conflict resolution, negotiation, social learning and collective decision-making towards concerted action" (Roling 2002, 39).

But a problem with Roling's definition is the inclusion of decision-making in the remit. Many MSPs are not vested with, nor do they claim, decision-making authority. To claim such authority may invite resistance

Table 9.1 Major river basins of the Mekong region

River basin		Irrawaddy	Salween	Mekong	Chao Phraya	Red
Countries in basin		China Myanmar	China Myanmar Thailand	Cambodia China Laos Myanmar Thailand Vietnam	Thailand	China Vietnam
Basin area	km^2	413,710	271,914	805,604	178,785	170,888
Ave. water yield	million m^3/year	410,000	151,000	475,000	29,800	177,000
Ave. population density	people/km^2	79	22	71	119	191
Water supply	m^3/person/year	18,614	23,796	8,934	1,237	3,083
Large cities in the basin	>100,000 people	6	1	9	3	3

SOURCES: Water Resources e-Atlas (WRI, UNEP, IWMI, IUCN), and Mekong Region Environment Atlas (ADB and UNEP 2004)

Figure 9.1 Key concepts of MSPS

Multi-Stakeholder Platforms (msps) *or* Dialogues
- ❖ actors with either a right, risk or general interest (stakeholders) are identified
- ❖ usually through representatives, infited & assisted to interact in a deliberative forum
- ❖ aiming for all participants to learn and understand alternative perspectives
- ❖ *possible* negotiate workable strategies and agreements

Desirable context	Desirable process	Desirable outcomes
✓ Well-intentioned	✓ Inclusive	✓ Options assessed
✓ Clear purpose & scope	✓ Facilitated	✓ Rights, risks, responsibilities established
✓ Sufficient political support	✓ Ethical	
✓ Sufficient time	✓ Visionary & focused	
✓ Sufficient resources	✓ Holistic	✓ More understanding
✓ Appropriate levels & scales	✓ Informed	✓ Workable agreements
	✓ Deliberative	✓ Discursive legitimacy
	✓ Communicative	✓ Constructive influence

Actors
People in the State-society complex, at various levels, "acting" individually or collectively in some type of group or coalition.

Institutions
Persistent, reasonably predictable, arrangements, laws processes, customs or organizations structuring aspects of the political social, cultural, or economic transactions and relationships in a society; although by definition persistent, institutions constantion evolve (as per Dovers)

Governance
Multi-layered interplay of negotiations, agenda-setting, preference-shaping, decision-making, management and administration between many actors and institutions in the State-society complex, at and between different levels and scales.

For example, governmence may involve: governments, bureaucracies, non-government organizations (NGOs) businesses, militaries, donors, lenders, lobbyists, community groups, active individuals, laws, treaties, policies, contracts, forman and informal agreements, commercial contracts, force-bearing dictates, common understandings.

Water governance
As per governance, but specifically water-related,

The interplay between the wide range of actors and institutions which may influence water and water use.

Water governance in the Mekong Region involves actors such as: political leaders, water and energy planners, storage and delivery authorities, military, agricultural irrigators, energy generators, fishers, navigators, ecologists, urban and rural dwellers; and institutions such as water-related legislation, river basin organizations, community-based water user associations, allocation policies, use and development agreements, regulations, quotas, pricing, and occasional use of armed force to ensure compliance etc.

NOTE: The definition for institutions is from Dovers (2001).

and be counter-productive. Hemmati (2002, 63), aware of the danger of including decision-making, has described MSPs as a "political phenomenon" which: "... aims to bring together all major stakeholders in a new form of communication, decision-finding (and possibly decision-making) on a particular issue."

Supporters of MSPs believe: "... there is integral value in messier, participatory arenas which value negotiating and social learning within a more open democratic process which encourages exploration and bounded conflict" (Dore et al. 2003, 176).

The most important characteristic of MSPs is that they be a site of "authentic deliberation"[7], meaning debate between people with different world views and priorities which "induces reflection upon preferences in non-coercive fashion" (Dryzek 2000, 2). But, there is a range of other desirable characteristics for each of context, process and outcomes that are introduced in figure 9.1 and elaborated in table 9.2.

Table 9.2 Desirable MSP characteristics

Desirable context	
Well-intentioned	Catalyzed by a genuine need or desire to do something constructive about a complex situation or problem.
Clear purpose, and scope	Clear articulation of: MSP purpose; political and practical boundaries to enquiry; the derivation, extent and duration of mandate; and justification as to how the MSP might improve existing governance.
Sufficient political support	Sufficient political space and momentum to permit or encourage establishment and support.
Sufficient time	Sufficient time for the MSP to make its contribution/s.
Sufficient resources	Adequate resources to pursue and achieve goals, including human, financial, informational, and intellectual.
Appropriate levels and scales	Cognizant that analysis and action may best occur at various levels and scales. The appropriate level for one MSP may be predominantly within government, for another at the local community. The appropriate scale of analysis may be local, provincial, watershed, national, basin, and regional; however, cross-scale issues may also be important.
Desirable process	
Inclusive	Enables "representation" of a wide range of "stakeholders" and their disparate interests via a flexible process which may have many different facets.
Facilitated	Exemplifies, to the extent possible, a fair and forward moving process, guided by an independent facilitator committed to transparency.
Ethical	Respectful of diverse "ethics"—ways of reasoning, world views and priorities of actors. However, also committed to privileging "goods", such as: respect and care for life, ecological integrity, social and economic justice; democracy, non-violence and peace.[8]

Visionary and focused	Encourages expression of alternative views of preferred, long-term visions for people and places, whilst also identifying and focusing on key issues.
Holistic	Takes an integrated or holistic view of issues taking account of: social, cultural, economic and ecological issues, their actions and interdependencies.
Informed	Utilizes and shares the best available information, building the knowledge base. While not essential to be integrated with them all, the MSP should become familiar with other relevant forums, plans, agendas etc..
Deliberative	Induces reflection upon preferences, without coercion, by representatives of competing points of view.
Communicative	Effectively communicates high-quality, honest information to MSP participants, and the wider public sphere, state or transnational authorities.
Desirable outcomes	
Options assessed	Assesses nuances of positive and negative aspects of alternative options.
Rights, risks & responsibilities established	Acknowledgement and scrutiny of the multiple rights and risks (borne voluntarily or involuntarily), and responsibilities of stakeholders.
More understanding	More learning, understanding and appreciation by all of the positions of other stakeholders.
Workable agreements	Depending on the mandate, negotiation of workable strategies and agreements for proposing to decision-makers.
Discursive legitimacy	MSP earns legitimacy by demonstrating these desirable characteristics.
Constructive influence	Has a constructive influence on the situation, enhancing the overall governance.

SOURCES: Adapted from Dore and Woodhill (1999, 43), Dovers and Dore (1999, 128), with additional ideas from Dryzek (2000, 2001)

Water governance forums

In all the waters of the Mekong region, local communities, governments, civil society organizations (local, national, regional and international), business interests, donors and international agencies have interests that they wish represented in governance. Few would claim that historical or current regional water governance is adequate, which partly explains the interest of some actors—but not all—to make genuine MSPs part of regional governance orthodoxy. There is a hope that using MSPs may contribute to greater transparency, and more informed, and equitable decisions.

For now, there are many regional water-related governance forums, but few MSPs. The forums are a starting point, and so how might they be better understood? Some of them are "old" style, state-centric and grounded in state interventions. However, some of them are qualitatively different and "new" with lead roles being taken by non-state actors. The new wave of younger regionalizations is coexisting with older types. The terminology of tracks 1–4 is one way of differentiating the forums (table 9.3). Track 1 depicts the "old" type of forum. But the spectrum in the Mekong region has widened to now include more examples akin to tracks 2, 3 and 4.

Each of the tracks can be discerned at the local/national scale, and also the regional scale. Each of tracks 1–4 can adopt an MSP approach to address any particularly complex problem. However, at the regional scale in the Mekong region, track 1 has shown little inclination to use an MSP approach, remaining for the most part hostage to the "traditional" political norms manifested in international diplomacy and national conventions where state actors see themselves as the only legitimate representatives of a country's citizens—in water issues, self-interested state approaches dominate. Track 2 and track 3 are more likely to take an MSP approach to tackle regional issues. Track 4 users are more likely to see regional platforms as advocacy stages. As with track 1, in track 4 the multi-stakeholder and deliberative elements tend to be downgraded, with other political strategies and approaches being considered more effective.

Table 9.3 Governance forums—tracks 1–4

	Track 1	Track 2	Track 3	Track 4
Summary	Formal and informal processes of governments and associated bureaucracy, including inter- and intra-state forums. In the eyes of states these are "official" and most legitimate.	Governance processes involving state, UN family, donor/lender, civil society, interactive forums but led by an actor closely aligned with states ensuring states remain privileged actors.	Research, dialogue and advocacy efforts led by civil society, less impeded by or subordinate to state actors.	Civil society organisations supporting (where possible) locally-led governance processes.
In eyes of states	Official	Semi-official	Unofficial	Unofficial
Dominant logic	For the most part, still implicitly accepting the dominance of rational, self-interested behavior, particularly in international affairs.	Trying to enhance the effectiveness of states by widening the field of ideas and influences.	Activist, optimistic about the potential of MSPs to find and assist negotiate better ways forward for society.	Activist, localist; low expectations of state capacity and intent; more explicit concerns about power imbalances, domination and co-option.

SOURCE: Adapted from Dore (2003, 412)

To illustrate the present situation, in the next few pages I will refer to a sample of the wide array of regional water governance forums in the Mekong region.[9] There is plenty of room for improvement, and no shortage of regional opportunities to experiment more with an MSP approach.

Track 1

There are many track 1 water-related governance forums in the Mekong region. Within countries the state government and bureaucracies dominate water governance. There are also many bilateral negotiations between government representatives which are pure track 1, vitally important, but not the focus of this chapter. The comments here are restricted to the most obvious transboundary example, that being the Mekong River Commission (MRC) that has a state government mandate in the Lower Mekong Basin i.e. the territory of the Mekong River basin, excluding Myanmar and China parts of the basin.

The 1995 Mekong River Agreement (Governments of Cambodia-Lao PDR-Vietnam-Thailand 1995) created a formal inter-government forum committing signatories to cooperate in all fields of sustainable development, utilization, management and conservation of the water and water-related resources of the Mekong River basin, including but not limited to irrigation, hydropower, navigation, flood control, fisheries, timber floating, recreation and tourism. Two items embedded on the MRC agenda by the 1995 Agreement are water utilization negotiations and basin development planning. Amongst others, a third agenda item that has emerged is the need for transboundary environment assessment in the Mekong region. Various dialogues—relatively exclusive—are occurring around each of these tasks. None resemble ideal-type MSPs.

All have thus far been primarily the domain of state agency officials, international donor representatives, many international consultants, and just a few local consultants. If you believe that these actors will adequately represent the interests of all Lower Mekong country citizens, such exclusiveness may be untroubling. However, many local and international actors do not have such confidence and are pressing the MRC secretariat to be more inclusive, meaning greater involvement by civil society, and more open to alternative knowledge and ideas. This is not so easy for the secretariat to do, as to a large extent their scope is set by their governing council, and most of the staff—from either riparian countries, or international recruits—is understandably cautious about moving out of sync with national processes. There is insufficient political support from the member states for the MRC to be proactive in controversial areas. Member states continue to act unilaterally whenever possible, and either bilaterally (stronger members—Thailand and Vietnam) or multilaterally (weaker members—Laos and Cambodia) as a last resort. Nevertheless, some complex interdependencies and donor support keep the MRC cooperation alive.

The non-membership of MRC by the governments of China and Myanmar further reduces the effectiveness of the organization, particularly at a time when China is building a substantial cascade of dams on the upstream portion (refer Dore et al. this volume). A united front from MRC member countries towards effective dialogue with China has also been scuttled, at least in part by effective bilateral diplomacy by the Chinese circumventing and undermining the MRC forum. China has demonstrated considerable power and influence over downstream countries to stop protests emanating from the MRC.

Indicative of the marginalization of the MRC within some of its own member states, the commission was also excluded from playing any role in the track 1 forum which negotiated the signing of a commercial navigation agreement for the Mekong River, between the four upstream riparian countries (Governments of China-Lao PDR-Myanmar-Thailand 2001). The signatories, from transport and communication ministries, have since presided over the installation of Chinese-funded extensive new navigation aids, and blasting of rocky navigation impediments. Improving the navigability[10] of the river, and the alteration to the natural flows—depending on the operations of the hydropower dams—will come at a cost to the integrity of the ecosystem, with as yet unquantified livelihood costs for river-dependent communities.

It would be reasonable to expect some level of protest, or at least enquiry, from downstream government elites via their river basin commission. However, Cambodia has pragmatically accepted Chinese offers for wide-ranging development support, and in exchange keeps quiet. Similarly, the Thailand government and associated bureaucracy has also refrained from supporting the MRC to become more proactively involved, accepting boat-building and river transport contracts from the Chinese, whilst at the same time continuing with plans for more tributary interventions of their own. Laos is caught in the middle of the navigation project between China and Thailand, un-empowered and with few obvious benefits to the country.

The Mekong River Commission will not proactively lead any MSP process relating to Thailand's resurgent plans for water resources development, which have Mekong (and other) basin implications. Thailand's reluctance to publicly share its national water resources development agenda with neighbors caused a crisis in the Mekong River cooperation in the early 1990s (Bui Kim Chi 1997, 302–316). Ten years later the MRC secretariat was still unable or unwilling to provide any comment whatsoever about the implications of the basin-wide, cross-basin and cross-border implications of various Thailand development possibilities. Of course, influential actors in Laos, Vietnam—and to a lesser extent Cambodia—have plans of their own which are already substantively changing the river basin.

The Mekong River Commission also struggled to find and sustain a proactive role in a recent high profile conflict between Cambodians and Vietnamese caused by loss of life and other problems stemming from the operation of the Yali Falls dam, situated on a stretch of the Se San River in Vietnam's territory (but note the track 3 example mentioned elsewhere in this chapter).

In theory, MRC would be able to play a key role in fostering deliberative processes which could lead to more informed decision making. In practice, due to a lack of political support, it has not yet been possible for the MRC secretariat to countenance leading MSPs which are fully informed and assess all options. However, since 2005, MRC has been showing an increased willingness to engage in events convened by others, which is a positive sign.

Track 2

Relevant to the Mekong region are the track 2 forums led or inspired by groups such as the UN's Economic and Social Commission for Asia and the Pacific (ESCAP), that have convened meetings exchanging information on issues such as water allocation policies and practices in Asia-Pacific, including all Mekong countries (ESCAP 2000). Between 2000 and 2005 ESCAP has continued leading national "strategic water planning" processes in partnership with others, such as Food and Agriculture Organization (FAO). Slightly less formal have been the track 2 regional forums held under the auspices of the Global Water Partnership, namely the Southeast Asia Regional Dialogue on Water Governance in 2002, and the ensuing South East Asia Water Forum in 2003. Both the ESCAP and GWP forums mostly involve government officials, UN agencies, natural sciences technical experts and international NGOs. Thus far there has been virtually no participation by local civil society.

The most important of the track 2 regional initiatives is the Greater Mekong Subregion (GMS) economic cooperation initiative facilitated by the ADB. This program has brought together the six countries to focus on the coordinated development of infrastructure (ADB 2001, 2002). Many "master plans" have been completed which are unrealistic dreams, or visionary guides, depending upon your point of view.

The GMS program was endorsed at the 2002 summit meeting of the political leaders from each of the Mekong region countries in Phnom Penh, and again at the second summit held in Kunming in 2005. The forward work plan includes flagship projects, intended as multi-disciplinary, large-scale interventions with high visibility and significant economic impact on the GMS economies. There are projects relating to: north-south, east-west and southern economic corridors (roads plus associated infrastructure); completion of a regional telecommunications "back bone"; regional power grid completion plus power trading arrangements; private sector participation and competitiveness boosting; cross-border trade and investments support; implementing a region-wide Strategic Environmental Framework (SEF) (SEI et al. 2002); and supporting country efforts to control floods and "manage" water resources; and tourism. In 2006, a GMS Core Environment Program was launched with an office in Bangkok.

The main participants in the GMS initiative have been state government representatives, ADB bank officials and consultants. A significant role is also played by shareholder member governments that contribute financially to the bank, principally the US and Japan, but more recently China also. A primary aim has been to entice the private sector to become more involved either supplying funds (e.g. money market) or implementing projects. In

Table 9.4 Recent regional water-related governance forums (tracks 1–2)

Track 1	Track 2
Mekong River Commission inter-government processes between Cambodia, Laos, Thailand and Vietnam.	ESCAP technical meetings about water allocation policies, GMS development cooperation 2001–2009 etc.
Negotiations between transport ministries leading to signing of Navigation Agreement between China, Myanmar, Laos and Thailand 2000, and subsequent river modifications.	Global Water Partnership regional "dialogues", such as the Chiang Mai First South East Asia Water Forum 2003, and Bali Second South East Asia Water Forum 2005, building on earlier national dialogues.
Greater Mekong Subregion (GMS) Leaders Summits which in 2002 signed an agreement to establish an electricity grid between Mekong region and some other ASEAN countries, and in 2005 launched the Biodiversity Conservation Corridors Initiative, and committed to regional power trading.	Asian Development Bank (ADB) processes, such as: the GMS program of economic cooperation activities 1992+ development of the Strategic Environment Framework (SEF) for the GMS 2001+
ASEAN Mekong Basin Development Cooperation 1996–2006 (abolished), which—despite the name—focused on railways, not water.	fostering establishment of Tonle Sap lake/basin management authority 2004+
Bilateral negotiations between governments, such as:	review of ADB policy on decision-making about large scale water resources projects 2005+
Thailand with its neighbors over proposed water diversions and associated dam and tunnel constructions	consultations surrounding the development of a GMS energy strategy 2006+
Vietnam and Cambodian governments formal meetings over Se San River dams downstream impacts 2000+	testing of Strategic Environment Assessment (SEA) on GMS program elements 2006+

recent years civil society has taken an active role on the periphery of this bank-led process e.g. parallel forums coinciding with the annual meeting of the bank's Board of Governors etc. Civil society has faced the question of whether to become more involved with ADB or to maintain its critical advocacy from outside. Critical advocacy has resulted in changes to the ways in which the GMS program operates, in particular with regard to transparency, expansion into social areas such as health, and willingness to engage with non-state actors. A wider range of development partners are now involved with the implementation of the GMS program. ADB has been showing increased willingness to engage with a wider range of partners.

Track 3

Lack of faith in tracks 1 and 2 by parts of civil society has led to the emergence of tracks 3 and 4, both of which may proceed with or without direct state involvement. In the eyes of states, track 3 is "unofficial" but this does not, and should not, deter activists optimistic about the power of discursive forums to enhance the quality of problem identification and solving, or, more positively, goal-setting and attainment.

There are an increasing number of examples in Mekong region countries of civil society led governance forums in water and water related areas, such as energy and fisheries. At the local/national level these have included MSPs about Se San hydropower, Cambodian fisheries law, and community-led research and watershed management (box 9.1).

Box 9.1 Recent civil society-led local/national MSPs

Cambodian fisheries law dialogue
The adoption of Cambodia's Community Fisheries Sub-decree, drafted between 2000 and 2004, is critical if there is to be non-violent and "sustainable" accessing of the extraordinary Tonle Sap fishery. The drafting has involved an MSP including small-scale fisher representatives, plus local and national officials. Critical facilitation has been provided by NGOs such as Oxfam Great Britain and the local Fisheries Action Coalition Team. The MSP has been supported by various international organisations such as the Environmental Justice Foundation, other Oxfams and the UN's Food and Agriculture Organisation. Critical context for the MSP was the political support provided by Prime Minister Hun Sen since 2000. Progress has been made in a process shaped by civil society actors working with sympathetic government officials.

Thai Baan action research and dialogue
Villager-led research groups are now operating in northern and northeast Thailand. This movement is commonly referred to as the Thai Baan research. The villagers are the researchers. Those helping them are

---

research assistants. Thus, traditional research hierarchies are being turned upside down. Thai Baan is boosting the understanding of communities and government officials of the links between rivers, wetlands and rural livelihoods. Thai Baan groups are being supported by partnerships between local organisations such as the Chiang Khong Conservation Group, regional NGOs such as the South East Asia Rivers Network (SEARIN), subdistrict and provincial officials, and other organisations such as Thailand's Maha Sarakam University, IUCN and Oxfam America. This chain of MSPs is focused on the local scale. Thai Baan has rapidly gained credibility by bringing in and respecting the knowledge of local fishers and farmers, and effectively communicating their knowledge to other actors through photo exhibitions, Thai and English booklets and videos.

Se San hydropower dialogue
The Se San Protection Network (see Hirsch and Wyatt 2004) is an initiative of downstream Cambodian villagers in the Se San River basin seriously affected by operations of Vietnam's Yali Falls dam. The network is gradually succeeding in working cooperatively with formal state actors such as the Cambodian National Mekong Committee Secretariat, and the Cambodian Standing Committee for Coordination on Dams and Canals along Cambodia—Laos, Vietnam, Thailand Borders. External support to the network is being provided by NGOs such as Both Ends, the Oxfams, and the Australian Mekong Resource Centre. Civil society groups have created and are sustaining their efforts to lead a constructive MSP. More recently, the initiative has expanded to include dam-affected villagers on the Srepok and Sekong, and there is now a "3s" working group, newsletter and events.

Yunnan community-based watershed management
The Lashi watershed management committee in Yunnan Province brings together local communities and government officials in an MSP to aid watershed decision making (Igbokwe et al. 2002, Lazarus 2003). The establishment process has been facilitated by Green Watershed, a local Chinese NGO, with support from Oxfam America. The MSP started in sixteen villages with awareness raising through watershed management trainings, participatory rural appraisal activities, gender training, historical reviews and trust building among two ethnic minority groups. It has now advanced to tackle more difficult subjects, such as an upcoming county-level project to raise the level of the small dam (dyke) to increase the water flow to Lijiang town and the potential impacts on local livelihoods (such as loss of fisheries, water, agricultural crops and land). Having established a solid base it is now scaling up to be more relevant to other townships and the whole of the watershed and is seen by parts of the Chinese government as a model learning site.

There have also been various track 3 initiatives focused on the regional scale (some examples are listed in table 9.6). Again, space precludes doing more than discussing one example, with its couple of offshoots. World Resources Institute (WRI) and Stockholm Environment Institute (SEI) were the drivers of the Resource Policy Support Initiative (REPSI)—mostly via a WRI office in northern Thailand, at which I was based. Our role was to support the construction and facilitation of a two year dialogue on environmental governance which emerged from a meeting about cooperation on international rivers, held in Yunnan in 1999 (He Daming et al. 2001). A wide range of regional actors were recruited/invited to participate in a process intended to learn about, and where necessary challenge, the ways in which decisions are made about "environment" issues in Mekong region countries (Badenoch 2001).[11] The Regional Environment Forum (REF) was a WRI-led evolution from REPSI which had a more explicit role for local organisations in the management of the initiative, with Thailand Environment Institute (TEI) and Cambodian Institute for Cooperation and Peace (CICP) taking leading roles. The initial outputs of this forum (REF participants 2002) closely mirrored the general WRI environmental governance agenda, exemplified in The Access Initiative (Petkova et al. 2002), which is a civil society strengthening initiative, drawing inspiration from the principles embodied in the European Aarhus Convention (UNECE 1998). In 2004 WRI closed its regional office, and SEI countered with its own new network initiative. Of the two, SEI in particular sees a niche for itself as a "boundary organization" occupying a mediating space between science, policy, business (Guston 1999, 2001) and perhaps even civil society advocacy groups.

The World Conservation Union (IUCN) is increasingly using its convening capacity in the Mekong region to focus on significant water-related governance challenges. An example was a recent high-level roundtable at the 2004 World Conservation Congress held in Bangkok. IUCN is an unusual hybrid organization being a union of some eighty state government and about one thousand non-state organization members. IUCN secretariat can use its membership base as a justification for a discussion format quite unlike the normal inter-government meetings on offer. Engaging in the Bangkok deliberation were Ministers from five of the six Mekong countries (excluding Myanmar), and many non-state representatives, some of whom delivered focused presentations on substantive and controversial issues such as Nu-Salween river development in China, Myanmar and Thailand; water basin diversions, with special reference to Thailand; and threats to the Tonle Sap freshwater lake in Cambodia. IUCN is committed to supporting water-related MSPs at different scales throughout the Mekong region, in part as the regional manifestation of its global Water and Nature Initiative (WANI) (see www.waterandnature.org). They recognize that MSPs need to have a diverse, but robust, knowledge base. For this reason IUCN remains keen to continue its support to local research institutions in the Mekong region. Many of these institutes, including IUCN, are now collaborating in the water governance network whose joint activities are undertaken via M-POWER (Mekong Program on Water Environment and Resources) which is coordinated from Chiang Mai University's Unit for Social and Environmental Research.

In 2006 IUCN, Thailand Environment Institute (TEI), International Water Management Institute (IWMI) and M-POWER colleagues have co-convened the Mekong Region Waters Dialogue (for all documentation, see www.mpowernet.org). The co-convenors intend to support this initiative for three years 2006–2008 in an attempt to institutionalize MSPs at the regional and national levels. The objectives of the first regional event, held in Vientiane July 2006, were to: 1) provide opportunity for state, civil society and business actors in the Mekong region to participate in water development dialogues to inform, and be informed; 2) assess national water resources development strategies, and the relevant regional strategies of the Asian Development Bank, Mekong River Commission, and the World Bank; and 3) enable the articulation of different perspectives about Mekong region water-related development to be considered in decision making.

Track 4

It is sometimes difficult to distinguish between track 2 and track 3 forums, but track 4 is quite different. It reflects the position of what are often called "localists," increasingly prominent in water governance. In general, civil society localists assert the significance of the rural community and local governance as an opposition to discourses propounding economic growth, urbanization and industrialism (Hewison 2001, 22). They usually have a greater emphasis on self-sufficiency and lower expectations of government, often believing that states and dominant elites are neither sufficiently legitimate, competent or inclined to adequately represent local communities. Suffice to say that there are numerous localists in the Mekong region acting constructively in communities where the state is largely absent, until such time as large projects or resource extraction opportunities arise.

An example of a track 4 water governance forum a few years ago was the "Dialogue on River Basin Development and Civil Society in the Mekong region" embodied in forums held in Australia and northeast Thailand in 2002. The forums included policy researchers, government agencies from Mekong countries, Mekong River Commission, Murray-Darling Basin Commission, NGOs and other advocates, farmers, fishers, plus representatives from many different people's movements and campaigns. The dialogue took a critical look at the types of knowledge included in decision-making processes and the development paradigms of states. It aimed to shakeup the track 1 river basin management commissions. The meeting in Thailand, in particular, provided a stage for airing the grievances of local communities negatively affected by some of the development in the region (Local people 2002). The Vietnamese National Mekong Committee (VNMC) attended and issued the first public apology from Vietnamese government officials to those affected by the Yali dam tragedy. The Ubon Ratchatani and Brisbane events did not emerge from a vacuum, and should be seen as just a part of an ongoing political struggle led by those opposed to a particular water resources development paradigm. They were moments when stakeholders with different views and interests came together, but these actors were already, and have since remained, involved in the highly political, often polarized, governance processes surrounding Mekong region development decision-making. Each participant has a history shaped by and shaping past events, represents particular views and has different objectives and preferred strategies for interacting and negotiating (or not).

The Second International Meeting of Dam Affected People and their Allies was also held in northeast Thailand the following year. Again a localist discourse dominated event (Dam affected people and their allies 2003). This is not meant to infer that track 4 leaders/participants only support their own forums and reject others. Rarely are issues so clearly cut. For example, the declaration from Rasi Salai expressed clear support for the track 3 World Commission on Dams process. However, regional-scale track 4 forums (some examples are listed in table 9.5) in the Mekong region have thus far been more associated with assembling and profiling public testimony for lobbying purposes and discourse-shaping, and less optimistic or interested in engaging in any genuine deliberation with most actors representing either developmental states or business interests.

Issues

An investigation of water forums, seeking an understanding of MSP prospects, turns up many issues. In this section just a few will be discussed. Comments are made about some of the issues related to context, process and outcomes.

Context—windows of opportunity

Proponents of MSPs have no magic formula to sweep away many hurdles that exist for the approach to be more widely tried in the Mekong region. The countries are now ruled by various forms of multi-party, single-party and military junta systems of government. Cambodia is a pseudo-democracy, trending back to authoritarianism, with internal violence on the increase. China is a single party system, but there is increasing political space permitted for questioning leadership decisions, and the media is

Table 9.5 Recent regional water-related governance forums (tracks 3–4)

Track 3	Track 4
Forums of the Mekong Learning Initiative 1998+, concentrating on community based natural resources management, and transboundary learning partnerships between a group of Mekong region universities.	Dialogue on River Basin Development and Civil Society in the Mekong 2002 run by coalition of NGOs including Towards Ecological Recovery and Regional Alliance (TERRA) and the Australian Mekong Resource Centre.
Forums of the Oxfam Mekong Initiative and its partners which have concentrated on trade, poverty reduction strategies, infrastructure and capacity building.	NGOs partnering in campaigns challenging the sensibility of the energy paradigm embedded in the ASEAN/GMS electricity grid proposal, as at 2004.
Annual meeting of the Regional Environmental Forum 2002+, driven by World Resources Institute, focused on environmental governance.	Meetings of the Dam Affected People and their Allies–Rasi Salai, Thailand 2003.
Mekong region water governance network 2003+ focusing on cross border research partnerships and dialogue about water and food, water and energy, water and nature via M-POWER (Mekong Program on Water Environment and Resources).	International Rivers Network advocacy against projects such as Nam Theun 2 Dam in Laos.
	Probe International advocacy against the approach being taken in projects such as the GMS/ASEAN electricity grid.
Southeast Asia consultations in World Commission on Dams, and followup, such as IUCN-supported Dams and Development dialogues in Mekong countries 2001+	Activities of the Rivers Watch East and Southeast Asia (RWESA) network which focuses on linking communities and advocacy efforts related to dams and river development.
IUCN-convened Mekong region roundtable at World Conservation Congress, Bangkok 2004.	
Mekong Region Waters Dialogue in Vientiane Laos, July 2006.	

increasingly opening up. Laos is a single party system, led by mostly military figures, where no internal public dissent about national policies is permitted—although it should be noted that very recently new types of citizen organizations are being allowed to form. The Myanmar military junta strictly controls internal media, and suppresses dissenting views as a threat to national security (or regime survival). Thailand's citizens have hard-won relative freedoms, even though the extent of "democracy" remains subject to debate. Vietnam is a single party system, but where recently there has been a substantial expansion of political space. The dominant political culture does not provide the most supportive setting for regional MSPs to realize their potential, however, already at the local/national and regional level there have been some praiseworthy MSP efforts which provide a basis for cautious optimism.

Advocates of "well motivated dissent" have also been encouraged by particular events in 2004 which may have opened the door for the MSP approach to be more seriously incorporated into regional water governance. In China, Premier Wen Jiabao responded to extensive domestic lobbying and suspended plans to develop the Salween River hydropower cascade until a more complete impact assessment of the proposed development is undertaken. In the following year more than sixty projects were halted in China by the State Environment Protection Agency (SEPA) and ordered to go through an impact assessment process, which has at least some deliberative character. These positive moves have been offset by a reassertion at the provincial level of the power of government officials, many of whom resent any interference by central government or civil society actors, and continued secrecy about the Salween development governance process.

In Thailand, protests resulted in the government altering its privatization plan for the Electricity Generating Authority of Thailand (EGAT) which is a major regional energy and water resources actor. In Cambodia, the government has finally joined the chorus of concerns from local and international actors about the future of the Tonle Sap Lake fishery in the Mekong River basin, which is threatened by upstream dams (and local over fishing). In Laos, debate about whether to build the Nam Theun 2 Dam spilled over regional borders, with the World Bank feeling compelled to conduct multi-stakeholder briefings, albeit in an attempt to "sell" the benefits of the now-approved project. All of these examples are connected threads of the Mekong region water and energy web. Key actors are now engaging more openly in a battle for transnational discursive legitimacy in which regional MSPs can play a valuable role.

In any regional MSPs, there is a need to clarify the scope for negotiations. In water governance the need to negotiate is integral due to "the mundane fact that modern societies are complex, multicultural, and populated by individuals who are often quite sensitive about their personal rights"

(Baber 2004, 333). However, formal negotiations are not an essential element of MSPs, as MSPs may not have any formal decision-making or formal negotiating mandate. Far from being problematic, this may actually give participants more space to explore options and propose workable agreements.

A concern for some people heavily committed to the learning possibilities of MSPs is that widening the scope to allow negotiation encourages MSP actors to act in a self-interested manner. This is seen as regressive by those committed to MSP participants being completely impartial, and MSPs being apolitical "time-outs" from an external world where all negotiations should take place. But, MSPs do not have to unrealistically deny that actors have interests that they will continue to pursue, inside or outside the MSP. Nor do MSPs have to function as an impartial jury. It is quite plausible for "parallel learning and negotiation trajectories (to be) taking place at more or less the same time" (Leeuwis 2000, 950) either in the same or separate forums. MSP facilitators need to be quite explicit about all this.

There are some general preconditions before substantive negotiations can take place: divergence of actors' interests; actors' recognition of mutual interdependence in resolving problems; and actors capability of communicating with each other (Leeuwis 2000, 951). At the regional scale, the first condition is invariably met—actors do have different interests. Mutual interdependence is another matter—in reality there is often independence-dependence. For example, an upstream water user such as China or Vietnam is able, with relative impunity, to act independently of dependent downstream neighbors, such as in Laos or Cambodia. The final point about communication is central to MSPs. A platform without effective modes of communication will be an MSP failure.

Process—legitimacy from representation and political responsibility

Legitimacy has been usefully defined as "moral justifications for political and social action" (Atack 1999, 855). A key aspect of MSP legitimacy relates to the inclusiveness of an MSP process. This relates to notions of accountability, representation and political responsibility.

For many commentators, actor participation in an MSP is only legitimate if they are, or are formally representing, a direct stakeholder. Agents of the state, such as government or bureaucracy officials, have a formal constituency whom they can usually claim to represent. Similarly, company executives are, or should be, accountable to shareholders they are entrusted to represent. However, this framing is often used to deny bestowing legitimacy on actors who do not claim to represent others, whose status as a stakeholder may be contested, but who have much to offer in improving the quality of public debate. Civil society groups in the Mekong region are often challenged in this way.

Political responsibility is a normative concept that differs slightly from accountability in that accountability has formal obligations embedded within its definition (Jordan and Van Tuijl 2000). The concept of political responsibility offers a way forward through the legitimacy impasse encountered when some actors challenge an actor's accountability, and right to be involved in an MSP.

The NGO Focus on the Global South (FOCUS) (http://www.focusweb.org), active in the Mekong region, is an illustrative example. FOCUS is neither bound—nor empowered—by an external mandate. In the absence of a formal legitimizing mechanism such as membership endorsement, they have to clearly define their position. FOCUS's commitment to addressing the marginalization of large numbers of people throughout "the South" has defined their constituency; however, they do not claim to "represent" these diverse peoples, as they recognize they have no such mandate. But, they do have their own accountability mechanisms, linked to political responsibility, acutely felt for particular interests. This argument has been persuasively made by an NGO member: "… the right to speak claimed by NGOs is not necessarily derived from a strict or formal notion of direct representation of particular group interests but rather from a commitment to a set of values and insights which form the basis for an analysis of particular situations and a strategy to act on that analysis. Sometimes these are best expressed as impacts on local people or environments… (For example) there would be no inherent contradiction for an NGO to make submissions and arguments relating to a proposed big dam even when no "local" group shares those views—the arguments should be taken up in public debate and dealt with on their own merits" (Greeff 2000: 75).

In the absence of formal accountability to constituents, and without necessarily claiming to represent another, the notion of political responsibility is sufficient to claim legitimacy as a social actor wishing to participate in regional MSP.

Outcomes—consensus, consent, consultations

In many MSPs, where diverse representation has been obtained, there is confusion about whether the goal is consensus. For example, the WCD sought consensus, at least between the commissioners, driven by a view that "without consensus, a commission will be seen to have reproduced divisions among stakeholders, rather than transcending them" (Dubash et al. 2001, 4). However, if consensus is "unanimous agreement not just on a course of action, but also on the reasons for it" it follows that "in a pluralistic world consensus is unattainable, unnecessary and undesirable. More feasible and attractive are workable agreements in which participants agree on a course of action, but for different reasons" (Dryzek 2000,170). Using this definition, failure by an MSP to reach a complete consensus should not be seen as a disappointment, provided that progress is made in the search for an acceptable and workable agreement.

Fundamental disagreements about rights will remain problematic. This is part of the MSP context, and is not a criticism of the approach. For example, water-related MSPs are still grappling with diverging opinions about the principle of free prior informed consent (FPIC) which is often now included in generic international declarations. If accepted, FPIC explicitly recognizes indigenous and tribal peoples' rights to give or withhold their consent to activities affecting their land and water resources. FPIC holds that consent must be freely given, obtained prior to implementation of activities and be founded upon an understanding of the full range of issues implicated by the activity or decision in question (MacKay 2004). In MacKay's view, articulated in a briefing note for the World Bank's Extractive Industries Review (EIR), but applicable also to the water resources development debate:

> Decisions about when, where and how to exploit natural resources are normally justified in the national interest, which is generally interpreted as the interest of the majority. The result is that the rights and interests of unrepresented groups, such as indigenous peoples and others, will often be subordinated to the majority interest: conflict often ensues and the rights of indigenous peoples are often disregarded (MacKay 2004).

The issue is whether the rights of local resource users/occupiers have primacy? If so, FPIC is a right to veto development. The final EIR report supported FPIC. The bank response was that they too support FPIC, but they "stole" the acronym and redefined it as free prior informed consultation (World Bank 2004 annexed responses—points 15–16). FPIC was also a hot issue for the World Commission on Dams (WCD). Adoption of "gaining public acceptance" as a strategic priority recommendation of the final WCD report represented a compromise by the commissioners and a restriction of the FPIC principle. FPIC becomes critically important to any MSPs that is mandated with decision-making powers. Non-acceptance of FPIC significantly reduces the negotiating power of local resource users/occupiers.

FPIC is closely related to the concept of "meaningful participation." Both are highly relevant to MSPs. According to Goodland (2004), meaningful participation became mandatory in World Bank assisted projects from the late 1980s-early 1990s. He claims the bank interpreted this to mean the people being consulted about a proposal had a right to say no. If this was the case, it would appear that the trend is now in reverse. As with Dryzek, the international financial institutions (IFIs) seem to be accepting that consensus is just not always possible.

ADB provide a good example of what is at stake. Their previous policy for large water resources projects said:

"ADB will adopt a cautious approach to large water resource projects—particularly those involving dams and storage—given the record of environmental and social hazards associated with such projects. All such projects will need to be justified in the public interest, and all government and non-government stakeholders in the country must agree on the justification. Where the risks are acceptable and ADB's involvement necessary, ADB will ensure that its environmental and social impact assessment procedures are rigorously applied. Any adverse environmental effects will be properly mitigated, the number of affected people in the project area will be minimized, and those adversely affected will be adequately compensated in accordance with ADB's policy on involuntary resettlement. In line with its energy sector policy, ADB will continue to extend its support for technically and economically feasible hydropower projects that form part of a country's least-cost energy development plan, provided their environmental (including impact on fisheries) and social effects can be satisfactorily managed in accordance with ADB policies" (ADB 2004, Paragraph 32).

The bank now sees this policy as unworkable because of (in the bank's words) the "impractical requirement for all stakeholders to agree on the justification of large water resources projects." In 2004 ADB proposed the following revision:

"... All such projects will need to be justified in the public interest and stakeholders must be provided the opportunity to comment regarding the justification with their views considered. The ADB will promote the participation of government, civil society and other stakeholders in the country towards this end. Where the risks are acceptable...."

This is a significant shift in approach by both The World Bank and the ADB. They have backed away from endorsing MSPs which have negotiating mandates. They now support only consultative/advisory MSPs. For a brief period, MSP policy of the IFIs had strengthened the negotiating positions of less powerful actors. However, the IFIs are now reaffirming the priority they attach to the decision-making authority of governments.

While noting the oscillation of the IFIs, it should be clearly noted that even a shift towards mandatory consultation and advisory MSPs in the Mekong region would be a significant step forward, as regional water governance is largely devoid of multi-stakeholder deliberative processes.

Opportunities

Something needs to be done to lift the standard of regional water governance in the Mekong region. Despite many types of regional water forums, large-scale water resources development has been deficient with negative domestic and transboundary impacts consistently ignored or outweighed by decision-makers.

Important next steps for the region would be to add robust regional MSP elements—giving space for the airing and scrutiny of all perspectives—to the governance of, for example: the Salween in China, Myanmar, and Thailand; the GMS/ASEAN electricity grid impacting on all six Mekong countries, and Thailand's nebulous water grid plans that directly affect several of its neighbors.

Salween River—prioritizing big business, natural heritage or human rights?

Substantial hydropower expansion is part of China's national planning and Yunnan province's role is key. Yunnan is seen as having 24 percent of China's hydropower potential for medium- and large-sized projects (He Jing 2002). In late 2003 much more information filtered into the public domain outlining extensive hydropower development proposed for the Salween which flows from China into Myanmar. The upper watersheds of the Salween, Mekong and Yangtze are known as the Three rivers region, was declared a World Heritage site by UNESCO in July 2003.

There are advanced plans for a cascade of thirteen dams on the Chinese reaches of the presently undammed Salween River that, if built, would have a profound impact. The China Huadian Corporation is one of the "big 5" power generation companies receiving assets from 2003 onwards which were previously "owned" by the giant State Power Corporation. The right to develop the Salween River is seen by Huadian as one of the transferred assets now in their portfolio. Since major energy industry reforms were announced late 2002 there has been a stampede by the "big 5 + 1"—not forgetting the Three Gorges development group—to secure their assets, principally coal-related, and move to develop their new assets, including "rivers for hydro" in various types of partnership with local authorities (see Dore et al this volume).

The decision-making and approvals processes have been far from transparent. The economic justification unspecified, and the ecological and cultural risks downplayed (both in China and further downstream). Moreover, the lines between public and private interest and ownership have become increasingly blurry as the energy companies blend state authority with private sector competitive opportunism. Remarkably, as the plans entered the public domain, broader civil society—beyond the usual officials, business operatives and experts—became much more involved. However, early optimism that the Premier's intervention in April 2004 might lead to a more open process has been diminished as secrecy continued to surround the formal impact assessment process, and some opponents in Yunnan have suffered extensive harassment.

There are five other dams being promoted downstream of China, including Ta Sang—planned to produce 7,000 megawatts. The Ta Sang dam, involving many actors including the Bangkok-based MDX Company, is already controversial due to numerous reports of human rights abuses of the Shan people in the dam area by the Myanmar military. Another two are planned for further downstream where the Salween forms the border between Myanmar and Thailand. Without any public debate, officials from both those countries committed in August 2004 to jointly develop the river (Pradit Ruangdit 2004).

All this has major implications for local livelihoods in each of these countries and a proposed regional electricity grid (see below). The situation is ripe for a regional MSP to ensure the driving assumptions, proposed development benefits, tradeoffs and transboundary impacts are more fully considered.

GMS/ASEAN electricity grid—the best option?

The Asian Development Bank (ADB) and the Electricity Generating Authority of Thailand (EGAT) are the major promoters of two overlapping schemes known as: the Greater Mekong Subregion (GMS) Power Interconnection and Trade, and the Association of Southeast Asian Nations (ASEAN) Power Grid. The leaders of the six Mekong region countries signed an inter-governmental agreement forming an electricity grid in 2002. ADB has prepared a list of USD 4.58 billion worth of loans and grants for financing 32 grid and grid-related projects in the Mekong region (Ryder 2003: 3). A further USD 43 billion would be needed for the twelve hydropower dams and the transmission system (IRN 2004: 10). Proponents cite the logic of no alternative. Opponents challenge the economic and technical justification. Embodied in the plan is a massive change in the way in which water resources are developed throughout the region.

In the last ten years of planning, there has been practically no involvement by civil society in any related governance process. This is now changing as local, national, regional and international actors are becoming involved. For the ADB, the grid should become a test case of their Strategic Environment Framework (SEI et al. 2002), intended to guide bank investments in the Mekong region water and transport sectors. A properly conducted, regional MSP focused on the electricity grid would be a very constructive governance intervention.

Thailand water grid—for irrigation, agribusiness transformation or urban supply?

At present contained primarily within the domestic political arena of Thailand, are the intra-government negotiations concerning the demand and distribution aspects of Thailand's proposed, but somewhat vague (at least in its publicly presented form) national water grid. A key driver for the grid is the increasing water scarcity in the Chao Phraya River basin which is the principal food bowl of Thailand, and provides much of the water for the capital city of Bangkok. Many parts of the grid have been previously conceived, designed and touted in the past. In 2004, new life was breathed into quite a few of the old plans by the regime of former Prime Minister Thaksin Shinawatra, but publicly available information was initially very scarce.

Numerous potential diversions have implications for the river dependent communities in Laos, Myanmar, Cambodia and Vietnam. If implemented, and at the time of finalizing this chapter political interest has again waned, the future of millions of Thai farmers is also unclear. The only way of funding such a scheme is if water pricing policies are introduced and agribusiness contract farming is given access to the "new water." So is it water for a new war on poverty, or water for agribusiness, or water for Bangkok? Whose water is it anyway? Many wished to shift debate about the water grid into the public sphere. A regional MSP about the Thailand water grid would have allowed these types of questions to be addressed.

World Bank's (and ADB's) Mekong Water Resources Assistance Strategy

The World Bank is now returned to funding large-scale water resources infrastructure. This is evidenced in the contents of the bank's Water Resources Sector Strategy (WB 2004), the substantial forward budget allocations, and the subsequent burst of efforts to develop national and/or regional strategies in places such as Pakistan, India and China. The Mekong River basin is one of the places designated to receive a regional strategy. In November 2004 there was a pseudo-consultative process involving donors, governments and civil society. A document was subsequently developed, primarily in consultation with governments and donors. ADB was brought in as a partner, and MRC also became more involved through time. Regional civil society saw the document, after a twenty-month hiatus, when it emerged on request in time for the Mekong Region Waters Dialogue. The implications for the region could be very significant. Again, it would seem that a more genuine consultation, coupled with an MSP, could lead to more informed public deliberation and choices.

Conclusion

MSPS are rooted in a belief in the added value provided by deliberation which is inclusive, information-rich and flexibly facilitated, actively promoting analysis of different views. However, MSPS are seen by some as disrespectful of, and at times subversive to, existing public decision-making structures. MSPS in the Mekong region led by civil society have been accused of being undemocratic, and too empowering of interest groups with policy positions which may differ from dominant policy positions within state governments or parts of their associated bureaucracy. Advocates claim the opposite, that in fact these types of processes are complementary to formal state decision-making processes, serving as a counter weight to many undemocratic water-related governance forums and, thus actually deepen democracy. The convenors of the new Mekong Region Waters Dialogue certainly adhere to this latter view.

There is some new political space in the Mekong region created by globalization, and corresponding new regionalisms, which is providing oxygen to MSP approaches. However, proponents will invariably continue to meet resistance from state actors and others with vested interests reinforced by the status quo. Many state actors still believe, or at least rhetorically pretend, that domestic-led criticism is unpatriotic, and—despite an emerging body of international water law—cross-border enquiry/criticism of water resources development plans is an unacceptable encroachment on hard-won state sovereignty. This political resistance to MSP approaches, grounded in self-interest and transboundary geopolitics, should not be underestimated. Other forms of advocacy will remain important to encourage more and less powerful actors to give MSPs a chance to fulfill their regional potential by being sites for authentic deliberation, learning by all actors, and (possibly) negotiation.

Box 9.2 Politics of participation: MSPs in Thailand
by Surichai Wun'gaeo

MSPS is a new phrase which seems to have only emerged in the last few years. Somehow the arena of development action and decision-making has become more complex. We used to talk of participation in terms of who decides, and who participates. But in recent years, it has become an issue of who decides who should participate at different levels in any specific development project. MSPS is a phrase that conveys an acceptance and support for more inclusive processes which should welcome new thinking. However, some people may still implement MSPS in a mechanical way. Real challenges remain in that some people don't or can't speak out; some are too poor, some too frustrated. These people are often left out from the consultation, participation or decision-making processes.

I think that MSPS is a phrase which is inherently supportive of a new inclusiveness of affected people in project deliberation and decision-making. I want to see MSPS that are more progressive than just engaging with visible participants at meetings. We should have an open, creative attitude when organising MSP processes.

Equivalent Thai term

We use *phu mi suan dai suan sia*— people who have benefit and losses in relation to a project—those who have a stake in the project—we can also say *phu mi suan kiao khong*—in someway they are related or involved to the project—the phrase has a relationship of power behind it —who says who is having a stake or not is the issue.

In reality, certain people are being automatically kept apart from the political decision-making process.

Definition of MSPS

For John Dore, MSPS are quite comprehensive. I agree on his definition and with many dimensions of this idea. Our society has entered an increasingly complex situation. I think MSPS might somehow better accommodate complex social relationships, which are not just horizontal or vertical.

We need to balance our understanding of an ideal process or situation with the need for concrete, substantive processes. Somehow we have to bring MSPS into experiential realities so that we don't make it just theory or catchword that does not resemble the application. Given very different contexts we also have to guard against MSPS being promoted as some cure-all, ready-made package.

Can MSPS work in Thailand?
There are different socio-political and cultural contexts in the Mekong region, and big differences between actors sharing parts of those contexts. But overall, we have this necessity of getting different actors on the same platform focusing on whatever are the critical issues.

In Thailand, when we talk of villagers in Mae Wang and the forestry department and local officials—somehow they have come to agreement to support and work together. Looking back, these are MSPS. But again with the forest issue, in some other areas, the same forestry people can be technocratic and not trust villagers. So even within the same organisation, in the same country, there are differences and it can be difficult to build trust.

We have to open up the possibility for participation. If the basic political structure still gives strong weight to state structure and bureaucratic authority then it is more difficult to have an influential MSP process. In my view, in terms of the socio-political context under former Prime Minister Thaksin Shinawatra, there was more possibility for MSP (or public deliberation) in the first year of his term but a lesser amount of room provided or allowed for in the later years. This is because of the so-called chief executive officer (CEO) management style that gives priority to business-like implementation, rather than MSP-like public deliberation.

In Thailand, state officials have not been serious about defining or discerning the various public interests. The CEO management policy has only made the bureaucracy more responsive to achieving targets set by the central government or even just satisfying the personal whims and desires of the prime minister. The CEO-style runs against public interest. It cannot be overcome unless through an MSP analysis or process.

The question is how to increase the participation of different and often marginalised voices affected by development projects into decision-making? If a society is interested in the negative effects of a project, that society needs something like MSPS to become more open, accept diverse opinions, and give legitimacy to other voices.

The challenge is not to take for granted that MSPS are an automatic medicine without making sense of the whole context but designing and encouraging MSPS which understand the context and find ways of enabling genuine participation.

In Thailand, MSPS was actualised in some ways in the National Reconciliation Commission (NRC) that was set up to seek peaceful solutions to the continuing ethnic violence in South Thailand. The situation in South Thailand has become more violent in the last few years. But this problem cannot be understood without seeing it in terms of the power relations between the political elite in Bangkok as well as the troubled history of the predominantly Muslim southern region. MSPS can help to broaden the decision-making process to better understand the region's multi-actor context.

> *On the issues of water governance and water resources in Thailand—for e.g. the recently proposed water grid*
> The water grid is different from the proposed energy power grid. Water is contextualised within different ecosystems, landscapes, and agricultural systems. We need to see water not only from a macro-perspective but rooted in different ecologies. The water grid, in fact, is an anti-people and anti-ecological idea. The grid represents concentration of power and decision-making in one entity. The word itself is very much a camouflage, an imposition; it hides its real insensitivity to the issues of people and water.
> For Thailand, MSPs could help sharpen our realization that state-society relations could be strengthened to overcome the different challenges of sustainable development and help open up our learning process.

Notes

This paper has benefited from interaction with, and many suggestions from, various colleagues, especially Louis Lebel, Mary Jane Real, Jeff Rutherford, Kate Lazarus, Rajesh Daniel and Masao Imamura. Others such as Mingsarn Kaosa-ard, Surichai Wun'gaeo, Yu Xiaogang, Steve Dovers, Jim Woodhill and Jeroen Warner have also helped shape the ideas. The writings of John Dryzek and Neils Roling have been especially helpful. Of course, all errors or misconceptions are my responsibility.

1 Some issues are of region-wide significance, still others: transboundary, transborder, cross-border, or interbasin. This chapter uses the term "regional" to encompass any issue involving at least one of these characteristics.

2 The concept of the state-society complex, which seems to have emerged from New Regionalism scholars at Sweden's Goteborg University, resonates well in the Mekong region. It transcends the more simplistic notion in which actors have often been classified as state, business, or civil society. Such a classification ignores many other key groups, such as the military and donors/funders, implies homogeneity within groups, and ignores multiple roles. For example, business or military actors may dominate government.

3 The conceptual difference between regionalisms and regionalisations is elaborated by Schulz et al. The point has been made that "the identification of new patterns of regionalization (co-existing with older forms) is more relevant than attempting to identify a new era of regionalization" (Hettne 1999, 8). The later section distinguishing between tracks 1–4 is an attempt to do just that.

4 There are many other social challenges which transcend Mekong region borders, such as: pressure on other natural resources such as forests and biodiversity, ethnic minority marginalisation, labor migration, human trafficking, HIV-AIDS, narcotics, dealing with the pressure to embrace agriculture biotechnology including genetically modified crops, and other impacts of international economic integration (see Mingsarn Kaosa-ard and Dore 2003).

5 The Salween, Mekong and—to a lesser extent—the Irrawaddy have their flow influenced by the annual Himalayan/Tibetan snow melt, in addition to the monsoon rains. The Chao Phraya and Red are shorter rivers which originate below

the snowline, hence their flow is dependent on the monsoonal climate. Across the region, there are also countless sub-basins–that is, catchments or watersheds– natural lakes, aquifers, and human-built dams and reservoirs. Plus there are many coastal river basins, some of which are quite large. Collectively, they comprise the visible and accessible freshwater "life source" or "resource."

6 I agree with the view that non-violent "conflict is not necessarily bad, abnormal or dysfunctional," but rather an inherent element of human interaction (Moore 1987: ix) due to the common incompatibility of goals, interests, perceptions or values. However, many Mekong actors prefer to speak of disputes, or differences, as the English word conflict is tainted by bad memories of the particularly troubled, not too distant past.

7 To the deliberative democrat, John Dryzek, deliberation is "multifaceted interchange or contestation across discourses within the public sphere" (2001, 652) where discourses are seen as "shared sets of assumptions and capabilities embedded in language that enables its adherents to assemble bits of sensory information that come their way into coherent wholes" (1999, 34). MSPs provide a mechanism for such "contestation across discourses." In so doing, they are in accord with the social learning perspective, the "building blocks" of which are: the constructivist paradigm, an orientation towards reflection and action, and commitment to a holistic approach (Maarleveld and Dangbgnon 2002, 70–75). Just as MSPs are diverse in their purpose and emphasis, so to is the "broad church" (Hay 2002, 208) of constructivism which "both seeks and serves to restore politics and agency to a world often constituted in such a way as to render it fixed and unyielding" (2002, 201). So it can be seen that the deliberative democrats, the social learning school, and constructivists, have much in common. Each emphasize the role of ideas as significant in reshaping the world.

8 These are the pillars of the Earth Charter (ECC 2000) which resonate well with the author. However, of course there are many other examples of ethical/ moral frameworks to which actors may aspire, whether determined by religion (e.g. Buddhist teachings), secular norms (e.g. UN Declaration of Human Rights), eco-centricity (e.g. Ecosystems Approach), or livelihoods (e.g. Sustainable Livelihoods Approach).

9 While this chapter is focused on the regional scale, it is not meant to deny or overshadow the existence of an equally diverse plethora of water governance forums focused on the national and sub-national scales. Tracks 1, 2, 3 and 4 are also discernible at this scale. To acknowledge these, some promising national/ sub-national MSP examples are included in the section discussing track 3. These examples are provided partly to inspire transboundary efforts which could be similarly motivated and constructed.

10 In combination with the Chinese-driven China-ASEAN free trade agreement— and an "early harvest" of products on which tariffs are being rapidly dismantled— trade between China and Thailand is escalating, as is the traffic on the Mekong River. The importance of river traffic to overall trade should not be over-stated. While increasing, it is from a low base. In 1999 it accounted for only about 1 percent of the value of goods traded between the two countries.

11 While to funders, REPSI was focused on the uplands, to encourage the participation of a wider range of regional actors it was necessary to broaden the geographic scope to encompass the Mekong region.

CHAPTER 10

SYNTHESIS: DISCOURSE, POWER AND KNOWLEDGE

Antonio P. Contreras

The Mekong region is a vast and geographically diverse territory, home to many cultural and social formations. Yet, it is also a region composed of countries and societies with experiences that are seemingly different at first glance but which upon scrutiny would reveal similarities, both subtle and apparent. Engagements between dominant and emerging power and knowledge are spread across the mountains, plains and waterways of the region.

This interplay is reflected in the manner social institutions are shaped and operate to produce knowledge and policies about water—seen either as an economic resource for hydropower and irrigation, or as a natural force that destroys and/or builds in the form of floods. Social institutions articulate their power through images and symbols that are in turn enabled or silenced by dominant forces. At the heart lie the rights to livelihoods of local communities and the political legitimacy and survival of the state. Here the structures and processes of society cleave along gender, class and ethnicity lines.

The media as instrument for ideological reproduction becomes a prime commodity as venues for legitimation by state or for resistance by civil society. Science, and its technocratic apparatus, is also a major source for ideological justification. In the Mekong region, all of the above-mentioned processes exist no longer as contained within the boundaries of nation-states, but are played amidst the backdrop of a growing regionalism not only of statist but also of civil society institutions.

The chapters in this volume collectively lend testimony both to the enormous power to control the production of discourses, and to the emerging practices that exist to provide alternatives. The chapters clearly illustrate three key themes that operate in the Mekong region: the dominance of statism, the emerging role of science in the dynamics of domination and resistance, and the challenges to create spaces for alternative discourses.

Statism in the context of regionalism

The emergence of the Mekong region as a geographical space for imagining development alternatives and as a political space for structuring power relations has revealed the challenges inherent in regionalism. The chapter on multi-stakeholder platforms (MSPS) indicates there is no singular form of regionalism in the Mekong region. Instead, what you see is a pluralism of engagements that clearly mirror the multiple nodes of interaction that deal with a wide array of issues, from issues of peace and security, to issues of environment, development, poverty and human rights.

Ideally, the emergence of regional institutions is supposed to reflect a desire to go beyond the boundaries and, logically, the authorities of nation-states. The complexity of the issues that regional institutions confront necessarily requires a broadening not only of the focus but also of the locus of the interactions. This enables the emergence of state-society nodes, where different actors from civil society and the state engage each other, and have learned to co-exist if not compete with each other. Thus, and ideally, the emergence of the Mekong region as a politically-constructed "state of mind" and "way of doing things" should enable a shift away from statist solutions to problems, and should gradually create a more defined and stronger space for civil society actors and processes that cross national boundaries. Indeed, there is some indication that this is happening.

Although, regionalism may have signaled the emergence of more civil society engagements, and the entry of transnational exchanges of knowledge and information, the chapters in this volume indicate that the rites are nevertheless dictated by statist imperatives. The state imprimatur remains dominant in multi-stakeholder negotiations and in the production of discourses, where externally imposed and state-sanctioned knowledge end up as dysfunctional, in that they do not help clarify issues, and/or are implicated in state legitimation, in that they are simply used by the state and its cohorts to further their interests. This is clearly illustrated in the cases of water management for irrigation purposes.

Similarly, the dominant constructs about water management for irrigation are mainly modeled from experiences outside the Mekong that are influenced by external agencies or development banks, and are actively promoted by national governments through their policies. Furthermore, economic changes manifested through industrialization and urbanization play a significant role in the transformation in irrigation technology and practices in the region. Even as nongovernmental organizations (NGOs) and civil society actors tend to resist these, through their active advocacy for irrigation practices that are more attuned with local traditions, culture and knowledge, the debate that ensues is not between these voices coming from civil society and the state actors, but is in fact between and among different state actors. NGO voices are not effectively factored into the policy process, and what are instead given privilege are the voices of technical consultants espousing the same voices but within the ambit of a state contract. In the end, calls for participatory reforms are co-opted by bureaucratized participation, even as line state agencies hijack alternative concepts in their attempts to relocate themselves in the new paradigm.

The visibility of state actors in directing the flow of discourses resides not only in their production and reproduction through policies within their borders, but also in the context of inter-state politics, where national interests dominate the agenda. This is clearly illustrated in the case of the Navigation Channel Improvement Project for widening the upper reaches of the Mekong River where the environmental impact assessment process and outcome were dominated by the politics of self-interest of spheres of influence within the states, and no serious negotiations existed along the science-policy boundary. The assessment team composed of a multinational group of "experts'" conducted a rapid two-day assessment, and quickly gave the project favorable ratings by pointing out that the blasting of "obstructions" or the reefs along the bed of the river will not have any significant adverse impacts, a conclusion that was not subjected to independent technical evaluation. There was also no serious effort to consult with stakeholders, which include local peoples and state agencies not directly involved in the project. The EIA team did not include technical skills one would normally expect from a serious assessment, and was dominated by the Ministry of Transport. This limited the technical capacity of the team and the political influence of environment/fisheries sectors in the process, and led to unclear focus of the exercise emanating from a failure to correctly scope the nature and extent of the project. This railroading was a direct outcome of the different interests from participating countries with China—Myanmar's (Burma) friendship, Thailand's desire to buy cheap energy, and Lao PDR's relative insecurity with its neighbor—to benefit from a conclusion that would be in China's interest, but eventually are also in their own interests.

The case of independent nation-states succumbing to dominant external forces is further illustrated in the case of hydropower development. However, new players emerged here in the form of rent-seeking transnational forces. These are able to influence national policy decisions to over-estimate the demand for energy, and thereby serve as a justification for hydropower projects, despite the evidence pointing out that energy drawn from these sources are not competitive compared with electricity drawn from other sources, such as natural gas and demand side management and other renewable energy options. In energy planning, hydropower projects end up being authorized by states as part of bilateral or regional cooperation initiatives, even if these are not warranted by cost-based analysis. What is tragic is that these projects entail enormous political and economic costs to state governments, in as much as they subsist on state subsidies as well as state intervention and involvement. The high cost of "transmission/distribution" systems are typically subsidized by states, thereby making hydropower firms economically viable. Thus, the self-interest of states is unwittingly subordinated to the regional transnational economic forces that operate outside their control and whose locus of accountability goes beyond the state, but whose main impetus for their operations heavily rely on state processes of legitimation and approval. This effectively makes hydropower operate in the context of a "state-firm" coalition. A feature of this complex political-economic relations is the fact that public interest is subordinated both by powerful domestic interests that stand to gain from lucrative contracts associated with hydropower expansion, and by the regional transnational forces who also stand to gain through legitimization of their role as well as through lending enormous sums of money.

The power of states to dictate and legitimize is even further strengthened, despite the seeming opportunity provided by regionalism, ironically through transnational structures and processes themselves. The Asian Development Bank (ADB) and World Bank, contrary to earlier practice of encouraging multistakeholder platforms (MSPS) with negotiating mandates, have reverted to the more statist practice of supporting only those MSPS that are consultative and advisory in character. This has reaffirmed the decision-making authority of governments to the detriment of those actors in civil society with weaker negotiation positions. There is, however, a silver lining to this in the context of the Mekong, where it is admitted that even just a general recognition of consultative/advisory mode for MSPS is good enough as a starting point in a region where multi-stakeholder processes are absent in water governance discussions.

Where states remain the dominant source of power and authority, even in cases where their interests may be held up for exposure to later risks such as in the case of hydropower, spaces remain to articulate a critique, if not to engage the statist discourses and practices. The recognition of MSPS, even for consultation and in advisory capacities may indeed open up a space for civil society participation, and for critical engagements between states and civil society actors. This would, however, entail vigilance among those whose positions are weakened by this accommodation. The media may become crucial in this regard. However, the media in the region remains captured by national interests, and seldom talk about regional and transboundary issues. This reality enables statist practices to remain dominant.

Science as power and knowledge

One of the forces that has the potential to restrain the state is the will to knowledge and truth, where the supposed objectivity and neutrality of science can provide the necessary brakes to the otherwise unhampered trajectory of the politics of self-interest propagated by the state elites and their cohorts. The rationality of science can provide the logic not only for resisting the absence of reason that clouds the objectivity of political actors, but also in providing saner alternatives to strategies that feed only the interests of economic rent-seekers and their collaborating bureaucrats. However, there is also the equally plausible scenario where the power and limitations of scientific knowledge becomes a tool of the dominant elites to justify their interests, and to lend legitimacy to their actions, and may be used to deflect criticism or to project good faith. Undeniably, the Mekong region is a fertile ground for these various possibilities.

The implication of science and its associated power in the maintenance of elite interests could not only be found beyond the willed manipulation of the political actors but may also be as an outcome of the very nature of scientific knowledge. This volume is full of examples of how the seemingly politically innocent and harmless array of scientific truth claims could lend legitimacy to practices that end up as exclusionary and harmful to local knowledge and power, and to the interests of the poor and the marginalized. For example, the chapter on gender pointed out that the failure to appreciate the fact that knowledge is gendered has serious implications to the manner such knowledge deals with women and their needs, thereby leading to policies and practices that are also gender-blind. The effects of the inherent structural biases of scientific knowledge is also made evident in flood management where most government and international efforts to reduce the risk of disasters from floods fail since they focus on structural and technical measures. This view projects the problem as apolitical, and tends to work on the "science" behind floods and less on the social dynamics that underpin the spatial location and the social practices of affected communities. The inherent bias of scientific knowledge in favor of certain kinds of analytical frames can have socially deleterious effects that may not necessarily be the outcome of a deliberate plan to exclude or marginalize.

Policy makers in the region also either ignore or remain unaware of existing, and potential for, "commons" arrangements, adhering to a conventional state/private sector approach for natural resources management that marginalizes local spaces of knowledge and power.

However, much as there is a lot of evidence to paint science as structurally challenged vis-à-vis social realities, it is also important to point out that there are certain kinds of scientific knowledge that can be beneficial, if only they are properly harnessed. State actors can deliberately use science as a tool for achieving power. However, it can also be said that the failure of state actors to effectively use the right kind of scientific knowledge can be traced from weak state capacity, and may have impacts that could lead to the further weakening of that capacity. This is clearly illustrated in the way institutions dealing with flood control have failed to adequately use scientific information in their work. There is evidence to show that institutional arrangements in the Mekong region prevent meaningful coordination and communication among agencies dealing with floods. Processes for utilizing scientific information about floods and disasters are evidently weak, if not absent. There is also no evidence of deliberate efforts to learn from previous disasters, as what has been shown to be the case in Thailand when the bureaucratic machinery failed to learn from a flood event in 1988 to establish mechanisms to correctly address and prepare for another flood event in 2001.

It is also apparent that scientific knowledge can be harnessed not only by the state, but also even by civil society and local communities, to develop their own capacities. Furthermore, the popular access to technology, such as the Internet and radio, has the effect of democratizing access to information that may have positive effects on the resilience of local communities and their capacity to take stock of their situations and the options available to them such as the case of the local commune in Vietnam that availed the internet to get advanced information about the arrival of storms. In addition, the use of various information technology by NGOs have provided alternative media venues to advocate for issues which otherwise would not be tackled by mainstream and mostly state-run or controlled media.

Alternatives at risk

The domination by the state of the processes by which discourses are produced and realized through policy intervention, and its effective use of science and the mass media in lending an air of legitimacy to such processes is by no means total. The different chapters in this volume reveal the dominant position of the state and the potential cooptation of science. However, they have also clearly shown the presence of alternative actors and institutions that confront and engage the dominant practices, and the challenges that they have to deal with. Alternative voices are able to create spaces for articulating discourses that give privilege to local communities and to alternative development perspectives. However, there are also evidences that these voices face the risk of cooptation, or of negation.

The sources of these alternative discourses in the Mekong region are usually the marginalized voices themselves. Examples of these are the civil society forces representing local communities whose livelihoods are threatened by poorly planned large-scale development like dams that deny the value of flooded forests and fisheries for local livelihoods. There is also evidence of the scaling up of partnerships and alliances, from village level to federation, suggesting that the "community" bearing the alternative discourse is more class-based than spatially based on geography.

Civil society activism has made its presence felt in the Mekong, particularly in Thailand where an active civil society has taken root. However, there is still much to be desired in terms of actual involvement of civil society and citizens' groups in processes of decision-making. Citizens' opposition to dam construction has been rarely taken into meaningful consideration. Participation of stakeholders in water policy-related meetings remains at best symbolic. As pointed out in the chapter on irrigation, while multilateral aid agencies and states are showing signs of guarded accommodation of civil society voices, most large-scale planning remains an exclusive domain for powerful interests. While this may be a direct manifestation of the lack of seriousness to meaningfully involve local voices, it may also be a result of the inability of local actors to scale-up their concerns to national and regional levels. Regional and national actors are also unable to scale-down their macro-views to more local contexts.

However, it is important to point out that civil society action is not limited to oppositional forms of politics. For example, civil society has an important role in reducing the vulnerability of local communities to disastrous floods, by organizing and rationalizing their operations to become effective institutions in dealing with disasters. An example is the innovative community-based disaster management program of the Asian Disaster Preparedness Center in Thailand. These types of civil society activities provide not only a counter-narrative to the dominant state practice, but in the end complement the state, and in case of state neglect or absence, perform functions which are more effective in dealing with the needs of local communities.

In both modes of activity, whether in oppositional or collaborative modes, alternative voices face risks. This is even made more real with the resurgence of statist discourses even in areas where it appeared that civil society was gaining ground, a particular example of which is Thailand. This development continuously threatens the deepening and broadening of alternative voices in the region. Alternative practices that work in opposition to the dominant practice may end up being de-legitimized by state authority and be subjected to censorship or persecution, as in the case of alternative media organizations, or they may be unable to or be denied access to necessary resources, as well as to their audiences. Proponents and advocates of MSPS, while being inspired by the on-going globalization process that permits and enables participatory governance even at regional and global scales, remain subjected to state surveillance, and are projected as agents of unrest, or at best seen as working against the interests of their own countries. This leads to a situation where the potential of MSPS within the Mekong region, particularly in water-related governance, remain unfulfilled.

Those practices that collaborate with the state face the risk of being co-opted where alternative strategies are manipulated to serve the interests of the dominant. Yet, a more insidious form of co-option occurs when alternative ideas and theories are appropriated or interpreted in ways that do not serve the interests of the marginalized. This is true in water management for irrigation, where state-contracted consultants effectively appropriated counter narratives that are being espoused by NGOs. This is also vividly illustrated in the issue of gender, where theories that are supposed to be promoting gender-fair practices are rendered counterproductive when they are mobilized for instrumental ends, or when they become embedded in discourses that reify women into stereotyped fields of subjectivity in being closer to nature and as victims of development.

Challenges for inquiry and political action

The power to control not only territories and spaces but also states of mind and the production of knowledge rests on a complex terrain of institutions. The Mekong region has become a "state of mind" about which images and discourses take shape. It has also become a laboratory for development intervention, one that is played amidst the backdrop of global environmental urgencies even as we deal with the resurgence of strong states, the increasing power of civil societies, and the emerging complexities brought upon by globalization not only of economies but also of cultures and identities. Democratization and decentralization processes have taken root in many areas. Private economic interests have flourished, some of which provide promising institutional arrangements for better governance, while others are implicated in rent-seeking activities. It is in this complex analytical and political territory where the discourses created by this volume must speak to, take root, and create new meanings through inquiry and political action.

This volume showed how statism is manifested in the discourses about water in the Mekong region. Development strategies in the region focus on modernization, infrastructures, and technocratic solution. Technical intervention and policy formulation receive much impetus from state-directives that are responding to bilateral or regional cooperation initiatives, the success of which largely depends on a combination of heavy state subsidies matched by state intervention and rent-seeking. The cooption of science, on the other hand, is evident when scientific warrants for policy interventions are projected as neutral, even if science is in fact recruited to justify exclusionary processes.

These operations of power and knowledge through an elite capture of the imperatives of the state and the rationality of science is matched by the emergence of alternative forces, narratives/discourses and structures that address the need to go beyond the state, to make policy making inclusive, and to link science to the agenda of local communities. However, there are certain risks, even as alternative structures and processes may also be problematic. The emergence of MSPS to enable participation of different actors deepens democracy, although they may also be captured by special interest groups that may influence decision making processes and work against the greater interest of the public. Alternative media practices remain hostage to economic pressures and to political persecution. Gender practices that offer alternatives face the risk of being subsumed under efficiency arguments that do not actually address the real logic of the problem that women face.

It is amidst this backdrop that the interplay between discourse, power and knowledge in the Mekong becomes a highly charged terrain for the unfolding drama, both overt and subtle, of domination and resistance.

The chapters in this volume have, in various ways, raised issues that warrant a response not only in the form of research, but also in the domain of political action. Of paramount concern is the creation of spaces within which civil society actors and local communities can engage the state, and how the various institutions in the region can harness these forces. Corollary to this would be the transformation of state and regional institutions to be able to nurture and engage civil society and local communities, and to make them work in modes where they are not poised to sequester power and constrain the potentials of these alternative voices. There are already examples of functional interactions between the state and civil society. Devolution of state power and decentralization of governance have begun to provide spaces for these interactions. Furthermore, private sector participation is now becoming a mode not only for the delivery of services, but also for proactive local mobilization towards environmental and natural resource management. What needs to be done is to inquire into the conditions in which these interactions exist to enable positive impacts, and to create these conditions through advocacy and political mobilization.

Another area of concern is the role of science and knowledge in political transformation in the region. There is some sense of urgency in strengthening science-policy connections. However, what is even more urgent, and will have to take precedence over this, is the transformation of science into a discourse that enables, and is inclusive of, the marginalized voices in the region, and not as a force whose imagined neutrality becomes an ideological blinder for its appropriation by powerful forces. We also need to transform policy processes that can allow for representation of more voices, to be improved by better science and equally consider the political dimensions to the construction of scientific knowledge. There is also the task of inquiring into the conditions that enable people-based science, and of mobilizing to realize these conditions. It has been shown in this volume that while science and knowledge can indeed be used by the powerful interests, they can also be harnessed to enable local communities and marginalized sectors and equip them with tools and skills to navigate the otherwise unfamiliar terrain dominated by the state and economic elites. In the end, this is not only about contesting what is good science, but also that good management may also depend more on genuine participation and dialogue.

REFERENCE LIST

CHAPTER 1
Introduction: Water governance in the Mekong region

Biswas, A. K. 2005. "Integrated Water Resources Management: A Reassessment." In *Integrated Water Resource Management in South and South-East Asia* edited by A. K. Biswas, O. Varis, and C. Tortajada. London: Oxford University Press.
Campbell, I. C. 2005. "Integrated Water Resource Management for the Mekong River Basin." In *Integrated Water Resource Management in South and South-East Asia* edited by A. K. Biswas, O. Varis, and C. Tortajada. London: Oxford University Press.
Deutsche Presse-Agentur (DPA). 2006. "Cambodian PM Lauds China as His Model Development Partner." July 26.
Evans, P. 2004. "Development as Institutional Change: The Pitfalls of Monocropping and the Potentials of Deliberation." *Studies in Comparative International Development* 38 (4): 30–52.
Ferguson, J. 1994. *The Anti-Politics Machine: "Development," Depoliticization, and Bureaucratic Power*. Lesotho: University of Minnesota Press.
Gay, C. 2004. "Thai Project Yields Graft and New Policies." *Far Eastern Economic Review*, July 29.
Goldman, M. 2001. "Constructing an Environmental State: Eco-governmentality and other Transnational Practices of a 'Green' World Bank." *Social Problems* 48 (4): 499–523.
Hirsch, P. and Wyatt, A. 2004. "Negotiating Local Livelihoods: Scales of Conflict in the Se San River Basin." *Asia Pacific Viewpoint* 45 (1): 51–68.
Noi, C. 2002. "Dirty Business in Samut Prakan." *The Nation* April 15, pp. 20.
Ojendal, J., V. Mathur, and M. Sithirith. 2002. "Environmental Governance in the Mekong: Hydropower Site Selection Processes in the Se San and Sre Pok Basins." Stockholm Environment Institute (SEI)/REPSI Report Series No. 4. Stockholm: SEI.
Perlez, J. 2006. "China Competes With West in Aid to Its Neighbors." *The New York Times* September 18.

Thomas, D. S. G. and C. Twyman. 2005. "Equity and Justice in Climate Change Adaptation amongst Natural-Resource-Dependent Societies." *Global Environmental Change* 15 (2005): 115–124.

World Bank (WB) and Asian Development Bank (ADB). 2006. "WB/ADB Joint Working Paper on Future Directions for Water Resources Management in the Mekong River Basin: Mekong Water Resources Assistance Strategy." June 2006, pp. 68. Washington DC: World Bank.

Online sources and electronic materials

International Water Power and Dam Construction (IWPDC). 2005. "Southeast Asia Turns Back to Hydro." November 5, http://www.waterpowermagazine.com/story.asp?sectioncode=166&storyCode=2032402 (accessed on September 21, 2006).

Jensen, K. M. 2005. "Response 1." *Mekong Update & Dialogue* 8 (2), April–June, http://www.mekong.es.usyd.edu.au/publications/mekong_updates/update8.2.pdf (accessed on September 21 2006).

Marwaan Macan-Markar, 2004. "Drought, not Dams, Behind Low River Levels—Experts." Inter Press Services (IPS), http://ipsnews.net/mekong/IPSWIRE/drought.html (accessed on September 21 2006).

The Mekong River Commission (MRC). 2004. "Mekong's Low Flows Linked to Drought, Says MRC Study." March 26. MRC, http://www.mrcmekong.org/free_download/report.htm (accessed on September 21, 2006).

People's Daily Online. 2004. "Thai Officials to Face Corruption Charges." October 20. http://english.people.com.cn/200410/20/eng20041020_160877.html (accessed on September 21, 2006).

World Bank (WB). 2004. "Mekong Regional Water Resources Assistance Strategy: Modelled Observations on Development Scenarios in the Lower Mekong Basin." November 2004, pp. 35, http://www.mrcmekong.org/free_download/report.htm (accessed on September 21, 2006).

World Bank. 2006 Lao PDR Economic Monitor, http://siteresources:worldbank.org LAOPRDETNX/Resources/LaoEconomicMonitorNov2006.pdf.

World Wildlife Fund (WWF). "Damming the Mekong." WWF, http://www.panda.org/about_wwf/what_we_do/freshwater/our_solutions/policies practices/removing barriers dams_initiative/examples/mekong/index.cfm (last accessed September 21, 2006).

CHAPTER 2
Irrigation and water policies: Trends and challenges

Abernethy, C. L. 2005. "Financing River Basin Management." In *Irrigation and River Basin Management: Options for Governance and Institutions* edited by M. Svendsen, D. J. Merrey, T. Shah. Wallingford: CABI.

Adamson, P. 2001. "The Potential Impacts of Hydropower Developments in Yunnan on the Hydrology of the Lower Mekong." *International Water Power and Dam Construction*, pp. 16–21.

Asian Development Bank (ADB). 2004. "Lao PDR: Water Resources Coordinating Committee." Country paper for Regional Meeting of National Water Sector Apex Bodies, Hanoi, Vietnam, May 18–21.

Bangkok Post. 2003. "Call to Build Water Supply Networks: Reservoirs Cannot Meet Agri Demand." December 28.

———. 2004. "Public to Get More Say in State Projects." February 13.

———. 2004. "B400 bn Water Management Scheme to be Proposed to Cabinet." February 18.

———. 2004. "New Projects to Ease Chronic Shortages." March 24.

———. 2004. "Government Policy Fails to Address Root Causes." May 3.

———. 2004. "Irrigation Head Air Doubts on Proposed National Grid." May 3.
———. 2004. "Military Units Conducting 'Psychological Operations.' " May 7.
———. 2004. "Water Crisis Looms, Says Grid Study." June 13.
Barrow, C. J. 1998. "River Basin Development Planning and Management: A Critical Review." *World Development* 26 (1): 171–186.
Berkoff, J. 2003. "China: The South-North Water Transfer Project—Is It Justified?" *Water Policy* 5 (2003): 1–28.
Bery, S. K. 1990. "Economic Policy Reform in Developing Countries: The Role and Management of Political Factors." *World Development* 18 (8): 1123–31.
Birch, A. 2004. "Direction and Experience in Water Sector Apex Body Development." Paper presented at the Regional Meeting of National Water Sector Apex Bodies, Hanoi, Vietnam, May 18–21.
Birch, A., M. H. Khan, and P. Taylor. 1999. "International Mentoring; Application of Australian Experience for Sri Lankan Water Sector Reforms under Technical Assistance of the Asian Development Bank." *Water International* 24 (4): 329–340.
Biswas, A. K. 2001. "Water Policies in the Developing World." *International Journal of Water Resources Development* 17 (4): 489–499.
———. 2004. "Integrated Water Resources Management: A Reassessment." *Water International* 29 (2): 248-256.
Both Ends. 2000. "Towards People Oriented River Basin Management: An NGO Vision." Input to the World Water Vision process, the Framework for Action and the World Water Forum. Netherlands: Both ENDS.
Boxer, B. 2001. "Contradictions and Challenges in China's Water Policy Development." *Water International* 26 (3): 355–341.
———. 2002. "Global Water Management Dilemmas Lessons from China." Resources for the Future. Winter 2002/Issue 146 Resources.
Cantor, J. 2003. "Setting up a River Basin Organization in the Cuu Long Delta in Vietnam." Paper prepared for the First Southeast Asian Water Forum, Chiang Mai, December 2003.
Chandler, D. 1996. A *History of Cambodia*. Chiang Mai: Silkworm Books.
Chenoweth, J. 1999. "Effective Multi-jurisdictional River Basin Management: Data Collection and Exchange in the Murray-Darling and Mekong River Basins." *Water International* 24 (4): 368–376.
Clark, T. W. 2002. The Policy Process. *A Practical Guide for Natural Resource Professionals*. Yale: Yale University Press.
Cleaver, F. 1999. "Paradoxes of Participation: Questioning Participatory Approaches to Development." *Journal of International Development* 11: 597–612.
Cleaver, F. 2000. "Moral Ecological Rationality: Institutions and the Management of Common Property Resources." *Development and Change* 31 (2): 361–383.
Cleaver, F. and T. Franks. 2003. "How Institutions Elude Design: River Basin Management and Sustainable Livelihoods." Paper prepared for The Alternative Water Forum, Bradford University, May 1–2.
Delli Priscoli, J. 2004. "What is Public Participation in Water Resources Management and Why Is It Important?" *Water International* 29 (2): 221–227.
Dore, J. 2003. "The Governance of Increasing Mekong Regionalism." In *Social challenges for the Mekong region* edited by Mingsarn Kaosa-ard and J. Dore. Bangkok: White Lotus.
Dore, J. and X. Yu 2004. "Yunnan Hydropower Expansion: Update on China's Energy Industry Reforms and the Nu, Lancang and Jinsha Hydropower Dams." Working Paper from Chiang Mai University's Unit for Social and Environmental Research, and Green Watershed.
Evans, P. 2003. "Development as Institutional Change: The Pitfalls of Monocropping and the Potentials of Deliberation." *Studies in Comparative International Development* 38 (4): 30–52 (Winter 2004).

Facon, T. 2002. "Downstream of Irrigation Water Pricing–The Infrastructure Design and Operational Management Considerations." Paper presented at conference on Irrigation Water Policies: Micro and Macro Considerations, Agadir, Morocco, June 15–17.

Frederiksen, H. D. 1998. "International Community Response to Critical World Water Problems: A Perspective for Policy Makers." *Water Policy* 1 (2): 139–158.

Giovalucchi, F. 2003. "Communauté, Pouvoir et Développement Dans les Campagnes Cambodgiennes: Brève Revue de la Littérature Disponible." Agence Française de Développement: Phnom Penh. Draft. Duplicated.

Halcrow and Partners, ARCADIS/Euroconsult. 2001. "Component C: Reorienting and Reorganising Service Delivery Operations in Irrigation." Final report Volume 3/3, Capacity Building in the Water Resources Sector project ADB-TA 3260-THA.

Heyd, H. and A. Neef. 2004. "Participation of Local People in Water Management: Evidence from the Mae Sa Watershed, Northern Thailand." EPTD discussion paper. Washington DC: International Food Policy Research Institute.

Hirsch, P. 2001. "Globalisation, Regionalisation and Local Voices: The Asian Development Bank and Rescaled Politics of Environment in the Mekong Region." *Singapore Journal of Tropical Geography* 22 (3): 237–251.

Hirsch, P. and A. Wyatt. 2004. "Negotiating Local Livelihoods: Scales of Conflict in the Se San River Basin." *Asia Pacific Viewpoint* 45 (1): 51.

International Water Management Institute (IWMI). 2003. "Development of Effective Water-Management Institutions: Final report, Volume II, Conceptual Framework." Colombo, Sri Lanka: IWMI.

Jaspers, F. G. W. 2001. "The New Water Legislation of Zimbabwe and South Africa—Comparison of Legal and Institutional Reform." *International Environmental Agreements* 1 (3): 305–325 (21).

Johnson, C. and T. Forsyth. 2002. "In the Eyes of the State: Negotiating a 'Rights-based Approach' to Forest Conservation in Thailand." *World Development* 30 (9): 1591–1605.

Jonch-Clausen and J. Fugl. 2001. "Firming Up the Conceptual Basis of Integrated Water Resources Management." *International Journal of Water Resources Development* 17 (4): 501–510.

Khamhung, A. 2001. *Land and Water Investment in the Lao PDR*. Rome: Food and Agriculture Organisation (FAO).

Kingdom of Cambodia (KOC). 2001. Draft Law on Water Resources Management of the Kingdom of Cambodia. Duplicated.

———. 2002. Draft National Water Resources Policy for the Kingdom of Cambodia. Duplicated.

Kolavalli, S. and J. D. Brewer. 1999. "Facilitating User Participation in Irrigation Management." *Irrigation and Drainage Systems* 13 (3): 249–273.

Lachapelle, P. R., S. F. McCool, and M. E. Patterson. 2003. "Barriers to Effective Natural Resource Planning in a 'Messy' World." *Society & Natural Resources* 16 (6): 473–490.

Lai, Nguyen Thai. 2002. Notes for Report on "National Water Resources Council and River Basin Organizations, Lessons and Issues." Meeting of ISG TAG2, September 11.

Malano, H. M., M. J. Bryant, and H. N. Turral. 1999. "Management of Water Resources: Can Australian Experiences be Transferred to Vietnam?" *Water International* 24 (4): 307–315.

Mehta, L., M. Leach, P. Newell, I. Scoones, K. Sivaramakrishnan and S. Way. 2000. "Exploring Understandings of Institutions and Uncertainty: New Directions in Natural Resource Management." Discussion paper no. 372. Environment Group, Institute of Development Studies. Brighton: University of Sussex.

Meinzen-Dick, R. M. Mendoza, L. Sadoulet, G. Abiad-Shields, and A. Subramanian. 1994. "Sustainable Water User Associations: Lessons from a Literature Review." Paper presented at World Bank Water Resources Seminar, Lansdowne, Virginia, US, December 13–15, pp. 91.

Merrett, S. 2003. "Virtual Water and the Kyoto Consensus: A Water Forum Contribution." *Water International* 28 (4): 540–542.
Miller, F. and P. Hirsch. 2003. "Civil Society and Internationalized River Basin Management." Working Paper No. 7. Sydney: Australian Mekong Resource Centre, University of Sydney.
Mingsarn Kaosa-ard and J. Dore. 2003. *Social challenges for the Mekong region*. Bangkok: White Lotus.
Mollinga, P. 2001. "Water and Politics: Levels, Rational Choice and South Indian Canal Irrigation." *Futures* 33 (2001): 733–752.
Mollinga, P., G. Hong, and A. M. Bhatia. 2003. "Leadership and Turnover: The Contradictions of Irrigation Management Reform in the People's Republic of China." Paper presented at conference on Asian Irrigation in Transition—Responding to the Challenges Ahead, Asian Institute of Technology, Bangkok, Thailand, April 22–23, 2002.
Ministry of Water Resources and Meteorology (MOWRAM) and Asian Development Bank (ADB). 2001. "National Water Sector Profile, Kingdom of Cambodia." Prepared by MOWRAM Taskforces in Association with M.Mac Donald & Partners and BCEOM. Project Report No. 7 (Revision 3). Phnom Penh: MOWRAM.
Nelson, N. and S. Wright. 1995. *Power and Participatory Development*. London: Intermediate Technology Publications.
Öjendal, J. 2000. "Sharing the Good: Modes of Managing Water Resources in the Lower Mekong River Basin." Dissertation at Department of Peace and Development Research. Göteborg University, Sweden. Göteborg: Vasastadens Bokbinderi AB.
Öjendal, J., V. Mathur and M. Sithirith. 2002. "Environmental Governance in the Mekong: Hydropower Site Selection Processes in the Se San and Sre Pok Basins." SEI/REPSI Report Series No. 4. Stockholm: Stockholm Environment Institute.
Ostrom, E. 2000. "Decentralization and Development: The New Panacea." In *Challenges to Democracy: Ideas, Involvement and Institutions* edited by Keith Dowding, James Hughes and Helen Margetts, pp. 237–56. New York: Palgrave Publishers.
Ovesen, J., I. B. Trankel and J. Öjendal. 1996. "When Every Household is an Island: Social Organisation and Power Structures in Rural Cambodia." Cited in Giovalucchi (2003).
Pahlman, C. 2000. "The Politics of Studies (and Economic Fairy Tales...)—The Role of the ADB in Hydro-power Development in the Mekong Region." Paper presented at the Mekong / ADB Symposium–Tokyo, September 2000.
Phan, Do Hong. 2003. "Towards an Effective Organization for River Basin Management in Vietnam." Paper prepared for the First Southeast Asian Water Forum, Chiang Mai, December.
Pheddara, Phalasack. 2003. "Water Rights in Lao PDR." Paper presented at the International working conference on Water Rights: Institutional Options for Improving Water Allocation. Hanoi, Vietnam, February 12–15.
Phonechaleun Nonthaxay, Chanthanet Boulapha and Choung Phanrajsavong. 2002. "National Water Vision to Action: A Framework for Integrated Water Resources Management in the Lao People's Democractic Republic." Water Resources Coordination Committee Secretariat, Lao PDR. (Second draft).
Pigram, J. J. 1999. "Projecting the Australian Experience in Water Reform." Hawaii: International Water and Resource Economics Consortium. Draft.
———. 2001. "Opportunities and Constraints in the Transfer of Water Technology and Experience between Countries and Regions." *International Journal of Water Resources Development* 17 (4): 563–579.
Radosevich, G. E. and D. Olson. 1999. "Existing and Emerging Basin Arrangements in Asia: Mekong River Commission Case Study." Third Workshop on River Basin Institution Development, June 24. Washington DC: The World Bank.
Richardson, M. 2002. "In its Water, Laos Sees Power to Cut Poverty." *International Herald Tribune*, March 11.

Rigg, J. 1991. "Grass-roots Development in Rural Thailand: A Lost Cause?" *World Development* 19 (2/3): 199–211.
Roling, N. and J. Woodhill. 2001. "From Paradigms to Practice: Foundations, Principles and Elements for Dialogue on Water, Food and Environment." In background papers prepared for Dialogue on Water for Food and the Environment: Workshop on Design for National and Basin Level Dialogues. Bonn, December 1–2.
Roth, R. 2004. "Spatial Organization of Environmental Knowledge: Conservation Conflicts in the Inhabited Forest of Northern Thailand." *Ecology and Society* 9 (3): 5.
Roux, J. 2004. "Participatory Irrigation Management and Development in Cambodia: Policy in the making and links to implementation." MSC Thesis in Agricultural Economics. Imperial College of London.
Sacha Sethaputra, Suwit Thanopanuwat, Ladawan Kumpa and Surapol Pattanee. 2001. "Thailand's Water Vision: A Case Study." In *From Vision to Action: A Synthesis of Experiences in Southeast Asia* edited by Ti and Facon. Rome, Bangkok: Food and Agriculture Organization/Economic and Social Commission for Asia-Pacific.
Saleth, R. M. and A. Dinar. 2000. "Institutional Changes in Global Water Sector: Trends, Patterns, and Implications." *Water Policy* 2 (3): 175–199.
Samad, M. and D. Vermillion. 1999. "Assessment of Participatory Management of Irrigation Schemes in Sri Lanka: Partial Reforms, Partial Benefits." International Water Management Institute (IWMI) Research Report 34. Colombo, Sri Lanka:. IWMI.
Sampath, R. K. 1992. "Issues in Irrigation Pricing in Developing Countries." *World Development* 20 (7): 967–977.
Schlager, E. and W. Blomquist. 2000. "Local Communities, Policy Prescriptions, and Watershed Management in Arizona, California, and Colorado." Paper presented at the Eighth Conference of the International Association for the Study of Common Property. Bloomington, Indiana, USA, May 31–June 4.
Shah, T., L. Makin and R. Sakthivadivel. 2001. "Limits to Leapfrogging: Issues in Transposing Successful River Basin Management Institutions in the Developing World." In *Intersectoral Management of River Basins* edited by C. Abernethy, 89–114. Colombo, Sri Lanka: International Water Management Institute; Deutsche Stiftung für Internationale Entwicklung.
Shao, X., H. Wang, and Z. Wang. 2003. "Interbasin Transfer Projects and their Implications: A China Case Study." *International Journal of River Basin Management* 1 (1): 5–14.
Shen, D. 2004. "The 2002 Water Law: Its Impacts on River Basin Management in China." *Water Policy* 6 (2004): 345–364.
Sinath, Chan. 2001. "Investment in Land and Water in Cambodia." Food and Agriculture Organization (FAO). Rome: FAO.
———. 2003. "Participatory Irrigation Management and Development of Cambodia." Paper prepared for the First Southeast Asia Water Forum, Chiang Mai, Thailand.
Tara, Theng, Ti Le-Huu and T. Facon. 2003. "National Water Vision to Action for the Kingdom of Cambodia." Ministry of Water Resources and Meteorology (MWRM). Phnom Penh: MWRM.
Towards Ecological Recovery and Regional Alliance (TERRA). 2002. "Creating Catastrophe: China and its Dams on the Mekong." *Watershed* 8 (2). Bangkok: TERRA.
The Nation. 2003. "Infrastructure Project: Tap Water Grid Planned by '05." June 23.
———. 2003. "National Water Grid: Holes in Pipeline Projects." September 14.
———. 2004. "Isaan Trip: PM Plays Lord Bounty." April 24, 2004.
———. 2004. "Irrigation Plan 'will Hurt Intended Beneficiaries'." September 24.
Thomas, J. W. and M. S. Grindle. 1990. "After the Decision: Implementing Policy Reforms in Developing Countries." *World Development* 18 (1): 1163–1181.
Ti, Le Huu Ti and T. Facon. 2004. "From Vision to Action in Least-developed Countries. A Synthesis of Experiences in Southeast Asia-2." The FAO-ESCAP Pilot project on National Water Visions.

Tiep, Nguyen Xuan. 2002. "Water Resources and Food Security in Vietnam." Paper presented at the national workshop on Water, Food and Environment.
Vermillion, D. L. 1997. "Impacts of Irrigation Management Transfer: A Review of the Evidence." International Irrigation Management Institute (IIMI) research report 11. Colombo, Sri Lanka: IIMI.
Watershed. 2001. "The Politics of Irrigation." 6 (3).
Wester, P. and J. Warner. 2002. "River Basin Management Reconsidered." In *Hydropolitics in the Developing World: A Southern African Perspective* edited by A. Turton, R. Henwood, 61–71. Pretoria, South Africa: African Water Issues Research Unit.
Wright, G. 1999. "River Basin Management and Irrigation in the Red River Basin of Viet Nam." DSE-MAF-MARD Workshop on Irrigators' Organisations.

Online sources and electronic material

Anonymous 2004a. "Lao PDR: Water Resources Coordinating Committee." Country paper, Regional Meeting of National Water Sector Apex Bodies, Hanoi, Vietnam, May 18–21, www.adb.org/Water/NWSAB/2004/Lao_PDR_Country_Paper.pdf.
———. 2004b. "Viet Nam: National Water Resources Council." National Water Sector Apex Body, www.adb.org/Water/NWSAB/2004/Vietnam_Country_Paper.pdf.
Apichart Anukularmphai. 2004. *River Basin Committees Development in Thailand: An Evolving Participatory Process (epp)*, http://www.adb.org/Water/NARBO/2004Training Program/country-paper-RBC development-THA.pdf.
Arriens, W. T. 2004. "ADB's Water Policy and the Needs for National Water Sector Apex Bodies." Asian Development Bank, www.adb.org/Water/NWSAB/2004/Arriens_Paper2.pdf.
Asian International Rivers Center (AIRC). 2003. *China: Water law 1988*, http://www.lancang-mekong.org/English_site/Eng_law/eng_law_ch_water.asp.
China International Electronic Commerce Network (CIECN). 2004. *Water Law of the People's Republic of China (the modified edition)* (August 29, 2002), http://en.ec.com.cn/pubnews/2004_03_24/200860/1004740.jsp.
Fu, C. and Z. P. Hu. 2002. "The Practice on Water Rights Allocation and Trade-off in China." Paper presented at the River Symposium, http://www.riverfestival.com.au/.
Molle, F. 2001. "Water Pricing in Thailand: Theory and Practice." DORAS Project, Kasetsart University, Bangkok, Research Report No. 7, pp. 78, http://std.cpc.ku.ac.th/delta/conf/Acrobat/Papers_Eng/pricing.pdf.
Molle, F., Nittaya Ngernprasertsri and Savakon Sudsawasd. 2002. "Are Water User Organisations Crucial for Water Management? A Post-mortem Analysis of Water User Groups in Thailand and the Prospect for Reincarnation." Paper prepared for the 6th Conference on Participatory Irrigation Management, Beijing, April 20–26, http://www.wca-infonet.org/iptrid/infonet/index.jsp.
World Bank. 2004. "Vietnam: World Bank helps Modernize Irrigation Schemes and Improve Dam Safety in Vietnam." Press release, http://web.worldbank.org wbsite/external/news/0,,contentmdk:20187138~menupk 34466~pagepk:64003015~pipk:64003012~thesitepk:4 607,00.htm.
World Water Council (WWC), Chinese Ministry of Water Resources (CMWR). 2003. "Country Report of the People's Republic of China. Marseilles: World Water Council," www.wwc.org.

CHAPTER 3
The politics of floods and disasters

Adam Fforde & Associates. 2003. "Report on Residential Clusters Research in An Giang, Dong Thap and Kien Giang Provinces in the Mekong Delta, Vietnam." In *At Risk: Natural Hazards, Peoples' Vulnerability and Disasters (second edition)* by B. Wisner, P. Blaikie,

T. Cannon and I. Davis, as report for CARE International, Hanoi, Vietnam. London: Routledge.

An, L., M. Linderman, J. Qi, A. Shortridge, and J. Liu. 2005. "Exploring Complexity in a Human–Environment System: An Agent-Based Spatial Model for Multidisciplinary and Multiscale Integration." *Annals of the Association of American Geographers* 95: 54–79.

Asian Disaster Preparedness Centre (ADPC). 2000. "Community Based Disaster Management. Trainer's Guide." Bangkok: ADPC.

Badenoch, N. 2001. *Environmental Governance: Principles and Practice in Mainland Southeast Asia*. Washington DC: World Resources Institute.

Bakker, K. 1999. "The Politics of Hydropower: Developing the Mekong." *Political Geography* 18: 209–232.

Bankoff, G. 2004. "In the Eye of the Storm: The Social Construction of the Forces of Nature and the Climatic and Seismic Construction of God in the Philippines." *Journal of Southeast Asian Studies* 35: 91–111.

Bhattacharjee, A. 2004. "India Battles the Red River Dragon." *Asia Times*.

Blaikie, P., T. Cannon, I. Davis, and B. Wisner. 1994. At risk: *Natural Hazards, People's Vulnerability, and Disaster*. Report for CARE International, Hanoi, Vietnam. London: Routledge.

Blaikie, P. M., and J. S. Muldavin. 2004. "Upstream, Downstream, China, India: The Politics of Environment in the Himalyan Region." *Annals of the Association of American Geographers* 94: 520–548.

Bonell, M., and L. A. Bruijnzeel, eds. 2005. *Forests, People and Water in the Humid Tropics: Past, Present and Future Hydrological Research for Integrated Land and Water Management*. Cambridge: Cambridge University Press.

Boyce, J. K. 2000. "Let Them Eat Risk? Wealth, Rights and Disaster Vulnerability." *Disasters* 24: 254–261.

Browne, M. J., and R. E. Hoyt. 2000. "The Demand for Flood Insurance: Empirical Evidence." *Journal of Risk and Uncertainty* 20: 291–306.

Dixit, A. 2003. "Floods and Vulnerability: Need to Rethink Flood Management." *Natural Hazards* 28: 155–179.

Dosch, J., and O. Hensengerth. 2005. "Sub-Regional Cooperation in Southeast Asia: The Mekong Basin." *European Journal of East Asian Studies (ejeas)* 4: 263–285.

Dudgeon, D. 2000. "Large-Scale Hydrological Changes in Tropical Asia: Prospects for Riverine Biodiversity." *Bioscience* 50: 793–806.

———. 2003. "The Contribution of Scientific Information to the Conservation and Management of Freshwater Biodiversity in Tropical Asia." *Hydrobiologia* 500: 295–314.

Economy, E. 2004. *The River Runs Black: The Environmental Challenge to China's Future*. Ithaca: Cornell University Press.

Few, R. 2003. "Flooding, Vulnerability and Coping Strategies: Local Responses to a Global Threat." *Progress in Development Studies* 3: 43–58.

Few, R., M. Ahern, F. Matthies, and S. Kovats. 2004. "Floods, Health and Climate Change: A Strategic Review." Working Paper No. 63. Tyndall Centre for Climate Change Research.

Forsyth, T. 1996. "Science, Myth and Knowledge: Testing Himalayan Environmental Degradation in Thailand." *Geoforum* 27: 275–292.

———. 1998. "Mountain Myths Revisited: Integrating Natural and Social Environmental Science." *Mountain Research and Development* 18: 126–139.

Fox, I.B. 2003. "Floods and the Poor: Reducing the Vulnerability of the Poor to the Negative Impacts of Floods." Manila: Asian Development Bank.

Government of Thailand. 1999. Natural Disaster Management Plan.

Gupta, S., A. Javed, and D. Datt. 2003. "Economics of Flood Protection in India." *Natural Hazards* 28: 199–210.

Kundzewicz, Z. W., and H.-J. Schellnhuber. 2004. "Floods in the IPCC TAR Perspective". *Natural Hazards* 31: 111–128.

Lang, G. 2002a. *Deforestation, Floods, and State Reactions in China and Thailand.* Hong Kong: City University of Hong Kong.

———. 2002b. "Forests, Floods, and the Environmental State in China." *Organization & Environment* 15: 109–130.

Lang, G., and C.H.W. Chan. 2006. "China's Impact on Forests in Southeast Asia." *Journal of Contemporary Asia* 36: 167–194.

Lebel, L., S. Khrutmuang, and J. Manuta. 2006b. "Tales from the Margins: Small Fishers in Post-Tsunami Thailand." *Disaster Prevention and Management* 15: 124–134.

Lebel, L., E. Nikitina, and J. Manuta. 2006c. "Flood Disaster Risk Management in Asia: An Institutional and Political Perspective." *Science and Culture* 72: 2–9.

Liu, A., H. Tan, J. Zhou, S. Li, T. Yang, J. Wang, J. Liu, X. Tang, Z. Sun, and S.W. Wen. 2006. "An Epidemiologic Study of Posttraumatic Stress Disorder in Flood Victims in Hunan China." *Canadian Journal of Psychiatry* 51: 350–354.

Manuta, J., S. Khrutmuang, D. Huaisai, and L. Lebel. 2006. "Institutionalized Incapacities and Practice in Flood Disaster Management in Thailand." *Science and Culture* 72: 10–22.

McCully, P. 1998. *Silenced Rivers: The Ecology and Politics of Large Dams.* London: Zed Books.

MRC-GTZ Cooperation Programme. 2003. "Mekong Flood Management and Mitigation Programme." Component 4: Emergency Management, Component 6: Land Management. MRC Programme Appraisal. Phnom Penh: Mekong River Commission (MRC).

Mekong River Commission (MRC). 2003. "Working Together on Flood Management." Phnom Penh: MRC.

Pacific Disaster Center (PDC). 2004. "Lower Mekong Basin: Flood Vulnerability Atlas." Final Report, Version 2.0. Maui: PDC.

Saroeun, B. 2000. "Huge Viet Dam Devastates Se San Valley and its People." *Phnom Penh Post*, June 10.

Saroeun, B., and C. Stormer. 2000. "Viet Dam Full of Lethal Surprises." *Phnom Penh Post.*

Sawitri Assanangkornchai, Sa-nguansri Tangboonngam, and J. G. Edwards. 2004. "The Flooding of Hat Yai: Predictors of Adverse Emotional Responses to a Natural Disaster." *Stress & Health* 20: 81–90.

Schultz, B. 2002. "Role of Dams in Irrigation, Drainage and Flood Control." *Water Resources Development* 18: 147–162.

Sodhy, P. 2004. "Modernization and Cambodia." *Journal of Third World Studies* 21: 153–174.

Takeuchi, K. 2001. "Increasing Vulnerability to Extreme Floods and Societal Needs of Hydrological Forecasting." *Hydrological Sciences Journal* 46: 869–881.

Tebakari, T., J. Yoshitani, and C. Suvanpimol. 2005. "Effects of Large-Scale Dams on the Hydrological Regime: A Case Study in Chao Phraya River Basin, Kingdom of Thailand." *Journal of the Japan Society of Hydrology and Water Resources* 18: 281–292.

Tingsanchali, T., S. Supharatid, and L. Rewtrakulpaiboon. 2003. "Institutional Arrangement for Flood Disaster Management in Thailand." Paper presented at First Southeast Asia Water Forum, Chiang Mai, Thailand.

Varis, O., and M. Keskinen. 2003. "Socio-Economic Analysis of the Tonle Sap Region, Cambodia: Building Links and Capacity for Targeted Poverty Alleviation." *Water Resources Development* 19: 295–310.

Walker, A. 2003. "Agricultural Transformation and the Politics of Hydrology in Northern Thailand." *Development and Change* 34: 941–964.

White, G. F., R. W. Kates, and I. Burton. 2001. "Knowing Better and Losing More: The Use of Knowledge in Hazards Management." *Environmental Hazards* 3: 81–92.

Wisner B., P. Blaikie, T. Cannon, and I. Davis. 2003. *At Risk: Natural Hazards, Peoples' Vulnerability and Disasters.* Second edition. London: Routledge.

Wong, K., and X. Zhao. 2001. "Living with Floods: Victim's Perceptions in Beijing." Guangdong, China. Area 33: 190–201.

Yodmani, S. 2001. "Disaster Risk Management and Vulnerability Reduction: Protecting the Poor." In Asia Pacific Forum on Poverty. Manila: Asian Development Bank (ADB).

Online sources and electronic material

Appleton, B., ed. H. van Schaik, and P. Kabat. (2003). "Climate Changes the Water Rules: How Water Managers can Cope with Today's Climate Variability and Tomorrow's Climate Change." Delft, The Netherlands, Dialogue on Water and Climate, http://www.waterandclimate.org/report.htm.

Dudgeon, D. 2005. "River Rehabilitation for Conservation of Fish Biodiversity in Monsoonal Asia." *Ecology and Society* 10 (15), http://www.ecologyandsociety.org/vol10/iss12/art15/.

Lebel, L., J. M. Anderies, B. Campbell, C. Folke, S. Hatfield-Dodds, T. Hughes, and J. Wilson. 2006a. "Governance and the Capacity to Manage Resilience in Regional Social-Ecological Systems." *Ecology and Society* 11 (1): 11–19, http://www.ecologyandsociety.org/vol11/iss11/art19/.

Seng, N. 2004. "Flood Documentary Maker Arrested." Irrawaddy, July 30, http://www.irrawaddy.org/aviewer.asp?a=3756&z=24 (accessed on November 17, 2006).

CHAPTER 4
China's energy reforms and hydropower expansion in Yunnan

Asian Development Bank (ADB). 2002. "The 2020 Project. Comprehensive Report Describing the Western Region Development Strategy." Manila: ADB.

Ball, A., A. Hansard, R. Curtotti, and K. Schneider. 2003. "China's Changing Coal Industry." Australian Bureau of Agricultural Economics (ABARE) eReport 03.3. Canberra: ABARE.

Beijing Review. . "Makeover for Takeovers." August 28.

———. 2003. "Beyond Three Gorges." September 3.

———. 2003. "China No. 4 in FDI Stock." September 4.

Blake, D. 2001. "Proposed Mekong Dam Scheme in China Threatens Millions in Downstream Countries." *World Rivers Review*, June, pp. 4–5.

Business Weekly. 2003. "Power Companies Rushing to Build New Plants." March 26.

Chapman, E.C. and D. He. 1996. "Downstream Implications of China's Dams on the Lancang Jiang (Upper Mekong) and their Potential Significance for Greater Regional Cooperation, Basin-Wide." In *Development Dilemmas in the Mekong Subregion* edited by B. Stensholt, pp. 16–24. Melbourne: Monash Asia Institute.

Chen, H. 2004. "Hydropower Generates Debates." *China Daily*, January 15.

China Daily. 2002. "Power Monopoly Broken Down, Electricity Regulatory Commission to set up." December 30.

———. 2003. "State Run Power Grid Reforms Underway." September 4.

———. 2003. "Monopoly Grid Switches to Private Firm." September 24.

———. 2003. "CLP Power to Invest in Thermopower Plants in Guangxi." October 15.

———. 2004. "Leaders Stress Development." March 6.

———. 2004. "New Way of Thinking Bodes Well for the Future." March 6.

China Economic Review. 2002. "China's Hydro Capacity to Double." December 2002/January 2003, 6.

China Power News (translated by Kevin Li). 2004. "Economic Vision: Hydropower Faces Dilemma again in China." February 10.

China West News. 2003. "China Plans Four Hydropower Plants on Drichu Source." February 1.

———. 2003. "Loan for Key Hydropower Project." February 19.

Daniel, R. 2003. "Thailand's Salween Dams to Fuel Southeast Asian Regional Power Grid at the Cost to Ethnic Communities Forests and Rivers." *Watershed* 9 (1). TERRA.

Dore, J. 2003. "The Governance of Increasing Mekong Regionalism." In *Social Challenges for the Mekong Region* edited by Mingsarn Kaosa-ard and J. Dore. Bangkok: White Lotus.

Dubash, N. K., M. Dupar, S. Kothari, and T. Lissu. 2001. *A Watershed in Global Governance? An Independent Assessment of the World Commission on Dams*. World Resources Institute, Lokayan and Lawyer's Environmental Action Team.

Dunning, J. H. 1988. *Explaining International Production*. London: Unwin Hyman.

Feng, J. 2003. "What a Waste." *Beijing Review* 46 (36): 12–15.

Forsyth, T. 1999. *International Investment and Climate Change: Energy Technologies for Developing Countries*. London: Royal Institute of International Affairs.

Deringer, F. B. 2003. "Restructuring China's Power Sector." *China Notes*, March.

Gao, S. 2000. "China." In *Rethinking Energy Security in East Asia* edited by P. B. Stares. Tokyo: Japan Centre for International Exchange.

Giddens, A. 1992. *Modernity and Self Identity: Self and Society in the Late Modern Age*. Cambridge: Polity Press.

He, D., G. Zhang and H. T. Kung, eds. 2001. "Towards Cooperative Utilization and Coordinated Management of International Rivers." Proceedings of International Symposium, June 25–30, 1999, Kunming, China. New York & Tokyo: Science Press & United Nations University.

He, J. 2002. "A Research on the Development Strategy of the 21st Century's Hydropower in China." *Electricity* 13 (1).

Hinton, P. 2000. "Where Nothing is as it Seems: Between Southeast China and Mainland Southeast Asia in the 'Post-Socialist' Era." In *Where China Meets Southeast Asia: Social & Cultural Change in the Border Regions* edited by G. Evans, C. Hutton and K. K. Eng, pp. 7–27. Bangkok: White Lotus.

International Energy Agency. 2002. "Press Release (02)32 on China's Oil Needs." December 12.

———. 2002. "Press release (02)24 on China's Energy Purchases and Infrastructure Needs to 2030." September 26.

International Rivers Network (IRN). 2002. "China's Upper Mekong Dams Endanger Millions Downstream." Briefing paper 3. Berkley: IRN.

Kattoulas, V. 2001. "Witnesses to a Crisis." *Far Eastern Economic Review*. September 27.

Lambropoulos, V. 1996. "Nomoscopic Analysis." *South Atlantic Quarterly* 95 (4): 855–879.

Landcare Research New Zealand. 2000. "Policies and Strategies for the Sustainable Development of the Lancang River Basin. Final Report of ADB TA 3139–PRC." Landcare Research New Zealand for the Asian Development Bank, Manila.

McCormack, G. 2001. "Water Margins: Competing Paradigms in China." *Critical Asian Studies* 33 (1): 5–30.

Medlock, K. B. and R. Soligo. 1999. "China and Long–Range Asia Energy Securities: An Analysis of Political, Economic and Technological Factors Shaping Asian Energy Markets." Rice University's James A Baker Institute for Public Policy.

Mingsarn Kaosa-ard and J. Dore, eds. 2003. *Social Challenges for the Mekong Region*. Bangkok: White Lotus.

Mekong River Commission (MRC). 2002. *Annual Report 2001*. Phnom Penh: MRC.

———. 2003. *State of the Basin Report*. Phnom Penh: MRC.

Mekong River Commission (MRC), United Nations Development Program (UNDP), Cambodia National Mekong Committee (CNMC), NEDECO and MIDAS (1998). "Natural Resources-Based Development Strategy for the Tonle Sap Area, Cambodia: Final Report, Volumes 1–3." Phnom Penh: MRC.

Nareerat Wiriyapong. 2003. "Egat wants China and Burma to Join in Huge Hydropower Project." *The Nation*, November 16.

Oil, A. and G. Connections. 2003. "Profile of China's Electric Power Industry." *News and Trends: East and Southeast Asia* 8 (2).

Plinston, D. and D. He. 1999. "Water Resources and Hydropower." Report for ADB TA-3139 Policies and Strategies for Sustainable Development of the Lancang River Basin. Manila: Asian Development Bank.

———. 2000. "Water Resources and Hydropower in the Lancang River Basin." Final Report of ADB TA-3139 Policies and Strategies for Sustainable Development of the Lancang River Basin. Manila: Asian Development Bank.

Roberts, T. R. 2001. "Killing the Mekong: China's Fluvicidal Hydropower-cum-Navigation Development Scheme." *Natural History Bulletin of the Siam Society* 49: 143–159.

Rungfapaisarn, K. 2003. "Yunnan Eyes S.E. Asia Trade & Investment." *The Nation*, October 22.

Sarkkula, J., J. Koponen, and others. 2003. "Modelling Tonle Sap for Environmental Impact Assessment and Management Support." Final report. Finnish Environment Institute and EIA Ltd., Helsinki and Espoo.

Scholte, J. A. 2000. *Globalisation: A Critical Introduction*. London: Palgrave.

Stares, P.B., ed. 2000. *Rethinking Energy Security in East Asia*. Tokyo: Japan Centre for International Exchange.

Towards Ecological Recovery and Regional Alliance (TERRA). 2002. "Creating Catastrophe: China and its Dams on the Mekong." *Watershed* 8 (2).

Vaitheeswaran, V. 2003. *Power to the People: How the Coming Energy Revolution will Transform an Industry, Change our Lives, and maybe even Save the Planet*. New York: Farrar Straus and Giroux.

van Zalinge, N., Nao Thuok and Sam Nuov. 2001. "Status of the Cambodian Inland Capture Fisheries with Special Reference to the Tonle Sap Great Lake." Cambodia Fisheries Technical Paper Series Volume 3. Phnom Penh: Inland Fisheries Research & Development Institute of Cambodia.

Vatcharasinthu, C. and Babel M. S. 1999. "Hydropower Potential and Water Diversion from the Salween Basin." In workshop on Transboundary Waters: The Salween Basin. Organized by AIT Regional Environmental Management Centre, Oregon State University, University of Victoria, Chiang Mai, September 13–16, 1999.

Watcharapong Thongrung. 2003. "EGAT Told to Suspend Dam Talks." *The Nation*, October 27, 2003.

Winchester, S. 1996. *The River at the Centre of the World: A Journey up the Yangtze and Back in Chinese Time*. London: Penguin Books.

World Commission on Dams (WCD). 2000. *Dams and Development: A New Framework for Decision Making*. Cape Town: WCD.

Xinhua News Agency, 2003. "World's Biggest Power Grid built in China." September 23.

Online sources and electronic material

China Development Bank (CDB). 2003. "China Development Bank Offers Loan of RMB 15 billion in Support of the Construction of the Xiaowan Hydraulic Power Station," http://www.cdb.com.cn (accessed on October 14, 2003).

People's Daily. 2003. "Regulator Sets Target for China's Power Sector Reform." March 26.

———. 2003. "China Steps up Development of Southern Power Grid." March 27.

2003. "Nuclear Energy to take 3 percent of China's Total by 2005." April 10.

———. 2003. "Energy Demand Set to Double by 2020." November 19.

———. 2003. "China's Grid Giant gives Shares to Huaneng Company." September 24.

International Commission on Large Dams (ICOLD). 2001. "A Brief Introduction to Dachaoshan Hydropower Project." ICOLD Web site, December 15, http://www.icold-cigb.net/.

Mulan, J. 2003. "Overview of Power Industry." March 10, http:// tdctrade.com.

World Bank (WB). 1998. China-East China (Jiangsu) 500kV Transmission Project, World Bank Infoshop Web, http:www.worldbank.org.cn/Chinese/content/81811198523 (accessed January 2, 2004).

CHAPTER 5
Electricity sector planning and hydropower

Anonymous. 2005. Personal communication. February.
Anonymous source within EGAT. Undated circa. 2001. "Information about IPP and SPP."
Bhargava, V. and E. Bolongaita. 2005. "Emerging Issues Analysis: Combating Corruption in Multilateral Development Banks—An Analysis of Key Issues and Recommendations Raised during the US Foreign Relations Committee Hearings." World Bank, International Affairs Unit, EXTVPU. July 25.
Business Day. 2003. "Government Plans to Increase Market Capital." November 30.
Chantanakome, W. 2005. "Electricity and Development: Key Challenges for ASEAN." Workshop on Electricity and Development, Asian Institute of Technology.
Chatikavanij, K. 1994. *The Life and Aspirations of Kasame Chatikavanij.* Bangkok: self-published.
Crispin, S. W. 2001. "Power Politics Trump Reform." *Far Eastern Economic Review*, September 27, 2001.
Dominguez, R., F. Manibog, et al. 2003. "Power for Development: A Review of the World Bank Group's Experience with Private Participation in the Electricity Sector." World Bank.
du Pont, P. 2005b. Personal Communication. February 13.
Electricity Generating Authority of Thailand (EGAT). 2006. "Preliminary Plan: Power Development Plan PDP 2006 (in Thai)." EGAT, May 30.
Hirsch, P. and C. Warren. 1998. *The Politics of Environment in Southeast Asia.* New York: Routledge.
Hydropower & Dams 2005. "Hydropower Plays a Leading Role in Myanmar's Power Development Plans." *Hydropower & Dams* 6 April: 119–123.
Imhof, A. 2005. Personal communication. July 26.
International River Network (IRN). 1999. "Power Struggle: The Impacts of Hydro-Development in Laos." IRN.
Lam Du Son. 2005. "Current Situation & Vietnam Electricity Development." Dam & Sustainable Energy Development: Challenges in Integration Period, Hanoi, Vietnam.
Lang, C. 1998. "Se Kong-Se san and Nam Theun: Too many Studies." *Watershed* Vol. 3 (2).
Li, K. 2005. "Lancang River's Hydropower Plan and Power Grid Connection within China." Paper presented at The role of the Mekong People's Council in Mekong Regional Development—to Coincide with the ADB-GMS Summit, Rimkok Resort Hotel, Chiang Rai.
Mallaby, S. 2004. *The World's Banker: A Story of Failed States, Financial Crises, and the Wealth and Poverty of Nations.* New York: Penguin.
Marbek Resource Consultants Ltd. and G. C. S. International. 2005. "Post-Implementation Impact Assessment: Thailand Promotion of Electrical Energy Efficiency Project TPEEE), Draft Report." Prepared for World Bank—GEF Coordination Team. April 8.
McCulley, P. 1996. *Silence Rivers: The Ecology and Politics of Large Dams.* London: Zed Books.
Myanmar Ministry of Electric Power. 2004. "Current Developments in the Power Sector of Myanmar." Second Meeting of the Regional Power Trade Coordination Committee RPTCC-2), Bangkok.
Noam, Z. 2006. Personal communication.
Norconsult. 2002a. "Indicative Master Plan on Power Interconnection in GMS Countries III-A." June.
———. 2002b. "Indicative Master Plan on Power Interconnection in GMS Countries III-B." June.
———. 2003. "Regional Indicative Master Plan on Power Interconnection in GMS — Executive Summary." Asian Development Bank. May 8.

Phongpaichit, P. 2000. *Why the Decision-Making Process on Big Projects has to Change.* Good Governance, Public Participation and Decision-making Process for Environmental Protection, Institute of Social and Economic Policy, Bangkok.

Regional Power Trade Coordination Committee. 2004. "Summary of Proceedings." Greater Mekong Subregion: Second Meeting of the Regional Power Trade Coordination Committee (RPTCC-2), Bangkok, Thailand.

Socialist Republic of Vietnam. 2000. *Master Plan on Power Development of Vietnam in period 2001–2010 with the vision to 2020.* Hanoi.

———. 2004. "Country Report: Recent Development in the Vietnam Power Sector." Greater Mekong Subregion Second Meeting of the Regional Power Trade Coordination Committee (RPTCC-2), Bangkok, Thailand.

Thai Load Forecast Subcommittee. 2004. January.

The Nation. 2003. "PM Pressing for Egat IPO this Year." *The Nation.* March 14.

United Nations. 1963. "A Report by the Panel of Experts on Rural Electrification in the ECAFE Region." United Nations Economic Commission for Asia and the Far East. February 12.

Vernstrom, R. 2005. "Nam Theun 2 Hydro Power Project Regional Economic Least Cost Analysis: Final Report." World Bank. March.

Williams, J. and N. Dubash. 2004. "Asian Electricity Reform in Historical Perspective." *Pacific Affairs* in review.

Wyatt, A. B. 2005. "Email communication." February 18.

Yeh, E. T. and J. I. Lewis. 2004. "State Power and the Logic of Reform in China's Electricity Sector." *Pacific Affairs* 77 (3): 437–491.

Online sources and electronic material

Akimoto, Y. 2004. "Hydro–powering the Regime." *Irrawaddy*, June, http://www.probeinternational.org/pi/Mekong/index.cfm?DSP=content&ContentID=10963.

Amornsakchai, S., P. Annez, et al. 2000. "Pak Mun Dam, Mekong River Basin, Thailand. A WCD Case Study prepared as an input to the World Commission on Dams," http://www.dams.org.

Asia Today. 2005. "Analysis—Thailand Considers Energy Import Options." February 21, http://asia.news.yahoo.com/050221/4/1wo2o.html.

Associated Press. 2005. "Laotian, Thai Prime Ministers Lay Cornerstone for Laotian Hydropower Dam." *AOL NEWS*, November 27, http://aolsvc.news.aol.com/news/article.adp?id=20051127075509990002.

Aylward, B., J. Berkhoff, et al. 2001. "Financial, Economic and Distributional Analysis, Thematic Review 3.1." Prepared as an Input to the World Commission on Dams, http://www.dams.org/docs/kbase/thematic/tr31anx.pdf.

Balls, A. K. a. A. 2005. "Dam Project in Laos Acts as Test Case for World Bank." *Financial Times*, February 17. http://www.namtheun2.com/mediangopdffiles/05%2002%2017-25%20Financial%20Times.pdf.

Bangkok Post. 2002. "Power Profligacy." January 6.

———. 2005. "Government to Push Egat to Invest in Myanmar (Burma) Dams Project." November 13, http://www.bangkokpost.com/breaking_news/breakingnewsphp?id=61672.

Bank of Thailand. 2006. "Key Economic Indicators," http://www.bot.or.th bothomepage/databank/EconData/Thai_Key/Thai_KeyE.asp.

Dieu, N. T. 2000. "Whose River, Whose Rights? Mekong Projects and their Environmental Impacts." Paper presented at the UNESCO International Workshop on Environmental Conflicts and Peace in East Asia, Republic of Korea, July 5–7, http://www.unesco.or.kr/kor/science_n/data/Nguyen.doc.

Dow Jones Newswires. 2006. "New Thai EGAT Unit to Invest in 4 Overseas Energy Projs." *Dow Jones Newswires*, August 24, http://www.easybourse.com/Website/dynamic/News.php?NewsID=45971&lang=fra&NewsRubrique=2.

D'Sa, A. 2005. "Integrated Resource Planning IRP and Power Sector Reform in Developing Countries." Energy Policy 33 (10): 1271–1285, http://www.iei-asia.org/IEIBLR-IRP-EnergyPolicy.pdf.

du Pont, P. 2005a. "Nam Theun 2 Hydropower Project (NT2) Impact of Energy Conservation, DSM, and Renewable Energy Generation on EGAT's Power Development Plan." World Bank. March 24, http://siteresources.worldbank.org/INTLAOPRD/Resources/DSMMARCH2005.pdf.

Duane, T. P. 2002. "Regulation's Rationale: Learning from the California Energy Crisis." *Yale Journal on Regulation* 19 (2): 471–540, http://proquest.umi.com/pqdlink?Ver=1&Exp=03-13-2003&FMT=TG&DID=000000144079031&REQ=1&Cert=dpri2JlX%2bxeOVg2lxsPwHT4DXpYkOU1AHhROcIscNZSS6dVyUPXQv%2foqFX02eANuoD1FitsiFLx21 3h%2f3H3n%2bA--.

Earthrights International. 2005. "Flooding the Future: Hydropower and Cultural Survival in the Salween River Basin." April 28, http://earthrights.org/Myanmar (Burma)/floodthefuture.shtml.

Environmental Defense. 2003. "The World Bank and Large Dams: Failure to Learn from History." September 2003, http://www.environmentaldefense.org/documents/3011_Gambling_Dams.pdf.

Electricity Generating Authority of Thailand (EGAT). 2005. "Why Nam Theun 2 Will Not Help the Poor in Laos." March, http://www.environmentaldefense.org/documents/4403_NT2WillNotHelpLaos.pdf.

Environmental Defense, Friends of the Earth, et al. 2003. "Gambling With People's Lives: What the World Bank's New 'High-Risk/High-Reward' Strategy Means for the Poor and the Environment," http://www.environmentaldefense.org/article.cfm?ContentID=3005.

Federal Research Division of the Library of Congress. 2005. "Thailand Electric Power," http://www.country-data.com/cgi-bin/query/r-13774.html (accessed on 7 Dec).

Garret, B. 2005. "Comments on GMS Regional Power Trade Operating Agreement." Palang Thai. July 2005, http://www.palangthai.org/docs/CommentsRPTOA.pdf.

Greacen, C. 2004. "The Marginalization of 'Small is Beautiful': Micro-hydroelectricity, Common Property, and the Politics of Rural Electricity Provision in Thailand." University of California, Berkeley: Energy and Resources Group, http://www.vidacom.org/chris/GreacenDissertation.pdf.

Greacen, C. and Chuenchom Greacen. 2004. "Thailand's Electricity Reforms: Privatization of Benefits and Socialization of Costs and Risks." *Pacific Affairs* 77 (4), http://www.palangthai.org/docs/PA77.3Thailand.pdf.

Greacen, C. and D. Sukkamnoed. 2005. "Laos: Did The World Bank Fudge Figures to Justify Nam Theun 2?" *World Rainforest Movement* No. 95 (June), http://www.wrm.org.uy/bulletin/95/Laos.html.

Hildyard, N. 2000. "Dams Don't Build Themselves." The Corner House. January 18, http://www.thecornerhouse.org.uk/item.shtml?x=51995.

Hirsch, P. 1998. "From Concept to Design: Creating an International Environmental Ombudsperson. The Nam Theun II Dam in Laos: Conflicts Over Development Plans for the Mekong River Region." San Jose, Costa Rica: The Earth Council, http://www.omced.org/cases/case_Hirsch.pdf.

Imhof, A. 1997. "World Bank, Undaunted by Thai Economy, Presses ahead with Nam Theun 2." *World Rivers Review*, http://www.irn.org/pubs/wrr/9712/nt2.html.

International Commission on Large Dams (ICOLD). 2000. "Position Paper on Dams and Environment." ICOLD, http://www.icold-cigb.org/chartean.html.

International River Network (IRN). 1994a. "The Legacy of Hydro in Laos." March 1994, http://www.irn.org/programs/mekong/Legacy_of_hydro_low.pdf.

International River Network (IRN). 1994b. "World Rivers Review." IRN, http://www.irn.org/pubs/wrr/9404/main.html.

Lang, C. 2003. "Laos: Nam Theun 2 Dam—Fighting Corruption World Bank Style." *WRM's BULLETIN* No. 67 (February), http://www.wrm.org.uy/bulletin/67/Laos.html.

REFERENCE LIST

Li, K. 2004. "China's State Council Approved Jinghong Dam Project." *Dianchi Chenbao*, http://www.probeinternational.org/pi/Mekong/index.cfm?DSP=content&ContentID=10220.

Nam Theun 2 Power Co. Ltd. 2004. "Nam Theun 2 Hydroelectric Project General Presentation." November, http://www.namtheun2.com/gallery/libr_press0410%20Briefing%20kit%20presentation.pdf.

Osborne, M. 2004. "River at Risk: the Mekong and the Water Politics of China and Southeast Asia." Lowy Institute for International Policy, http://www.lowyinstitute.org/PublicationGet.asp?i=160.

Permpongsacharoen, W. 2005. "Lao Power may not be the Best Buy." *Bangkok Post* March 15, http://www.bangkokpost.com/News/15Mar2005_opin42.php.

Perrin, A. 2005. "Options under Water." *Time Asia*. March 28, http://www.time.com/time/asia/magazine/article/0,13673,501050404-1042503,00.html.

Petty, M. 2005. "Environmentalists Lose the Dam Battle in Laos." *Thai Day* December 1, http://www.manager.co.th/IHT/ViewNews.aspx?NewsID=9480000165853.

Phumaraphand, N. 2001. "Evaluation Methods and Results of EGAT's Labeling Programs." A presentation at Lessons Learned in Asia: Regional Conference on Energy Efficiency Standards and Labeling. Organized by Collaborative Labeling and Appliance Standards Program (CLASP) and the United Nations Economic and Social Commission for Asia and the Pacific (ESCAP). Bangkok, Thailand, http://www.un.org/esa/sustdev/sdissues/energy/op/clasp_egatppt.pdf.

Porter, I. 2005. "Letter to Japanese NGOs," http://siteresources.worldbank.org INTLAO-PRD/Resources/Japanese-NGOS-letter.pdf

Ryder, G. 1994. "Thirsty for the Rivers of Laos." *World Rivers Review, Special Mekong Issue*, http://www.nextcity.com/ProbeInternational/Mekong/articles/94-12-2 World Rivers.htm.

———. 2004. "Ten Reasons Why the World Bank Should Not Finance the Nam Theun 2 Power Company in Lao PDR." June, http://www.probeinternational.org/pi/documents/mekong/nt10reasons.pdf.

Samabuddhi, K. 2004. "China's Dams Linked to Low Water Levels—Green Group Rejects Climate Change Claim." *Bangkok Post*. March 5, http://www3.sympatico.ca/nearovi/potins24.html.

Sant, G., S. Dixit, et al. 1998. "Re-Assessing the Role of Large Dams in Meeting Power Demand: Presentation to the World Commission on Dams." December, http://www.prayaspune.org/energy/14_WCD_Paper.pdf.

Sharp, T. 2001. "The Last Great Hydro Power Frontier." *International Water Power and Dam Construction*. October 15, http://www.waterpowermagazine.com/story.asp?storyCode=2010165.

———. 2004. "Hydro in China–to be or not to be?" *International Water Power and Dam Construction*, http://www.threegorgesprobe.org/tgp/index.cfm?DSP=content&ContentID=11118

Shi, L. 2005. "Comment: Electricity Agency Lacks Power." *China Daily*. March 6, http://www.chinadaily.com.cn/english/doc/2005-03/06/content_422124.htm.

Shoemaker, B. 1998. "Trouble on the Theun-Hinboun: A Field Report on the Socio-Economic and Environmental Effects of the Nam Theun-Hinboun Hydropower Project in Laos." International Rivers Network (IRN), http://www.irn.org/programs/mekong/threport.html.

Swisher, J. N. and G. d. M. Jannuzzi. 1997. "Tools and Methods for Integrated Resource Planning." Roskilde, Denmark, Riso Laboratory, http://www.uneprisoe.org/IRPMANUAL/.

Thailand Development Research Institute (TDRI). 2005. "Macroeconomic Policy Program (MEP)," http://www.nectec.or.th/bureaux/tdri/mep.htm (accessed on August 5).

Thai Ministry of Energy. 2005. "Strategy to Reform the Country's Energy Consumption: Presentation to the Prime Minister (in Thai language)." November 23. www.palangthai.org/docs/PMENERGY23.11.05 2.

Vernstrom, R. 2004. "Nam Theun 2 Hydro Power Project Regional Economic Least-Cost Analysis Draft Final Report." World Bank. June, http://siteresources.worldbank.org/IN TLAOPRD/4917611094074854903/20251513/Economic.pdf.

World Bank. 2003. Thailand Economic Monitor. Bangkok, World Bank: 58, http://siteresources.worldbank.org/INTTHAILAND/Resources/Economic-Monitor/2003oct.pdf.

World Commission on Dams. 2000a. "Case Study—Thailand: Pak Mun Dam and Mekong/Mun River Basins." November, http://www.dams.org/kbase/studies/th/th_exec.htm.

———.2000b. Chapter 2: Technical, Financial and Economic Performance. The Report of the World Commission on Dams. W. C. o. Dams. London: Earthscan Publications Ltd, http://www.dams.org/report/contents.htm.

World Wildlife Fund (WWF). 2004. "Rivers at Risk: Dams and the Future of Freshwater Ecosystems," http://www.panda.org/downloads/freshwater/riversatriskfullreport.pdf.

Wyatt, A. B. 2002. "Power Sector Restructuring in Vietnam: The Construction and Transfer of Risk." Asia Power Sector Reforms Workshop, Bangkok, Thailand, http://prayaspune.org/energy/41_06viet.pdf.

Xinhua. 2005. "Biggest Vietnamese-invested Project goes to Laos." *People's Daily*. December 6, http://english.people.com.cn/200512/06/eng20051206_225996.html.

CHAPTER 6
Mathematical modeling in integrated management of water resources

Adamson, P. T. 2001. "Hydrological Perspectives on the Lower Mekong Basin—the Potential Impacts of Hydropower Developments in Yunnan on the Downstream Flow Regime." *International Water Power and Dam Construction* 53 (3): 16–21.

Bonheur, N. 2001. "Tonle Sap Ecosystem and Value." Technical Coordination Unit for Tonle Sap. Phnom Penh, Cambodia: Ministry of Environment.

Dao, T. and T. Dac. 2000. "Modeling of Flow and Salinity in the Mekong Delta by SAL 99." Paper presented at workshop on Hydrologic and Environmental Modeling on the Mekong Basin, Phnom Penh, Cambodia.

Dutta, D., M. J. Alam, K. Umeda, M. Hayashi, and S. Hironaka. 2004. "Physically Based Distributed Modeling Approach for Urban Flood Simulation in the Lower Mekong Basin." Paper presented at international conference on Advances in Integrated Mekong River Management, Vientiane, Laos.

Global Water Partnership (GWP). 2000. "Integrated Water Resources Management." Technical Advisory Committee Background paper No. 4. Stockholm: GWP.

Hapuarachchi, H. A. P., A. S. Kiem, K. Takeuchi, H. Ishidaira, J. Magome, I. Struthers, M. Zhou, and A. Tianqi. 2004. "Application of a Distributed Hydrological Model YHYM to the Mekong River Basin." Paper presented at international conference on Advances in Integrated Mekong River Management, Vientiane, Laos.

Herath, S. and D. Yang. 2000. "Distributed Hydrologic Modeling in Mekong Basin." Paper presented at workshop on Hydrologic and Environmental Modeling on the Mekong Basin, Phnom Penh, Cambodia.

Ibbit, R. 2000. "Modeling the Nam Gnouang Catchment, Lao PDR." INCEDE Report-2000–4, Mekong Basin Studies—Proceedings of the AP FRIEND workshop.

Inoue, K., K. Toda, and O. Maeda. 2000. "Overland Inundated Flow Analysis for Mekong Delta in Vietnam." In *Hydraulic Engineering Software* pp. 123–132. Southampton: WIT Press.

Jakeman, A. J. and R. A. Letcher. 2003. "Integrated Assessment and Modeling: Features, Principles and Examples for Catchment Management." *Environmental Modeling & Software* 18 (6): 491–501.

Janssen, W. and P. Goldsworthy. 1996. "Multidisciplinary Research for Natural Resource Management: Conceptual and Practical Implications." *Agricultural Systems* 51 (3): 259–279.

Jirayoot, K. and L. D. Trung. 2004. "Hydrological and Basin Simulation Models for Water Utilization Programme on the Mekong River Commission." Paper presented at international conference on Advances in Integrated Mekong River Management, Vientiane, Laos.

Keskinen, M. 2006. "The Lake with Floating Villages: A Socio–Economic Analysis of the Villages around the Tonle Sap Lake." *International Journal of Water Resources Development*—Special Issue: Integrated Water Resources Management on the Tonle Sap Lake, Cambodia, 22 (3).

Keskinen, M., J. Koponen, M. Kummu, J. Nikula, and J. Sarkkula. 2005a. "Integration of Socio-economic and Hydrological Data in the Tonle Sap Lake, Cambodia." Proceedings of the 2005 International Conference on Simulation & Modeling, SimMod'05, edited by V. Kachitvichyanukul, U. Purintrapiban and P. Utayopas, pp. 309–318. Bangkok, Thailand.

Keskinen, M., M. Kummu, N. Pok, H. Rath, and Y. Sambo. 2005b. "Where Water Equals Life—Analysing Water–Livelihoods Interconnections in the Mekong Floodplain of Cambodia." Paper presented at workshop on Water in Mainland Southeast Asia, the Centre for Khmer Studies (CKS) and the International Institute for Asian Studies (IIAS), Siem Reap, Cambodia.

Kite, G. 2000. "Developing a Hydrological Model for the Mekong Basin: Impacts of Basin Development on Fisheries Productivity." Working paper 2, International Water Management Institute(IWMI), Colombo, Sri Lanka, pp. 141.

———. 2001. "Modeling the Mekong: Hydrological Simulation for Environmental Impact Studies." *Journal of Hydrology* 253 (1–4): 1–13.

Kudo, M., S. Kazama, K. Suzuki, and M. Sawamoto. 2004. "Study on Sediment Movement in the Middle Mekong River Basin." Paper presented at international conference on Advances in Integrated Mekong River Management, Vientiane, Laos.

Kummu, M., J. Sarkkula, J. Koponen, and J. Nikula, 2006a. "Ecosystem Management of Tonle Sap Lake: Integrated Modeling Approach." *International Journal of Water Resources Development*—Special Issue: Integrated Water Resources Management on the Tonle Sap Lake, Cambodia, 22 (3).

Kummu, M., J. Sarkkula, and O. Varis. 2006b. "Sediment-related Impacts due to Upstream Reservoir Trapping, the Lower Mekong River." *Geomorphology*, in press.

Lamberts, D. 2001. "Tonle Sap Fisheries: A Case Study on Floodplain Gillnet Fisheries in Siem Reap, Cambodia." FAO Regional Office for Asia and the Pacific, Bangkok, Thailand. RAP Publication 2001/11, pp. 133.

Liu, H., Unpublished. "Water Resources Simulation Model of the Lancang River (In Yunnan Portion of China)." Nanjing Institute of Hydrology and Water Resources, Nanjing, China.

Nancarrow, B. E. 2005. "When the Modeller Meets the Social Scientist or Vice–versa." In MODSIMO5—International Congress on Modeling and Simulation, Modeling and Simulation Society of Australia and New Zealand, edited by A. Zerger and R. M. Argent, Melbourne, December.

Nikula, J. 2005. "Lake and its People—Review and Integration of Hydrological, Ecological and Socio-Economic Information in the Tonle Sap Lake." Master's Thesis, Helsinki University of Technology, Espoo, Finland.

Parker et al. 2002. "Progress in Integrated Assessment and Modelling." *Environmental Modeling & Software* 17 (3): 209–217.

Poulsen, A. F., O. Poeu, S. Viravong, U. Suntornratana, and N. T. Thung. 2002. "Fish Migrations of the Lower Mekong River Basin: Implications for Development, Planning and Environmental Management." Mekong River Commission (MRC) Technical Paper, pp. 62. Phnom Penh: MRC.

Rotmans, J. 1998. "Methods for IA: The Challenges and Opportunities Ahead." *Environmental Modeling and Assessment* 3 (3): 155–179.

Sarkkula, J., E. Baran, P. Chheng, M. Keskinen, J. Koponen, and M. Kummu. 2004. "Tonle Sap Pulsing System and Fisheries Productivity." SIL XXIX International Congress of Limnology. Lahti, Finland.

Sarkkula, J., M. Kiirikki, J. Koponen, and M. Kummu. 2003. "Ecosystem Processes of the Tonle Sap Lake." Ecotone II–1 workshop. Phnom Penh/Siem Reap, Cambodia.

Somlyódy, L. 1994. "Water Quality Management: Can We Improve Integration to Face Future Problems?" Working paper WP-94-34, IIASA.

Sutherland, J.W. 1983. "Normative Predicates of Next-Generation Management Support Systems." *IEEE Transactions on Systems, Man and Cybernetics* 13: 279–297.

Tanaka, H. 1998. "Flood Forecasting of the Mekong River in 1997." Paper presented at regional workshop on Flood Management and Mitigation in the Mekong River Basin, Vientiane, Laos.

Tes, S. and L. D. Trung. 2004. "Application of the MRC Decision Support Framework as Tools to Help in Flood Management in the Lower Mekong Basin." Paper presented at international conference on Advances in Integrated Mekong River Management, Vientiane, Laos.

Tran, D. D. 2000. "VRSAP Model and its Application." Paper presented at workshop on Hydrologic and Environmental Modeling on the Mekong Basin, Phnom Penh, Cambodia.

Tonle Sap Lake and Vicinities (TSLV) Project, 2004. "Consolidation of Hydro-Meteorological Data and Multi-functional Hydrologic Roles of Tonle Sap Lake and its Vicinities, Phase-III Project Final Report." MRCS, Vientiane, Laos.

Varis, O. 1998. "A Belief Network Approach to Optimization and Parameter Estimation: Application to Resource and Environmental Management." *Artificial Intelligence* 101 (1/2): 135–163.

Varis, O., and S., Fraboulet-Jussila. 2002. "Water Resources Management in the Lower Senegal River Basin Conflicting Interests, Environmental Concerns, and Policy Options." *International Journal of Water Resources Development* 18 (2): 245–260.

Varis, O., and M. Keskinen. 2006. "Policy Analysis for the Tonle Sap Lake, Cambodia A Bayesian Network Model Approach." *International Journal of Water Resources Development*—Special Issue: Integrated Water Resources Management on the Tonle Sap Lake, Cambodia, 22 (3).

Wolanski, E., N. N. Huan, L. T. D. N. H. Nhan, and N. N. Thuy. 1996. "Fine-sediment Dynamics in the Mekong River Estuary, Vietnam." *Estuarine, Coastal and Shelf Science* 43 (5): 565–582.

WUP-A. 2003. "Knowledge Base and DSF Application Software." Water Utilisation Project Component A (WUP-A): Development of Basin Modeling Package and Knowledge Base, Mekong River Commission (MRC), Phnom Penh (WUP-A/MRC, Working paper 13).

WUP-FIN. 2003. "Modeling Tonle Sap for Environmental Impact Assessment and Management Support." MRCS/WUP-FIN Project, Final Report, Mekong River Commission (MRC), Phnom Penh, Cambodia.

CHAPTER 7
Forums and flows: Emerging media trends in the region

Economy, E. 2005. China's Environmental Movement, testimony before the Congressional Executive Commission on China Roundtable on Environmental NGOs in China: Encouraging Action and Addressing Public Grievances. Council on Foreign Relations, Publication No. 7770, February 7, 2005.

Mooney, P. 1993. "China Wages a New War on Academic Dissent." In The Rhetoric of Empire: Colonial Discourse in Journalism, Travel Writing and Imperial Administration by David Spurr, pp. 25. Durham: Duke University Press.

Hawkins, V. 2000. "The Other Side of the CNN factor: The media and conflict." Journalism Studies 3 (2): 255-245.

Hirsch, P. and C. Warren, eds. 1998. The Politics of Environment in Southeast Asia: Resources and Resistance. London: Routledge.

Economy, E. "The Grass-roots Greening of China," International Herald Tribune April 22, 2004.

The Lahu National Development Organisation (LNDO). 2003. "Aftershocks along Burma's Mekong: Reef-blasting and Military-style Development in Eastern Shan State". Chiang Mai.

CHAPTER 8
Gender myths in water governance: A survey of program discourses

Agarwal, B. 1997. "Environmental Action, Gender Equity and Women's Participation." Development and Change 28 (1): 1-44.

———.2001. "Participatory Exclusions, Community Forestry, and Gender: An Analysis for South Asia and a Conceptual Framework." World Development 29 (10): 1623-1648.

Asian Development Bank (ADB). 2002. "Report and Recommendation of the President to the Board of Directors on a Proposed Loan and Technical Assistance Grant to the Kingdom of Cambodia for the Tonle Sap Environmental Management Project." Manila: ADB.

Cleaver, F. 1999. "Paradoxes of Participation: Questioning Participatory Approaches to Development." Journal of International Development 11: 597–612.

———. 2003. "Bearers, Buyers and Bureaucrats: The Missing Social World in Gender and Water." Paper presented at Gender Myths and Feminist Fables: Repositioning Gender in Development Policy and Practice, Institute of Development Studies (IDS), University of Sussex, July 2–4.

Community Capacities for Development (CCD). 2003. "Program for the Development of Community Fisheries Phase II." Kampong Chhnang Province: CCD.

Community Fisheries Development Office—Department of Fisheries (CFDO–DOF). 2004. CFDO Strategic Plan. Phnom Penh: DOF.

Francis, E. 2002. "Gender, Migration and Multiple Livelihoods: Cases from Eastern and Southern Africa." Journal of Development Studies 38: 167–190.

Gauld, R. 2000. "Maintaining Centralised Control in Community-based Forestry: Policy Construction in the Philippines." In Forests: Nature, People, Power edited by M Doornbos, A Saith and B White, pp 223–248. Oxford: Blackwell Publishers.

Hart, G. 1991. "Engendering Everyday Resistance: Gender, Patronage and Production Politics in Rural Malaysia." Journal of Peasant Studies 19 (1): 93–121.

Hampshire, K. 1999. "Fulani on the Move: Seasonal Economic Migration in the Sahel as a Social Process." Journal of Development Studies 38: 15-36.

Hirsch, P. and A. Wyatt. 2004. "Negotiating Local Livelihoods: Scales of Conflict in the Se San River Basin." Asia Pacific Viewpoint 45 (1): 51–68.

Huyen Thi Do. 2003. "Women's Participation in Natural Resources Management and Environmental Protection in Vietnam: Experiences and lessons from the Sida Environmental Fund Project." Paper presented at the Politics of the Commons on Articulating Development and Strengthening Local Practices, Chiang Mai, Thailand, July 11–14.

Jackson, C. 1998. "Gender, Irrigation and Environment: Arguing for Agency." *Agriculture and Human Values* 15 (4): 313–324.

———. 2000. "Rescuing Gender from the Poverty Trap." In *Feminist Visions of Development: Gender Analysis and Policy* edited by C. Jackson and R. Pearson, London: Routledge.

Manorom, K. 1999. *Socio-cultural Impacts of the Construction of the Pak Mun Dam*. Ubon Ratchathani: Ubon Ratchathani University Press.

Kotavinon, S. 2000. "Women in the Marginal People's Movement: A Case Study of Mae Mun Man Yuen Community Two and Three at Rasi Salai Dam." Master's thesis, Thammasat University, Bangkok.

Leach, M. 1992. "Gender and environment: Traps and Opportunities." *Development in Practice* 2 (1): 12–22.

Locke, C. 1999. "Constructing a Gender Policy for Joint Forest Management in India." *Development and Change* 30 (2): 265–285.

Mehta, L., M. Leach, P. Newell, I. Scoones, K. Sivaramakrishnan, and S. A. Way. 1999. "Exploring Understandings of Institutions and Uncertainty: New directions in Natural Resource Management." *IDS Discussion Paper 372*. Sussex: Institute of Development Studies.

Mosse, D. 1997. "The Symbolic Making of a Common Property Resource: History, Ecology, and Locality in a Tank-irrigated Landscape in South India." *Development and Change* 28 (3): 467–504.

———. 2001. *The Rule of Water: Statecraft, Ecology and Collective Action in South India*. New Delhi: Oxford University Press.

Narayan, D. 1995. *The Contribution of People's Participation. Evidence from 121 Rural Water Supply Projects*. Washington DC: World Bank.

Nguyen Huu Chiem, et al. 2004. "Towards Holistic and Sustainable Community Development-fish Conservation and Organic Farming in An Binh Village, Vietnam." Paper presented at the Mekong Learning Initiative Reflection Meeting in Pakse, Laos, October 5–7.

Ostrom, E. 1990. *Governing the Commons: The Evolution of Institutions for Collective Action*. Cambridge: Cambridge University Press.

Palmer, I. 1985. *The Impact of Male-Outmigration on Women in Farming*. West Hartford: Kumarian Press.

Prokopy, L. S. 2004. "Women's Participation in Rural Water Supply Projects in India: Is it Moving Beyond Tokenism and does it Matter?" *Water Policy* 6: 1–14.

Resurreccion, B., M. J. Real, and P. Pantana. 2004. "Officialising Strategies. Participatory Processes and Gender in ADB's Capacity-building in Thailand's Water Resources Sector." *Development in Practice* 14 (4): 521–533.

Singh, N., P. Bhattacharya, G. Jacks, and J. E. Gustafsson. 2003. "Women and Water: A Policy Assessment." *Water Policy* 5: 289–304.

Thongchanh S., et al. 2004. "Integrated Problems, Integrated Responses: Improving Livelihoods and Encouraging Conservation in Hanghee Village, Champassak Province, Southern Lao PDR." Paper presented at the Mekong Learning Initiative Reflection Meeting in Pakse, Laos, October 5–7.

Ubon Ratchathani University. 2002. "Project to Study Approaches to Restoration of the Ecology, Livelihood and Communities Receiving Impact from Construction of Pak Mun Dam." Team research, Ubon Ratchathani University.

World Bank. 1992. *World Development Report*. New York: Oxford University Press.

Online sources and electronic material
Assembly of the Poor, Pak Mun Dam Affected People, Thailand and Southeast Asia Rivers Networks (SEARIN). 2002. "The Return of Fish, River Ecology and Local Livelihoods of the Mun River. Case study of Pak Mun and Rasi Salai Dams." In *Livelihood and Contemporary Civil Movement* edited by Pasuk Ponhpaichit. Bangkok: Thailand Research Fund, http://www.searin.org/Th/PMD/PMDRESEARCH.htm.
Both ends/Gomukh. 2003. "Case Study: The Case of the Se San River Basin, Cambodia and Vietnam." In water@bothends.org, June.
NGO Forum on Cambodia (NGOF). 2001. "Annual Progress Report 2001," http://ngoforum.org.kh/Core/annual_report_2001%20text.html.
Oxfam America. 2004. "Se San Protection Network Celebrates a Year of Progress," http://oxfamamerica.org/newsadpublications/news_updates/archive2004.
Southeast Asia Rivers Network (SEARIN). 2004. "Thai Baan Research at Chiang Kong," http://www.searin.org/Th/Mekong/mek_tb_research.pdf (accessed November 13, 2006).

CHAPTER 9
Multi-stakeholder Platforms (MSPS): Unfulfilled potential

Asian Development Bank (ADB). 2001. "Building on Success: A Strategic Framework for the Next 10 Years of the GMS Programme." Endorsed by the Tenth Ministerial Conference held in Yangon, Myanmar on November 29. Manila: ADB.
———. 2002. "Economic Cooperation in the Greater Mekong Subregion: An Overview." Manila: ADB.
———. 2004. "Proposed Revision in ADB's Water Policy Regarding Large Water Resources Projects." Manila: ADB.
——— and United Nations Environment Programme (UNEP). 2004. *Greater Mekong Subregion Atlas of the Environment*. ADB and the UNEP Regional Resource Centre for Asia and the Pacific.
Atack, I. 1999. "Four Criteria of Development NGO Legitimacy." *World Development* 27 (5): 855–864.
Baber, W. F. 2004. "Ecology and Democratic Governance: Towards a Deliberative Model of Environmental Politics." *Social Science Journal* 41: 331–346.
Badenoch, N. 2001. "Environmental Governance: Principles and Practice in Mainland Southeast Asia." Washington DC: World Resources Institute.
Bui Kim Chi. 1997. "From Committee to Commission? The Evolution of the Mekong River Agreements with reference to the Murray-Darling Basin Agreements." PhD thesis, University of Melbourne.
Dam Affected People and their Allies. 2003. "Rivers for life! The Rasi Salai Declaration." Statement from the Second International Meeting of Dam Affected People and their Allies, Rasi Salai, Thailand, November 28–December 4.
Dore, J. 2003. "The Governance of Increasing Mekong Regionalism." In *Social Challenges for the Mekong region* edited by Mingsarn Kaosa-ard and J. Dore, pp. 405–440. Bangkok: White Lotus.
Dore, J., and J. Woodhill. 1993. "Sustainable Regional Development." Canberra: Greening Australia.
Dore, J., J. Woodhill, K. Andrews, and C. Keating. 2003. "Sustainable Regional Development: Lessons from Australian Efforts." In *Managing Australia's Environment* edited by S. R. Dovers and S. Wild River. Canberra: Federation Press, in collaboration with Land & Water Australia.
Dovers, S. 2001. "Institutions for Sustainability." Melbourne: Australian Conservation Foundation.

Dovers, S., and J. Dore. 1999. "Adaptive Institutions, Organisations and Policy Processes for River Basin and Catchment Management." Proceedings of the 2nd International River Management Symposium, September 29–October 2. Brisbane.

Dryzek, J. S. 1999. "Transnational Democracy." *The Journal of Political Philosophy* 7 (1): 30–51.

———. 2000. *Deliberative Democracy and Beyond: Liberals, Critics, Contestations*. Oxford: Oxford University Press.

———. 2001. "Legitimacy and Economy in Deliberative Democracy." *Political Theory* 29 (5): 651–669.

Dubash, N. K., M. Dupar, S. Kothari, and T. Lissu. 2001. "A Watershed in Global Governance? An Independent Assessment of the World Commission on Dams." World Resources Institute (WRI), Lokayan and Lawyer's Environmental Action Team. Washington DC: WRI.

Economic and Social Commission for Asia and the Pacific (ESCAP). 2000. "Proceedings of Principles and Practices of Water Allocation among Water-use Sectors." *Water Resources Series 80*. Bangkok: ESCAP.

Goodland, R. 2004. "Roundtable Comments on 'Prior Informed Consent' and the World Bank Group." Proceedings of Prior Informed Consent Conference, March 2, convened by American University, Centre for International Environmental Law, and Washington College of Law. Washington DC: World Bank.

Governments of China-Lao PDR-Myanmar-Thailand 2001. *Agreement on Commercial Navigation on the Lancang-Mekong River*. Signed in Tachilek, Myanmar, April 20, 2000.

Greeff, L. 2000. "Comments Submitted January 2000 Responding to December 1999 Draft Version of Participation, Negotiation and Conflict Management in Large Dams Projects." *Thematic Review V. 5*. A thematic review prepared by RESOLVE Inc et al. as an input to the World Commission on Dams (WCD). Cape Town: WCD.

Guston, D.H. 1999. "Stabilising the Boundary between US Politics and Science." *Social Studies of Science* 29 (1): 87–111.

———. 2001. "Boundary Organisations in Environmental Policy and Science: An Introduction." *Science Technology and Human Values* 26 (4): 399–408.

Hay, C. 2002. *Political Analysis: A Critical Introduction*. Hampshire: Palgrave.

He, D., G. Zhang, and H.T. Kung, eds. 2001. "Towards Cooperative Utilisation and Coordinated Management of International Rivers." Proceedings of International Symposium, June 25-30, 1999, Kunming, China. New York & Tokyo: Science Press & United Nations University.

He, J. 2002. "A Research on the Development Strategy of the 21st Century's Hydropower in China." *Electricity* 13 (1).

Hemmati, M. 2002. "The World Commission on Dams as a Multi-stakeholder Process." *Politics and the Life Sciences* 21 (1).

Hettne, B. 1999. "Globalization and the New Regionalism: The Second Great Transformation." In *Globalization and the New Regionalism* edited by B. Hettne, A. Inotai, and O. Sunkel, pp. 1–25. Houndmills: Macmillan Press.

Hewison, K. 2001. "Nationalism, Populism, Dependency: Southeast Asia and Responses to the Asian Crisis." *Singapore Journal of Tropical Geography* 2 (3): 219–236.

Hirsch, P. and A. Wyatt. 2004. "Negotiationg Local Livelihoods: Scales of Conflict in the Se San River Basin." *Asia Pacific Viewpoint* 45 (1): 51–68.

Igbokwe, K. N., M. B. Espinelli, X. Yu, and K. Lazarus. 2002. "Towards Developing and Implementing a Multi-stakeholder Capacity Building Program for Participatory Watershed Management: A Case of Lashi Watershed, Yunnan Province." In Third Symposium on Montane Mainland South East Asia, edited by J. Xu et al. Kunming: Yunnan Science and Technology Press.

International Rivers Network (IRN). 2004. "Sizing up the Grid: How the Mekong Power Grid Compares against the Policies of the Asian Development Bank." Berkely, CA: IRN.

Jordan, L. and P. Van Tuijl. 2000. "Political Responsibility in Transnational NGO Advocacy." *World Development* 28 (12): 2051–2065.

Lazarus, K. 2003. "A Multi-stakeholder Watershed Management Committee in Lashi Watershed: A New Way of Working." Commentary in China Environment, Series No. 6. Washington DC: Woodrow Wilson Centre.

Leeuwis, C. 2000. "Reconceptualising Participation for Sustainable Rural Development: Towards a Negotiation Approach." *Development and Change* 31: 931–959.

Local people. 2002. "Declaration by the Local Communities of the River Basins in Thailand." In Press Release from the Dialogue on River Basin Development and Civil Society in the Mekong Region. Distributed by TERRA, Ubon Ratchatani, Thailand, November 9–12.

Maarleveld, M. and C. Dangbegnon. 2002. "Social Learning: Major Concepts and Issues." In *Wheelbarrows Full of Frogs* edited by C. Leeuwis and R. Pyburn. The Netherlands: Koninklijke Van Gorcum, Assen.

MacKay, F. 2004. "Indigenous Peoples' Right to Free Prior and Informed Consent, and the World Bank's Extractive Industries Review." Briefing note from Forest Peoples Programme, March 17.

Mingsarn Kaosa-ard and J. Dore, eds. 2003. *Social Challenges for the Mekong Region*. Bangkok: White Lotus.

Moore, C. W. 1987. *The Mediation Process, Practical Strategies for Resolving Conflict*. San Francisco: Jossey-Bass Publishers.

Petkova, E., C. Maurer, N. Henninger, and F. Irwin. 2002. "Closing the Gap: Information, Participation and Justice in Decision Making for the Environment." Based on the findings of The Access Initiative, World Resources Institute. Washington DC: WRI.

Pradit, R. 2004. "No Backing for Rebels, PM Tells Junta." *Bangkok Post*, August 26.

Regional Environmental Forum (REF) participants 2002. "Regional Environmental Forum Consensus Statement." In Press Release from the First Annual Regional Environmental Forum for Mainland Southeast Asia. Distributed by World Resources Institute, Phnom Penh, November 14–15.

Roling, N. 2002. "Moving Beyond the Aggregation of Individual Preferences." In *Wheelbarrows Full of Frogs* edited by C. Leeuwis and R. Pyburn, The Netherlands: Koninklijke Van Gorcum, Assen.

Ryder, G. 2003. "Behind the ASEAN Power Grid." Toronto: Probe International.

Stockholm Environment Institute (SEI), United Nations Environment Programme (UNEP), Asian Development Bank (ADB), Mekong River Commission (MRC). 2002. "Strategic Environmental Framework for the Greater Mekong Subregion: Integrating Development and Environment in the Transport and Water Resources Sectors." Executive Summary, SEF Main Report Volume I, Issues and Trends Volume II, GMS Hotspot Profiles Volume III, SEF Case Study Reports Volume IV, SEI, UNEP, ADB, MRC. Manila: ADB.

The Economist. 2004. *Pocket World in Figures*. London: Profile Books.

World Bank (WB). 2004. "Water Resources Assistance Strategy." Washington DC: WB.

———. 2004. "Draft response of the World Bank to the Final Report of the Extractive Industries Review." Posted on the web June 4 2004 to be available for public comment for 30 days.

Online sources and electronic material

Dore, J. and X, Yu. 2004. "Yunnan Hydropower Expansion: Update on China's Energy Industry Reforms and the Nu, Lancang and Jinsha Hydropower Dams." Working Paper from Chiang Mai University's Unit for Social and Environmental Research, and Green Watershed, http://www.sea-user.org/pubs/user-wp-2004-04.pdf.

Earth Charter Commission (ECC). 2000. "The Earth Charter." ECC c/o University for Peace, Costa Rica, http://www.earthcharter.org.

Governments of Cambodia-Lao PDR-Vietnam-Thailand. 1995. *Agreement on the Cooperation for the Sustainable Development of the Mekong River Basin.* Signed in Chiang Rai, Thailand, April 5, http://www.mrcmekong.org.

United Nations Economic Commission for Europe (UNECE). 1998. *Convention on Access to Information, Public Participation in Decision-making and Access to Justice in Environmental Matters.* Geneva: UNECE, http://www.unece.org/pub_cat/lpenv0.html.

ABOUT THE CONTRIBUTORS

Bach Tan Sinh is Acting-Director of the Department of Science Policy Studies at the National Institute for Science and Technology Policy and Strategy Studies—a policy advisory institution to the Ministry of Science and Technology. Sinh has more than fifteen years experience on policy analysis in the field of science, technology, environment and development in Vietnam. He is currently leading a research component on reducing the risk of flood-related disasters in M-POWER.

Antonio P. Contreras is Full Professor at the Department of Political Science and also currently the Dean of the College of Liberal Arts at the De La Salle University in Manila. He has a Ph.D. in Political Science from the University of Hawaii.

Rajesh Daniel is a researcher with USER, Chiang Mai University, Thailand. His research interests are upper tributary watersheds and ethnic communities with focus on local livelihoods and natural resources management in the Mekong region. He is working with M-POWER on the "watershed" research area.

John Dore is responsible for the development of IUCN Asia Water Program, and as a political economy and governance researcher works with M-POWER leading the "dialogues, deliberation and diplomacy" research area.

Po Garden is a researcher with USER, Chiang Mai University, Thailand. He is working on water governance and upland livelihoods.

Chris Greacen works on power sector issues in the Mekong region, with a focus on renewable energy, and electricity policy and planning in Thailand. His Ph.D. from the Energy and Resources Group at University of California, Berkeley focused on community-managed micro-hydroelectricity in Thailand.

Masao Imamura is a researcher with USER, Chiang Mai University, Thailand. Currently he is also coordinator of the Mekong Program on Water, Environment and Resilience (M-POWER). He is strongly interested in cross-disciplinary and multi-national research networking in the Mekong region. His research focuses on issues of representation and legitimacy.

Kanokwan Manorom is Assistant Professor, Faculty of Liberal Arts, Ubon Ratchathani University, Thailand. Her Ph.D. from the University of Missouri focused on gender aspects of village life which was concerned with community forest resource management. Most of her work relates closely with local people and natural resources management, community development, community studies, and local participation in action research. Her work endeavors to understand and support village communities articulate their needs and opinions to policymakers at national scale such as in the "Pak Mun Dam Management and People's Environmental and Social Impact Assessment" and "Social Assessment on Integrated Basin Flow Management of the MRC."

Marko Keskinen is a Ph.D. candidate at the Water Resources Laboratory of Helsinki University of Technology, Finland. He studies the interconnections between water and society in the Lower Mekong Basin, and looks at multi- and cross-disciplinarity of water resources management, and of modelling and impact assessment in particular. He has been working in the WUP-FIN Project since 2002 as a socio-economist.

Jorma Koponen is the deputy team leader and the main modeller of the WUP-FIN Project, having a long-term experience in development, validation, use, and practical application of hydrological, hydrodynamic, water quality and ecosystem simulation models. He has been developing the EIA 3D model over the last twenty years.

Matti Kummu is a Ph.D. candidate at the Water Resources Laboratory of Helsinki University of Technology, Finland. His Ph.D. topic is "Simulating the long-term morphological changes in alluvial system." He has been working in the WUP-FIN Project for the last four years as a modeller.

Louis Lebel is currently the director of USER, Faculty of Social Sciences, Chiang Mai University. Over the past thirteen years he has carried out and helped coordinate research on natural resources management, institutional change, public health, global environmental change and development politics in Thailand and neighboring countries in Southeast Asia.

Kevin Yuk-shing Li was involved in environmental campaigns in Hong Kong for over sixteen years. He joined the Berkeley-based International Rivers Network as a consultant, and worked closely with the environmentalists in Beijing and Yunnan in highlighting the negative impacts of dam construction in the transboundary rivers of China, namely Nu-Salween River and Lancang-Mekong River.

François Molle is a senior researcher at the Institut de Recherche pour le Développement, France, with a joint appointment with the International Water Management Institute, Colombo. He has experience from South America, Africa and Asia on irrigation and river basin management and now focuses his research on water policy and governance issues in the Mekong region, particularly on issues of participatory management, river basin management, and policy processes.

Shawn L. Nance is an independent journalist and geopolitical risk consultant based in Bangkok, Thailand specializing in foreign investment, security and human rights in the Mekong region. He is also the former deputy editor of the Irrawaddy news magazine, which focuses on Myanmar [Burma] and Southeast Asia.

Jussi Nikula works at Gaia Consulting Ltd. in Finland. He is also a Researcher in the Water Resources Laboratory at the Helsinki University of Technology. In 2005 he completed his Master's Thesis with the WUP-FIN Project on integration of socio-economic, ecological and hydrological information in the Tonle Sap Area.

Apsara Palettu is the pseudonym of an independent researcher in the Mekong region.

Bernadette P. Resurreccion is currently the Coordinator of Gender and Development Studies at the Asian Institute of Technology (AIT) in Thailand and has worked extensively on issues of gender, policy and natural resource management in Thailand, Cambodia, Vietnam and the Philippines.

Juha Sarkkula is the team leader of the WUP-FIN Project and has been working in the Lower Mekong Basin, particularly in the Tonle Sap Lake, over five years. He has long-term experience in hydrological, hydrodynamic, sediment and water quality modelling projects for water resources management and environmental impact assessment.

Surichai Wun'gaeo is Associate Professor, Faculty of Political Science, Chulalongkorn University, Thailand. He has many years experience in social issues especially in relation to policy dialogue and deliberation processes in Thailand.

Olli Varis is a senior researcher at the Water Resources Laboratory of Helsinki University of Technology, Finland and a policy analyst in the WUP-FIN Project. He holds a PhD degree in Water Resources Management and is the author of more than 200 scientific papers. His current research is concentrated on environmental and social impacts of water policies and integrated water resources management in developing countries.

Markku Virtanen works at EIA Ltd., Finland and has a long-term experience in development and practical application of hydrological, hydrodynamic, water quality and ecosystem simulation models. He also works as a hydrological modeller of the WUP-FIN Project.

Yang Saing Koma is currently the director of Cambodian Center for Study and Development in Agriculture (CEDAC). Over the past eleven years he has been involved in coordinating and implementing research, extension, education and publication in the field of ecological agriculture and participatory natural resources management and farmer organizations.

Yu Xiaogang is the founder and director of Green Watershed, the Chinese NGO started in 2002 that works to promote participatory watershed management with local communities in Southwest China. In 2003 he helped form the China Rivers Network, the first Chinese network of environmental activists dedicated to protecting China's rivers. He pioneered watershed protection by creating the Lashi Watershed Project to bring together residents, local government authorities and private entrepreneurs to rebuild that area, and has played a key role in the movement to protect the Nu River, one of only two undammed major rivers in China. In 2006, he won the Goldman Prize for his watershed protection work.

ABOUT M-POWER

M-POWER stands for the Mekong Program on Water, Environment and Resilience (see http://www.mpowernet.org). M-POWER was initiated by the Unit for Social and Environmental Research (USER), Chiang Mai University, Thailand, for action-research to improve the quality of water governance in ways which support sustainable livelihoods in the Mekong region.

M-POWER is bringing together a high-caliber group of individuals and leaders from state, nongovernmental organizations and academia to explore water governance issues in the Mekong region. Based on a common grounding of social and ecological concern about the Mekong region, the group is engaged in a 4–year action-research plan funded by the CGIAR Challenge Program on Food and Water.

The ultimate goals of the program are improved livelihood security, human and ecosystem health in the Mekong region through democratizing water governance. The proximate goal of M-POWER is to contribute to efforts to democratize water governance through action research.

Action research means that the work often involves being engaged in the political debates and actions the project is analyzing and commenting upon. This significantly increases the levels of responsibility for doing the work well. The program aims to draw lessons from these experiences through critical comparison and exchange of experiences. The action-research case studies are comparative or regional. Each "case" is therefore usually composed of several studies. The themes are meant to help organize thinking about the broad lessons of governance which may cut across several or all water politics situations represented in the cases.

The case studies are organized around:
- Fisheries: negotiating sustainable livelihoods;
- Floods: reducing the risks of disaster; Irrigation: alternatives to large-scale infrastructure;
- Hydropower: meeting energy needs fairly and sustainably;
- Watersheds: resilient livelihoods in the uplands;
- Water works: secure water supply and treatment for households.

The four governance themes are:
- Dialogue: deliberation, diplomacy and negotiation;
- Social justice: gender, ethnicity and class;
- Knowledge: assessment, practice and communication;
- Policies: integration, decentralization and privatization.

The action-research program is expected to produce empirical experiences, critique and analysis of water use, sharing and management, and local livelihood concerns as well as synthesis of the pressing social and political challenges for water governance in the countries of the Mekong region.

INDEX

acid rain, 58
activists
　energy. *See* energy activists
　opposition to Salween dam plans, 171
adaptive capacity
　managing floods, 53
adjust discourse, 40
agencies
　effect of repositioning, 29
agricultural production
　Yunnan Province, 56
Agriculture Sector Program Loan (ASPL), 16
Amazon basin, 144
Anbinh
　fish sanctuary in, 190
Apex bodies, 18
　focus of, 19
　step-by-step approach, 19
applied meteorology
　use of numerical models, 136
ASEAN electricity grid
　proposal for, 220
Asia-Pacific Economic Cooperation (APEC), 140
Asian Development Bank (ADB), 9, 15, 62, 91, 94, 101, 121, 177, 178, 198, 211, 220, 230
　approach in water resource projects, 218
　board of governors, 208
　Mekong Water Resources Assistance Strategy, 221
　Strategic Environment Framework, 220
　Technical Assistance (TA), 182
　water forum, 166
Asian Disaster Preparedness Centre (APDC), 48
Asian financial crisis, 115, 160
Asian Wall Street Journal, 160
Asiaweek, 161
Assembly of the Poor (AOP), 186

Association of Southeast Asian Nations (ASEAN), 140, 198
Australian Agency for International Development (AUSAID), 25
Australian experience
　transferring of, 36
Australian Mekong Resource Center, 209
Australian Mekong River Commission (AMRC), 185
Ayutthaya Province, 42

Bach Tan Sinh, 158
balanced development path, 31
Bangkok, 76
Bangkok Post, 11
Banqiao, 47
Basin Development Plan (BDP), 140
basin management
　macro-level, 31
Bayesian Causal Networks, 148, 149
Beijing hydropower forum, 87
best practice, 18
　easy transplantation of, 30
Bhumipol Dam, 44, 97
bilateral agencies, 27
Bina Agarwal, 179
Bing Zhong Luo, 91
biomass, 64
　grid connected, 124
Board of Investment, 113
British Broadcasting Service (BBC) World Service
　East Asia Today, 161
British Columbia, 125
Burmese ethnic nationalities
　relaying news back home, 162
Burmese online rap group, 167

California, 121
Cambodia, 2, 4, 11, 20, 21, 41, 51, 80, 99, 122, 138, 140
　community fisheries, 182, 188–189

Cambodia (cont.)
   draft of water law, 15
   fisheries department, 189
   ADB, 189
   hydropower, 110
   irrigated area, 2
   limits to free expression, 159
   mainstream mass media in, 171
   Ministry of Environment, 36
   Ministry of Water Resources and Meteorology (MOWRAM), 15, 16, 35
   priorities, 23
   radio station owners in, 171
   Tonle Sap Lake, 144
   water policy of, 13
   water resource development, 185–186
   Women's Media Center, 165
   Yali Falls Dam, 185
Cambodian fisheries law dialogue, 208
Cambodian Institute for Cooperation and Peace, 210
Cambodian Mekong Floodplains, 150
Cambodian National Mekong Committee, 51, 209
Cambodian reporters
   paying with lives, 159
Cambodia's People Party, 159
Cam Kim commune, 44
Canada
   economy of, 120
Can Tho University, 190
CARE International, 50
cascade dams, 3
catchment organizations
   establishment of, 30
Central China Television (CCTV), 76
Champassak Province
   Lao PDR, 44
challenges
   spiritual side, 154
changes
   using bottom-up approach, 33
Channel Financing Agreement, 98
channel modification, 38
Chao Phraya, 44
Chao Phraya Flood Management Master Plan, 44
Chao Phraya River basin, 220
Chen Dongping, 58
Chiang Khong Conservation Group, 209
Chiang Kong district, 186, 187
Chiang Mai, 162, 169
Chiang Rai Province, 26

Chiang Saen, 79
China, 10, 24, 51, 64, 102, 122
   coal reserves, 91
   commercialization of media, 172
   deregulation of, 62
   electricity supply, 3
   energy development governance, 89
   energy industry reforms, 67, 69
   energy policy, 89
   energy production, 67
   energy reforms, 55–92
   global energy market, in, 63
   "greening" of media, 172, 173
   hydropower, 57–60
   hydropower potential, 58, 59
   hydropower production, 58
   Internet police, 173
   investors interested in, 61
   irrigation in, 35
   key issues, 84
   largest oil importer outside OECD, 63
   Ministry of Water Resources, 24
   non-membership of MRC, 205
   public awareness of disasters, 172
   projected supply of primary energy, 60, 66
   renewable energy sources, 64
   shift to market economy, 61, 62
   South-North transfer project, 14
   State Environment Protection Agency (SEPA), 214
   water law, 15, 17
China Atomic Energy Agency, 91
China Construction Bank, 82
China Development Bank, 78, 82
China Environmental Culture Association, 75
China Gezhouba Group, 70
China Huandian Corporation, 74, 75, 219
China Water Conservancy and Hydropower Construction Group, 70
China Yangtze Electric Power Corporation (CYPEC), 82
China-ASEAN free trade agreement, 226
Chindwin basin
   off limits, 5
Chinese Sino Hydro Corporation, 108
Chou Chetarith, 159
Chuan Leekpai, 175
CITIC Technology Company, 108
civil society, 49, 208
civil society groups

legitimacy of, 215
clean water
  access to, 4
climate change
  impact of, 52
climate variability, 4
coal-fired power plants, 58
Cold War era, 122
collection of primary information, 153
colonization
  history of, 163
Committee for Coordination of Investigations of the Lower Mekong Basin, 96
Committee to Protect Journalists, 159
Common Property Resource management, 31
Common Property Resources (CPR) approach
  call for greater institutional building, 181
  creation of local institutions, 180
  efficiency in managing resources, 180–182
  participation of women, 179–180
  water resources management, 178–179
communications infrastructure, 52
communication problems, 131
communications
  central issue, 130
community fisheries, 178
  Cambodia, 188
Community Fisheries Development Office Master Plan, 189
community sector participation, 44
community-based natural resource management (CBNRM), 191
community-based radio stations, 162
competing discourse, 41
competition
  value of, 6, 7
conflict resolution mechanisms, 178
conservationists, 32
Construction Bank of China, 78
consultative meetings, 30
consumers
  lower income, 165
control discourse, 40
conventional structural measures, 50
Core Environment Program, 207
cost-recovery, 10
Cuu Long RBO, 25

Dachoashan, 77, 110
dam developers
  entrepreneurial, 68
dams
  alternatives to, 86
  cross border environmental impact, 87
  source of risk, 46
databases
  analysis of, 146
debate over, 86
Decentralized Irrigation Development and Management Project, 187
decision-making framework, 88
decision-making process
  assessment, 89
definitions
  independent, 121
  models, 131
deforestation, 46
deliberative development, 31
delta areas, 40
demand forecast, 119
  realistic, 123
demand management, 91
demand side management (DSM), 122, 230
Democratic Voice of Burma, 161
Department of Disaster Prevention and Mitigation, 45
Department of Dykes Management, Flood and Storm Control, 44
development
  preferred type of, 84
Development Cooperation Department, Ministry of Foreign Affairs of Finland, 156
development cooperation projects, 139
development goals
  methods of achieving, 84
development banks
  mainstream approaches, 28
  support of, 34
development bureaucracy, 6
development and management
  difficulty, 1
Dialogues. *See* multi-stakeholder platforms (MSPS)
directive models, 132
disaster
  mitigation of damages, 45
disaster management, 38
disaster mitigation, 53
disaster rhetoric, 49

Disaster Self Reliant Fund system, 44
disasters
  national security issues, 51
  political challenge, 49
donor-driven publications, 165
downstream erosion, 79
Dujiangyan irrigation scheme, 172
dry season, 37
dry-season rice area, 13
Dulong, 57

early warning system, 52
Earth Charter, 226
East Asia
  monsoons, 37
ecofeminism, 194
economic assessment
  Yunnan dams, of, 90
economic disparity
  people of Mekong countries, 163
economic growth, 43
economic integration
  international, 61
economic planning
  least cost, 123
economic reforms, 30
economic reorganizations, 29
ecosystem model, 131
ecosystem processes, 144
EGAT International Co., 119
EGAT-STRATEGIST modeling, 119
Electric Power Designing Institute, 70
Electric Power Law, 69
Electrical Generation Authority of
  Thailand (EGAT), 11, 78, 80, 97, 112, 220, 214
  building of Pak Mun Dam, 175
Electricite de France, 104, 166
Electricite du Camboge, 11
electricity
  alternative sources, from, 230
  fulfillment of needs, 123
  increased tradability, 3
  non-storability, 121
  peak demand, 95
  regional demand, 94
Electricity Generating Public Company of Thailand, 166
electricity sector
  planning, 93–125
Electricity of Vietnam (EVN), 102
Electricity Generating Authority of
  Thailand, 91

Eleventh Five-Year Plan, 64, 65
embankments, 50
empirical post-event surveys
  need for, 52
energy activists
  Thailand, 118
energy demand
  increases in, 68
Energy Research Institute, 62
engineering applications, 131
engineering capacity, 37
engineers
  paradigmatic backgrounds, 131
English-language media, 160
environment
  definition of, 86
environment modeling, 131
Environmental Impact Assessment (EIA), 86, 87
Environmental Impact Assessment Centre
  of Finland, 156
environmentalists, 32
  dismay of, 11
ethnic groups
  Yunnan Province, 56
ethnic identity
  reinforcing of, 169–170
expert-driven approaches, 32
European Commission (EC), 134
European Espoo Convention, 92
European Forum for Integrated
  Environmental Assessment (EFIEA), 129

Far Eastern Economic Review, 160
Farmer Water User Communities (FWUCS), 20
financial sustainability, 10
Finnish Environment Institute, 156
fisheries ecology
  disturbance to, 79
Fisheries Programme, 143
flash flooding, 39, 52
flood
  becoming disasters, 42
  damage to property, 42
flood disasters, subject to bureaucratic
  competition, 50
Flood Management and Mitigation
  Agreement, 51
Flood Management and Mitigation
  Programme (FMMP), 143
flood protection, 50

flood protection measures, 45
flood regimes
  importance of, 41
flood risks
  discourses relating to management of, 54
flood-resistant varieties of rice, 42
floodplain manipulation, 38
floodplains, 38
floods, 38
  adverse impacts, 39
  adverse impacts of, 41
  benefits from, 43
  coordinating recovery, 47
  diversity of, 39
  economic losses of, 47
  managing using adaptive capacity, 53
  nutrient and sediment loads, 38
  politics of, 53
  reducing risks, 43
  treatment of, 37, 38
Food and Agricultural Organization (FAO), 15, 178, 206
food production
  effect of floods, 42
forecasts
  demand, 119
  demand forecasts, 123
  load forecast overestimation, 115
  successive base-case, 115
foreign-based broadcasting, 174
foreign direct investment (FDI), 91
  China, in, 61
free expression
  limits to, 159–160
freedom of expression
  creative solutions to limits placed, 167–168
  limits to, 159–160
freshwater lake
  Tonle Sap, 144
fundamental disagreements
  problematic, 217

Ga Lai province, 185
Ganlanba, 79
geothermal, 64
GIS-based socioeconomic database, 146
Global Environment Facility (GEF), 124, 140
global initiatives
  water management, 8
global warming, 37

Global Water Partnership, 206
globalization, 60–61, 90
good governance
  definition in Thailand, 7
Gonguoqiao, 79
governance
  China's energy policy, 89
  debate over dams, 86
  energy development, 89
  vague and generic term, 2
governance challenges, 4–6
governance patterns, 31
  emergence of, 32
government
  role in fulfilling electricity needs, 123
government agencies
  pro-active approach, 53
grassroots movement, 32
Great Lake, 80
Greater Mekong Subregion (GMS), 99, 140, 172, 206
Green Watershed, 75, 92, 209
Guangdong Province, 64, 65, 108
Guotai Junan Securities Co., 91

Haestad Methods and Danish Hydraulic Institute, 134
Hanoi, 43
Hat Gyi Dam, 108
health educators
  educating public about HIV/AIDS, 167
health services
  aftermath of flood disasters, 49
Helsinki University of Technology, 156
highways
  constructed on flood plains, 50
High Pa Mong project, 96
historical enmity
  people of Mekong countries, 163
Hmong Lao Radio, 161
Ho Chih Minh City, 4, 43
Homi Kharas, 99
Honghe, 57
households
  marginalized, 38
Hu Jintao, 84
Huai River, 47
Huai River Basin Commission, 47
Huandian Corporation, 110
Huaneng, 77
Huaneng Power International, 78
Huari, 83
Hun Sen, 3, 80, 159

Hydraulic Design Institute, 70
hydraulic network, 10
hydrodynamic modeling, 155
hydrological model
    trade-off scenarios, 1
hydrological indicators, 151
hydrological modeling, 155
hydrological models, 152
hydrological regimes, 152
hydropower, 2
    China's potential, 59
    development in Vietnam, 102
    electricity generation, of, 93–125
    expansion of, 58
    importance in region, 111
    social and environmental costs, 68
hydropower dam plans, 71, 71–73
hydropower development, 3, 121, 122
    sensitive issue, 85
hydropower governance, 85
hydropower imports, 119
hydropower projects
    future plans for, 123
    Lao, 120
    matter of national security, 169
    rapid development, 102
    transmission costs, 119

IA modeling, 130
ignorance discourse, 42, 43
Impact Assessment, 85
    framework for, 151
impact process, 151
incompetence discourse, 42, 43
independent
    definition of, 121
independent media 164, 165
independent publications, 166
independent regulator, 122
Indicative Master Plan on Power
        Interconnection in GMS Countries,
        124
Industrial & Commercial Bank, 78
Industrial & Commercial Bank of China,
        82
industrial-sector livelihoods, 40
industrialization, 4
infrastructural development
    decision making on, 30
Ital-Thai Development Company, 104
injustice discourse, 42, 43
inquiry
    challenges for, 234–236

institutional changes, 49
institutional mechanisms, 50
institutional monocropping, 30
Integrated Assessment (IA), 129
Integrated Basin Flow Management (IBFM),
        140
Integrated Modeling and Assessment (IMA),
        129
integrated management, 149
integrated management of water resources,
        149
integrated model
    Tonle Sap system, 144
integrated resource planning, 121
Integrated Resource Planning (IRP), 118,
        122
integrated water resource management
        (IWRM), 1, 7, 10, 23, 129, 140, 142
    vague and generic, 2
integration of information, 149
International Energy Agency (IEA), 63
International Financial Institutions (IFIS),
        98
    critic, 101
International Rivers Network (IRN), 76
International Rivers Symposium, 79
International Water Management Insitute
        (IWMI), 211
International Water Power & Dam
        Construction, 105
International Water Power and Dam
        Construction (2005), 2, 3
Internet
    limited reach, 161
    method of delivering news, 158
intolerance, 131
Irrawady River
    effect of Himalayan snow melt, 226
irrigated land
    area of, 13
    increase in, 2
irrigation
    trends and challenges, 9–36
irrigation development, 187–191
    Cambodia community fisheries,
        188–189
    Laos, 187–188, 191
    Vietnam, 190, 191
irrigation infrastructure, 11
irrigation management transfer (IMT), 187
irrigation practices, 33
irrigation schemes, 10
Italian-Thai Development Public
        Company, 166

IUCN, 27, 32, 209
IWRM, 29
   effect of repositioning of line agencies, 29

Japan Bank for International Cooperation (JBIC), 16
Jinghong, 78
Jinghong dam, 78, 79
Jinsha, 57, 83
Jinsha River, 55, 82
Joint Committee of the MRC, 142
journalists
   sources of information, 163

Kanchanaburi Province, 97
karaoke
   favorite pastime, 170
Karenni State, 106
Kasame Chatikavanij, 112
Khamhung, 35
Kok River, 26
Kon Tun Province, 185
Kunming, 162
   Kunming Hydropower Design and Planning Institute, 74

Lancang, 55, 57
Lancang dams, impact on fisheries, 81
Lancang River, 77–81
   damming of, 172
   See also Mekong River
Lancang-Mekong
   Chinese hydropower projects, 109
Lancang-Mekong Basin, 79
land development
   via removal of trees, 46
land-holders
   misuse of flood plain concessions, 49
Lao Holding State Enterprise, 166
Lao PDR, 2, 7, 11
   See also Laos
Laos, 22, 26, 26, 35, 51, 96, 99, 102, 106, 138, 140
   agricultural sector, 13
   battery of Asia, 103
   disaster reduction strategy, 45
   Environmental Protection Law, 15
   fish sanctuary development, 191
   foreign currency, 13
   gas-fired combined cycle plants, 105
   hydropower projects, 104, 120
   impact of radio, 161

Information and Culture Ministry, 161
irrigation schemes, 13
low-level infrastructures, 13
national leaders, 103
single party system, 214
Water Resources Coordination Committee (WRCC), 19
Water Resources Law, 15
least-costs economic planning, 123
legitimacy
   definition, 215
Lijiang Prefecture, 82
limits to free expression, 159
   Ministry of Information and Culture, 159
living with discourse, 40
living with floods, 41
Liu Ku dam, 74
load forecasting
   overestimation, 115
load forecast overestimation
   Thailand, 115
local power/gender relations
   overlooking of, 193
local stakeholders
   limitations of, 34
logging, ban in Sichuan, 46
Lop Buri, 183
Lower Mekong Basin, 13, 43, 96, 128, 140, 144
Lower Mekong Basin countries, 51
Lower Mekong Modeling Project, 156
lowland
   residents from, 38
Luang Prabang, 79
lut, 40

Macn-Markar, 5
Maha Sarakam University, 209
management paradigms, 1
management transfer, 20
Manila, 162
Manwan, 77
Manwan dam, 87, 108, 110
Mao Zedong, 47
Master Plan for the Ping River, 24
Mathematical models, 127–155
MDX Company, 219, 220
media
   donor driven, 164–165
   foreign-based broadcasting, 174
   governance issues for, 162–163
   issues in accountability, 163–164

INDEX

media (cont.)
    reaching to audience, 161–162
    role in reinforcing ethnic identity, 169–170
    role of, 227
    subscription revenues, 165
    taking advantage of, 170–173
media consolidation
    problems of, 173
media development
    challenges in, 171
media producers
    role of, 163
media trends, 157–176
Mekong, 5, 122
    effect of Himalayan snow melt, 226
    hydropower development, 98
    low water level, 5
    Nam Theun 2 Power Co., 111
Mekong Agreement, 140
Mekong Agreement (1995), 140, 142
Mekong basin development planning, 141
Mekong Delta, 12
Mekong Learning Initiative (MLI), 190
Mekong region, 2–4, 15, 94, 122
    foreign aid in, 3
    problems, 33
    selected modeling efforts, 155–156
    spectrum of issues, 33
Mekong Region Waters Dialogue, 222
Mekong River, 26
    diverse territory, 227
    diversity of fish, 81
    major river basins, 199
    modeling of, 137
    See also Lancang River
    water concerns, 198
Mekong River Agreement, 26, 129
Mekong River Agreement (1995), 204
Mekong River basin, 140, 152
    infrastructure expansion, 2
Mekong River Commission (MRC), 5, 8, 26, 44, 51, 80, 92, 129, 133, 177, 178, 206, 211
    agenda in agreement, 204
    Decision Support Framework (DSF), 130
    hydropower plans, 95
    Joint Committee of, 142
    modeling activities at, 140
    non-membership of China and Myanmar, 205
Mekong River Commission (MRC)
    Secretariat, 96, 153, 205

Mekong River Commission's Indicative Basin Plan, 124
Mengsong, 79
mental health problems, 50
Ministry of Agriculture and Rural Development (MARD), 20
minority groups
    use of media, 164
model base
    impact assessment, for, 141
    strengthening of, 141
model categories, 132
model development, frustration with, 137
model users, 133
    role of, 133
models
    decision making, 131
    definition of, 131
    development cooperation, in, 139
    key lessons learnt, 138
    for management and decision making, 127
    management of water resources, 127
    Mekong-related, 139
    selection and evaluation, 136
    standardization, effect of, 136
    standardized, 134
    standardized packages, 135
    tailored versus standardized, 135
    tailoring of, 135
model system, 153
modelers, 152
modeling
    difficulties, 153
    purpose of, 134
    regulatory needs, 134
    reliability of results, 135
    way forward for, 137
modeling activities
    Mekong River Commission, at the, 140
Mon Literature and Culture Association, 168
MOWRAM, 20, 23
MRC Basin Development Plan (BDP), 142
MRC Decision Support Framework (DSM), 141
MRC Environment Programme (EP), 140
multi-stakeholder dialogues, 31
multi-stakeholder platforms (MSPs), 197–225, 228
    civil society-led, 208–209
    definition, 199
    definition of, 223

desirable characteristics, 201
governance, 200
institutions involved, 200
key concepts, 200
learning possibilities of, 215
legitimacy of, 215
outcomes, 216–218
predominance of the state in negotiations, 228
recognition of, 230
regional governance, part of, 202
regular meetings, 199
supporters, 201
Thailand, in, 223
water governance, 200
whether workable in Thailand, 225
windows of opportunity, 212–213
multidisciplinary information
 challenges for, 128
 integrating of, 128
multilateral agencies, 27
multilateral banks
 conditions set, 29
multilateral organizations, 178
multilaterals
 aid from, 99
Mun River, 175
Murray-Darling Basin Commission, 211
music recordings
 reinforcing ethnic identities, 174
mutual interdependence, 215
Myanmar, 5, 11, 36, 51, 56, 95, 99, 120
 assertion of Shan identity, 168
 control by military junta, 214
 Department of Hydroelectric Power, 106
 export to other countries, 105
 hydropower, 105–108
 human rights abuse of Shan people, 220
 limits to free expression, 159, 160
 Literary Works Scrutinizing Committee, 159
 military junta in, 169
 Motion Picture and Video Censor Board, 160
 National Water Vision to Action, 17, 18
 non-membership of MRC, 205
 population, 4
Myanmar Electric Power Enterprise, 106
Myanmar Future Generation
 online rap group, 167

Nakai plateau, 104

Nakon Sawan, 119
Nam Choan Dam, 97
Nam Ngum Dam, 103
Nam Ngum River basin, 23
Nam Ngum valley, 14
nam pass lai lak, 39
Nam Theun 2 dam, 3, 8, 14, 22, 99, 100, 103, 105, 112, 119
Nam Theun 2 Dam Consortium, 166
nam tuam, 39
Nan River, 44
National Development and Reform Commission, 110
National Disaster Management Committee, 45
National Energy Policy Council, 117
National Pump Installation management Project (NPIMP), 14
National Reconciliation Commission (NRC), 224
National Water Resource Council, 17
National Water Resources Committee (NRWC), 16
National Water Vision for Laos, 23
natural flood disturbance regime, 41
natural gas, 119
 alternative source of fuel, 230
 consumption, 62
natural heritage
 risk assessment, 90
natural resources
 joint management, 22
navigation aids
 Chinese-funded, 205
Navigation Channel Improvement Project, 229
news
 methods of delivery, 158
 state approved, 166
NGO Focus on the Global South (FOCUS), 216
non-governmental organizations (NGOS), 27, 32, 100, 189, 198
 growth of, 32
 help in broadcasting news, 162
Norconsult, 94, 101, 102, 110
North America
 massive blackout, 121
North China plain, 14
Nouzhadu, 110
nuoc noi, 40
Nu, 55, 57
Nu River, 74, 75, 76, 94

Nu River (cont.)
    development of, 87
Nu-Salween river development, 210
Nujian Lisu Nationality Autonomous
    Prefecture, 76
Nujiang Lisu Nationality Autonomous
    Prefecture, 56
numerical model, 132
Nuozhadu, 79

OECD, 63
oil
    demand for, 62
Ontario, 121
operational models, 132
overestimation
    load forecasting, 115
Oxfam America, 209

Pa Mong dam, 7
Pa Mong project, 124
Pacific Disaster Centre, 43
Pak Mun Dam, 118
Participatory Irrigation Management and
    Development (PIMD), 20
    essential principles of, 21
    top-down program, 21
Participatory Irrigation Management (PIM),
    20
participatory rhetoric
    limits of, 33
Pa Sak River, 23, 183
Pa Sak River Basin Development Project,
    183, 184
Pak Mun Dam, 186
    controversy, 173, 175
past interventions
    learning from, 1
Pattaya Post, 159
People's Army Forces, 17
People's Committees
    Vietnam, 21
Pham Hong Son, 159
Phnom Penh, 4
Ping River, 44
    master plan, 24
Ping River basin, 182
Ping River project, 184
Plain of Reeds
    reclamation, 12
policies
    implementation of, 34
policy analysis, 148

policy initiatives
    poorer households, for, 47
Policy Model, 149
policy-making, 10
political action
    challenges for, 234–236
political economy
    assessment of, 90
political reorganizations, 29
politics of floods, 53
post-traumatic stress disorder, 50
poverty reduction, 192
poverty/efficiency approach, 192
power plants
    natural gas, 119
Power Purchase Agreements (PPAs), 93
power relations
    local, 181
poverty
    plan to eradicate, 11
Prek Dam, 145
primary information
    collection of, 153
private property
    increase in value, 43
private sector
    nature of involvement, 34
private sector participation, 44
    Private Sector Participation Options in
        Water and Electricity, 91
professionalization
    scope for, 33
project managers, 28
Provincial Bureau of Hydrology and Water
    Resources, 52
public hearings
    essential safeguard mechanism, 122
public interest
    subordination of, 230
public property
    increase in value, 43
Public Services International, 167
public utilities
    privatization of, 62
publications
    donor driven, 165

Quang Nam Province, 44

radio
    importance of, 170
    method of delivering news, 158
    popularity, 162

Radio Free Asia, 161
radio stations
  community based, 162
  impact of, 161
rainfall
  floods caused by, 38
  variations in, 37
Rasmei Kampuchea, 161
Ratanakiri, 47
Red River, 12
  seasonal water levels, 46
Red River Basin Organization (RRBO), 183
Reform of the Water Sector (RWS), 16
reforms
  failed, 33
  prompting of outsiders, 28
Regional Dialogue on Water Governance, 206
Regional Environment Forum (REF), 210
regional media consolidation, 160–161
regional institutions
  emergence of, 228
regional overview
  demand for electricity, 93
Regional Power Trade Coordination Committee, 111
Regional Trade Operative Agreement (RPTOA), 120, 122
regional water-related governance forums, 207
regionalism, 228–230
regionalizations, 203
regulation
  need for independence, 121
rehabilitation programs, 28
relief operations, 47
reporters
  shortage of trained, 161
Reporters Without Borders, 158
research issues, 32
resource planning
  integrated. *See* integrated resource planning
renewable energy options, 230
Renewable Energy Promotion Law, 64
reservoirs, development of, 10
Residential Cluster Program, 50
resources management, 10
rice
  flood-resistant varieties, 42
rice farming
  expansion of, 50
rice-growing cultures, 39

risk creation, 46
risk-adjusted economic least-cost alternatives, 122
River Basin Committees (RBCS)
  establishment of, 16
river basin development
  policy-making in, 187
river basin management
  role of women, 185
  Vietnam, 24
risk management, 43
risk redistribution, 45
risks
  assessment of, 43
  unfair distribution of, 53, 54
River Basin Organizations (RBOS), 10, 32
  attemps to set, 29
  evolution of, 29
River Basin Planning Management Boards, 25
river regulation
  ecological impact of, 38
Robert and Patricia Switzer Foundation, 124
Royal Cambodian Government, 188
run-off
  floods caused by, 38
  increasing, 41
rural households, 41

Salween Dam plans
  opposition to, 171
Salween River, 5, 94, 169
  data on streamflow, 8
  effect of Himalayan snow melt, 226
  hydropower potential, 110
  opportunities for development, 219, 220
Salween River basin
  hydropower projects, 107
Samut Prakan
  wastewater project, 3
San Jiang, 60
Santi Lamaneenil, 159
Saraburi, 183
science
  power and knowledge, 231–232
Se San 3 hydropower dam, 102
Se San hydropower dialogue, 209
Se San Protection Network (SPN), 186
Se San River, 5, 27, 46, 85, 186
Se San Working Group (SWG), 185
Second Greater Mekong Subregion (GMS) Summit, 120

Second International Meeting of Dam Affected People and their Allies, 212
Second Red River Basin Sector Project, 177, 184
sediment loads
  effect of, 50
sedimentation results
  depending on land use, 147
Sekong Province, 102
SEPA, 76
Shan community
  ethnic identity, 169
  human rights abuses against, 220
  own media solutions, 170
Shan Herald Agency for News (S.H.A.N.), 167
Shan identity
  assertion of, 168
Shigu, 83
Shimantan, 47
Sichuan Province
  ban on logging, 46
  dam project in, 172
Sida Environmental Fund Projects
  Vietnam, in, 188
Sittoung River basin, 23
Sirikit Dam, 44
social and cultural assessment
  dams in the Mekong region, 90
social relationships
  lack of attention to, 179
socioeconomic analysis, 146
socioeconomic modeling, 131
sociological challenges, xv
social choice
  better definition of, 31
social institutions
  shaping of, 227
Songkhram River
  floodplain of, 41
solar power, 64
Son La, 7
Son La Pak Num dam, 85
Southeast Asia
  economic development indicators, 2
  gross domestic product, 2
  peace, stability and growth, 2
Southeast Asia Rivers Network (SEARIN), 76, 186, 209
Southeast Asia Water Forum, 36, 92, 206
Southern Power Grid Company, 69
Soviet Union, 64, 122
SRDC, 75

SRDC-ERI, 65
Sre Pok, 85
standardized model packages
  limits of, 135
stakeholders
  local. *See* local stakeholders
state
  domination by, 232–234
state agencies
  better understanding of constrains andallocation, 31
  top-down mode of, 34
state-approved news, 166
State Electricity Regulatory Commission (SERC), 68, 70
State Electriciy Regulation Commission (SERC), 67
State Environment Protection Administration (SEPA), 75
State Power Corporation, 58
  establishment of, 69
State Power Corporation (SPC), 67, 74, 76
State Power Grid Company, 69, 92
State Reform and Development Commission, 69
State Reform and Development Commission (SRDC), 62, 68
strategic models, 132
statism
  regionalism, in context of, 228–230
Strategic Environmental Framework (SEF), 207
subsidiarity
  antagonistic to macro-level basin management, 31
successive base-case forecasts, 115
sulphur dioxide, 58
Surapong Rithi, 159
sustainability losses
  risk of, 153
Sweden
  Goteborg University, 225
Swedish Environment Secretariat in Asia (SENSA), 90
Swedish International Development Agency (SIDA), 90

Ta Sarng dam, 106, 169, 219
tactical models, 132
technical challenge, 52
technological devices
  small and low-tech, 4
Tennessee Valley Authority, 26

Tenth Five-Year Plan, 64
Thai Baan action research and dialogue, 208
Thai Baan research, 186
Thai bureaucracy, 22
Thailand, 10, 16, 22, 41, 48, 51, 94, 96, 99, 119, 138, 140
  agreement with Myanmar, 106
  Chao Phraya basin, 2
  comparison of load forecast to actual demand, 116
  Constitution (1997), 158
  definition of good governance, 7
  Department of Disaster Prevention and Mitigation (DDPM), 48
  Department of Water Resources, 16, 23
  Electricity Generating Authority of Thailand (EGAT), 11, 78, 80, 97, 112, 214, 220
  downstream communities, 51
  effect of Asian financial crisis, 160
  energy activists, 118
  flood management, 45
  generation planning, 113
  hydropower, 96
  importing hydropower from Laos, 97
  limits to free expression, 159
  load centers, 95
  load forecast overestimation, 115
  load forecasting, in, 112
  Ministry of Natural Resources and Environment, 20
  Ministry of Energy, 108
  National Economic and Social Development Board (NESDB), 114
  northeast region, 186
  northern region, 186, 187
  Pak Mun Dam, 185
  peak demand, 124
  Power Development Plan (PDP), 117
  proposal for water grid, 225
  Rasi Salai Dam, 185
  Seventh National Plan, 23
  severe flooding, 49
  water grid, 2, 220–221
  water grid project, 12
  Water Law, 16
Thailand Development and Research Institute, 114
Thailand Environment Institute (TEI), 210, 211
Thaksin Shinawatra, 11, 35, 103, 118, 160, 162, 221, 224

Theun-Hinboun project, 22
Three Gorges dam, 14, 58, 82
  financing of, 82
Three Gorges Development Group, 68
Three Gorges Project Development Corporation, 83
Three Rivers
  hydropower status, 74
Three Rivers region, 60
three-tier institutional design, 18–20
Time Asia, 161
Time Warner, 161
Tonle Sap, 80
  fisheries, 81
  floodplains, 144, 145
Tonle Sap Lake, 130, 145, 148, 152, 156, 188
  future of, 214
Tonle Sap region, 41
Tonle Sap River, 145
Tonle Sap system
  integrated model, 144
top-down model for demand forecasting, 115
transboundary effects assessment, 90
Transboundary Environment Assessment (EA), 80
transboundary water related governance, 197
transmission grid, 119
tree cover
  decrease in, 41

Ubon Ratchathani University
  study by scholars, 185
UN Convention on the Law of the Non-Navigational Uses of International Watercourses, 80
UN Declaration of Human Rights, 226
UN Economic and Social Commission for Asia and the Pacific (ESCAP), 206
uncritical copycat replication, 36
United Nations Committee on the Development of Trade, 61
United Nations Development Program, 44
United Nations Economic, Social and Cultural Organization (UNESCO), 60
World Heritage, 172
Upper Paunglaung Hydro-Electric Power Project, 108
urban lifestyles, 40
urbanization, 4, 43
  effect of, 211

United States
  standardized models, 134
United States Environmental Protection
  Agency (EPA), 134
US Agency for International Development
  (USAID), 96
US Senate Foreign Relations Committee,
  99
video disc
  method of delivering information, 158
Vietnam, 2, 7, 10, 45, 94, 95, 96, 99, 138,
  140
  apex bodies, 35
  area of irrigated land, 13
  Central Government Agencies, 25
  flood management in, 44
  hydropower development, 102
  limits to free expression, 159
  load forecasts, 117
  Ministry of Agriculture and Rural
    Development (MARD), 177, 183
  Ministry of Energy, 103
  mountainous north, 40
  National Hydropower Master Plan, 98
  People's Army Forces, 17
  People's Committees, 25
  rapidly urbanizing areas, 46
  relief assistance in, 48
  resettlement policies, 41
  river basin management, 24
  rural water infrastructures, 12
  Second Red River Basin Sector Project,
    177, 183
  single party system, 214
  support from government, 48
  thermal and gas powered plants, 102
  Water Law, 17, 35
  water resource management, 190–191
Vietnam National Water Resources
  Council, 19
Vietnam Women's Union, 188
Vietnamese National Mekong Committee
  (VNMC), 212
village user associations, 178
Voice of America, 161

Water and Nature Initiative (WANI), 210
water concerns, 198
  disparate regionalism, 198
water distribution, 10
water governance
  achievement of, 192
  gender myths in, 177–195

water governance forums, 202–212
  Track 1, 204–205
  Track 2, 206–208
  Track 3, 208–211
  Track 4, 211–212
  tracks, 203, 213
water governance programs, 181
  need to rethink gender roles, 194
water governance network, 35
water grid, 2
  proposal by Thailand, 225
water institutions
  uniformity, 27
Water Law of Vietnam, 21
water laws, 15–18
water management, global initiatives, 9
water mode, 131
water policy, 15–18
  attributes, 23
  contested domain, as a, 34
  reforms, 30
water politics
  challenges, 162–163
water resource management
  use of mathematical modeling, 127–154
water resource projects
  ADB's approach, 218
Water Resource Management
  Departments, 19, 20
water resources
  assessment of, 128
  development and management, 1
  managing, xv
  planning and development, 10–18
Water Resources Bureaus, 17
Water Resources Coordination Committee
  (WRCC), 15
water resources development
  aid for, 3
  Cambodia, 185, 186
  northeast Thailand, 186
  northern Thailand, 186
  opportunities in, 218, 219
  Thailand, 182–183
  Vietnam, 183–185
Water Resources Law, 18
water resource management
  caricature on women's responsibilities,
    180
  common property resources (CPR)
    approach, 178–179
  discourse in different sectors, 192
  involvement of direct users, 177

water resources
  management of, 177
Water Resources Laboratory
  Helsinki University of Technology, 156
water sectors, 33
water shortages
  recurring, 9
Water Utilization Programme (WUP-FIN),
  142, 156
  funded by Global Environment Facility
    (GEF), 140
water user associations, 178, 187
  quota for women, 188
Water User Groups (WUGS), 22, 28
Water Vision, 23
water-related governance
  transboundary, 197
Wen Jiabao, 76, 110, 214
Western Region, 64
  energy exports, 65
Western Region Development Strategy, 56,
  60, 64, 65, 77, 91
wet season, 37
wetland
  destruction of, 46
wind power, 64
women
  actual practices of engagement, 193
  encouraging active participation of, 188
  generation of disposable household
    income, 182
  harnessing for conservation activities,
    192
  inclusion in community fisheries, 191
  involvement in community
    participation, 182
  role in river basin management, 185
women's role
  assumptions, 190
word-of-mouth
  effectiveness of, 170
World Bank 9, 15, 23, 94, 96, 98, 99, 100,
  101, 102, 116, 118, 181, 198, 218,
  221, 230
  assistance from, 105
  details of, 100
  gender concerns, 194
  loan for Bhumipol Dam, 112
  loan to Thailand, 97
  Public-Private Infrastructure Advisory
    Facility (PPIAF), 62
World Bank Report (2004), 5

World Commission on Dams, 59, 85, 87,
  88, 97, 120, 212, 217
  framework, 89
World Conservation Union (IUCN), 210
World Heritage site, 76
world natural heritage
  Yunnan Province, 57–60
World Resources Institute (WRI), 210
World Wildlife Fund (WWF), 5, 27, 32, 172
WUP-FIN models, 144, 145
WUP-FIN Policy Model, 148, 150
WUP-FIN Project, 142, 143

Xiaowan, 77, 87, 110

Yali Falls hydropower dam, 46, 47, 102,
  185, 209
Yangtze River, 14
Yangtze River floods, 46
Yellow River, 14
Yunnan, 17, 83, 94, 99, 108, 120
  community-based watershed
    management, 209
  hydropower, 58
  key drivers for hydropower expansion,
    60
  key role, 219
Yunnan dams, 85
Yunnan Development Investment, 75
Yunnan Huandian Hydropower
  Development Company, 75
Yunnan Huaneng Lancangjiang
  Hydopower Company (YHLHC)
  Limited, 78
Yunnan Huaneng Lancangkiang
  Hydropower Company Limited, 92
Yunnan hydropower
  economic impact of development, 87
  expansion, 84, 89
  governance, 89
Yunnan Machinery & Equipment Import
  & Export Co., 108
Yunnan Province, 55, 56
  population, 56
Yuxi Tobacco Factory, 92

Zhu, 57